SCHOLASTIC

The Great BIG Book of Funtastic MATH

200+ Super-Fun Activities, Games, and Puzzles That Help Students Master Must-Know Math Skills and Concepts

New York • Toronto • London • Auckland • Sydney
Mexico City • New Delhi • Hong Kong • Buenos Aires

Teaching Resources

Formerly published as part of the Funtastic Math! series: *Multiplication and Division*, written by Joyce Mallery; *Decimals and Fractions*, written by Cindi Mitchell; *Measurement and Geometry*, written by Marcia Miller and Martin Lee; *Probability* and *Algebra Readiness*, written by Sarah Jane Brian; *Problem Solving and Logic*, written Martin Lee and Marcia Miller.

Editor: Mela Ottaiano
Cover design: Maria Lilja
Interior design: Ellen Matlach for Boultinghouse & Boultinghouse
Interior illustrations: pages 14–62 and 289–311 by Ellen Joy Sasaki, pages 69–118 and 181–230 by Kate Flanagan, pages 125–176 and 235–285 by Michael Moran; additional illustrations by Manuel Rivera

ISBN-13: 978-0-545-23140-4
ISBN-10: 0-545-23140-X

Printed in the U.S.A.

2 3 4 5 6 7 8 9 10 40 16 15 14 13 12 11 10

Contents

Introduction 6
Connections to the NCTM Standards 8

Activities below that include a student reproducible are indicated with a ✸.

Basic Facts: Multiplication & Division
Multiplication Bingo 12
✸ Go to Bat for Facts 13
Triple Toss 16

Factors, Related Facts & Multiples
Find the Factors 17
Factor Facts 18
That's a Fact 19
✸ Don't Four-Get Multiples 20
Multiplication Buzz 22

Exploring Patterns: Multiplication & Division
✸ Greetings From Space 23
Dot to Dot 25
Star Cards 26

Estimating Products & Quotients
Can You Dig It? 27
✸ Riddle Round-Up 28

Multiplying by 1-Digit Factors
Productive Draws 30
Time to Grow Up 31
✸ Believe It or Not! 32
Car Facts 34
Weigh up in Space 35

Dividing by 1-Digit Divisors
✸ What Do You Know? 36
Your Table Is Ready 38
✸ Career Changes 39
✸ Continue Her-story 41
✸ You're in Jeopardy 43

Multiplying by 1-, 2- & 3-Digit Factors
✸ River Rapids 45
✸ Road Rally 47
What's New in the News? 49

Dividing by 2-Digit Divisors
Me First! 50
✸ Food for Thought 51

Multiplying & Dividing Money
✸ Sandwich by the Slice 53
✸ Shop 'Til You Drop 55
✸ Party Problems 57

Mental Math: Multiplication & Division
✸ A-mazing Multiplication Patterns 59
✸ Treasure Hunt 61

Multiplication & Division Problem Bank 63

Equivalent Fractions
✸ The Mysterious Fraction Zone 68
Fraction Snowflakes 70

Fractions: Lowest Terms
✸ The Wheel of Fractions 71
✸ Optical Illusions 73

Comparing & Ordering Fractions
✸ Sensational Surveys 75
Fraction Line-Up 77

Mixed Numbers
Shoot for the Stars 78
The Great Fraction Race .79

Fractions: Addition & Subtraction
LIKE FRACTIONS
✸ Four in a Row Fractions .80
✸ Shout It Out! 82
UNLIKE FRACTIONS
✸ Teacher Troubles 84
Fraction Trios 86

Fractions: Multiplication & Division
✸ Tangram Fractions 87
✸ Ladybug Fractions 89
Don't Let Fractions Drive You Buggy 91

Relating Fractions With Mixed Numbers & Decimals
✸ Clowning Around 92
Battling Decimals 94

Reading & Writing Decimals
✸ Stumpers 95
Name That Decimal 97

Decimals: Place Value
Guess That Decimal 98
✸ Every Number Has Its Place 99

Comparing & Ordering Decimals
* "Weighty" Problems 101
* Wacky Presidential Firsts 103
Who's First? 105

Rounding Decimals
* Decimal Roundup 106
Top Secret Numbers 108

Equivalent Decimals
Bag Math 109
Guarded Treasure 110

Decimals: Addition & Subtraction
* Absolutely Magical 111
* Shopping in the "Good Old Days" 113
* Running for the Gold 115

Decimals: Multiplication & Division
* Decimal Points Everywhere 117
Decimal Puzzlers 119

Fractions & Decimals Problem Bank 120

2-Dimensional Figures
* Inside Out 124
* What's the Angle? 126
Musical Math 128
Eye Spy 129
* Tangram Investigations 130

3-Dimensional Figures
Bulletin Board Logic 132
Models in Space 133
Any Way You Slice It 134
* Mapping Up 135
Are You Sure? 137
Icosa-Questions 138
Figure With Figures 139
* Geometry Jumble 140

Coordinate Geometry
Right Angle Tic-Tac-Toe 142
Finger Twister 143
Rectangle Hunt 144
* Shark Stretch 145

Transformational Geometry
Art Explosion 147
Partner Symmetry 148
* Pentominetris 149
* Creative Compass Constructions 151

Weight, Capacity & Mass
Measurement Scavenger Hunt 153
* Measuring Across and Down 154

Length
* Hidden Meters 157
* Lengthy Words 159

Perimeter/Area/Volume
Pin That Area 161
* Area Irregulars 162
Have a Ball! 164
* Gourmet Pet Problems 165
Design a Wall Unit 167
* Geometry Jeopardy 168

Time/Temperature
Analog Angles 170
* Cuckoo Clocks 171
Warmth War 173

Geometry & Measurement Problem Bank 174

Probability of a Simple Event
* Toy Joy 178
* Guess 'n' Go 180
Flip for Probability 182
* Odds and Evens 183

Probability as Fraction, Decimal, Percent & Ratio
* Probability at Play 185
* Go for a Spin 187
Sweet Experiments 189

Sample Space
Take a Sample 190
* Lost in Sample Space 191

Counting Outcomes
TREE DIAGRAMS & FUNDAMENTAL COUNTING PRINCIPLE
* Clothes Combo 193
Tree-Licious Diagrams 195
Count on Sports Schedules 196
* Pet Peeves 197
* School Daze 199

PERMUTATIONS
Gold, Silver, Bronze 201
* Career Day Conundrums 202

COUNTING OUTCOMES VISUALLY
* MAKING AN AREA MODEL: Turnover Turns 204
* MAKING A VENN DIAGRAM: Join the Club 206
ARRANGEMENTS: Stamp to It! 208

Making Predictions
SIMULATIONS
* Spin to Win 209
False Hopes 211

- ✱ The Real Meal Deal 212
- ✱ What's Behind Door Number 2? 214

SAMPLING

- Elective Detective 216

RELATIVE FREQUENCY

- Picky, Picky 217

Probability of a Compound Event

INDEPENDENT EVENTS

- Trick-or-Treat Numbers .218
- ✱ Game Show Showdown .219

DEPENDENT EVENTS

- Bon Voyage 221
- ✱ Critter Cards 222

MUTUALLY EXCLUSIVE EVENTS

- Card Tricks 224

Real-World Applications

- ✱ Wheel of Fortune 225
- Above Average 227
- Rain, Rain, Go Away 228
- ✱ Collect All Six 229

Probability Problem Bank 231

Properties

- ✱ Tasty Properties 234
- Opposites Subtract 236
- ✱ Olympic Flips 237
- ✱ Have No Fear 239

Order of Operations

- ✱ Order Up! 241

Using a Number Line

- ✱ Numbers of Invention 243

Inequalities

- Inequality Mix-Up 245
- ✱ Amazing Animal Inequalities 246

Formulas

- Happy Birth Day! 248
- The Shadow Knows 249
- ✱ Bone Up on Formulas 250

Variables & Expressions

- Party With Variables 252
- ✱ Variable Bingo 253
- Magical Memorizing Math Teacher 255
- ✱ Train Trouble 256
- ✱ Express Yourself 258

Equations

- Equations Are the Name of the Game 260
- ✱ The Amazin' Equation Game 261
- On Sale Now—Algebra! .263
- ✱ Step "Two" It! 264

Factors

- ✱ Factor Falls 266
- ✱ Let's Make a Factor! 268

Coordinate Plane

- Cool Off With Coordinates 270
- ✱ Grid Giggles 271
- Scatterplot Scores 273

Integers

- ✱ Integer Football 274
- Mouthwatering Math 276

Squares & Square Roots

- ✱ Square Off 277
- ✱ Laboratory Labyrinth 279

Patterns, Relations & Functions

- Paper Patterns 281
- Function Detective 282
- Crunchy Functions 283
- ✱ Missing Museums 284

Algebra Readiness Problem Bank 286

Problem Solving

- ✱ What, No Numbers? 288
- ✱ Pets Step Up 290
- ✱ Car for Rent 292
- Laces 294
- On the Beaten Path 295
- ✱ Following Directions .296
- Piece of the Pie 299
- ✱ Mapmaker, Mapmaker 300
- ✱ Think Again! 302

Logic

- ✱ Logically Speaking 304
- ✱ Let's Be Reasonable .306
- Chili Challenge 308
- Toast French 309
- ✱ Talent Show 310

Problem Solving & Logic Problem Bank 312

- Answer Key 314
- Student Self-Evaluation 319
- Assessment Form—With Scoring Rubric 320

Introduction

With this book of activities, we hope to make teaching and understanding key math skills fun, creative, engaging, and exciting.

An Overview of the Book

There are several ways to find what you need to target specific math concepts. As you look through the table of contents, you'll notice the activities are grouped by math topic and skill, and that a star (✱) indicates an activity with a student reproducible. When thumbing through the book itself, you will also find the topic and skill labeled at the top of each teaching page.

The activities in this book correspond to the standards recommended by the National Council of Teachers of Mathematics (NCTM). For quick reference, the chart on pages 8–11 shows how each activity connects to the *Principals and Standards for School Mathematics* (2000). In addition to repeated practice with key mathematics content, students will also exercise their mental math skills, develop automaticity with computation, engage in problem-solving and communication skills, and much more.

Teaching Pages

Everything you need to know is on the teaching page, but you also have the option of tailoring the activities to meet students' individual needs and to address the various levels displayed in your classroom.

Learning Objective

The learning objective clearly states the primary aim of the activity.

Grouping

This states whether the whole class, individual students, pairs, or cooperative groups should perform the task. If an activity lends itself to more than one grouping, the choices are indicated. Again, if you feel that a different grouping is more appropriate to your classroom, feel free to alter the activity accordingly.

Materials

To cut your preparation time, all materials necessary for the main activity and its extension are listed. Most of the materials are probably already in your classroom. If an activity has a student reproducible with it, the page number of the reproducible is listed here as well.

Advance Preparation

A few activities require some minimal advance preparation on your part. All the directions you need are given here. You may also let students take over some or all of the preparation.

Directions

The directions usually begin with suggestions on how to introduce or review the topic, including any terms and/or formulas you should address. Step-by-step details on how to do the activity follow. When pertinent, specific strategies that might help students in solving problems are suggested.

Taking It Further

This section on the teaching page offers suggestions on how you can extend and enrich the activity. Students who require extra help and those who need a challenge will both benefit when you take the activity to a different level. This is also where you will find additional ideas for reaching students of all learning styles.

Assessing Skills

The key questions and/or common errors pointed out in this section will help alert you to students' progress. (In fact, you may want to jot down more questions on the page.) Use the information you gather about students here in conjunction with the Assessment Form that appears on page 320.

Student Reproducibles

About one-third of the activities have a companion student reproducible page for you to duplicate and distribute. These activities are marked with a star (*) in the Table of Contents and are listed in the Materials section on the teaching page.

Problem Bank

These pages at the end of each section are filled with fun and challenging problems that you may use in a variety of ways. Post a Problem of the Day (or Problem of the Week for the more challenging ones). Have them readily available as self-starters or extra-credit brain-teasers, or assign them as homework. Read problems aloud to help students practice their listening skills. You can even invite students to come up with similar problems to add to the bank!

Answer Key

You will find answers to the problems on the reproducible activity pages (when they are called for) and all of the Problem Bank exercises in the Answer Key on pages 314–318.

Assessment

Student Self-Evaluation

At the end of the activity, hand out these forms for students to complete. Emphasize that their responses are for themselves as well as you. Evaluating their own performances will help students clarify their thinking and understand more about their reasoning.

Assessment Form With Scoring Rubric

The sign of a student's success with an activity is more than a correct answer. As the NCTM stresses, problem solving, communication, reasoning, and connections are equally important in the mathematical process. How a student arrives at the answer—the strategies she or he uses or discards, for instance—can be as important as the answer itself. This assessment form and scoring rubric will help you determine the full range of students' mastery of skills.

Connections to the NCTM Standards

The grid below shows how the activities in this book correspond to the standards recommended by the National Council of Teachers of Mathematics. In most cases the activities address multiple standards.

Activity Title	Page	Number & Operations	Algebra	Geometry	Measurement	Data Analysis & Probability	Problem Solving	Reasoning & Proof	Communication	Connections	Representation
Multiplication Bingo	12	x							x		
Go to Bat for Facts	13	x							x		
Triple Toss	16	x							x		
Find the Factors	17	x							x		
Factor Facts	18	x							x		
That's a Fact	19	x							x		
Don't Four-Get Multiples	20	x		x					x		
Multiplication Buzz	22	x							x		
Greetings From Space	23	x	x						x		
Dot to Dot	25	x							x		
Star Cards	26	x	x						x		
Can You Dig It?	27	x	x						x		
Riddle Round-Up	28	x	x						x		
Productive Draws	30	x	x					x	x		
Time to Grow Up	31	x							x		
Believe It or Not!	32	x	x								
Car Facts	34	x							x		
Weigh up in Space	35	x			x				x	x	x
What Do You Know?	36	x							x		
Your Table Is Ready	38	x					x		x		
Career Changes	39	x									
Continue Her-Story	41	x								x	
You're in Jeopardy	43	x							x		
River Rapids	45	x									
Road Rally	47	x							x		
What's New in the News?	49	x				x			x		
Me First!	50	x									
Food for Thought	51	x									
Sandwich by the Slice	53	x			x					x	
Shop 'Til You Drop	55	x			x	x				x	
Party Problems	57	x			x	x			x		
A-mazing Multiplication Patterns	59	x	x								
Treasure Hunt	61	x									
The Mysterious Fraction Zone	68	x		x			x				
Fraction Snowflakes	70	x					x				x
The Wheel of Fractions	71	x							x		
Optical Illusions	73	x									
Sensational Surveys	75	x				x	x		x		x
Fraction Line-Up	77	x							x		x
Shoot for the Stars	78	x							x		x
The Great Fraction Race	79	x							x		x

Activity Title	Page	Number & Operations	Algebra	Geometry	Measurement	Data Analysis & Probability	Problem Solving	Reasoning & Proof	Communication	Connections	Representation
Four in a Row Fractions	80	x					x	x	x		
Shout It Out!	82	x							x		x
Teacher Troubles	84	x									x
Fraction Trios	86	x							x		x
Tangram Fractions	87	x									
Ladybug Fractions	89	x							x		
Don't Let Fractions Drive You Buggy	91	x							x		
Clowning Around	92	x									x
Battling Decimals	94	x							x		x
Stumpers	95	x						x			
Name That Decimal	97	x							x		
Guess That Decimal	98	x						x	x		
Every Number Has Its Place	99	x									
"Weighty" Problems	101	x				x					
Wacky Presidential Firsts	103	x									
Who's First?	105	x							x		
Decimal Roundup	106	x							x		
Top Secret Numbers	108	x							x		
Bag Math	109	x							x		x
Guarded Treasure	110	x							x		x
Absolutely Magical	111	x					x		x		
Shopping in the "Good Old Days"	113	x			x						
Running for the Gold	115	x							x		
Decimal Points Everywhere	117	x									x
Decimal Puzzlers	119	x									
Inside Out	124			x			x				
What's the Angle?	126	x		x							
Musical Math	128				x				x	x	
Eye Spy	129	x		x			x				
Tangram Investigations	130			x							x
Bulletin Board Logic	132			x				x	x		
Models in Space	133			x						x	x
Any Way You Slice It	134			x					x	x	x
Mapping Up	135			x				x	x		
Are You Sure?	137			x					x		
Icosa-Questions	138			x			x		x		
Figure With Figures	139			x			x		x		
Geometry Jumble	140			x			x				
Right Angle Tic-Tac-Toe	142			x					x		x
Finger Twister	143			x					x		x
Rectangle Hunt	144			x				x	x		x
Shark Stretch	145			x				x		x	
Art Explosion	147			x				x			x
Partner Symmetry	148		x	x					x		x
Pentominetris	149			x					x		
Creative Compass Constructions	151		x	x							x

Activity Title	Page	Number & Operations	Algebra	Geometry	Measurement	Data Analysis & Probability	Problem Solving	Reasoning & Proof	Communication	Connections	Representation
Measurement Scavenger Hunt	153			x	x				x		x
Measuring Across and Down	154			x	x						x
Hidden Meters	157	x			x						x
Lengthy Words	159	x		x	x						
Pin That Area	161			x	x				x		x
Area Irregulars	162	x		x	x						
Have a Ball!	164			x	x			x	x		
Gourmet Pet Problems	165	x		x	x			x		x	
Design a Wall Unit	167	x		x	x	x			x	x	
Geometry Jeopardy	168	x		x	x			x	x		
Analog Angles	170	x		x	x			x		x	
Cuckoo Clocks	171	x			x			x		x	
Warmth War	173	x			x	x			x		
Toy Joy	178					x					
Guess 'n' Go	180	x				x			x		
Flip for Probability	182	x	x			x			x		
Odds and Evens	183	x	x			x			x		
Probability at Play	185	x				x					x
Go for a Spin	187	x	x			x			x		
Sweet Experiments	189	x	x			x			x		x
Take a Sample	190	x	x			x			x	x	
Lost in Sample Space	191	x			x	x				x	
Clothes Combo	193	x				x			x	x	x
Tree-Licious Diagrams	195					x			x	x	x
Count on Sports Schedules	196	x	x			x			x	x	
Pet Peeves	197	x	x			x	x	x			x
School Daze	199	x	x			x		x	x		
Gold, Silver, Bronze	201	x				x	x		x	x	
Career Day Conundrums	202	x				x					
Turnover Turns	204	x			x	x			x		x
Join the Club	206	x		x		x					x
Stamp to It!	208			x		x	x				x
Spin to Win	209	x				x			x		x
False Hopes	211	x				x		x		x	
The Real Meal Deal	212	x				x			x	x	x
What's Behind Door Number 2?	214	x				x	x		x		x
Elective Detective	216	x				x			x		x
Picky, Picky	217	x				x			x		
Trick-or-Treat Numbers	218	x				x			x	x	
Game Show Showdown	219	x				x			x		x
Bon Voyage	221	x				x		x	x	x	
Critter Cards	222	x				x		x		x	
Card Tricks	224	x				x			x	x	
Wheel of Fortune	225	x	x			x				x	
Above Average	227	x			x	x			x	x	
Rain, Rain, Go Away	228	x				x			x	x	x
Collect All Six	229	x				x			x	x	x

Activity Title	Page	Number & Operations	Algebra	Geometry	Measurement	Data Analysis & Probability	Problem Solving	Reasoning & Proof	Communication	Connections	Representation
Tasty Properties	234	X	X								
Opposites Subtract	236	X	X						X	X	
Olympic Flips	237	X	X							X	
Have No Fear	239	X	X								
Order Up!	241	X	X								
Numbers of Invention	243	X	X								X
Inequality Mix-Up	245	X	X								X
Amazing Animal Inequalities	246	X	X								
Happy Birth Day!	248	X	X		X						
The Shadow Knows	249	X	X		X				X		
Bone Up on Formulas	250	X	X		X				X		
Party With Variables	252	X	X		X			X	X	X	
Variable Bingo	253	X	X						X		
Magical Memorizing Math Teacher	255	X	X					X	X		
Train Trouble	256	X	X			X			X		
Express Yourself	258	X	X						X		
Equations Are the Name of the Game	260	X	X				X		X		
The Amazin' Equation Game	261	X	X				X		X		X
On Sale Now—Algebra!	263	X	X						X	X	X
Step "Two" It!	264	X	X							X	
Factor Falls	266	X	X				X				
Let's Make a Factor!	268	X	X				X		X		
Cool Off With Coordinates	270	X	X						X	X	X
Grid Giggles	271	X	X				X			X	X
Scatterplot Scores	273	X	X			X			X	X	X
Integer Football	274	X	X						X	X	X
Mouthwatering Math	276	X	X				X		X		
Square Off	277	X	X								X
Laboratory Labyrinth	279	X	X				X				
Paper Patterns	281	X	X	X		X			X	X	
Function Detective	282	X	X				X	X	X		
Crunchy Functions	283	X	X	X	X				X		
Missing Museums	284	X	X					X	X		
What, No Numbers?	288	X					X	X	X	X	
Pets Step Up	290	X			X		X		X		X
Car for Rent	292	X	X		X		X		X	X	
Laces	294	X			X		X		X		
On the Beaten Path	295	X			X		X		X	X	X
Following Directions	296	X		X	X		X				
Piece of the Pie	299	X	X	X			X		X		X
Mapmaker, Mapmaker	300			X			X				
Think Again!	302	X		X			X			X	
Logically Speaking	304					X		X	X	X	
Let's Be Reasonable	306	X				X		X			
Chili Challenge	308	X			X			X		X	X
Toast French	309		X					X	X	X	
Talent Show	310				X			X	X	X	X

Multiplication Bingo

In this multiplication game, students team up to practice facts to 9 and find the products on their bingo cards.

Directions

1. Ask students to form two teams. Have them sit on opposite sides of the room.
2. Students make their own game boards by drawing two vertical and two horizontal lines to divide their papers into nine boxes. Then they write one of the following numbers in any order in each box: 0, 2, 3, 4, 5, 6, 7, 8, 9, 10, 12, 14, 15, 16, 18, 20, 21, 24, 25, 27, 28, 30, 32, 35, 36, 40, 42, 45, 48, 49, 54, 56, 63, 64, 72, 81.
3. Say a multiplication fact to 9, such as 4 × 8 = 32, but do not give the product. (Keep track of the facts you say.) Students solve the fact. If the product is on their game board, they place a counter in that box. The first student to place counters in three boxes horizontally, vertically, or diagonally wins for the team. Allow students to play several games.

30	12	81
21	45	0
48	4	54

LEARNING OBJECTIVE

Students practice basic multiplication facts.

GROUPING

Two teams

MATERIALS

- game counters, such as dried lima beans
- paper
- markers
- extra counters (optional)

Taking It Further

Vary this game by using facts to 12.

Assessing Skills

If students have difficulty solving facts, allow them to use extra counters to model the multiplication.

Go to Bat for Facts

Students make a hit by practicing division facts and devising strategies to win a game!

Directions

1. Duplicate the two reproducibles for each pair of students and distribute.
2. Write the following division sentence on the board: 15 ÷ 3 = 5. Ask volunteers to identify the dividend, divisor, and quotient.
3. Explain to students that they will play a game to practice division facts.
4. Players sit next to each other and take turns choosing a number on a ball as a dividend and a number on a bat as a divisor. He or she crosses out the numbers and writes the division sentence on his or her scorecard. That player earns the same number of runs as the quotient.
5. If remaining numbers do not form basic division facts, students may write their own division facts using the dividends or divisors. For instance, if the numbers 40 and 7 were left, students could write 40 ÷ 5 = 8 or 63 ÷ 7 = 9.
6. After all the numbers are used, players calculate their total number of runs. Have them use calculators as necessary.

Taking It Farther

Encourage students to play again. Ask them to consider strategies they can use to achieve higher scores.

Assessing Skills

Observe whether students understand the terms *dividend* and *divisor* and use the terms correctly in their division sentences.

LEARNING OBJECTIVE

Students practice basic division facts.

GROUPING

Pairs

MATERIALS

- *Go to Bat for Facts* reproducibles (pp. 14–15)
- calculators (optional)

 Name ____________________ Date ____________

Go to Bat for Facts

Choose a number on a ball as a dividend. Then choose a number on a bat as a divisor. Cross out these numbers. Write and solve the division sentence on your scorecards. You earn the same number of runs as the quotient. Take turns and then tally your final scores!

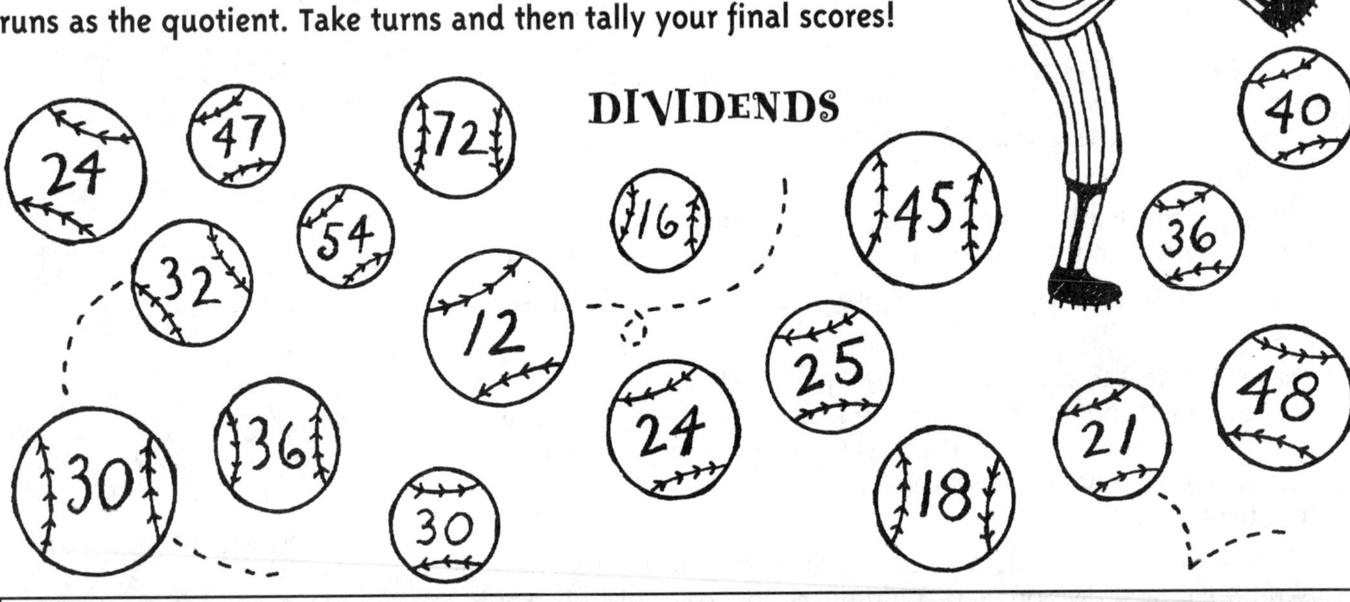

SCORECARD: Player 1

DIVISION SENTENCE	NUMBER OF RUNS SCORED

Name ______________________ Date ______________

Go to Bat for Facts

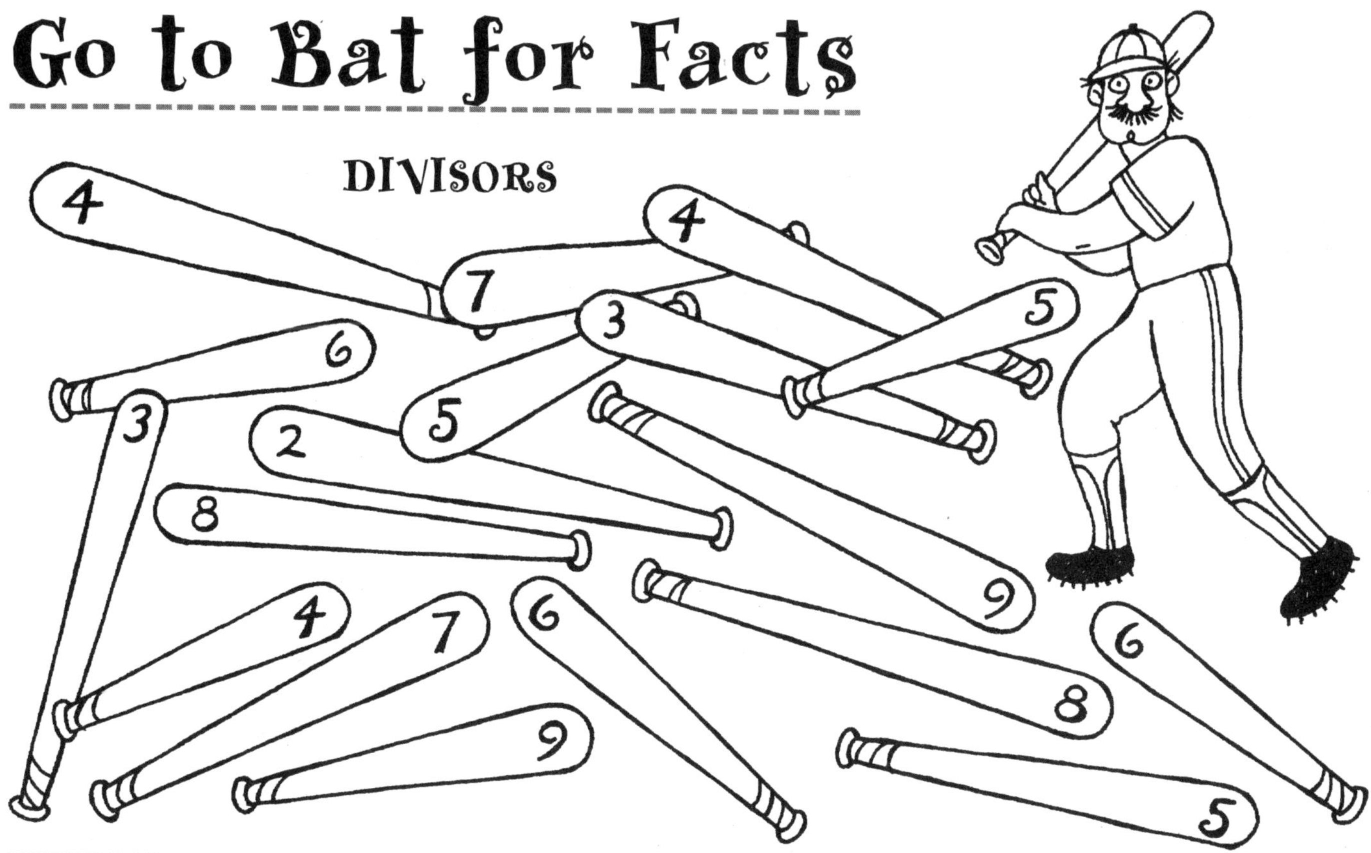

SCORECARD: Player 2

DIVISION SENTENCE	NUMBER OF RUNS SCORED

Triple Toss

Students play a fast-paced game to review the properties of multiplication and division.

LEARNING OBJECTIVE

Students use the properties of multiplication and division.

GROUPING

Pairs

MATERIALS

For each pair:

- 6 number cubes
- masking tape
- 2 small cups
- counters (optional)

Directions

1. Use the masking tape to cover the dots on one face of two different number cubes. Give three cubes to each player: two regular cubes and one with the face covered. Explain that the "blank" face represents zero.
2. Review the Identity Property and the Property of Zero, and the Associative Property of Multiplication.
3. Explain to students that first they will play a multiplication game with six rounds. They will write multiplication sentences whose products result in the highest possible answers.
4. Designate students as Player 1 and Player 2. Both players put the three cubes in a cup. Each player shakes and rolls the cubes. Player 1 quickly decides if they should "switch" and exchange the cubes with each other, or keep the numbers that each has rolled.
5. Each player writes a multiplication sentence using three factors. They should use all three numbers shown, and then multiply.
6. The game continues for six rounds, with students taking turns calling "switch" or "keep." After six rounds, students add the products to find the total scores. The higher score wins the game.
7. To play the division game, players take turns tossing all six number cubes. They use two of the cubes as the dividend and divisor in a division sentence. The object of this game is to get the highest score possible. Play continues for six rounds.

Taking It Further

Have students play the multiplication and division games. This time, the lower final score wins the game.

Assessing Skills

Watch for students who need more work multiplying three factors. Review the Associative Property by asking students to group the factors in two different ways. As necessary, use counters to illustrate the Identity Property and the Property of Zero.

Find the Factors

Students will have fun testing their concentration as they look for factors of certain products.

Directions

1. Write each of the following numbers in red on index cards: 1, 3, 3, 4, 4, 5, 5, 6, 6, 7, 7, 8, 8, 12, and 16. Write each of the following numbers in blue on index cards: 24, 42, 45, 48, and 56.
2. Ask students to form two teams. Have them sit on opposite sides of the room.
3. Shuffle the red cards and place them facedown to form a 5-by-3 grid. These are the factor cards. Shuffle the blue cards and place them to the right of the other cards to form a final 5-by-4 grid. These are the product cards. Leave some space between the sets of cards to distinguish them.

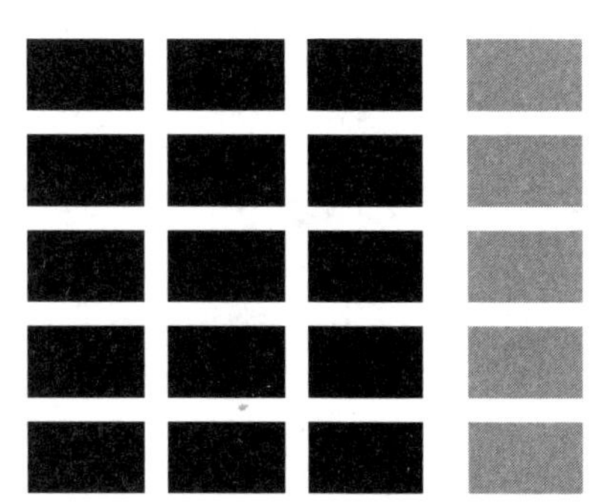

4. The first player turns over two factor cards and one product card. The student says whether the factors give that product. If the factors do give that product, and the student answers correctly, then the team takes the two factor cards and turns the product card facedown again. The next player on the same team turns over two factor cards and one product card in a similar manner. If the factors do not give the product, he or she turns all the cards over again. Play goes to the other team.
5. Continue until all factor cards are gone. The team with more factor cards wins.

LEARNING OBJECTIVE

Students recognize factors for specific numbers.

GROUPING

Two teams

MATERIALS

- large index cards
- red and blue markers

Taking It Further

Depending on the ability of the class, you can vary this game by using more difficult multiplication facts.

Assessing Skills

Are students having difficulty matching factors with the products? You may want to have them write the factors of each product on the board.

Factor Facts

The fact is that this multiplication game reinforces the concept of factors and related facts.

Directions

1. For each group, make a set of cards listing numbers that students are able to factor. Numbers may include 10, 12, 16, 18, 20, 24, 30, 36, and 45.
2. Review the concept of factor pairs—numbers that, when multiplied, give the same product. Write the number 12 on the board and ask students to list all of the factor pairs. [1 × 12, 12 × 1, 2 × 6, 6 × 2, 3 × 4, 4 × 3] Then choose one of the factor pairs such as 2 and 6, and ask a volunteer to write a multiplication and division fact family for the numbers. [2 × 6 = 12, 6 × 2 = 12, 12 ÷ 2 = 6, 12 ÷ 6 = 2]
3. Explain to students that they will be playing a game involving factors. They begin the game by stacking the cards and then turning over the top card. Each player in the group writes a factor pair for that number and the fact family. Then players show their pairs. An example of factor pairs for the number 12 is given below.

Player A	**3, 4**
Player B	**6, 2**
Player C	**3, 4**

4. Players score 1 point for each correct factor pair and 2 points for a correct fact family. (You may want to provide calculators for students to check their answers.) Players score 3 points for factor pairs that are not listed by any other player. In the above example, Players A and C score 1 point, while Player B scores 3 points for factor pairs. If all players wrote a complete and correct fact family, each would score 2 additional points.
5. Students continue playing until all of the cards are used. The highest score wins the game.

Taking It Further

Provide students with one factor and the product, such as 3 and 12. Challenge them to supply the missing factor.

Assessing Skills

If students have difficulty finding factors, provide them with counters. They may use the counters to model the given number and make equal groups to show the factors. Make sure students understand that the number of counters in a group and the number of groups are factors.

LEARNING OBJECTIVE

Students find factors for a specific number and write the fact family.

GROUPING

Cooperative groups of 3

MATERIALS

- index cards
- marker
- paper and pencil
- calculators (optional)
- counters (optional)

That's a Fact

Students clear the decks and search for fact families.

Directions

1. Distribute a deck of cards to each group. Have students remove all face cards and aces from their decks, leaving the cards 2 through 10 in all four suits, and then shuffle the cards well. They place the cards facedown in the center of the group.
2. Explain that they will be using the number cards to play a fact family game. Players take turns turning over two cards and saying a related fact for the numbers. For instance, if a player draws a 2 and an 8, the related fact might be $2 \times 4 = 8$, $2 \times 8 = 16$, or $16 \div 2 = 8$.
3. The other group members write another related fact on a sheet of paper. If there are duplicate related facts, the player who turned over the cards must complete the fact family. That player receives 1 point for each related fact he or she contributes.
4. Play continues for five rounds. Groups may reshuffle the cards as necessary.

Taking It Further

Let students play the game verbally. Each takes a turn saying a related fact. Encourage them to say the facts as quickly as they can.

Assessing Skills

Do students understand the relationship among the three numbers in the fact family?

LEARNING OBJECTIVE

Students write fact families for groups of three numbers.

GROUPING

Cooperative groups of 4

MATERIALS

- 1 deck of cards for each group
- paper and pencil

Don't Four-Get Multiples

To solve this puzzle, students reinforce the concept of multiples and geometry.

Directions

1. Duplicate the reproducible for each student and distribute. Review the concept of multiples: The multiples of a number are the products of that number and other numbers. Ask students to list multiples for the number 3 [3, 6, 9, 12, 15, 18, 21, 24, 27, 30, and so on].
2. Then have students look carefully at the reproducible to find triangles within the large triangle containing dots that add up to a multiple of 4. Point out that the triangles may be of any size.
3. Invite pairs of students to compare their results.

Taking It Further

Encourage students to make similar puzzles with multiples of 5. They may exchange puzzles with classmates.

Assessing Skills

- If students have difficulty finding multiples of 4, display a chart before they begin.
- If students are unable to visualize the different triangles, you may want to have them begin by outlining triangles that they see with colored markers or pencils.

LEARNING OBJECTIVE

Students review multiples, focusing on the number 4.

GROUPING

Individual

MATERIALS

- *Don't Four-Get Multiples* reproducible (p. 21)
- colored markers or pencils (optional)

Name ______________________ Date ______________

Don't Four-Get Multiples

There are multiple ways to solve this multiple puzzle! But you'll need to sharpen your eyes and look carefully.

Think about how to find multiples for the number 4. Then find triangles in the large triangle that contain dots adding up to a multiple of 4. The triangles may be of any size—even upside down!

Use a marker to show your triangles. Then compare your results with those of a friend.

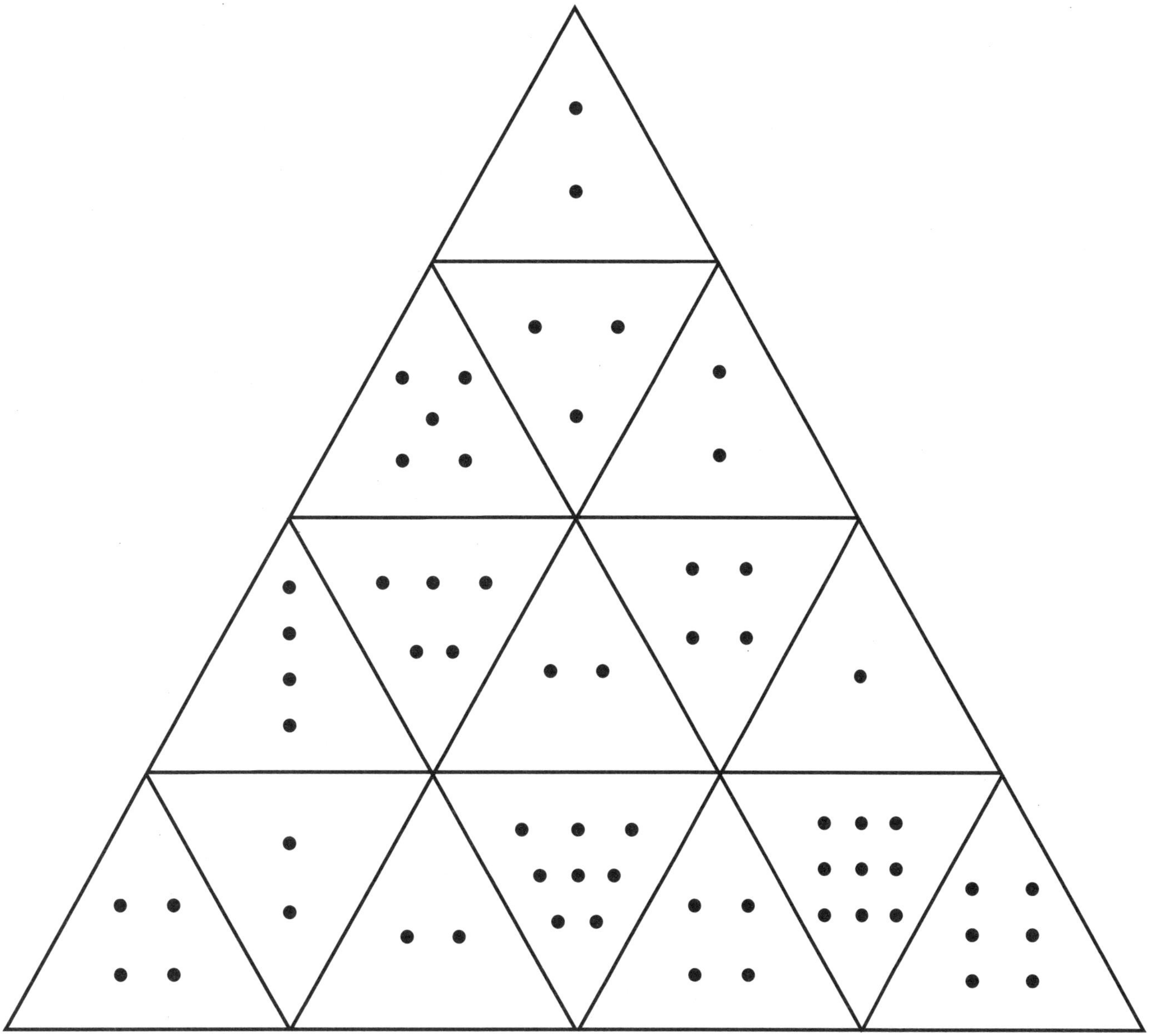

Multiplication Buzz

Students will enjoy this multiplication counting game as they recognize multiples of numbers.

Directions

1. Have students sit in a large circle. Ask them to choose a number to be "It." Explain that they cannot name "It" or any multiple of "It." For example, if 3 is "It," then they must substitute the word "buzz" for all 3s, all multiples of 3, or whenever a 3 appears.
2. Suppose 3 is "It." Ask someone to start the game by saying "1." The next student says "2," the next says "buzz," and so on around the group. The counting continues as follows: 4, 5, buzz (2 × 3 = 6), 7, 8, buzz (3 × 3 = 9), 10, 11, buzz (4 × 3 = 12), buzz (3 appears in 13), and so on. You may wish to have students say the multiplication fact after saying "buzz."
3. A student who fails to say "buzz" at the proper time, or says it at the wrong time, or says an incorrect number, is out of the game and leaves the circle. The last student remaining is the winner.
4. Play several games, using different numbers for "It."

Taking It Farther

As you go around the circle in order, some students may count ahead to prepare for their turn. To avoid this, you can have them toss a beanbag or ball to select the next player. Thus, the first player says "1" and tosses the ball to another student who says "2" and then tosses the ball to another student.

Assessing Skills

Ask students to explain which numbers chosen as "It" will produce the most buzzes and why. For example, if 1 were chosen as "It," what would happen?

LEARNING OBJECTIVE

Students recognize multiples of numbers.

GROUPING

Whole class

MATERIALS

- beanbag or ball (optional)

Greetings From Space

Students create numbers to multiply and complete a spacey story.

Directions

1. Duplicate the reproducible for each student and distribute. Make sure students understand that they write one digit in each space below the blank, creating 1-, 2-, or 3-digit numbers.
2. After students create numbers, they exchange stories and multiply. Discuss the patterns that occur when multiplying by multiples of 10.
3. Encourage students to read the stories aloud to each other. Talk about the similarities and differences in the completed stories.

Taking It Further

Ask partners to work together to write similar types of letters about fantasy vacations. They then exchange letters and solve.

Assessing Skills

- Determine whether students are able to identify patterns when multiplying.
- Observe whether they write the correct number of zeros in the products.

LEARNING OBJECTIVE

Students explore patterns when multiplying by multiples of 10.

GROUPING

Pairs

MATERIALS

- *Greetings From Space* reproducible (p. 24)

 Name ______________________ Date ______________

Greetings From Space

Harry had a strange trip this summer.

Help him write a postcard to his friend. Write a 1-digit, 2-digit, or 3-digit number in the space(s) below each blank. Then give to a friend to solve.

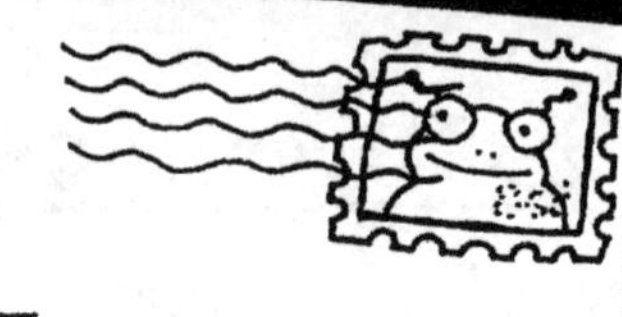

Hi, Mel! This space trip has been totally strange. The first day,

we traveled __________ miles. We landed on the planet Mojomo,
_ _ × 20

and about __________ aliens were there. We must have looked
100 × _ _

hungry, because they brought us about __________ sandwiches.
30 × _ _ _

We didn't want to be rude, so we ate as many as we could.

Then we were tired, so we slept for __________ hours under
10 × _ _

a beautiful tree. But when we woke up, there were about

__________ wild animals circling around us! We didn't want to be
100 × _

their lunch, so luckily we had some sandwiches left to give them.

We ran to our spaceship and traveled back to Earth. As they

say, there's no place like home!

Dot to Dot

This game utilizes patterns to sharpen students' mental math skills.

Directions

1. Make a spinner out of tagboard like the one shown for each pair. Divide each spinner into three equal sections, labeled 0, 00, and 000. Distribute the spinners, dominoes, and calculators (optional) to pairs of students.
2. Explain to students that they will play a multiplication game. The object is to score the greatest number of points.
3. Players make an array of dominoes facedown. The first player turns over a domino and writes the two numbers represented by dots on its face. The player chooses one number to be the first factor. To form the second factor, she or he spins the spinner and writes that number of zeros after the other number.
4. The player mentally multiplies the factors and says the product. If both players agree that the product is correct, the player records the product. The product is the player's score for that round.
5. Students take turns. After five rounds, they add to find their total scores. You may want to have students use calculators to check the scores for each round as well as the total scores.

Taking It Farther

Talk about strategies students developed to gain higher scores. Then let them play again. This time, the lower score wins the game. Compare the strategies students used to play each game.

Assessing Skills

Assess students' ability to use mental math to multiply. If they seem unsure at any stage, write the following on the board:

4×3

4×30

4×300

Allow them to use models to understand the relationships.

LEARNING OBJECTIVE

Students multiply multiples of 10, 100, and 1,000.

GROUPING

Pairs

MATERIALS

- tagboard
- scissors
- markers
- pencils
- paper clips

For each pair:

- set of dominoes
- paper and pencil
- calculators (optional)

Star Cards

Are students starstruck? They'll find out when they play this fast-paced division game.

Directions

1. Shuffle each group of cards. Place the divisor and dividend cards facedown in two stacks on a desk or table.
2. Have the class count off 1 and 2 to form two teams. Designate one student as the scorekeeper and another student as the checker. Each team stands in a line before the stacks of cards.
3. The first player on each team takes the top card from one stack and displays the card. The two players divide mentally and write the quotient on the board.
4. The first player to write the correct quotient scores 1 point for the team. When a player picks a card with a star, he or she scores 2 points for a correct answer for that round. The checker verifies the accuracy of the answers with a calculator. The scorekeeper uses tallies to record the scores.
5. Place the cards in a discard pile, reshuffling and incorporating them into the game as necessary. Play continues until everyone has had a turn.

Taking It Farther

Have students make additional cards and add them to the stacks. Groups of three students can play the game. The roles of the scorekeeper and checker are combined; students rotate the roles with each turn.

Assessing Skills

Note students who are experiencing difficulty with multiples. If necessary, pause during the game and provide some practice equations, relating the number of zeros in the factors to the number of zeros in the product.

LEARNING OBJECTIVE

Students divide multiples of 10, 100, and 1,000.

GROUPING

Two teams

MATERIALS

- large index cards
- markers
- calculators

ADVANCE PREPARATION

1. Write the following divisors on index cards, then stack them: 3, 3, 4, 4, 6, and 6.
2. Make another set of cards with the following dividends:

   12; 24; 120; 240; 1,200; 2,400; 12,000; and 24,000.
3. Draw a star in a corner of one of the divisor cards and on two of the dividend cards.

Can You Dig It?

If someone asked you to "dig it," would you get a shovel? For this game, students use front-end estimation and discover some '60s phrases.

Directions

1. Discuss how the same words can mean different things to different people and how words change meanings at different times. Ask students to share some slang expressions that they use.
2. Review how to use front-end estimation using the example below.

Multiply. 37 × 281	Use front-end estimation. 30 × 200	The estimate is 6,000.

3. Partners place the cards facedown in a 4-by-4 grid and play a Concentration-type memory game. The first player turns over two cards and uses front-end estimation to multiply any multiplication problem. The object is to match the multiplication problem ('60s slang) with the estimated product (its definition). Encourage students to try to remember the location of the estimated products. [Pad, Home (46 × 389; estimate, 12,000); Hairy, Scary (56 × 89; estimate, 4,000); Do a number, Persuade (426 × 7; estimate, 2,800); Scene, Where the fun is (295 × 471; estimate, 80,000); Hang me up, Keep me waiting (97 × 51; estimate, 4,500); Get down, Have fun (628 × 43; estimate, 24,000); Trash, Destroy (578 × 382; estimate, 150,000); Flower Power, Peace and love (87 × 7; estimate, 560)]
4. Players keep matches, and the player with more cards wins. Groovy!

Taking It Further

Let students create their own modern version of the game, using contemporary slang for the multiplication problems and definitions for the estimated products.

Assessing Skills

Note whether students have trouble relating place value to front-end estimation. Have them use place-value charts to estimate.

LEARNING OBJECTIVE

Students estimate products using front-end estimation.

GROUPING

Pairs

MATERIALS

* index cards
* markers

ADVANCE PREPARATION

Make a set of 16 index cards with the following written on them:

Pad 46 x 389	Hairy 56 x 89
Do a number 426 x 7	Scene 295 x 471
Hang me up 97 x 51	Get down 628 x 43
Trash 578 x 382	Flower Power 87 x 7
Have fun 24,000	Destroy 150,000
Keep me waiting 4,500	Peace and love 560
Persuade 2,800	Home 12,000
Scary 4,000	Where the fun is 80,000

Riddle Round-Up

Estimating can be a laughing matter when students round and divide.

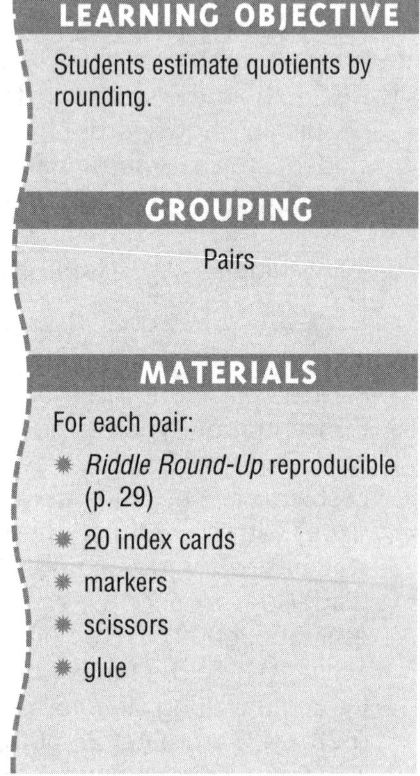
LEARNING OBJECTIVE

Students estimate quotients by rounding.

GROUPING

Pairs

MATERIALS

For each pair:

- *Riddle Round-Up* reproducible (p. 29)
- 20 index cards
- markers
- scissors
- glue

Directions

1. Write 267 ÷ 5 on the board. Review and discuss how to estimate the quotient by rounding and using compatible numbers.

ROUNDING	COMPATIBLE NUMBERS
Round dividend to the greatest place and divide. 267 ÷ 5 ↓ 300 ÷ 5 = 60	Use basic division facts. 267 ÷ 5 ↓ 250 ÷ 5 = 50

2. Give partners a copy of the reproducible and have them cut out and glue a riddle and division problem to the front of an index card. Then they cut out the quotient and answer. Students should fold the quotient/answer so that the quotient appears on one side of the index card and the answer to the riddle is on the back. The riddle and division problem go on one card. The quotient and answer appear on a separate card.

5,000

3. One student chooses a riddle card and estimates the quotient by using compatible numbers. The partner finds the matching card with the estimated quotient and reads the answer to the riddle. Students use the answer to the riddle to make sure the estimate is sensible.
4. Students take turns and continue until all the riddles have been solved.

Taking It Further

Invite students to choose some of the problems and estimate the quotients by rounding. Have them compare the estimates derived by both methods. Talk about situations where each type of estimation might be appropriate.

Assessing Skills

- Do students use the closest basic division fact?
- Are they putting the correct number of zeros in the quotients?

 Name ______________________________ Date ______________

Riddle Round-Up

Estimating can be a laughing matter!

Cut out and glue a riddle and division problem to the front of an index card. Cut out, fold, and glue a quotient and answer to the front and back of an index card.

Now you're ready to play! Estimate by *using compatible numbers*, find the matching estimation card, and see if you can answer the riddles.

Riddles and Division Problems

Why did the man bring a rope to the baseball game?	$8\overline{)3,719}$
What does a shark eat with peanut butter?	$57 \div 3$
What has four legs and flies?	$711 \div 9$
What did one eye say to the other?	$7\overline{)462}$
What do you call the time of prehistoric pigs?	$5,680 \div 6$
Why can't a bicycle stand by itself?	$5\overline{)16,102}$
What kind of jam cannot be eaten?	$4\overline{)2,620}$
What did one math book say to the other?	$42,888 \div 9$
When is a black dog not a black dog?	$8\overline{)741}$
Why did the boy put an alarm clock in his shoe?	$3,707 \div 9$

Quotients and Answers

20	5,000
jellyfish	Boy, I've got problems!
900	400
Jurassic Pork	so his foot wouldn't fall asleep
3,000	500
because it's two tired	to tie up the game
80	90
a horse	when it's a greyhound
70	600
There's something between us that smells.	a traffic jam

Productive Draws

Students sharpen critical-thinking skills and decide which factors will give the highest product.

LEARNING OBJECTIVE

Students use logical reasoning and practice multiplying by a 1-digit number.

GROUPING

Two teams

MATERIALS

* deck of cards
* paper and pencil
* calculator (optional)

ADVANCE PREPARATION

Remove all tens and face cards from a deck of cards. The number cards 2 through 9 and the aces should remain.

Directions

1. Write the multiplication sentence 35 x 9 on the board. Review the regrouping process as follows:

Multiply the ones. Regroup if necessary.		Multiply the tens. Add any new tens.	
$\begin{array}{r} {}^{4} \\ 35 \\ \underline{\times\ 9} \\ 5 \end{array}$	$(9 \times 5 = 45)$	$\begin{array}{r} {}^{4} \\ 35 \\ \underline{\times\ 9} \\ 315 \end{array}$	$(9 \times 3 = 27)$ $(27 + 4 = 31)$

2. Ask students to form Team A and Team B. Have teams sit on opposite sides of a table.
3. Explain that the object of the game they will play is to use factors to make the highest product possible.
4. Shuffle the cards and place them facedown in a stack on the table. The first player on each team draws three cards. The first player on Team A places two cards faceup on the table to form a 2-digit factor of his or her choice. Then the first player on Team B places one card below the two to form a multiplication problem.
5. Students multiply to find the product. Team A records the product as its first score. Players place their cards in a discard pile.
6. Repeat the process, with the second player on Team B going first to form a 2-digit factor and the second player on Team A going second to select a 1-digit factor. Team B records the product as its score. Play continues until all students have drawn cards. (You may need to reshuffle the discard pile before the game ends.) Teams add their scores. They may use calculators if you wish. The team with the higher score wins.

Taking It Farther

For an additional challenge, the second player of each round can place two cards below the first factor to form a 2-digit factor. You can also have students draw five cards and form 3- and 2-digit factors.

Assessing Skills

* Observe what kinds of strategies students are developing.
* Ask them to explain how to obtain the highest scores.

Time to Grow Up

Students use the gestation or incubation periods of different animals displayed on a bulletin board to create multiplication problems.

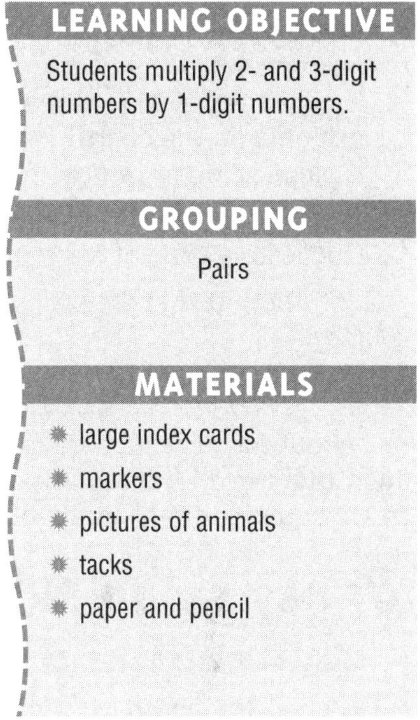

LEARNING OBJECTIVE

Students multiply 2- and 3-digit numbers by 1-digit numbers.

GROUPING

Pairs

MATERIALS

- large index cards
- markers
- pictures of animals
- tacks
- paper and pencil

Directions

1. Make the bulletin board as shown below. On six cards, draw a picture of an animal or write its name. Using six more cards, list the average gestation or incubation time.

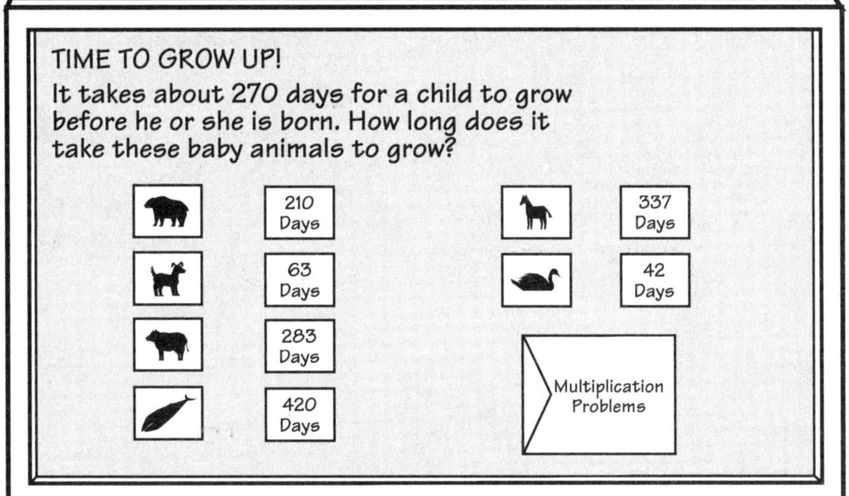

2. You may want to explain that animals can grow inside their mothers, which is called gestation, or they can grow in eggs outside their mothers, which is called incubation.
3. Students then make up multiplication problems, such as the following: *If a mother horse is pregnant 2 times in her life, how many days will she be pregnant?* [674 days] Challenge students to solve each other's problems.

Taking It Further

Invite students to research the gestation or incubation times for other animals. Let them include these animals on the bulletin board.

Assessing Skills

Make sure students are using the correct numbers to solve the problems.

Believe It or Not!

Students find out interesting facts by multiplying and completing some strange sentences.

Directions

1. Review multiplying with regrouping by writing the following example on the board: 3 × 39. Have students write the multiplication in vertical form and solve. Work through the regrouping process using models if necessary.
2. Duplicate a copy of the reproducible for each student and distribute.
3. Tell students that they will multiply to complete each fact.

Taking It Farther

Talk about the facts that are most surprising to students. Encourage them to make a list of unusual facts that they come across. Help them to create equations to fill in the blanks as appropriate.

Assessing Skills

- Note whether students use mental math.
- Observe whether they make common errors such as forgetting to regroup, regrouping incorrectly, or errors with basic facts.

LEARNING OBJECTIVE

Students multiply 2-digit and 3-digit numbers by 1-digit numbers.

GROUPING

Individual

MATERIALS

- *Believe It or Not!* reproducible (p. 33)

Name ______________________ Date ______________

Believe It or Not!

Chances are you won't know the answers to these wacky facts! Multiply and then write the product in the blank. What you find out may surprise you!

1. Even without its head, a cockroach can live up to ________ days.
(10 × 1)

2. When you sneeze, the air rushes through your nose at about ________ miles per hour.
(50 × 2)

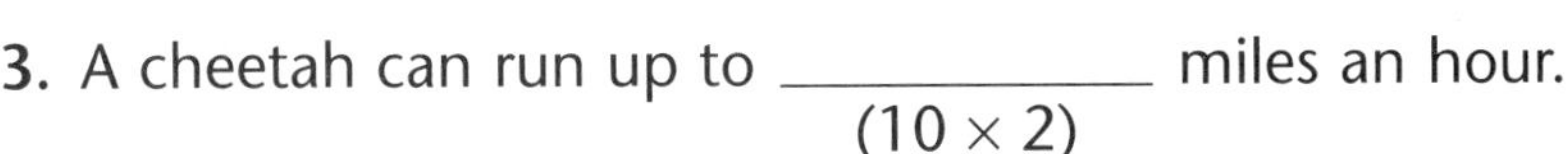

3. A cheetah can run up to ________ miles an hour.
(10 × 2)

4. If you weigh 100 pounds on Earth, you would weigh ________ pounds on Mars.
(19 × 2)

5. The top speed for a sailfish has been recorded at ________ miles per hour.
(17 × 4)

6. A large order of French fries has about ________ calories.
(120 × 3)

7. The figure of the Statue of Liberty is about ________ feet high.
(30 × 5)

8. There are ________ muscles in the body.
(213 × 3)
These muscles make up about ________ percent of the body weight.
(10 × 4)

Car Facts

Students multiply and create a timeline to show the history of the automobile.

Directions

1. Write the following facts on one side of the index cards and the multiplication problems on the back. Have students multiply and write the products on the front beside the event. The products will show the years in which the events took place.

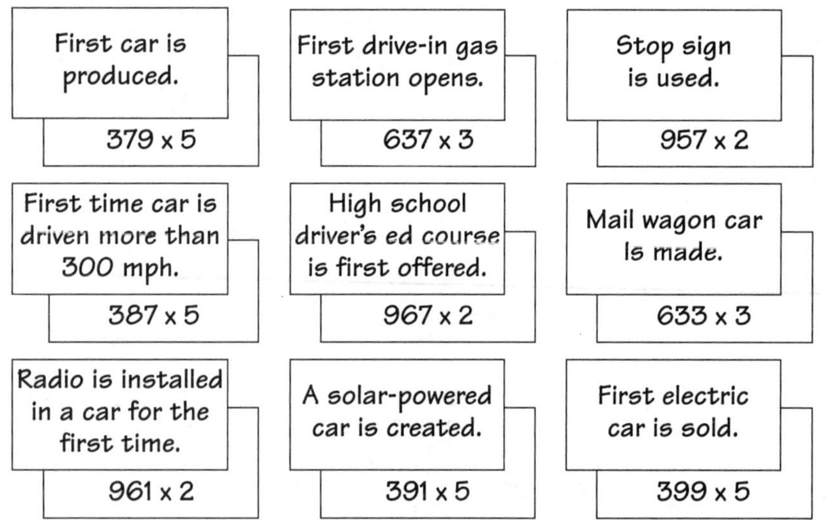

2. Help students tape the cards on the appropriate place on the timeline as necessary. Encourage them to draw illustrations for the timeline. [1895—First car is produced. 1899—Mail wagon car is made. 1911—First drive-in gas station opens. 1914—Stop sign is used. 1922—Radio is installed in a car for the first time. 1934—High school driver's ed course is first offered. 1935—First time a car is driven more than 300 mph. 1955—A solar-powered car is created. 1995—First electric car is sold.]

Taking It Further

Invite students to research other automobile history facts for the timeline. Encourage them to include facts from the automobile's first 100 years as well as those that extend to the present.

Assessing Skills

Observe if students place the dates correctly on the timeline. Point out how a timeline is like a number line. If necessary, have students practice placing 2-digit numbers on number lines.

LEARNING OBJECTIVE

Students multiply 3-digit numbers by 1-digit numbers.

GROUPING

Small cooperative groups

MATERIALS

- chart paper
- index cards
- markers
- tape

ADVANCE PREPARATION

Use chart paper and markers to make a timeline showing ten-year increments from 1895 through 1995. Leave ample space so that students can tape index cards on the timeline. If desired, leave space to extend the timeline from 1995 to the present day.

Weigh up in Space

Students multiply to learn about size and weight of planets as they help to make a bulletin board.

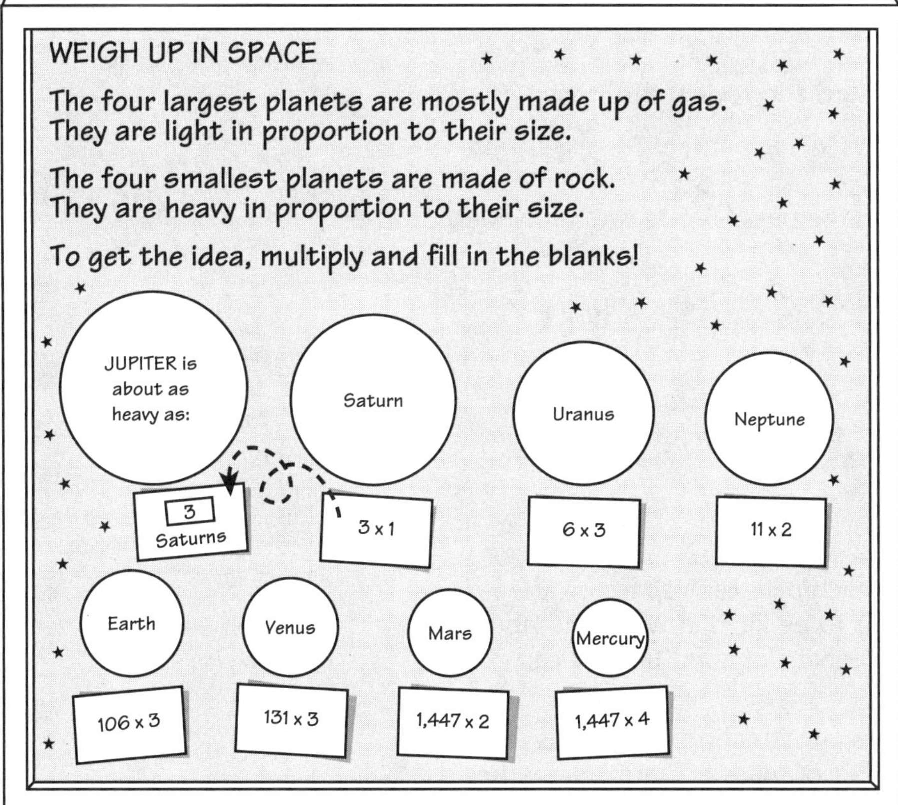

Directions

Students multiply and write the products in the rectangles on the back of the cards. Then they reattach the cards to the appropriate planets. You may want to have them check their work by using a calculator. [Jupiter is about as heavy as 3 Saturns; 18 Uranuses; 22 Neptunes; 318 Earths; 393 Venuses; 2,894 Marses; 5,788 Mercuries.]

Taking It Further

Invite students to find out the diameter in miles of each planet. Have them order the numbers and make up problems for others to solve.

Assessing Skills

Ask students to describe the regrouping process when multiplying 4- and 5-digit numbers.

LEARNING OBJECTIVE

Students multiply by 1-digit numbers.

GROUPING

Small cooperative groups

MATERIALS

- bulletin board
- markers
- index cards
- art paper
- tacks
- calculator (optional)

ADVANCE PREPARATION:

Prepare the bulletin board as shown. Cut out proportionate circles to show the planets and label them accordingly. Write the matching multiplication problem on an index card. On the other side of the card draw a rectangle followed by the planet's name in plural (for example, Earths, Neptunes). Place the card under the appropriate planet.

131 x 3

Venuses

What Do You Know?

Students think of numbers they already know as they play a division game.

LEARNING OBJECTIVE

Students divide by 1-digit numbers.

GROUPING

Pairs

MATERIALS

For each pair:

- *What Do You Know?* reproducible (p. 37)
- number cube
- 2 counters
- calculator (optional)
- correction fluid (optional)

Directions

1. Write the example shown on the board and review the steps involved in the division.

Step 1
Determine where to place the first digit in the quotient. Divide.

4 > 1
4 < 15 Divide tens.

$$\begin{array}{r} 3 \\ 4\,\overline{)159} \\ -12 \\ \hline 3 \end{array}$$

Step 2
Bring down the ones. Divide.

$$\begin{array}{r} 39 \\ 4\,\overline{)159} \\ -12 \\ \hline 39 \\ -\,36 \\ \hline 3 \end{array}$$

Step 3
Write the remainder.

$$\begin{array}{r} 39 \text{ R3} \\ 4\,\overline{)159}\phantom{\text{ R3}} \\ -12\phantom{\text{ R3}} \\ \hline 39\phantom{\text{ R3}} \\ -\,36\phantom{\text{ R3}} \\ \hline 3\phantom{\text{ R3}} \end{array}$$

2. Give a copy of the reproducible to each pair. Each space on the game board has a square that needs to be filled in with a number. The number can be part of a book, movie, or song title, or can complete a phrase.
3. Players use counters for game pieces, and the first player rolls the number cube and moves that number of spaces. That player writes the correct number in the square and divides that number by the number represented on the number cube. For example, if Player 1 rolls 4, he or she divides 13 by 4.
4. The partner checks the division. If the division is correct, the player stays in the space. If it is incorrect, he or she moves back to START.
5. Players must roll the exact number to reach FINISH.

Taking It Farther

Use correction fluid to make some blank spaces on a photocopy of the game board. Have students create their own phrases for the game and play again.

Assessing Skills

You may want to have some students fill in the blanks on the game board before playing the game. Then these students can focus on the division as they play.

Name ______________________________ Date ________________

What Do You Know?

You'll need to think of numbers you already know to play this division game!

Roll the number cube and then move that many spaces on the game board. Fill in the square with the correct number. Then make and solve a division sentence with the number you rolled and the number in the square.

Your Table Is Ready

There's no need for students to fly by the seats of their pants when they figure out how many tables their classroom will need.

Directions

1. Explain to students that they will plan a new seating arrangement for the classroom. They may consider the following types of desks and tables:
   - desks that seat 2 students
   - tables that seat 3 students
   - tables that seat 4 students
   - tables that seat 5 students
   - tables that seat 6 students
2. Ask students to choose one type of desk or table and then determine how many of each your class will need.
3. Divide students according to the type of desk or table each chose. Let the groups compare work, especially focusing on how they dealt with remainders when dividing. For instance, a class of 32 students would need 7 tables that seat 5 students each.
4. Allow time for the groups to present their ideas to the class.

Taking It Farther

Present the class with the total number of students in your school. Ask them to choose cafeteria tables that seat 4, 6, or 8 students each and determine how many tables your school would need.

Assessing Skills

- Are students taking remainders into account in their orders?
- Can they verbalize the strategies they used?

LEARNING OBJECTIVE

Students divide 2-digit numbers by 1-digit numbers and work with remainders.

GROUPING

Individuals and then groups

MATERIALS

- paper and pencil

Career Changes

Students match a president of the United States with a former career and practice division skills.

Directions

1. Duplicate the reproducible for each student and distribute.
2. Have students complete the page individually. You may want to let pairs compare their answers and talk about facts about the presidents that surprised them.

Taking It Further

Encourage students to research the lives of other presidents. They can use the information to write their own multiplication matches for other students to solve.

Assessing Skills

- Ascertain whether students place the first digit correctly in the quotient.
- Ask students why the remainder cannot be larger than the divisor.

LEARNING OBJECTIVE

Students divide 2- and 3-digit numbers by 1-digit divisors.

GROUPING

Individual

MATERIALS

- *Career Changes* reproducible (p. 40)

Name ______________________ Date ____________

Career Changes

Many Americans will change careers during their lives.
Even presidents of the United States have had different jobs!

What careers do you think these presidents had before they moved into the White House? Your job is to find out! First, take a guess. Then divide, match the quotient, and see if your guess is correct.

DIVIDE:

1. Andrew Jackson

   75 ÷ 6 = ________

2. Woodrow Wilson

   193 ÷ 4 = ________

3. Ronald Reagan

   462 ÷ 7 = ________

4. John F. Kennedy

   469 ÷ 5 = ________

5. Andrew Johnson

   432 ÷ 8 = ________

6. Lyndon Johnson

   843 ÷ 9 = ________

7. Jimmy Carter

   72 ÷ 2 = ________

8. Thomas Jefferson

   755 ÷ 5 = ________

QUOTIENT AND CAREER:

66 Actor

151 Writer

93 R6 Teacher

12 R3 Soldier

36 Peanut farmer

54 Tailor

48 R1 Teacher

93 R4 Newspaperman

Continue Her-story

Students discover some amazing women in history as they practice division.

Directions

1. Review division that results in a zero in the quotient.
2. Duplicate the reproducible for each student or pair and distribute.
3. Explain to students that they need to find the sentence in the second column to continue the story begun in the first column. After dividing the number in the first column by the number in the second column, they check the list of women at the top of the page to find the matching quotient. Do the first exercise together, reviewing the division process as necessary.
4. You may want to have students work in pairs. They can take turns matching the story sentences and doing the division.

Taking It Farther

Ask each student to interview a woman to find out about something she has accomplished. Students can work in groups to prepare a similar set of exercises.

Assessing Skills

Watch for students who do not find the matching quotient after they divide. Help them use logical reasoning to determine if the factors do not match, or if they made a division error.

LEARNING OBJECTIVE

Students divide 4- and 5-digit numbers by 1-digit numbers.

GROUPING

Individual or pairs

MATERIALS

- *Continue Her-story* reproducible (p. 42)

Name ______________________ Date ____________

Continue Her-story

Elizabeth Blackwell 2,958
Nellie Bly 4,232
Lydia Pinkham 4,319
Ida B. Wells 6,307
Sarah Edmonds 1,065

Many women have done deeds that have made history, but we don't always hear about it! Here's your chance to find out more.

Read about the deed in the first column. Then find the sentence in the second column that continues the story. Divide the number in the first column by the number in the second column and match the quotient to find the accomplished woman.

This woman was called "the best reporter in America." (12,696)

This woman disguised herself as a man to fight in the Civil War. (2,130)

About 20,000 people came to watch her become the first woman to receive an M.D. (a doctor's degree). (14,790)

When she was 18, this woman was forced to leave a train because she wouldn't sit in the "colored only" section. (18,921)

In 1875, this woman started selling an herbal medicine and offering advice about women's health. (25,914)

Her medicine sales started earning $300,000 a year! (6)

When she couldn't find an American hospital that would hire her, she began her own hospital. (5)

She wrote a book about her war adventures that sold 175,000 copies. (2)

Once she pretended to be mentally ill so she could write a news story about mental hospitals. (3)

She sued the railroad and continued to write about problems in the South. (3)

You're in Jeopardy

The answers are the easy part—it's the questions that are tricky!

Directions

1. Review the terms *dividend, divisor,* and *quotient* by writing the example on the board and having students identify and label each term: 250 ÷ 7 = 35 R5.
2. Explain to students that they will play a division Jeopardy game. The answers will be given, and the players must supply the questions in the categories of "Dividends," "Divisors," and "Quotients." One student will be the game host and read the answers and questions out loud; another student will keep score; and the remaining 2 or 3 students will be contestants.
3. Distribute a copy of the reproducible to each group. On index cards, they write five questions and answers for each category. The cards should have the format shown.
4. Students cut apart the Jeopardy category pieces. On the back of the matching pieces, they write only the answers from their corresponding index cards. Groups then exchange sets of index cards and game categories.
5. The contestants take turns choosing categories and money amounts. The game host turns over the appropriate pieces and reads aloud the answers. All contestants may respond by raising their hands. The host determines who raised his or her hand first and refers to the index cards for the correct questions. Contestants may use paper and pencils to solve the problems. If the contestant gives the correct question to the answer, he or she earns that amount of money. The scorekeeper records the amount. That contestant may choose another category.
6. Play continues until all the category pieces have been turned over and read.

QUOTIENTS $100	
Answer:	**The dividend is 40.**
	The divisor is 8.
Question:	**What is 5?**

LEARNING OBJECTIVE

Students identify dividends, divisors, and quotients.

GROUPING

Cooperative groups of 4 or 5

MATERIALS

For each group:

- *You're in Jeopardy* reproducible (p. 44)
- 15 index cards
- markers
- scissors
- calculators
- paper and pencil

Taking It Further

Expand the game categories to include the multiplication terms *factors, products,* and *multiples.*

Assessing Skills

Are students able to connect the category terms to the proper parts of the division sentence?

Name ____________________ Date ____________

You're in Jeopardy

How about Divisors for $200? Don't forget to give your answer in the form of a question!

Cut out the game pieces below. Write an answer on the back of each one.

Dividends $100	**Divisors $100**	**Quotients $100**
Dividends $200	**Divisors $200**	**Quotients $200**
Dividends $300	**Divisors $300**	**Quotients $300**
Dividends $400	**Divisors $400**	**Quotients $400**
Dividends $500	**Divisors $500**	**Quotients $500**

River Rapids

Students take a "rapid" trip as they multiply and divide to make their way through a maze.

Directions

1. Duplicate and distribute the reproducible. Explain that the object is to follow the maze by forming correct multiplication sentences. If the path is correct, the answer to one sentence will be the first number in the next sentence.
2. Point out that if a sentence in the maze is not correct, students should try another path.

Taking It Farther

Pair students of similar abilities and challenge them to time each other to see how "rapidly" they can complete the maze.

Assessing Skills

Determine how effectively students are able to backtrack if they make a multiplication error or go down the wrong path.

LEARNING OBJECTIVE

Students multiply by 1-, 2-, and 3-digit numbers.

GROUPING

Individual

MATERIALS

- *River Rapids* reproducible (p. 46)

Name ______________________ Date ______________

River Rapids

Multiply to find your way out of the river rapids. If the path is correct, the answer to the first multiplication sentence will be the first factor in the next sentence, and so on.

Road Rally

The road to solid multiplication skills can take a lot of practice! With this multiplication game, students are well on their way.

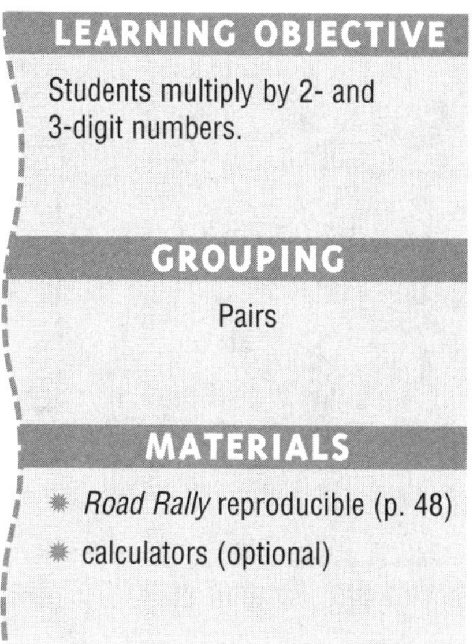

LEARNING OBJECTIVE

Students multiply by 2- and 3-digit numbers.

GROUPING

Pairs

MATERIALS

- *Road Rally* reproducible (p. 48)
- calculators (optional)

Directions

1. Duplicate the reproducible for each pair and distribute.
2. Discuss multiplying by 2-digit numbers, focusing on the regrouping process as follows:

Multiply by the ones. Regroup if necessary.

$$\begin{array}{r} ^{1} \\ 35 \\ \times\ 62 \\ \hline 70 \end{array} \quad (2 \times 35 = 70)$$

Multiply by the tens. Regroup if necessary.

$$\begin{array}{r} ^{3} \\ ^{\cancel{1}} \\ 35 \\ \times\ 62 \\ \hline 70 \\ 2100 \end{array} \quad (60 \times 35 = 2{,}100)$$

Add the products.

$$\begin{array}{r} ^{3} \\ ^{\cancel{1}} \\ 35 \\ \times\ 62 \\ \hline 70 \\ +\ 2100 \\ \hline 2170 \end{array}$$

Ask students to give you a 3-digit number and a 2-digit number. Write a multiplication sentence on the board and let volunteers explain the multiplication process.

3. Review the terms *odd* and *even* and ask students to give examples of each.
4. Have partners play the game. You may want to let students check their answers with calculators.

Taking It Further

Talk about strategies that students used during the game. Then have them write four more numbers on the billboard and play a bonus round.

Assessing Skills

- Do students complete the regrouping process from ones to tens and so on as necessary?
- Do they remember to regroup and add?

Name ______________________ Date ______________

Road Rally

Play this game with a partner. Pick two numbers from the billboard and multiply them. Cross out the numbers and then find your score below. Play five rounds.

32	45	519	26	279
23	350	81	486	94
75	237	52	148	663
68	37	104	389	74

The product is even.
1 point

The product is odd.
2 points

The product is greater than 3,000.
3 points

Player 1

PRODUCT	POINTS
TOTAL	

Player 2

PRODUCT	POINTS
TOTAL	

What's New in the News?

Students "report" on numbers and practice multiplying.

Directions

1. Ask students to look through newspapers and magazines and cut out two articles or ads that mention 2- and 3-digit numbers.
2. Divide the class into groups. Extra students will be fact checkers. The first student "reports" and reads the sentence that uses a number. The second student does the same. The third student multiplies, using the numbers as factors. A student checker verifies the product with a calculator. If the product is correct, the third student scores a point.
3. Group members change roles and continue until each person has a chance to multiply at least three times. You may also want to let checkers and group members exchange roles.

Taking It Farther

Challenge students to find 3-, 4-, or 5-digit numbers to use in a division game. The rules are the same as for the game above except that students divide these numbers by 2-digit numbers from articles or ads that they already have.

Assessing Skills

Observe students who are having difficulty multiplying. Take time to review the multiplication process, using models if necessary. Encourage students to explain each step of the process.

LEARNING OBJECTIVE

Students multiply by 2- and 3-digit numbers.

GROUPING

Cooperative groups of 3

MATERIALS

- local and/or national newspapers
- magazines
- scissors
- calculators

Me First!

Almost everyone wants to go first! Students divide, order numbers and discover some interesting "firsts."

Card	Front	Back
1	First elevated railroad 580 ÷ 29	First elevator 2,112 ÷ 64
2	Root beer is invented 1,116 ÷ 36	First bottle cap with a cork 2,250 ÷ 45
3	First cookbook 702 ÷ 13	First children's magazine 1,364 ÷ 22
4	First ballpoint pen 1,062 ÷ 18	First pencil with an eraser 1,067 ÷ 11
5	First bicycle 2,556 ÷ 71	First roller skates 774 ÷ 18
6	First alarm clock 532 ÷ 38	First wristwatch 575 ÷ 25

Directions

1. Shuffle the cards before distributing to pairs.
2. Have students guess which fact on each card came first. Encourage them to use estimation.
3. Students take turns and divide. After they write the quotients, they order the numbers on each card. The number that is less, or "comes first," matches the event that came first. See the answers at right.

Taking It Further

Invite students to write two events in their own lives, with matching division problems to show which came first. Partners exchange cards, divide, and order the events.

Assessing Skills

You may want to have students use calculators to check their work. If they discover errors, ask them to explain each step of the division process.

LEARNING OBJECTIVE

Students divide by 2-digit divisors and order numbers.

GROUPING

Pairs

MATERIALS

- large index cards
- markers
- calculators (optional)

ADVANCE PREPARATION

Write the facts and division sentences on the front and back of the index cards as shown so each pair has a set of 6 cards. Each card will contain two different facts and sentences.

ANSWERS

Card 1— 20 (elevated railroad)
33 (elevator)

Card 2— 31 (root beer)
50 (bottle cap)

Card 3— 54 (cookbook)
62 (magazine)

Card 4— 59 (pen)
97 (pencil)

Card 5— 36 (bicycle)
43 (skates)

Card 6— 14 (clock)
23 (wristwatch)

Food for Thought

Students learn some fascinating food facts as they practice dividing by 2-digit numbers.

Directions

1. Begin by reviewing odd and even numbers. Write several 3-digit numbers on the board and have students classify them as odd or even.
2. Write the following example on the board: 17,595 ÷ 85. Have students explain the division process, especially focusing on the zero in the quotient (207). Ask students to determine whether the quotient is odd or even and to explain how they know.
3. Duplicate the reproducible for each student or pair and distribute. Go over the directions and make sure they understand that if the quotient is odd, the fact is true.

Taking It Further

Ask students to develop rules that tell when quotients will be odd or even. Have them experiment with different combinations of odd and even dividends and divisors.

Assessing Skills

Some students may forget to place a zero in the ones place of the second partial product. Provide a multiplication sentence and have them write the second factor in expanded form. Point out that the first factor is multiplied by the value of each digit in the second factor.

LEARNING OBJECTIVE

Students divide by 2-digit numbers.

GROUPING

Individual or pairs

MATERIALS

- *Food for Thought* reproducible (p. 52)

Name ______________________________ Date ______________

Food for Thought

These food facts may or may not be true! Divide and decide if the quotient is odd or even. If the quotient is odd, then oddly enough, the fact is true!

1. The shape of a pretzel was invented by a priest who gave "pretzels" to children when they memorized prayers.

   18,543 ÷ 21 = __________ **True** **False**

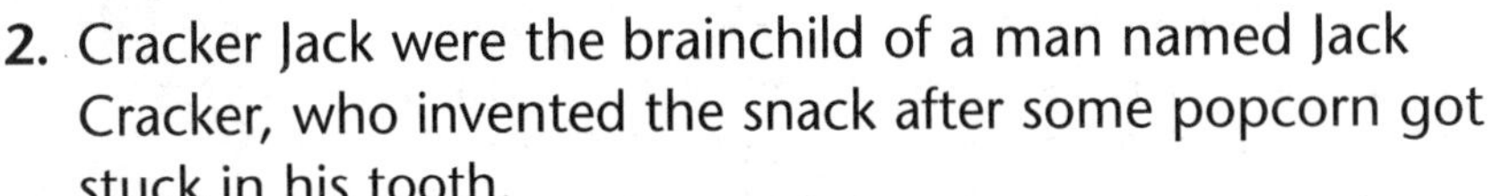

2. Cracker Jack were the brainchild of a man named Jack Cracker, who invented the snack after some popcorn got stuck in his tooth.

   25,546 ÷ 53 = __________ **True** **False**

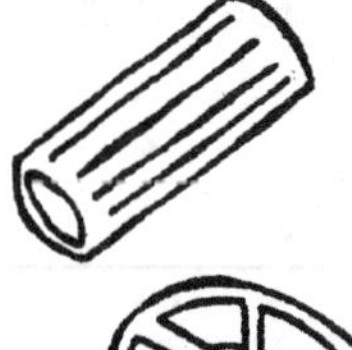

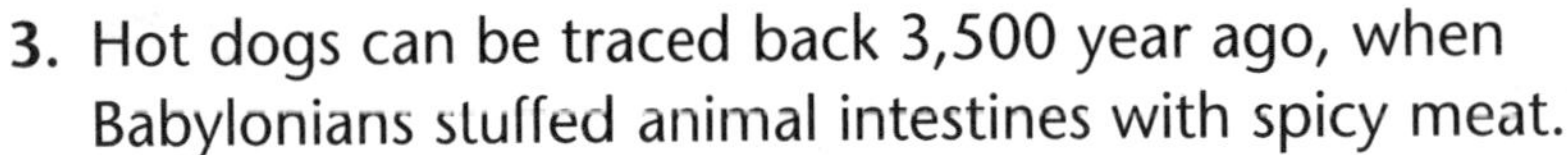

3. Hot dogs can be traced back 3,500 year ago, when Babylonians stuffed animal intestines with spicy meat.

   19,703 ÷ 61 = __________ **True** **False**

4. Pasta was first made in China from rice and bean flour.

   9,845 ÷ 11 = __________ **True** **False**

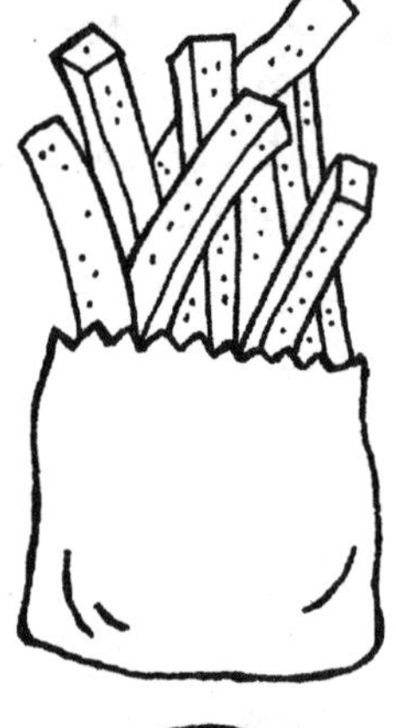

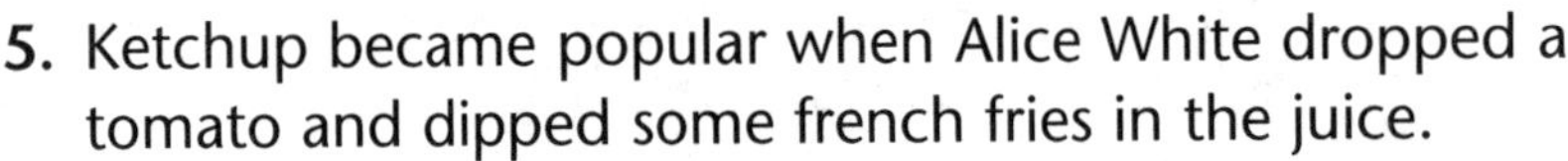

5. Ketchup became popular when Alice White dropped a tomato and dipped some french fries in the juice.

   9,204 ÷ 78 = __________ **True** **False**

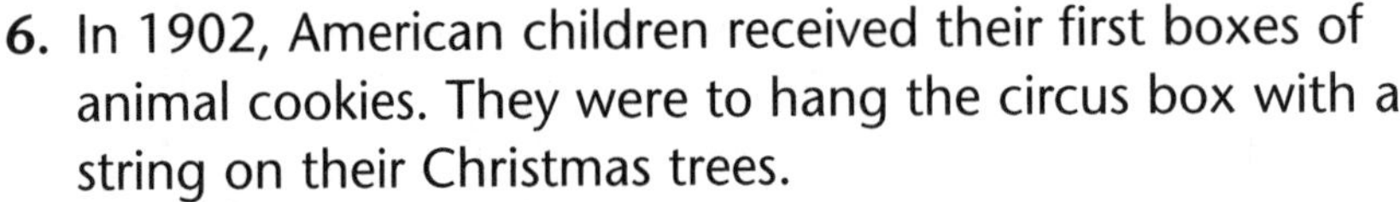

6. In 1902, American children received their first boxes of animal cookies. They were to hang the circus box with a string on their Christmas trees.

   28,035 ÷ 45 = __________ **True** **False**

7. Frank Fleer's first try at creating bubble gum was called Blibber-Blubber Bubble Gum.

   43,097 ÷ 71 = __________ **True** **False**

Sandwich by the Slice

No matter how you slice it, this activity will help students take a bite out of multiplying money.

Directions

1. Copy and distribute the reproducible. Explain to students that they can ask 6 to 10 classmates to choose types of filling for their sandwiches. Each person can choose three slices of the same type of filling, or any combination of the three.
2. After compiling the data, students multiply to find the totals and the cost.
3. When students complete the tables, have them compare results.

Taking It Further

Ask students to estimate before they find the total cost, using front-end estimation and rounding. Discuss which method gave a more accurate estimate.

Assessing Skills

Observe the steps that students use to solve the problems.

LEARNING OBJECTIVE

Students take a poll and multiply to solve problems.

GROUPING

Individual

MATERIALS

- *Sandwich by the Slice* reproducible (p. 54)
- calculators (optional)

Name ____________________ Date ____________

Sandwich by the Slice

You're planning a party! You can invite from 6 to 10 classmates. You're going to order a sub sandwich from the Sandwich by the Slice Shop.

Each friend can order 3 fillings for the sandwich. Take a poll and find out what kinds of sandwiches your friends like. Then multiply to find out how many slices the sandwich will have and the cost. (Don't forget to include yourself!)

Specials

Sandwich by the Slice
Turkey .... 25¢
Roast Beef....... 29¢
Cheese........... 18¢

FRIEND'S NAME	TURKEY	ROAST BEEF	CHEESE

		Cost
Slices of Turkey	________	$________
Slices of Roast Beef	________	$________
Slices of Cheese	________	$________
Total slices	________	
Total cost		$________

Which type of filling is the most popular? ____________

Shop 'Til You Drop

Students compare prices by buying in bulk and buying single items. Let them decide how to shop smart!

Directions

1. Duplicate a copy of the reproducible for each student or group and distribute.
2. Students use newspaper ads to find the price of a single item and the price of the same item in a multi-pack. You may also want to have students research prices at the grocery store the next time their families go shopping, or supply prices yourself. Explore with them how to determine the amount saved. If necessary, help students find the savings by following either of these methods:
   a. Multiply the price of the single item by the total number of items in a multi-pack. Then subtract the cost of the multi-pack from that amount.
   b. Divide the price of the multi-pack by the number of items in it. Then subtract the cost of each multi-pack item from the price of a single item.
3. Discuss the results, including other items that students added to the table.

Taking It Farther

Ask students to think of other types of items that are sold in bulk, such as socks, T-shirts, or barrettes. Encourage them to investigate savings and incorporate their findings in a newspaper or television ad for one of the products. Are multi-packs always the smarter buy?

Assessing Skills

Determine whether students understand the computation to find the savings. If necessary, help them to analyze each step using a calculator for the computation.

LEARNING OBJECTIVE

Students develop consumer skills as they multiply and divide money amounts.

GROUPING

Individual or groups

MATERIALS

* *Shop 'Til You Drop* reproducible (p. 56)
* newspaper ads
* calculator (optional)

Name ______________________ Date ____________

Shop 'Til You Drop

More and more people shop at warehouse-type stores where they can buy products in large quantities. Some grocery stores also sell items the same way.

How much do shoppers really save? Do some research to find out. Visit a store or look at newspaper ads to find some of the items listed below. Add some items of your own to the table. Then complete the table to find out if you're shopping smart.

ITEM	Cost of Single Item	Cost of Multi-pack	Number of Items in Multi-pack	SAVINGS
Paper Towels				
Canned Dog Food				
Bars of Soap				
Ballpoint Pens				
Canned Soda				

Party Problems

Students plan a party and multiply money amounts. The problem is figuring out the best way to spend $80!

Directions

1. Duplicate a copy of the reproducible for each student or pair and distribute.
2. To begin, students make decisions regarding food, decorations, and other items that they would like to include in their party plan. Then they use information from local stores and restaurants to find appropriate prices. Students multiply as needed; they may also use calculators to determine the total cost.
3. If the total amount is more than $80, students should reassess their choices and make the appropriate changes. If the total is less than $80, they divide the cost by the number of students on the team to determine how much was spent for each student. Students round amounts to the penny as necessary.
4. Draw a blank check on the board and fill it in so students can refer to it when filling out their own checks. They may also draw additional checks on a separate sheet of paper.
5. Allow time for students to share and compare their results.

Taking It Farther

Invite groups of students to plan a class party, spending as little money as possible. Challenge them to think about how they could make low-cost snacks and decorations.

Assessing Skills

If students have difficulty multiplying money amounts, let them use bills and coins to review the regrouping process.

LEARNING OBJECTIVE

Students make decisions and multiply money amounts.

GROUPING

Individual or pairs

MATERIALS

- *Party Problems* reproducible (p. 58)
- paper
- markers
- calculators (optional)

Name ______________________ Date ______________

Party Problems

You're planning the end of the season party for the basketball team. Seven players, including you, are coming. (Don't forget to invite the coach!) You can spend up to $80.

Use data from nearby stores and restaurants to make your plans. Decide what you will spend on decorations, food, and anything else you want to include. Then fill out the check from the coach! (If you need more than one check, you may draw them on a separate sheet of paper.)

Item	Cost	Number of Items	TOTAL

Paula Ramsey
34 Court Street
Oakton, IL

______________ 19 ___

$ ______________

Pay to the order of ______________________________

______________________________ Dollars

Memo ______________________ Paula Ramsey

How much did you spend on each player? ______________________

A-mazing Multiplication Patterns

Students look for multiplication patterns as they follow a maze to escape from a snake-infested desert.

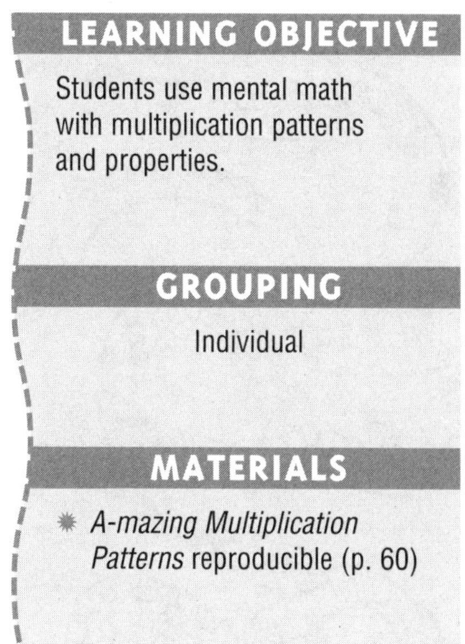

LEARNING OBJECTIVE

Students use mental math with multiplication patterns and properties.

GROUPING

Individual

MATERIALS

- *A-mazing Multiplication Patterns* reproducible (p. 60)

Directions

1. Duplicate the reproducible for each student and distribute.
2. Write the following pattern on the board:

$$4 \times 2 = 8$$
$$4 \times 20 = 80$$
$$4 \times 200 = 800$$

   Discuss the pattern and ask students to continue it.
3. Explain that students can look for patterns to help them through the maze on the reproducible. They begin with any multiplication examples at the left and find a path to the exit at the right. You may want to have students begin by finding the products for the examples on the rocks and looking for patterns before they begin the maze. If the path is correct, they will see a pattern. You may want to suggest that students make a list as they progress to verify the pattern.
4. An alternate approach is to have students complete the maze and then solve the examples to see if they form a pattern.

Taking It Farther

Have students create different multiplication patterns for the rocks on the path of the maze.

Assessing Skills

Observe whether students are able to use and verbalize their mental math strategies.

Name ______________________ Date ______________

A-mazing Multiplication Patterns

There aren't any gold or silver treasures in this desert—only snakes!

Enter the desert by any path on the left. To find your way out as quickly as possible, look for a multiplication pattern on the rocks.

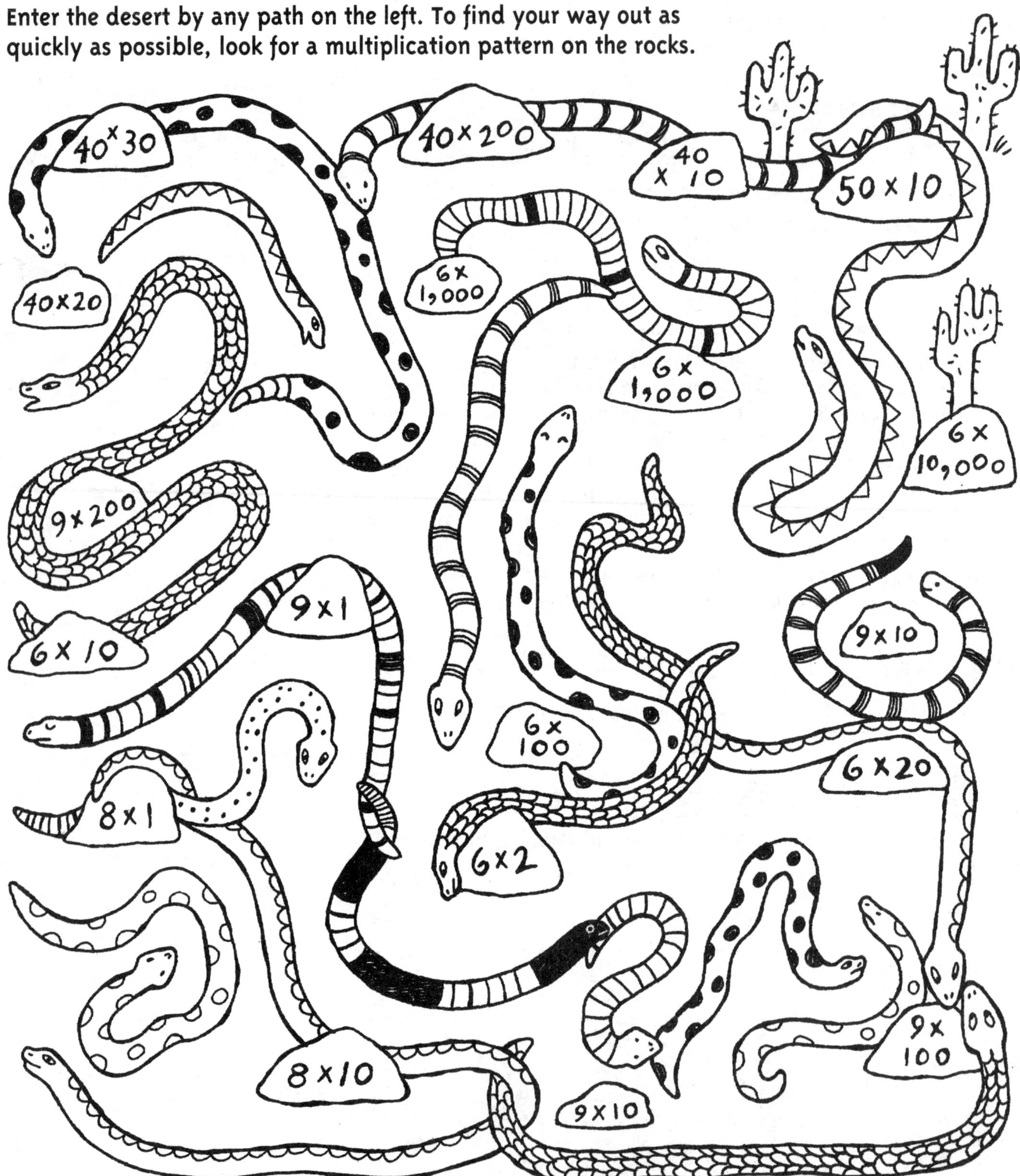

Treasure Hunt

Will students fall into Luckless Lagoon, or will they find the treasure? It all depends on their mental math skills!

Directions

1. Write 15,000 ÷ 3 on the board and discuss how to use mental math to divide. Talk about using patterns and attaching the correct number of zeros.
2. Pairs write 10 division problems such as 6,400 ÷ 8, where the dividend is a multiple of 10, 100, or 1,000 and the divisor is a 1-digit number. Each pair exchanges a set of cards with another pair of students.
3. Distribute counters and a copy of the reproducible to each student pair and explain how the game is played. The pairs make a stack of the cards. The first player chooses a card and uses mental math to find the quotient. The partner uses a calculator to check.
4. If the quotient is correct, the player rolls the number cube and moves that number of squares on the map. The player may move horizontally or vertically. If the player lands on Brigadoon Island, Craggy Caverns, or Luckless Lagoon, he or she loses a turn. If he or she lands on Frightful Falls, the player "slides" down.
5. Players need an exact number to reach the treasure at Finish.

Taking It Farther

Let students make more cards with different numbers and play the game again. Challenge them to include 5-digit multiples.

Assessing Skills

Ask students to describe the relationship between the number of zeros in the dividend and in the divisor.

LEARNING OBJECTIVE

Students divide using mental math.

GROUPING

Pairs

MATERIALS

For each pair:

- *Treasure Hunt* reproducible (p. 62)
- 10 index cards
- 2 counters
- markers
- calculator
- number cube

Name ____________________ Date ____________

Treasure Hunt

Ahoy there, mates! Are ye searching for buried treasure? It's not a matter of luck—it's all in your mind!

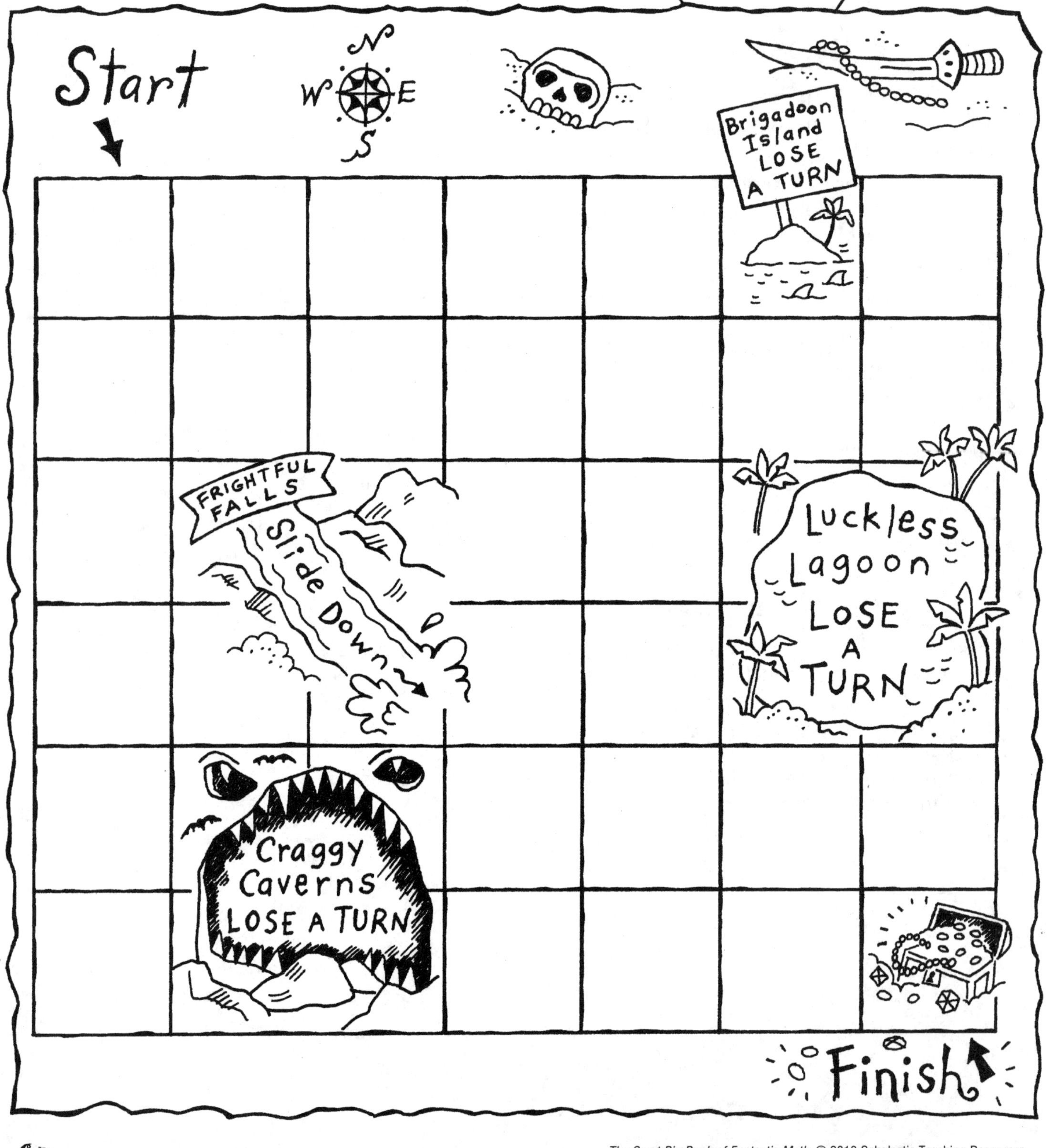

Start

N
W E
S

Brigadoon Island LOSE A TURN

FRIGHTFUL FALLS

Slide Down

Luckless Lagoon LOSE A TURN

Craggy Caverns LOSE A TURN

Finish

Multiplication & Division Problem Bank

Use these quick skill-builders as self-starters, homework, or just for a fun break from the textbook.

1. CROSSNUMBER PUZZLE

Multiply and divide to solve the puzzle.

a.	b.		c.	d.	
e.		f.		g.	h.
		i.	j.		
k.	l.		m.	n.	
	o.	p.			
		q.			

ACROSS

a. 72 ÷ 3 =
c. 5 × 13 =
e. 12 × 24 =
g. 9 × 8 =
i. 3 × 8 =
k. 490 ÷ 14 =
m. 8 × 31 =
o. 9 × 5 =
q. 1,000 ÷ 10 =

DOWN

a. 11 × 2 =
b. 3,120 ÷ 65 =
d. 3 × 19 =
f. 738 ÷ 9 =
h. 4 × 52 =
j. 6 × 7 =
l. 9 × 6 =
n. 8 × 55 =
p. 1,020 ÷ 20 =

2. BODY OF BONES

How many bones are in the human body?
Find the products and then the sum.

Skull	1 × 29 =	_____
Spine	2 × 13 =	_____
Chest	5 × 5 =	_____
Hands	2 × 27 =	_____
Arms	2 × 5 =	_____
Legs and Feet	2 × 31 =	_____

Total

There are _____ bones in the body!

3. PUZZLING POUNDS

Petra has 126 pounds of apples to sell. She has 39 bags in all.
Some are 2-pound bags and some are 5-pound bags.
How many of each does Petra have?

4. BOXED IN

Find the numbers that complete each multiplication box.

×	2	7		5	8
4	8				
1			3		
	0				
5				25	
6					

5. CALCULATED GUESS

Use different combinations of the given numbers to complete each multiplication sentence. Use a calculator to help you find the missing numbers.

1 3 5 8

__ __ × __ __ = 630

__ __ × __ __ = 1,245

__ __ × __ __ = 1,938

__ __ × __ __ = 2,835

6. SHAPE UP

Each shape represents a number. Find the missing factor or divisor and write it inside in each shape.

△ × □ = 24

□ × □ = 64

⬡ × ○ = 64

△ × ⬡ = 48

7. MATCH GAME

Find each product and dividend. Draw a line to match them.

96 × 62 = _______	_______ ÷ 12 = 484
72 × 84 = _______	_______ ÷ 12 = 496
24 × 242 = _______	_______ ÷ 36 = 168

8. GREATEST POSSIBLE PRODUCT

Find the number of digits in the greatest possible product of a 2-digit factor and a 3-digit factor. Write the factors and the product.

__ __ × __ __ __ = __________

How many digits? _____

9. Multiplication Maze

Draw a line connecting correct multiplication sentences from the entry arrow to the exit arrow of the maze.

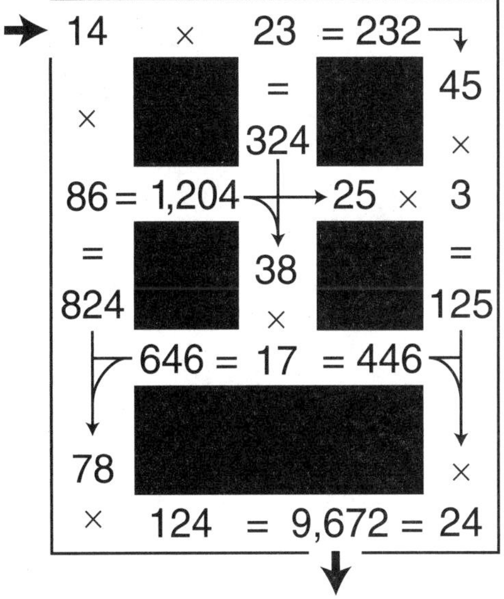

10. Pyramid Products

Each number in the pyramid is the product of the two numbers below it. Complete the pyramid.

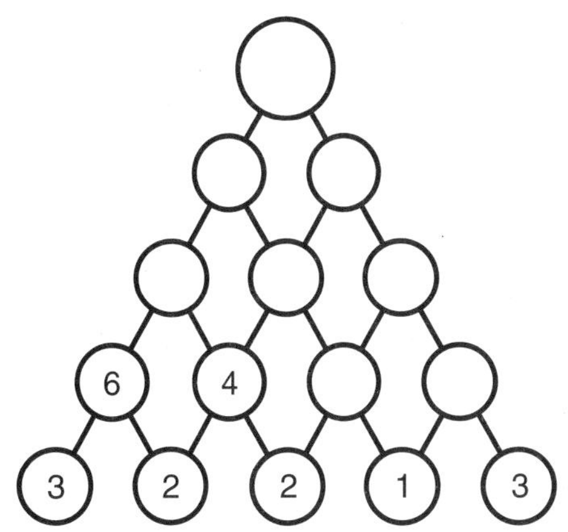

11. Picnic Planning

a. Alyssa is buying sandwiches from Dan's Deli for a class picnic. She has orders for 8 tuna, 12 turkey, and 5 egg sandwiches. How much money will she need to cover the cost of sandwiches? (Dan is not charging her tax.)

b. Dan sold $112.00 worth of tuna sandwiches, $174.25 worth of turkey sandwiches, and $65.00 worth of egg sandwiches on Tuesday. How many of each kind of sandwich did Dan sell?

Dan's Deli Menu

Tuna . . $3.50
Turkey $4.25
Egg . . $3.25

12. FIND THE KEYS

Each key unlocks a door that is marked by factors that match the product on the key. Each box represents a room. To mark the path out of the house, shade the boxes that have factors that match a key. There are no diagonal moves.

ENTER

576 × 1	36 × 16	24 × 24	52 × 36	105 × 10
26 × 72	150 × 7	21 × 50	23 × 41	144 × 13
34 × 18	250 × 5	36 × 24	48 × 12	36 × 16
83 × 26	144 × 12	18 × 32	25 × 42	48 × 52
55 × 11	17 × 82	78 × 24	150 × 4	62 × 31

LEAVE

13. SIX-FACED CUBE

- Write a multiplication sentence to describe how many squares are on each face of the cube.
- Write a multiplication sentence to describe how many squares there are on all faces of the cube.

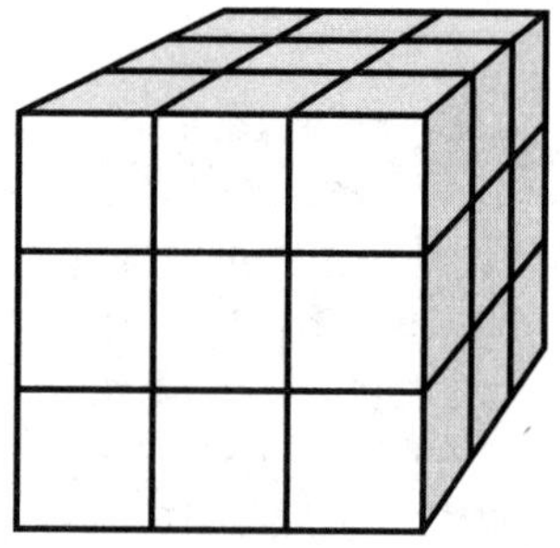

14. TARGET FACTORS

Circle the two numbers on each target that have a product closest to the score.

TARGET 1

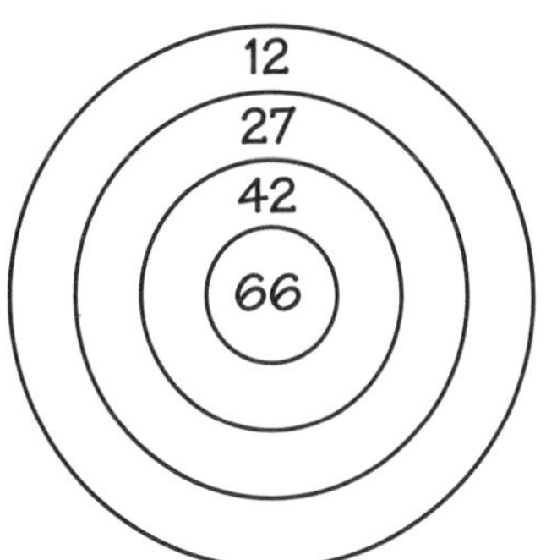

Score 800

TARGET 2

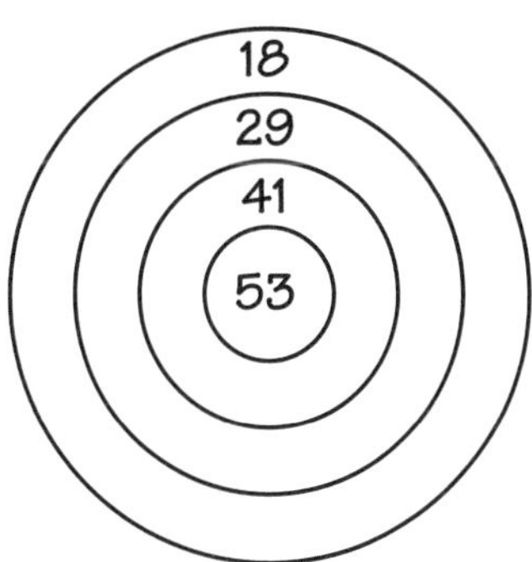

Score 1,200

TARGET 3

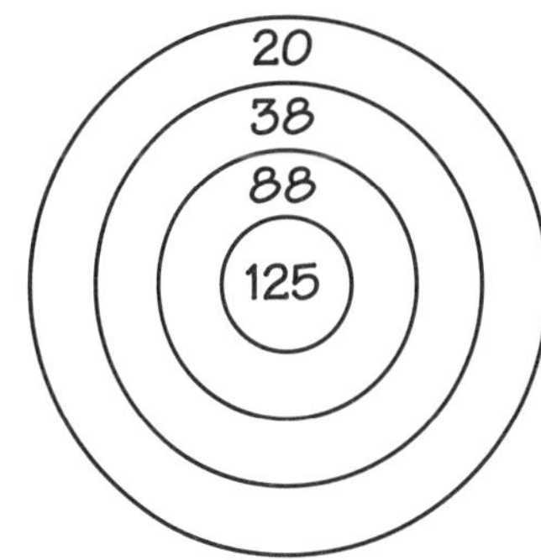

Score 4,800

15. MULTIPLICATION COUNT

Use multiplication to find the number of squares in each section in the diagram to the right. Write and solve a multiplication sentence for each section.

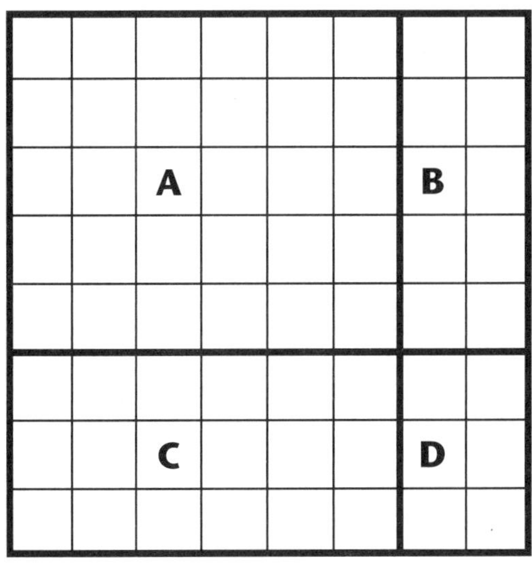

A. ______________________________

B. ______________________________

C. ______________________________

D. ______________________________

- Add to find the total number of squares in the diagram.
- Write a multiplication sentence to find the total number of squares in the diagram.

16. MULTIPLICATION WHEEL

Complete the multiplication wheel by finding each product.

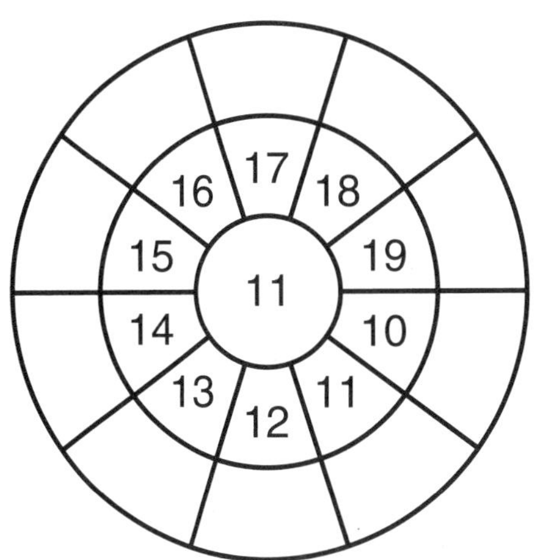

The Mysterious Fraction Zone

What do learning about equivalent fractions and investigating the Bermuda Triangle have in common? Fun and intrigue!

Directions

1. Duplicate the reproducible for each student and distribute.
2. Review the term *equivalent fractions.* Remind students that equivalent fractions have the same value, such as $\frac{1}{3}$ and $\frac{2}{6}$.
3. Fold a piece of paper in half and shade one half lightly with a marker. Ask a volunteer to tell what fraction represents the shaded area. [$\frac{1}{2}$]
4. Fold another piece of paper in half, and then in half again, to create fourths. Shade two sections, $\frac{2}{4}$, lightly with a marker. Ask a volunteer to tell what fraction represents the shaded area. [$\frac{2}{4}$] Discuss with students what the two fractions have in common.
5. Remind students that they can write an equivalent fraction by multiplying the numerator and denominator by the same number.
6. To rename a fraction that is not in lowest terms, they can find the greatest common factor and then divide the numerator and denominator by it.

LEARNING OBJECTIVE

Students find equivalent fractions.

GROUPING

Individual

MATERIALS

- 2 pieces of paper
- markers

For each student:

- *The Mysterious Fraction Zone* reproducible (p. 69)
- paper and pencil

Taking It Farther

Encourage students to find more facts about the Bermuda Triangle or other unsolved mysteries. They can write their own equivalent fractions to match the facts.

Assessing Skills

- Observe whether students are taking the original fraction and multiplying the numerator and denominator randomly to find equivalent fractions, or if they are dividing the numerator and denominator to rename the fraction in lowest terms.
- If students are dividing the numerator and denominator to reduce fractions to lowest terms, are they randomly dividing or using the greatest common factor?

Name ____________________ Date ____________

The Mysterious Fraction Zone

Welcome to the Mysterious Fraction Zone—where every fraction is equivalent to an unexplained mystery!

Hundreds of planes and ships have vanished without a trace in an area of the Atlantic Ocean known as the Bermuda Triangle. Pilots have reported spinning compasses, loss of electric power, and jammed equipment.

Some people think the triangle has unusual magnetic or gravitational forces. Others conclude that the disappearances are due to weather, pilot error, or other explainable conditions. Decide for yourself.

WHAT TO DO:

- **Match the fraction under each picture to the two equivalent fractions in the Fact Bank. These facts reveal a mystery.**
- **Write the equivalent fractions and mystery facts on a separate sheet of paper. The order of the facts isn't important.**

FACT BANK

$\frac{50}{100}$ In 335 B.C. Plato wrote about an ancient empire, Atlantis, that after a day and night of rain sank to the bottom of the ocean.

$\frac{8}{10}$ Five Avenger torpedo bombers in perfect working order left Fort Lauderdale Naval Air Station with full loads of fuel on a clear day.

$\frac{6}{12}$ Underwater expeditions in the Bermuda Triangle have uncovered stone heads, carved pillars, and pyramids believed to be part of the lost civilization of Atlantis.

$\frac{6}{21}$ The USS *Cyclops*, a 19,600-ton Navy boat, left the West Indies bound for Norfolk, Virginia, but it never arrived.

$\frac{40}{50}$ Several hours after takeoff, the Avengers radioed the control tower, saying that everything was strange and they were not sure of their directions . . . then, silence.

$\frac{10}{30}$ The *Mary Celeste*, a 103-foot-long ship, was found perfectly intact and abandoned at sea. There was no sign of bad weather or foul play.

$\frac{4}{14}$ The navy boat—and its 309 crew members—disappeared without a trace in fair weather, without sending an SOS.

$\frac{3}{9}$ What mysterious event would lead Captain Briggs, his wife, his daughter, and eight crew members to leave their ship with a meal still on the table?

Fraction Snowflakes

Students create a whole roomful of unique snowflakes while exploring equivalent fractions.

LEARNING OBJECTIVE

Given a fraction, students find equivalent fractions.

GROUPING

Individual

MATERIALS

For each student:

- scissors
- sheet of grid paper
- yarn

Directions

1. Review finding a missing numerator in equivalent fractions. Write the example below on the board. Remind students that 4 is multiplied by 25 to get 100, so the 1 must be multiplied by 25 to get 25.

$$\frac{1}{4} = \frac{n}{100} \qquad \frac{1 \times 25}{4 \times 25} = \frac{25}{100}$$

2. Have students find the number of squares on their grid paper without counting every square. They can count the number of squares down, the number of squares across, and multiply the two to find the total number of squares.
3. Tell students that they are going to cut away $\frac{1}{4}$ of their grid paper to make a snowflake. Using their knowledge of equivalent fractions, they can find the number of squares they should cut away.
4. Instruct students to fold their grid paper in half lengthwise with the grid squares showing, then fold the paper in half again. If the paper were opened, there would be four equal squares.

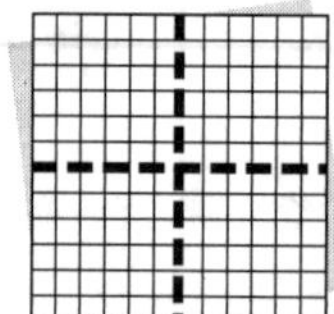

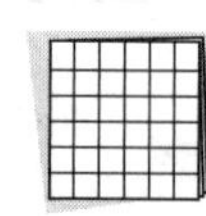

5. As students begin cutting out their snowflakes, remind them that they are cutting out 4 squares at a time. If they are cutting away a number of squares that is not divisible by 4, they may need to slightly adjust the number. For instance, if they are cutting away 25 squares, they would adjust the number to 24, which is easily divisible by 4. Therefore, they would cut away 6 squares.
6. Remind students to take care when cutting along the sides that are fold lines. If they cut down both fold lines, the paper will be cut into four separate pieces.
7. Attach yarn to the snowflakes and display them around the classroom.

Taking It Farther

Encourage students to make snowflakes with $\frac{1}{2}$ or $\frac{3}{4}$ of the squares cut away. Discuss which snowflakes are the easiest to make and which are the most intricate.

Assessing Skills

Are students able to apply their knowledge of equivalent fractions and find the number of squares they need to eliminate?

The Wheel of Fractions

Renaming fractions in this easy-to-assemble game spells nothing but fun!

Directions

1. Duplicate the reproducible for each pair and distribute.
2. To make the Wheel of Fractions, students cut out the two game pieces. They also cut out the window and window flap as directed. Then they place Figure 1 on top of Figure 2, punch a hole in the middle of both figures, put the paper fastener into the hole, and spread the tabs flat. **Tip:** To make the wheel easier to spin and the game longer lasting, laminate it, print it on oak tag, or glue the printed page to paper plates.
3. Students decide who will go first. In turn, a player spins the Wheel of Fractions with the spinner tab and reads the fraction in the window.
4. The player renames the fraction in lowest terms and opens the answer flap to see if the answer is correct.
5. If the answer is correct, that player collects the amount of money shown in the window. If the answer is incorrect, no money is collected. Then the next player takes a turn.
6. The first player to earn $100 wins the game.

Taking It Further

Encourage students to make their own games. They can trace the circle in Figure 2 and write questions and answers. Some topic suggestions include changing improper fractions to mixed numbers, changing fractions to decimals, or finding a missing number in equivalent fractions.

Assessing Skills

Are students using the greatest common factor to rename the fraction, or repeated division?

LEARNING OBJECTIVE

Students rename fractions in lowest terms.

GROUPING

Pairs

MATERIALS

For each pair:

- *The Wheel of Fractions* reproducible (p. 72)
- scissors
- 1 brass paper fastener
- play money (up to $200 in ones, fives, tens, and twenties)
- oak tag or paper plates (optional)

Name ______________________ Date __________

The Wheel of Fractions

Renaming fractions spells nothing but fun!

Figure 1

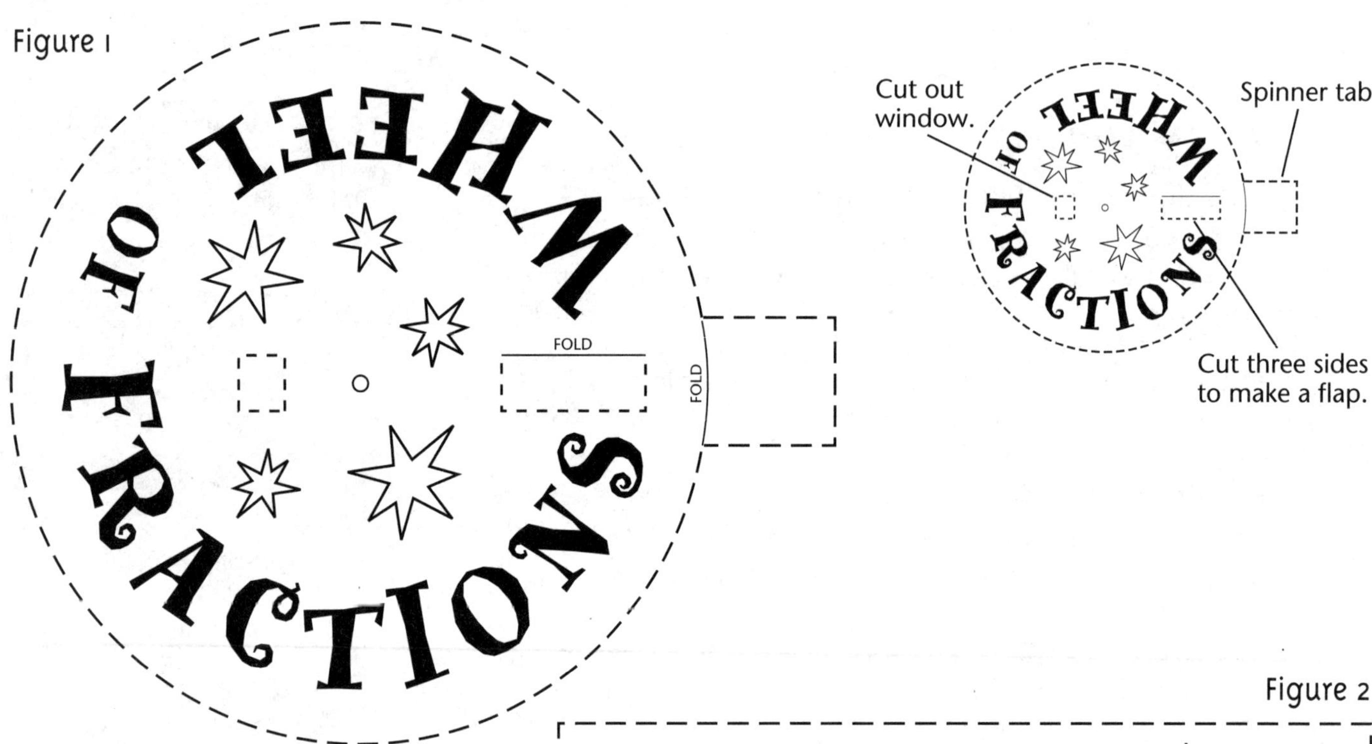

Figure 2

$12.00 $\frac{4}{6}$ · $7.00 $\frac{2}{3}$ · $8.00 $\frac{4}{5}$ · $9.00 $\frac{1}{3}$ · $13.00 $\frac{1}{3}$ · $6.00 $\frac{2}{3}$ · $9.00 $\frac{1}{4}$ · $8.00 $\frac{1}{3}$ · $11.00 $\frac{2}{6}$ · $7.00 $\frac{1}{5}$ · $14.00 $\frac{1}{3}$ · $5.00 $\frac{1}{2}$

Optical Illusions

As fractions are renamed and colored, the flower blossoms and becomes three-dimensional.

Directions

1. Duplicate the reproducible for each student and distribute.
2. Draw the following lines of equal length on the board:

   Ask students which line looks longer. Then have a volunteer measure the length of each line with a ruler.
3. Explain that the two lines are an example of an optical illusion. The line on the left only appears to be longer than the line on the right.
4. Write the following fractions on the board: $\frac{1}{3}$ and $\frac{311}{933}$. Ask students which fraction they believe is larger. Guide them as necessary in determining that the two fractions are equivalent.
5. Allow students to complete the reproducible on their own.

Taking It Further

- Direct students to find other fractions that are equivalent to $\frac{1}{2}$, $\frac{1}{3}$, and $\frac{1}{4}$. They may make their own optical illusions for classmates to solve.
- After the fractions have been renamed, challenge advanced students to add all of the fractions and find the sum for the reproducible.
- Students enjoy solving patterns using the concept of equivalent fractions. Present the following for them to solve:

  $\frac{1}{4}, \frac{3}{12}, \frac{9}{36}, \frac{?}{?}, \frac{?}{?}, \frac{?}{?}$

  $\frac{304}{416}, \frac{152}{208}, \frac{?}{?}, \frac{?}{?}, \frac{?}{?}$

Assessing Skills

Are students using the greatest common factor or repeated division?

LEARNING OBJECTIVE

Students rename fractions and find their lowest terms equivalent.

GROUPING

Individual

MATERIALS

For each student:

- *Optical Illusions* reproducible (p. 74)
- ruler
- crayons or colored pencils

Name ______________________ Date ______________

Optical Illusions

Color the fractions equivalent to $\frac{1}{2}$ dark blue. Color the fractions equivalent to $\frac{1}{3}$ red. Color the fractions equivalent to $\frac{1}{4}$ light blue.

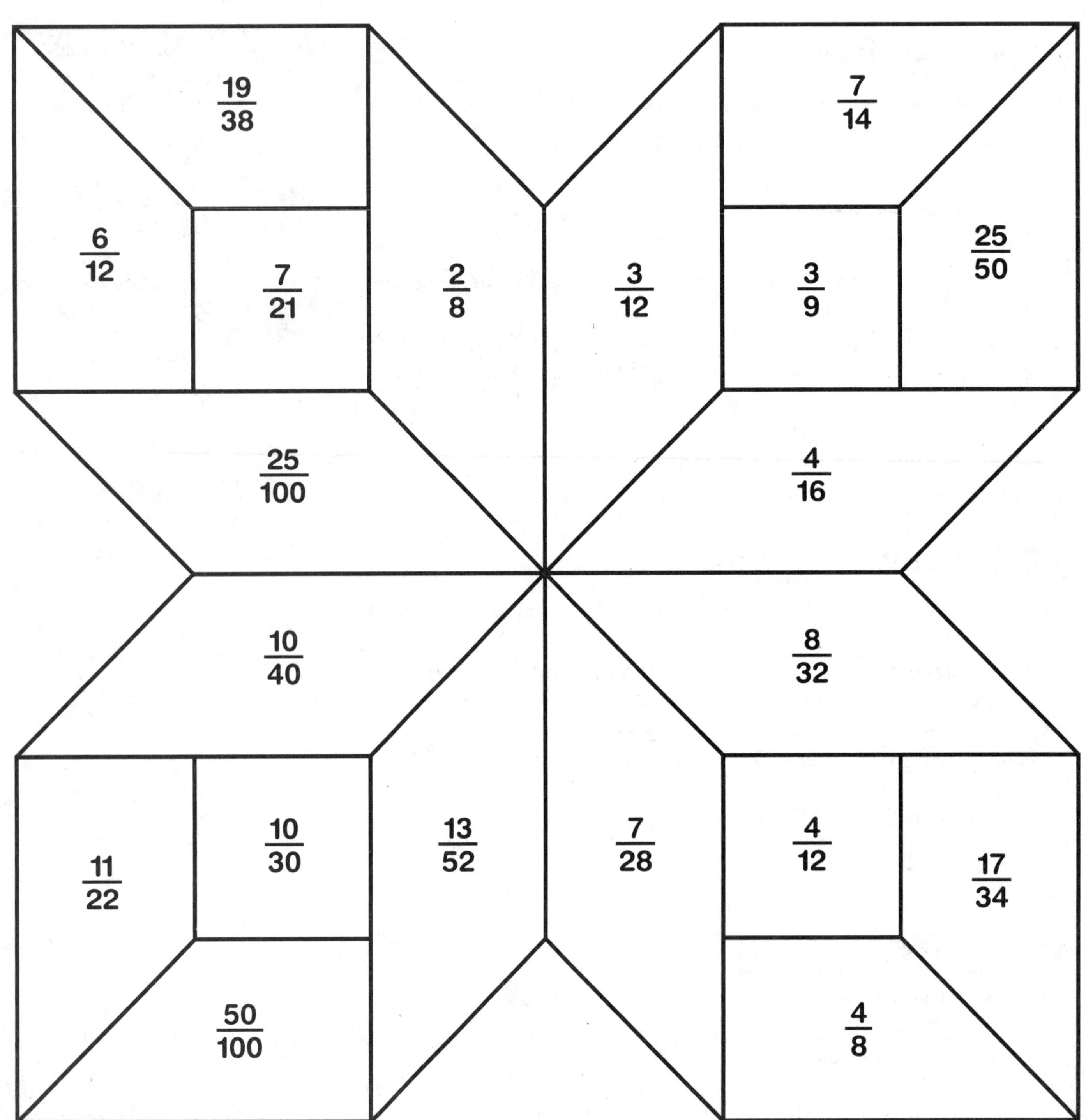

Sensational Surveys

Students work in groups to design a survey, gather information, graph data, and share their results. They see that fractions have real-life applications.

Directions

1. Review stating information in fractional form.
   a. Twenty people were asked which pets they liked the best with the following results: cats (5), dogs (10), turtles (1), birds (1), snakes (2), and mice (1).
   b. Here are the data written in fractional form:
   cats ($\frac{5}{20} = \frac{1}{4}$), dogs ($\frac{10}{20} = \frac{1}{2}$), turtles ($\frac{1}{20}$), birds ($\frac{1}{20}$), snakes ($\frac{2}{20} = \frac{1}{10}$), and mice ($\frac{1}{20}$)
2. Review writing data on circle graphs. If you have access to computers with graphing software, familiarize students with this process. If computers are not available, follow the steps below.
   a. Divide a 12-inch cardboard circle into fourths with a light erasable line. You may also want to draw a large circle to display.
   b. Using the data above, dogs would fill $\frac{1}{2}$ of the graph, and cats would fill $\frac{1}{4}$ of the graph. Draw dark lines to define those sections.
   c. Lightly divide the remaining fourth into five equal sections. The turtles, birds, and mice each fill one section, and snakes fill up two sections. Record the information.
   d. Color each section a different color and give the graph a title.
3. Go over the *Sensational Surveys* reproducible with the class.

LEARNING OBJECTIVE

Students compare and order fractions.

GROUPING

Cooperative groups of 3 or 4

MATERIALS

For each group:

- markers
- crayons or colored pencils
- poster paper
- 12-inch cardboard circle
- scissors
- *Sensational Surveys* reproducible (p. 76)

Taking It Further

Have students monitor their activities for 24 hours and record the data on a circle graph. To divide a circle into 24 equal parts:

- Draw a 12-inch circle on poster paper and cut it out.
- Divide the circle into sixths by folding. (See illustration.) First, fold the circle in half. Then fold $\frac{1}{3}$ of the top half on top of the other $\frac{2}{3}$. Next fold over the other $\frac{1}{3}$. The circle is now divided into sixths.
- Fold this triangle twice, and the circle is divided into 24 equal parts.

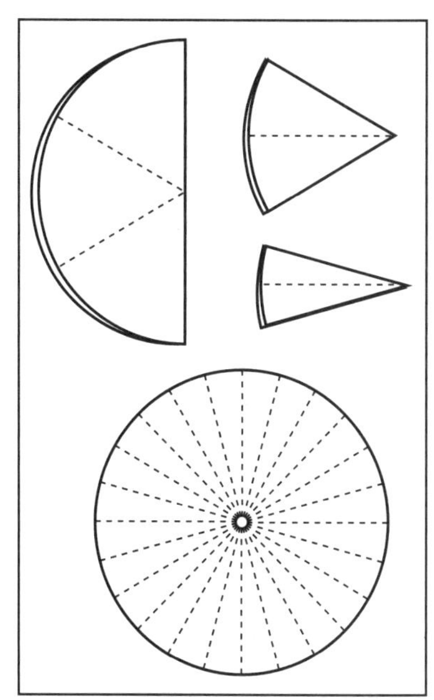

Assessing Skills

- Do students understand that adding all the fractional parts of a circle graph equals 1?
- Do students use equivalent fractions to help them divide the circle graph more accurately?

Name ______________________ Date ______________

Sensational Surveys

This is your chance to get the scoop on your classmates. Find out who likes anchovies, who has a pet alligator, or who hates spiders. You design the survey, ask the questions, graph the data, and share the results.

CHOOSING A TOPIC

1. Brainstorm survey topics. Remember to keep the ideas simple. Record your ideas on a sheet of paper.
2. Write your survey topic.

   ____

3. Write the exact questions you will be asking on a separate sheet of paper. (Each question should be specific. What is your favorite color, for instance, is a general question. Which color do you like best—red, blue, or green, is a specific question.)

CONDUCTING THE SURVEY

Assign a job to each group member.

- **Speaker:** This person tells the class what the survey questions will be.

  ____

- **Data Collector:** This person counts the number of responses.

  ____

- **Data Recorder:** This person writes down the information.

  ____

- **Presenter:** This person is not directly involved in the survey but shares the final results with the class.

  ____

GRAPHING THE DATA

1. Write the data collected in fractional form. For instance, if 5 people out of 20 surveyed liked the color red, the fraction would be $\frac{5}{20}$, or $\frac{1}{4}$.
2. Transfer the data to a circle graph.

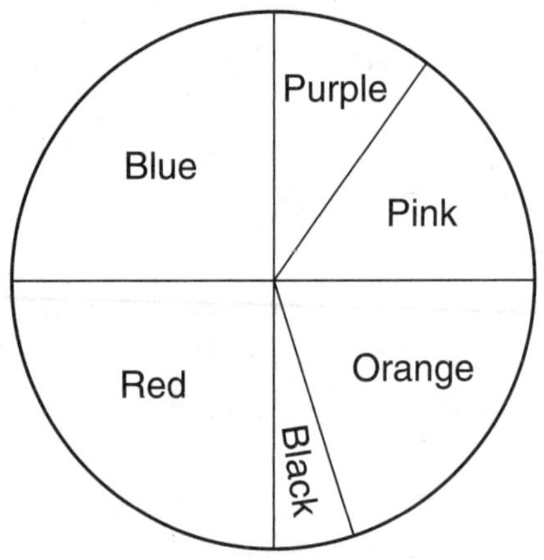

3. Give your graph a title and color it.

SHARING THE RESULTS

The presenter shares the results of the survey with the class. The following information must be included.

- How many people were surveyed?
- Share the circle graph. Talk about each portion of the graph and tell what information is given.
- Tell what the surveyed students liked most and what they liked least.
- Tell what strategy the group used to divide the graph into representative parts.

Fraction Line-Up

Students race to get their fractions in order from least to greatest before their opponents beat them to it!

Directions

1. Tell students they will be playing a game. The goal is to order fractions from least to greatest before their opponent does.
2. Distribute half an egg carton to each student and a set of cards to each pair.
3. Direct pairs to sit facing each other with the draw pile of fraction cards facedown between them. They place the "least fraction" card next to the far left section of the egg carton and the "greatest fraction" card next to the far right section.
4. Each player draws six cards, placing them from left to right in his or her egg carton as the cards are chosen. Another card is placed faceup next to the card pile. This is the discard pile.
5. In turn, a player chooses one card from either the draw or discard pile. That card may be used to improve the least-to-greatest order in the egg carton. If the card drawn is used, the replaced card is discarded. If the card drawn is not used, it is discarded. Cards already in the egg carton can never be moved from one cup to another. The turn ends when player discards the unused or replaced card.
6. If a player draws a card that is equivalent to a fraction in his or her egg carton, this is considered a bonus card. The player may discard the card and take two free turns in a row.
7. The first player who can put the fractions in order wins the game.

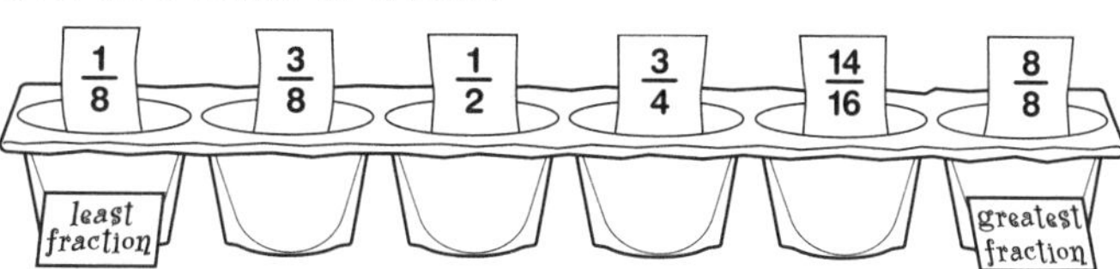

8. Save these egg cartons for the *Name That Decimal* activity on page 97 and the *Guess That Decimal* activity on page 98.

Taking It Further

Increase the level of difficulty by adding cards with improper fractions and fractions with many different denominators.

Assessing Skills

Are students developing strategies? Are they spacing fractions so there is a high probability that they can fill the sections that are out of order?

LEARNING OBJECTIVE

Students compare and order fractions with like and unlike denominators.

GROUPING

Pairs

MATERIALS

- marker
- scissors

For each pair:

- 1 egg carton
- 40 index cards
- paper and pencils

ADVANCE PREPARATION

1. Remove the lid of the egg carton, and cut the base in half lengthwise so that you have two separate rows with six sections.
2. Cut the index cards into 1-inch by 2-inch strips and write the following fractions on one side:

   $\frac{1}{2}, \frac{2}{2}, \frac{1}{4}, \frac{2}{4}, \frac{3}{4}, \frac{4}{4},$

   $\frac{1}{8}, \frac{2}{8}, \frac{3}{8}, \frac{4}{8}, \frac{5}{8}, \frac{6}{8}, \frac{7}{8}, \frac{8}{8},$

   from $\frac{1}{16}$ to $\frac{16}{16}$ ($\frac{1}{16}, \frac{2}{16}, \ldots$),

   from $\frac{1}{32}$ to $\frac{10}{32}$ ($\frac{1}{32}, \frac{2}{32}, \ldots$).

   You also may let students create the cards.
3. For each egg carton, write two cards, "least fraction" and "greatest fraction."

Shoot for the Stars

This fraction game doubles as a bulletin board and can be displayed all year.

Directions

1. Give two white stars to each student. Have students write an improper fraction on one star. On the other star they write the corresponding mixed number. They should not rename the mixed number in lowest terms.
2. Mix the white stars and tack each one facedown to a yellow star on the bulletin board. Place the white stars randomly.
3. Divide the class into two even teams and decide which team will go first. If you have an odd number of students in your class, choose one student to be the scorekeeper. If not, take that role yourself.
4. The players must match improper fractions to their equivalent mixed numbers. They choose two white stars and read the fractions aloud. If there is a match, remove the white stars from the bulletin board. The scorekeeper gives one point to the team. Then the other team takes a turn.
5. The game continues until all of the matches have been made. The team with more points wins.
6. At the end of the game, replace the white stars on the bulletin board.

Taking It Farther

This game can be adapted to any subject or theme. Students may enjoy matching math vocabulary words to definitions, decimal names to their numeric equivalent, or geometric shapes to their names.

Assessing Skills

Are students reversing the numerator and denominator? If so, the initial use of concrete models can help eliminate this error.

LEARNING OBJECTIVE

Students change improper fractions to mixed numbers and mixed numbers to improper fractions.

GROUPING

Whole class

MATERIALS

- yellow construction paper
- white paper
- black markers
- scissors
- stapler
- thumb tacks
- cardboard or star cookie cutter for star template

ADVANCE PREPARATION

1. Make a star template out of cardboard or use a cookie cutter to trace 28 stars on yellow construction paper. Cut out the stars. Laminate them if you want.
2. Staple the 28 yellow stars to the bulletin board as placeholders.
3. Trace 28 stars on white paper and cut them out.

The Great Fraction Race

This outdoor game will inspire even the most reluctant math students.

Directions

1. Divide the class into groups of 5 or 6.
2. Write the following whole and mixed numbers on the board vertically:

   $3\frac{2}{7}$, 3, $9\frac{1}{2}$, 7, $2\frac{1}{9}$, $4\frac{2}{9}$, 9, 4, $6\frac{1}{4}$, $10\frac{2}{8}$, 8, 3, $9\frac{5}{7}$, $4\frac{9}{12}$, 5, $1\frac{6}{7}$, $4\frac{1}{7}$, $7\frac{1}{11}$, $7\frac{2}{9}$, $19\frac{2}{4}$, $9\frac{1}{4}$, $13\frac{1}{5}$, 4, 2, $3\frac{2}{9}$, 20, $9\frac{6}{9}$, $2\frac{4}{5}$, 2, and $4\frac{5}{7}$

   One member of each group copies them on a piece of notebook paper.
3. Take students to the playground and give them the start signal. The objective is for each group to find as many hidden milk cartons as possible. Then they write the improper fraction found in the milk carton beside the corresponding number on their number list. (The mixed number has not been renamed in lowest terms.)
4. After the group completes the task, each member sits down.
5. When all of the groups are sitting down, the group with the largest number of correct matches wins the game. That group hides the milk cartons for the next, or a future, game.

Taking It Further

Here are two variations on the game:

* Play the game with two sets of fractions that equal the number 1.
* Have students match a set of fractions that, when reduced, equals the other set.

Assessing Skills

* Are students working cooperatively to complete the task?
* Can students change a mixed number to an improper fraction without first looking at the improper fractions on the list?

LEARNING OBJECTIVE

Students match improper fractions to equivalent mixed numbers.

GROUPING

Cooperative groups of 5 or 6

MATERIALS

* 30 empty milk cartons
* several sheets of notebook paper
* scissors
* markers

ADVANCE PREPARATION

1. Cut a piece of notebook paper into 30 narrow strips along the writing lines.
2. Write one of the following fractions on each strip of paper:

   $\frac{23}{7}$, $\frac{15}{5}$, $\frac{19}{2}$, $\frac{28}{4}$, $\frac{19}{9}$, $\frac{38}{9}$, $\frac{27}{3}$, $\frac{16}{4}$, $\frac{25}{4}$, $\frac{82}{8}$, $\frac{88}{11}$, $\frac{75}{25}$, $\frac{68}{7}$, $\frac{57}{12}$, $\frac{45}{9}$, $\frac{13}{7}$, $\frac{29}{7}$, $\frac{78}{11}$, $\frac{65}{9}$, $\frac{78}{4}$, $\frac{37}{4}$, $\frac{66}{5}$, $\frac{100}{25}$, $\frac{12}{6}$, $\frac{29}{9}$, $\frac{80}{4}$, $\frac{87}{9}$, $\frac{14}{5}$, $\frac{50}{25}$, $\frac{33}{7}$
3. Place a fraction strip in each milk carton and close the top. Hide the milk cartons on the playground.

Four in a Row Fractions

This fast-action game pairs addition and subtraction of fractions with problem-solving strategies to create a winning combination.

Directions

1. Duplicate the reproducible for each pair of students and distribute.
2. Give students the following oral instructions:
   a. The game is played by two players. Decide who will go first and which kind of game counter each of you will use.
   b. The first player searches for two fractions in the boxes at the top of the page that when added or subtracted equal one of the fractions on the game board. Answers are always in lowest terms.
   c. Each fraction can be used only once. Draw lines through the fractions used.
   d. After locating the fraction on the game board, the first player covers that space with a counter.
   e. The second player takes a turn. Players alternate turns.
   f. The first player to cover a row horizontally, vertically, or diagonally with his or her counters wins.

LEARNING OBJECTIVE

Students add and subtract like fractions.

GROUPING

Pairs

MATERIALS

- *Four in a Row Fractions* reproducible (p. 81)
- 16 game counters (8 of one kind, 8 of a different kind)

Taking It Further

For an extra challenge, make your own fraction boxes and game board that use unlike fractions.

Assessing Skills

Do students randomly add or subtract fractions, hoping to find one that is on the game board? Or do they look at the board and try to find fractions that, when added or subtracted, provide the needed answers?

 Name ______________________ Date ______________

Four in a Row Fractions

Can you add and subtract fractions at lightning speed? Do you have mighty powers of logic and reasoning to help you develop game strategies? This fast-action game will put your skills to the ultimate test.

To play the game, follow your teacher's instructions.

$\frac{4}{12}$	$\frac{4}{18}$	$\frac{1}{8}$	$\frac{7}{50}$	$\frac{5}{18}$	$\frac{1}{30}$	$\frac{7}{9}$	$\frac{1}{8}$	$\frac{1}{3}$
$\frac{5}{6}$	$\frac{9}{10}$	$\frac{3}{7}$	$\frac{4}{13}$	$\frac{3}{4}$	$\frac{2}{6}$	$\frac{1}{3}$	$\frac{3}{6}$	$\frac{2}{10}$
$\frac{4}{4}$	$\frac{5}{8}$	$\frac{3}{15}$	$\frac{1}{12}$	$\frac{4}{6}$	$\frac{3}{8}$	$\frac{11}{12}$	$\frac{2}{9}$	$\frac{3}{12}$
$\frac{2}{15}$	$\frac{3}{13}$	$\frac{1}{7}$	$\frac{12}{50}$	$\frac{1}{4}$	$\frac{2}{5}$	$\frac{7}{30}$	$\frac{1}{5}$	

$\frac{3}{4}$	$\frac{1}{6}$	$\frac{5}{9}$	$\frac{7}{10}$
$\frac{2}{3}$	$\frac{7}{13}$	$\frac{7}{12}$	$\frac{1}{18}$
$\frac{4}{7}$	$\frac{1}{5}$	$\frac{19}{50}$	$\frac{1}{2}$
$\frac{5}{6}$	$\frac{4}{15}$	$\frac{1}{3}$	$\frac{1}{4}$

Shout It Out!

This exhilarating, fast-paced fraction game will bedazzle students from start to finish.

Directions

1. Distribute at least one fraction sentence to each student. (Give the sentences with an asterisk to advanced students.) Depending upon the number of students in the class, add or delete fraction sentences at the end.
2. The student with the beginning sentence reads it aloud. Emphasize that students must listen carefully and respond quickly, and that *only* the student with the correct answer should "Shout it out."
3. If several seconds have passed and no one has responded, say, "Who has it? Shout it out!"
4. If the holder of the sentence still fails to respond, read the previous sentence again.
5. Play until the last sentence is read.

Taking It Farther

Challenge students to make a set of Shout It Out cards for adding and subtracting fractions with unlike denominators.

Assessing Skills

Do any students seem confused or unable to concentrate? Some visual learners may benefit from writing the sentences down as they are read.

LEARNING OBJECTIVE

Students add and subtract like fractions.

GROUPING

Whole class

MATERIALS

- *Shout It Out!* reproducible (p. 83)
- scissors
- 23 index cards, tape (optional)

ADVANCE PREPARATION

Cut apart the fraction sentences on the photocopy of page 83. You may want to let students tape the sentences to index cards for durability.

$3\frac{1}{2} + 8\frac{1}{6} + \frac{1}{8} = ?$ ✸ $\frac{1}{2} = \frac{2}{4} = \frac{4}{8}$ ✸ $0.5 = 0.50 = 0.500$ ✸ $123.456789 + 9876.54321 = ?$

Shout It Out!

Beginning Card

My fraction is $\frac{2}{30}$. Who has $\frac{2}{30}$ and $\frac{2}{30}$ more?	My fraction is $\frac{4}{30}$. Who has $\frac{4}{30}$ and $\frac{5}{30}$ more?	My fraction is $\frac{9}{30}$. Who has $\frac{9}{30}$ and $\frac{2}{30}$ more?
My fraction is $\frac{11}{30}$. Who has $\frac{11}{30}$ and $\frac{5}{30}$ more?	My fraction is $\frac{16}{30}$. Who has $\frac{16}{30}$ and $\frac{5}{30}$ more?	My fraction is $\frac{21}{30}$. Who has $\frac{21}{30}$ and $\frac{4}{30}$ more?
My fraction is $\frac{25}{30}$. Who has $\frac{25}{30}$ in lowest terms?	✸ My fraction is $\frac{5}{6}$. Who has $\frac{5}{6}$ and $\frac{1}{6}$ less?	My fraction is $\frac{4}{6}$. Who has $\frac{4}{6}$ and $\frac{1}{6}$ less?
My fraction is $\frac{3}{6}$. Who has $\frac{3}{6}$ and $\frac{2}{6}$ less?	My fraction is $\frac{1}{6}$. Who has $\frac{1}{6}$ and $\frac{2}{6}$ more?	My fraction is $\frac{3}{6}$. Who has $\frac{3}{6}$ in lowest terms?
✸ My fraction is $\frac{1}{2}$. Who has $\frac{1}{2}$ and $\frac{1}{2}$ more?	My fraction is $\frac{2}{2}$. Who has $\frac{2}{2}$ as a whole number?	My number is 1. Who has 1 and $\frac{5}{16}$ less?
✸ My fraction is $\frac{11}{16}$. Who has $\frac{11}{16}$ and $\frac{2}{16}$ more?	My fraction is $\frac{13}{16}$. Who has $\frac{13}{16}$ and $\frac{1}{16}$ more?	My fraction is $\frac{14}{16}$. Who has $\frac{14}{16}$ in lowest terms?
✸ My fraction is $\frac{7}{8}$. Who has $\frac{7}{8}$ and $\frac{1}{8}$ less?	My fraction is $\frac{6}{8}$. Who has $\frac{6}{8}$ and $\frac{1}{8}$ less?	My fraction is $\frac{5}{8}$. Who has $\frac{5}{8}$ and $\frac{1}{8}$ less?
My fraction is $\frac{4}{8}$. Who has $\frac{4}{8}$ in lowest terms?	✸ My fraction is $\frac{1}{2}$. We are done! Want to start again?	**Last Card**

Teacher Troubles

Students solve addition and subtraction fraction problems while they unravel a riddle.

Directions

1. Duplicate the reproducible for each student and distribute.
2. Review with students addition and subtraction of fractions with unlike denominators.

Step 1	Step 2	Step 3
Find the common denominator. $\frac{3}{8} = \frac{}{8}$ $+\frac{1}{2} = \frac{}{8}$	Find the equivalent fractions. $\frac{3}{8} = \frac{3}{8}$ $+\frac{1}{2} = \frac{4}{8}$	Add or subtract. $\frac{3}{8} + \frac{4}{8} = \frac{7}{8}$

3. Students should be able to complete the reproducible on their own.

Taking It Farther

- Challenge students to add fractions whose sum is greater than 1.
- Advanced students may apply the same concepts used in this lesson to solve this fraction magic square. Each row, column, and diagonal must have the sum of 1. [All squares can be filled with $\frac{4}{12}$.]

$\frac{1}{3}$	$\frac{4}{12}$	
$\frac{2}{6}$		
		$\frac{5}{15}$

Assessing Skills

- Are students using the least common denominator (LCD)?
- Do students realize that in some exercises one of the fractions contains the LCD so that only the other fraction needs to be renamed?

LEARNING OBJECTIVE

Students add and subtract unlike fractions.

GROUPING

Individual

MATERIALS

- *Teacher Troubles* reproducible (p. 85)

Name ______________________________ Date ________________

Teacher Troubles

Teachers never want to see these animals in their classes unless, of course, they can watch them every minute of the day. Which animals aren't trustworthy?

Add or subtract the fractions. Rename if necessary. Next to the answer space is a letter. When you find your answer in the riddle box, place that letter above it to solve the riddle.

$\frac{1}{3} + \frac{2}{6}$ = **C**	$\frac{3}{4} + \frac{2}{12}$ = **E**	$\frac{7}{9} + \frac{3}{18}$ = **A**	$\frac{5}{8} + \frac{1}{4}$ = **S**
$\frac{1}{10} - \frac{1}{15}$ = **D**	$\frac{5}{6} - \frac{2}{30}$ = **O**	$\frac{5}{6} - \frac{3}{24}$ = **N**	$\frac{3}{4} - \frac{1}{3}$ = **I**
$\frac{1}{3} + \frac{2}{5}$ = **H**	$\frac{3}{4} - \frac{2}{8}$ = **T**	$\frac{4}{7} - \frac{1}{3}$ = **L**	$\frac{3}{8} + \frac{1}{4}$ = **!**

Fraction Trios

Adding and subtracting fractions is fun and easy to understand after you've played a few hands of Fraction Trios!

Directions

1. Explain that the goal of the game is to get two three-card sets before the opponent does. Each set consists of an addition or subtraction sentence, the corresponding answer, and a picture.
2. Distribute the sets of index cards to pairs. Ask them to shuffle the cards and place them in a pile. Each player chooses six cards.
3. Players take turns drawing cards from the pile. If a player chooses to keep the card he or she draws, one card must be discarded from that player's hand. The next player can then draw one card from the pile or take the discarded card.
4. The first player to get two three-card sets calls the game. The player displays the hand for the opponent to see. Before a winner is declared, both players must agree that the mathematics is correct.

Taking It Further

Play a similar game with mixed-number pairs. On one set of 15 cards, students write problems for multiplication of two mixed numbers. On the other set of 15 cards, they write the answers to the problems. The game is played the same way. The first person to have three two-card sets wins the game.

Assessing Skills

- Can students match the pictorial representations of the addition and subtraction of fractions to the written problems and answers?
- Can students explain the meaning of the pictorial models?

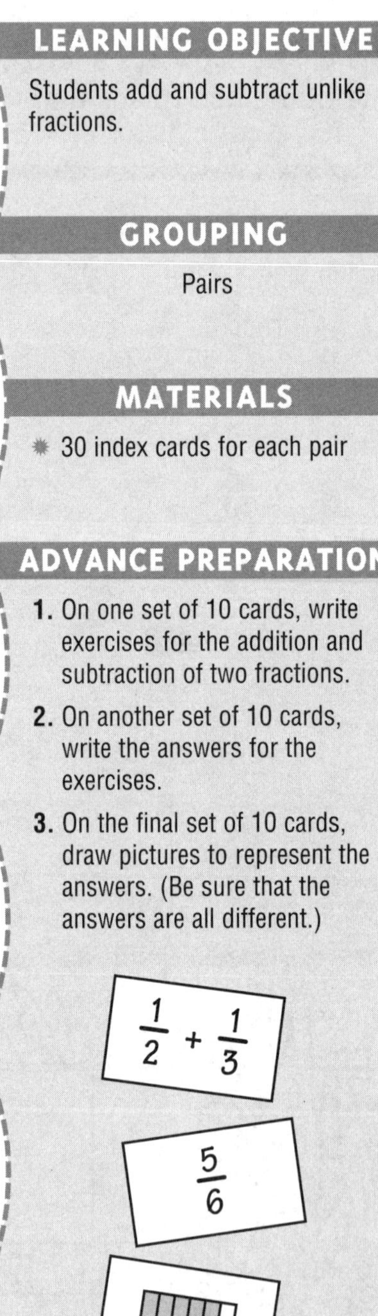

LEARNING OBJECTIVE

Students add and subtract unlike fractions.

GROUPING

Pairs

MATERIALS

- 30 index cards for each pair

ADVANCE PREPARATION

1. On one set of 10 cards, write exercises for the addition and subtraction of two fractions.
2. On another set of 10 cards, write the answers for the exercises.
3. On the final set of 10 cards, draw pictures to represent the answers. (Be sure that the answers are all different.)

Tangram Fractions

Add variety to your mathematics instruction with this art project that not only encourages creativity but also teaches students to multiply and divide fractions.

Directions

1. Review multiplication and division of fractions. Write examples such as the following on the board:

$$\frac{2}{3} \times \frac{1}{5} \qquad \frac{1}{6} \div \frac{5}{6}$$

2. Ask volunteers to show the steps in solving each example. In the multiplication example, they should point out that first the numerators are multiplied and then the denominators are multiplied. For division, students may use common denominators or multiply by the reciprocal of the divisor (e.g., $\frac{1}{6} \times \frac{6}{5}$) and reduce the fraction to lowest terms.
3. Distribute a copy of the reproducible to each student and go over the directions with the class. You may want to cut out the tangram pieces and either show how to create the swan yourself or call on volunteers to do so.
4. After students have constructed their designs, direct them to trace around the outer outlines on construction paper. Encourage them to give titles to their designs and sign their masterpieces. Trace over the lines with a black marker. Laminate the finished products and place them in your math learning center with sets of tangram pieces. Students will enjoy puzzling over their classmates' tangram creations.

LEARNING OBJECTIVE

Students multiply and divide fractions.

GROUPING

Individual

MATERIALS

- black marker

For each student:

- *Tangram Fractions* reproducible (p. 88)
- one zippered plastic bag
- scissors
- construction paper

Taking It Further

Have students work in cooperative groups and combine tangram designs to create an amusement park, playground, or city. They can even use tangram designs to illustrate books the class is studying in literature.

Assessing Skills

- Are students placing a problem and solution at every meeting point?
- When students divide by common fractions, do they understand that the quotient may be larger than the dividend?

Name ______________________ Date ______________

Tangram Fractions

A tangram is an ancient Chinese puzzle with seven pieces. For centuries people have been using tangrams to create shapes and designs. Today it's your turn!

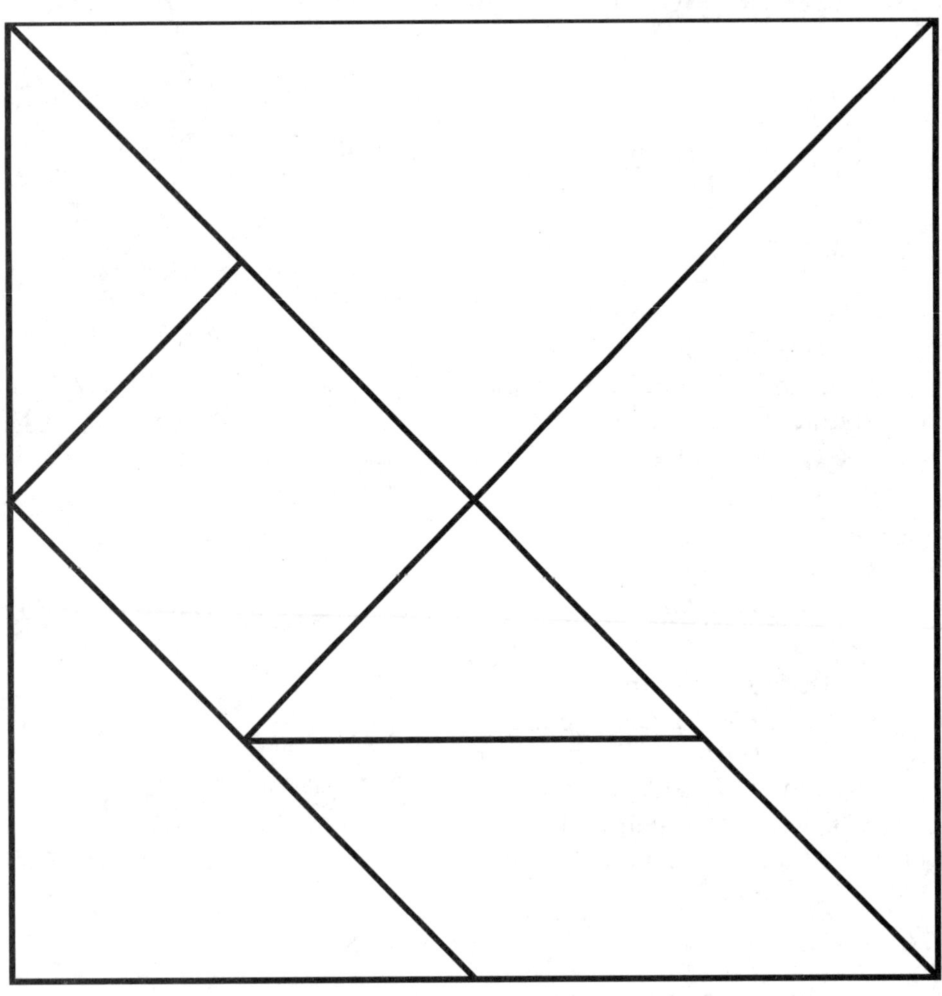

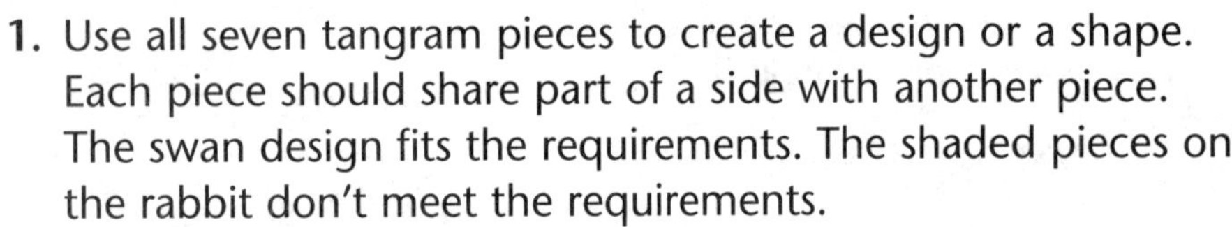

1. Use all seven tangram pieces to create a design or a shape. Each piece should share part of a side with another piece. The swan design fits the requirements. The shaded pieces on the rabbit don't meet the requirements.

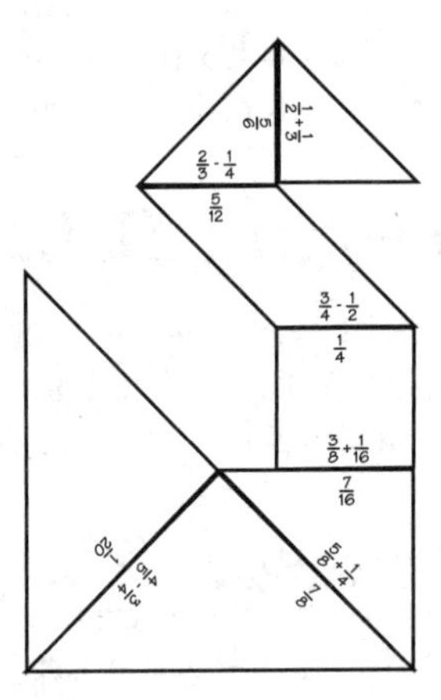

2. Locate the places on your design where two pieces touch. On one side of the meeting point, write a multiplication or division problem using only fractions. On the other side of the meeting point, write the answer. Make sure you have a problem and answer at every meeting place. (See the swan diagram.)

3. Place your tangram pieces in a zippered bag. Give it to another student. He or she can pair the problems with the correct answers and reconstruct your design or picture!

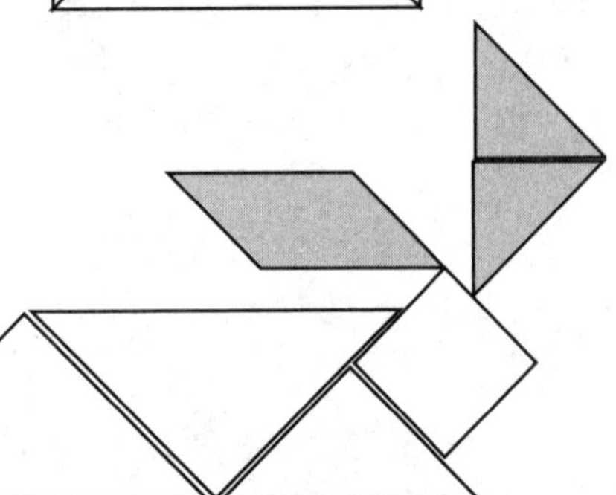

Ladybug Fractions

Students soar to new heights of understanding as they create their own ladybug fractions.

Directions

1. Duplicate the reproducible for each group.
2. Divide the class into groups of 4 or 5 and pass out the materials. Have a volunteer in each group cut out the pattern. Each member of the group makes a ladybug.
3. Students trace the pattern onto construction paper as indicated by color and cut out the construction paper. They glue three small circles to each wing and then punch a hole in the areas indicated on the pattern. Finally, students attach the wings and the body with the paper fastener.

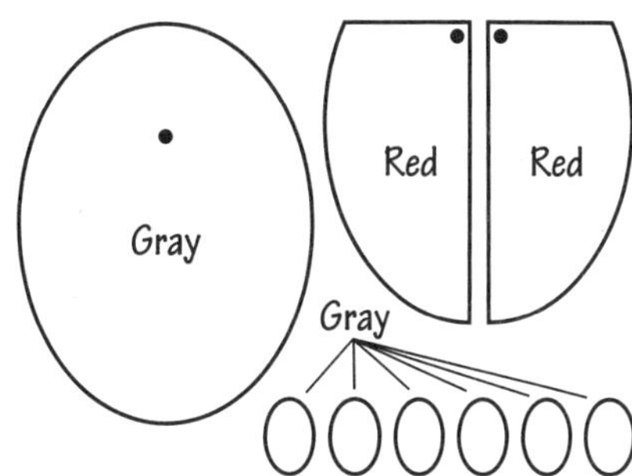

4. Ask students to write a fraction multiplication problem in the circles on one wing. Have them write a fraction division problem in the circles on the other wing.
5. Show students how to pull back each wing and write the answer to the fraction problems.
6. Attach the ladybugs to pieces of yarn and display them in the classroom. Periodically during the day have students solve the problems.
7. The activity *Don't Let Fractions Drive You Buggy* (p. 91) is an interactive bulletin board that uses the ladybugs constructed in this activity.

Taking It Further

Ask students to write a lowest-term fraction under the wing of the ladybug. Then challenge them to write three equivalent fractions on the circles attached to the wings.

Assessing Skills

Do students understand that when they divide common fractions the quotient may be larger than the dividend?

LEARNING OBJECTIVE

Students multiply and divide fractions.

GROUPING

Cooperative groups of 4 or 5

MATERIALS

For each group:

- *Ladybug Fractions* reproducible (p. 90)
- scissors
- glue
- markers

For each student:

- 1 sheet of red construction paper
- 1 sheet of gray construction paper
- 1 brass paper fastener
- yarn

 Name ______________________ Date ______________

Ladybug Fractions

Each time the ladybug flies home, she reveals the answers to the math problems written on her wings.

Cut out the pattern and trace it on construction paper. Punch a hole in the pattern as shown. Attach the wings to the body with a brass paper fastener. Now you're ready to write your multiplication and division problems.

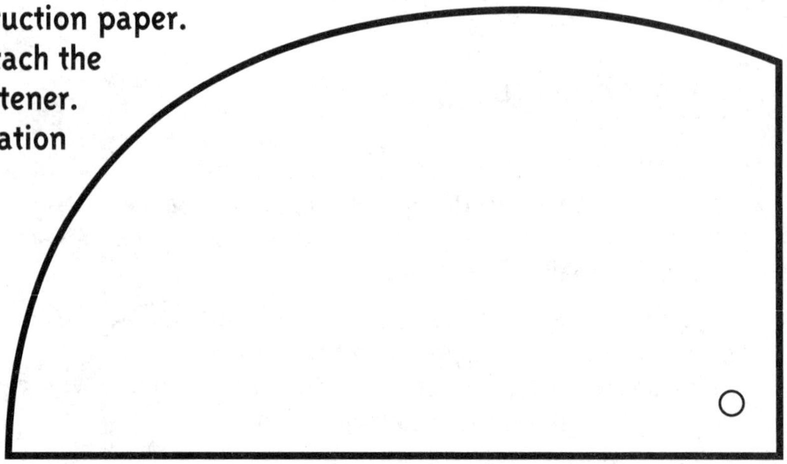

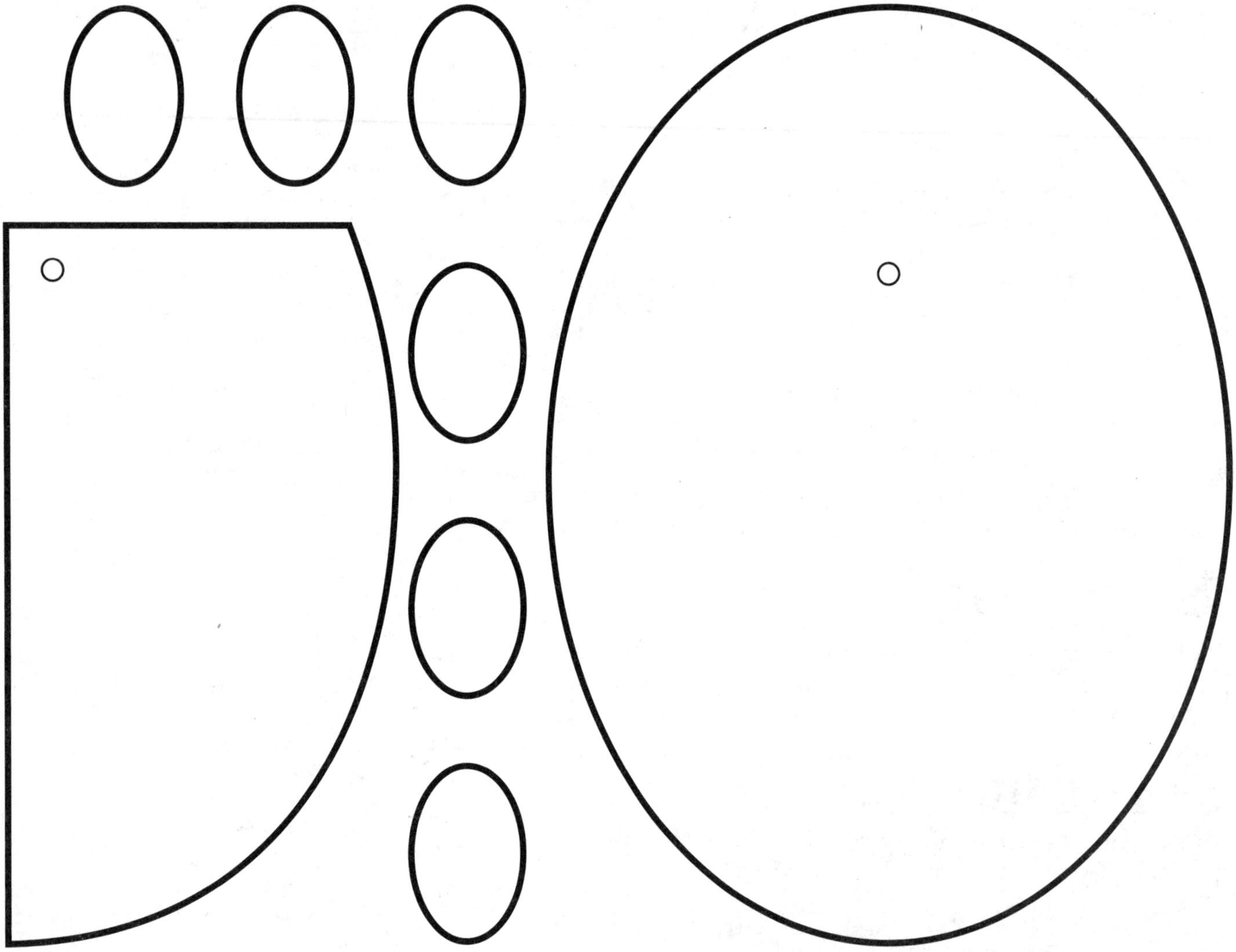

Don't Let Fractions Drive You Buggy

This interactive bulletin board gets the whole class involved in a lively game of multiplying fractions.

Directions

1. Ask the class to choose a game leader. Then divide the class into two even teams and assign a scorekeeper to each team. Each team tries to be the first to spell the word *ladybug.* Each scorekeeper draws seven lines on the chalkboard. As the team accumulates letters, the scorekeeper puts the letters on the lines to spell the word *ladybug.*

2. Decide which team will go first. The first player on that team chooses a ladybug and computes the answer to the problem. (Once a ladybug has been used, it can not be chosen again.)
3. The game leader pulls back the ladybug's wings and verifies that the answer is correct.
4. The letter next to the correct answer goes to that player's team. The scorekeeper writes the letter on the appropriate line. If the team already has that letter, the scorekeeper does not record it.
5. The game continues until one team completes the word *ladybug.*

Taking It Further

Have students extend the length of the game by spelling several words or a phrase. The difficult part is making words or phrases that have the same letters found in *ladybug.* Let the class experiment and have fun creating their own unique titles. One class came up with the title *Bad, Bad, Daddybug.*

Assessing Skills

Are students renaming the fractions in lowest terms?

LEARNING OBJECTIVE

Students multiply fractions.

GROUPING

Whole class

MATERIALS

- Ladybug constructions from the *Ladybug Fractions* activity (p. 90)
- poster paper
- white construction paper
- black marker
- thumb tacks

ADVANCE PREPARATION

1. Cover the bulletin board with poster paper and an attractive border. Affix construction paper letters to the board that read, "Don't Let Fractions Drive You Buggy!"
2. Open the wings on the ladybug constructions. Beside each answer, write one of the following letters: L, A, D, Y, B, U, G. Distribute the letters as evenly as possible, so that there are not too many of one letter.
3. Close the wings and attach the ladybug constructions to the bulletin board.

Clowning Around

Relating fractions and decimals is sure to be a laughing matter when students shade decimal shapes and watch the clown Wearie Willie come to life!

Directions

1. Duplicate the reproducible for each student and distribute.
2. Review the concept of fractions and equivalent decimals. Write the following fractions and equivalent decimals in random order on the board:

   $3\frac{3}{10}$ 3.3 $\frac{96}{100}$ 0.96 $17\frac{8}{100}$ 17.08 $\frac{9}{10}$ 0.9

   Call on volunteers to match the fractions with the equivalent decimals and explain how they matched the two.
3. Allow the students to complete the page on their own.

Taking It Further

Students can easily make their own picture puzzles for classmates to solve. Give one piece of centimeter graph paper to each student. They may use the graph paper to sketch their pictures and then write the decimals that will fit their drawings on notebook paper. After students list the matching fractions, they exchange puzzles.

Assessing Skills

- Can students differentiate between decimals such as 0.5 and 0.05?
- Do students realize that 1.20 and 1.2 are equivalent?

LEARNING OBJECTIVE

Students match fractions with equivalent decimals.

GROUPING

Individual

MATERIALS

- *Clowning Around* reproducible (p. 93)
- colored pencils
- centimeter graph paper

Name ______________________________ Date ______________

Clowning Around

What do Wearie Willie and the man Emmett Kelly have in common? They're different names for the same person. Emmett Kelly spent hours putting on makeup to magically transform himself into the sad circus clown known as Wearie Willie.

Create your own transformation. Match the fractions in the data bank with the equivalent decimals in the picture puzzle and then shade them. The first one has been done for you.

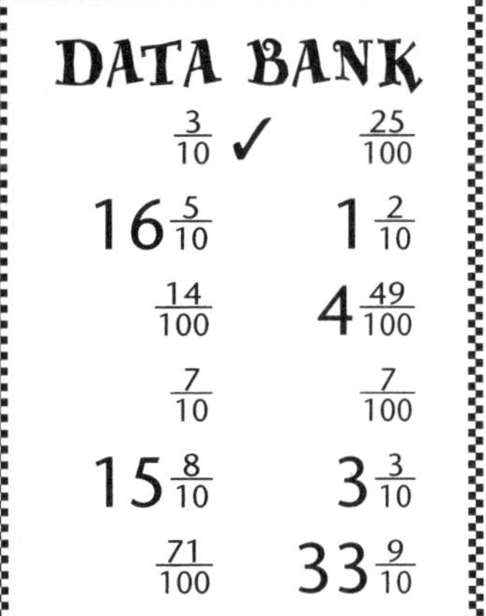

DATA BANK

$\frac{3}{10}$ ✓	$\frac{25}{100}$
$16\frac{5}{10}$	$1\frac{2}{10}$
$\frac{14}{100}$	$4\frac{49}{100}$
$\frac{7}{10}$	$\frac{7}{100}$
$15\frac{8}{10}$	$3\frac{3}{10}$
$\frac{71}{100}$	$33\frac{9}{10}$

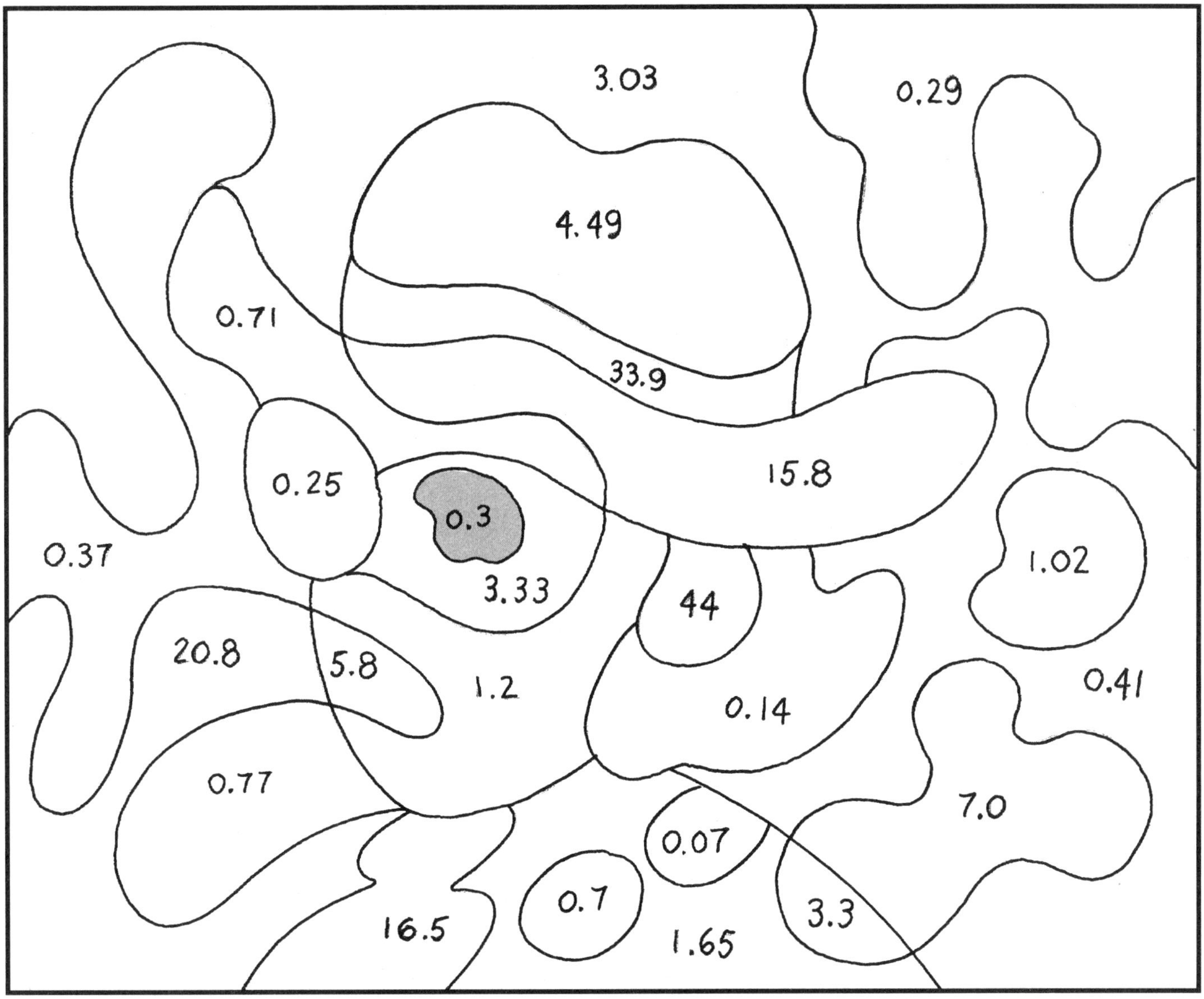

3.03 0.29
4.49
0.71
33.9
0.25 0.3 15.8
0.37 3.33 1.02
44
20.8 5.8 1.2 0.41
0.14
0.77
7.0
0.07
0.7 3.3
16.5 1.65

Battling Decimals

Two players match wits and try to be the first to cross a fraction game board.

Directions

1. Explain to students that the goal of the game is to make a path with their game cards across the game board before their opponent does. Decimal game cards must be placed on corresponding fraction and mixed number squares. Each piece must be connected by at least a corner. You may want to show the following arrangements using game boards and game cards.

Vertical Path

$1\frac{1}{10}$	0.4	$12\frac{7}{100}$	$\frac{5}{10}$	$193\frac{1}{10}$
$6\frac{5}{100}$	$\frac{1}{10}$	56.1	$\frac{3}{10}$	$\frac{1}{100}$
$\frac{9}{100}$	6.4	$16\frac{8}{1000}$	$\frac{6}{10}$	$\frac{16}{100}$
$8\frac{2}{100}$	1.9	$5\frac{4}{1000}$	$9\frac{3}{10}$	$\frac{47}{100}$
$57\frac{2}{10}$	$\frac{7}{10}$	3.16	$6\frac{2}{10}$	$1\frac{57}{100}$

Horizontal Path

$1\frac{1}{10}$	$\frac{4}{10}$	$12\frac{7}{100}$	$\frac{5}{10}$	$193\frac{1}{10}$
6.05	$\frac{1}{10}$	$56\frac{1}{10}$	$\frac{3}{10}$	$\frac{1}{100}$
$\frac{9}{100}$	6.4	$16\frac{8}{1000}$	$\frac{6}{10}$	$\frac{16}{100}$
$8\frac{2}{100}$	1.9	5.004	$9\frac{3}{10}$	$\frac{47}{100}$
$57\frac{2}{10}$	$\frac{7}{10}$	$3\frac{16}{100}$	6.2	1.57

Incorrect Path

$1\frac{1}{10}$	0.4	12.07	$\frac{5}{10}$	$193\frac{1}{10}$
$6\frac{5}{100}$	$\frac{1}{10}$	$56\frac{1}{10}$	$\frac{3}{10}$	0.01
$\frac{9}{100}$	6.4	$16\frac{8}{1000}$	$\frac{6}{10}$	$\frac{16}{100}$
$8\frac{2}{100}$	$1\frac{9}{10}$	$5\frac{4}{1000}$	$9\frac{3}{10}$	0.47
$57\frac{2}{10}$	$\frac{7}{10}$	3.16	$6\frac{2}{10}$	$1\frac{57}{100}$

2. Pairs shuffle the game cards and place them facedown in a pile. They also decide which player will travel horizontally and which player will travel vertically. Each player draws three cards.
3. Pairs determine who goes first. Player 1 chooses a new card from the pile and places any one of her or his four game cards on the game board. That player discards one card.
4. Player 2 takes a turn. The game continues until one player makes a path across the game board.

Taking It Further

Follow the same directions and have students pair improper fractions to mixed numbers.

Assessing Skills

Can students differentiate among 1.02, 1.2, and 1.20?

LEARNING OBJECTIVE

Given fractions and mixed numbers, students match equivalent decimals.

GROUPING

Pairs

MATERIALS

- 2 pieces of tagboard
- thin-tipped marker
- scissors

ADVANCE PREPARATION

1. To make a game board, cut tagboard to measure $8\frac{1}{2}$ by $8\frac{1}{2}$ inches. Divide the game board into 25 squares that measure $1\frac{1}{2}$ inches by $1\frac{1}{2}$ inches. Outline the squares with a thin-tipped marker.
2. To make game cards, follow the same directions and cut the squares into separate pieces.
3. Copy the numbers from the examples below onto the game board and game cards.

Game Board

$1\frac{1}{10}$	$\frac{4}{10}$	$12\frac{7}{100}$	$\frac{5}{10}$	$193\frac{1}{10}$
$6\frac{5}{100}$	$\frac{1}{10}$	$56\frac{1}{10}$	$\frac{3}{10}$	$\frac{1}{100}$
$\frac{9}{100}$	$6\frac{4}{10}$	$16\frac{8}{1000}$	$\frac{6}{10}$	$\frac{16}{100}$
$8\frac{2}{100}$	$1\frac{9}{10}$	$5\frac{4}{1000}$	$9\frac{3}{10}$	$\frac{47}{100}$
$57\frac{2}{10}$	$\frac{7}{10}$	$3\frac{16}{100}$	$6\frac{2}{10}$	$1\frac{57}{100}$

Game Cards

1.1	0.4	12.07	0.5	193.1
6.05	0.1	56.1	0.3	0.01
0.09	6.4	16.008	0.6	0.16
8.02	1.9	5.004	9.3	0.47
57.2	0.7	3.16	6.2	1.57

Stumpers

Challenge students with these weekly decimal problems.

Directions

1. Review decimal place value.

Tens	Ones	Decimal Point	Tenths	Hundredths
2	1	.	4	5
3	7	.	0	8
	5	.	6	

   Go over how each decimal is read and written:
   We say, "Twenty-one and forty-five hundredths."
   We write 21.45.
   We say, "Thirty-seven and eight hundredths."
   We write 37.08.
   We say, "Five and six tenths."
   We write 5.6.

2. Students use the clues in each problem to find the mystery number.
3. They write the answers using both numbers and words. For instance, 13.97 is also written as thirteen and ninety-seven hundredths.

Taking It Further

Students may enjoy making their own decimal problems to stump classmates. Place the new Stumpers in your learning center.

Assessing Skills

Are students writing six tenths as 0.06 or as 0.6? Many students incorrectly reason that since tens are two places to the left of the decimal, tenths must be two places to the right of the decimal.

LEARNING OBJECTIVE

Students use logical reasoning and knowledge of place value to solve number puzzles.

GROUPING

Whole class

MATERIALS

- *Stumpers* reproducible (p. 96)
- construction paper
- scissors
- glue
- paper and pencil

ADVANCE PREPARATION

Duplicate one *Stumpers* reproducible. Cut along lines. Attach each problem to construction paper and display weekly in your math learning center or on the bulletin board.

Name ____________________ Date ____________

Stumpers

Write your answers on a separate piece of paper in both number and word form; for example, 14.37 (number form), fourteen and thirty-seven hundredths (word form).

1. Who Am I?
- **a.** I have 4 digits, and they all are different.
- **b.** All of my digits are odd.
- **c.** I have a 1 in the hundredths place.
- **d.** I have a 7 in the ones place.
- **e.** The number in the tens place is less than the number in the tenths place.
- **f.** None of my digits are 9.

2. Who Am I?
- **a.** I have 4 digits, and they are all odd.
- **b.** The number in the tenths place is greater than 3. It is a factor of 36.
- **c.** The number in the hundredths place is less than 4 and greater than 1.
- **d.** The numbers in the ones and tens places are the same and are also factors of 25.

3. Who Am I?
- **a.** I have 4 digits, and they are all different and even.
- **b.** The number in the hundredths place is half of the number in the tenths place.
- **c.** The number in the hundredths place is greater than 3.
- **d.** The number in the ones place is 6.
- **e.** The number in the tens place is 2.

4. Who Am I?
- **a.** I have 4 digits.
- **b.** Each digit is either a 2 or a 4.
- **c.** The numbers in the ones place and tenths place are the same.
- **d.** The numbers in the tens place and hundredths place are the same.
- **e.** I have a 4 in the hundredths place.

5. Who Am I?
- **a.** I have 3 even digits.
- **b.** The number in the tenths place when subtracted from 3 equals 1.
- **c.** The number in the ones place is 8.
- **d.** Divide the number in the ones place by 2 and you will have the number in the hundredths place.

6. Who Am I?
- **a.** I have 4 digits, and they are all odd.
- **b.** The 2-digit whole number is greater than 10 and less than 20. When this number is divided into 121, the quotient is also that number.
- **c.** The digit in the tenths place is 3.
- **d.** Add 4 to the number in the tenths place and you will have the number in the hundredths place.

Name That Decimal

Learning decimal place value is fun and egg-citing with this simple egg carton game.

Directions

1. Distribute egg cartons, number cubes, and counters to students. Have them form pairs. Explain that they will be playing a game. The goal of the game is for each player to create a greater number in her or his egg carton than her or his opponent.
2. Players roll number cubes to determine order of play; the player with the higher number goes first.
3. Player 1 rolls the number cube. Suppose a 4 is rolled. Then 4 counters may be put in any empty section in that player's egg carton.
4. Player 2 rolls the number cube. Suppose a 6 is rolled. Then 6 counters may be put in any empty section in that player's egg carton.
5. Play continues until all the sections in both egg cartons are filled.
6. Students write and read the number represented by the counters in their egg cartons. The player with the greater number wins the game.

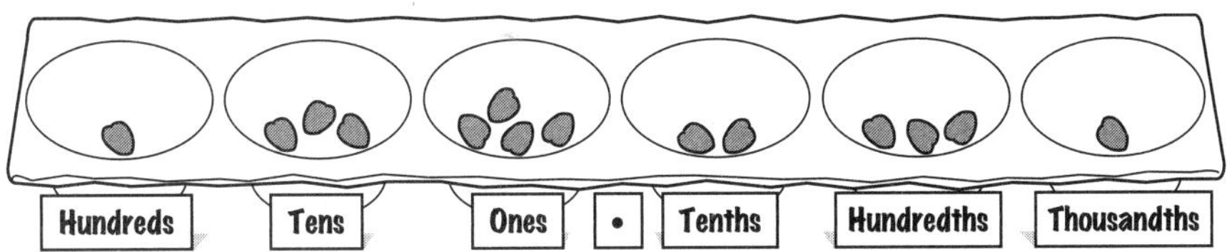

The number in the egg carton above is 134.231.

Taking It Further

Glue two egg cartons together, end to end, and increase the decimal to the millionths.

Assessing Skills

- Are students developing a strategy or randomly placing the counters in the egg cartons?
- Do students read and write the decimals correctly?

LEARNING OBJECTIVE

Students read and write decimals to the thousandths.

GROUPING

Pairs

MATERIALS

- marker
- index cards

For each student:

- half an egg carton (Use the egg cartons from the *Fraction Line-Up* activity on page 77, or see directions for making them. Be sure to save these egg cartons and place-value labels for the *Guess That Decimal* activity on page 98.)
- 1 number cube labeled 1–6
- 30 counters, such as dried beans

ADVANCE PREPARATION

1. Use index cards to label the sections of each egg carton from left to right as follows: Hundreds, Tens, Ones, Tenths, Hundredths, and Thousandths.
2. Place a decimal point between the Ones and Tenths.

Guess That Decimal

This guessing game helps students develop their logical-reasoning skills and teaches decimal place value.

Directions

1. Explain to students that they will be playing a game with partners. The goal of the game is to ask yes and no questions to determine their opponent's secret number.
2. Distribute half an egg carton and one stack of numbered cards to each student and then pair them.
3. Partners sit facing each other. They place a number card in each section of the egg carton to make a 6-digit secret number. The number on each card stands for the number of units in that place.
4. After deciding who goes first, players ask one yes or no question per turn, such as, "Is there an odd number in the ones place?" or "Is the number in the tenths place greater than 5?" Students may record responses on a separate sheet of paper.
5. The first person to correctly guess the opponent's secret number wins the game.

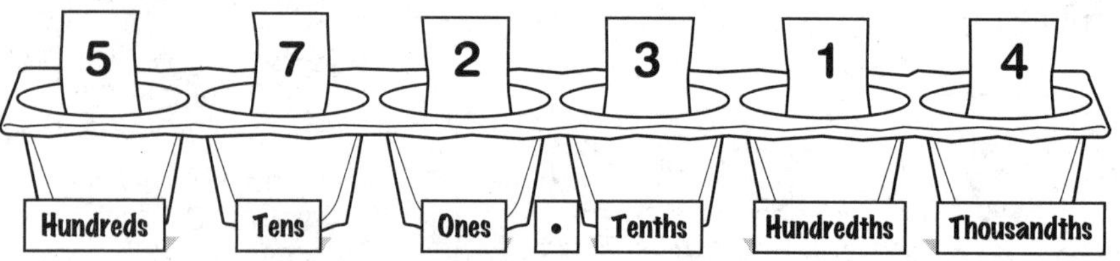

The number in the egg carton above is 572.314.

Taking It Further

Have students use the egg cartons to create more secret numbers and then develop a list of clues that will lead others to identify the number. Post the list of clues in your math learning center or on the bulletin board and see how many students can guess the correct answer.

Assessing Skills

Are students able to formulate good questions that eliminate many possible answers?

LEARNING OBJECTIVE

Students identify place value to the thousandths.

GROUPING

Pairs

MATERIALS

- marker

For each student:

- half an egg carton (Use the egg cartons and place-value labels from the *Name That Decimal* activity on page 97, or see directions for making them.)
- 10 index cards
- paper and pencil

ADVANCE PREPARATION

Write each number, 0 through 9, on the ten index cards.

Every Number Has Its Place

Kids love a challenge. This decimal place-value puzzle will put them to the ultimate test.

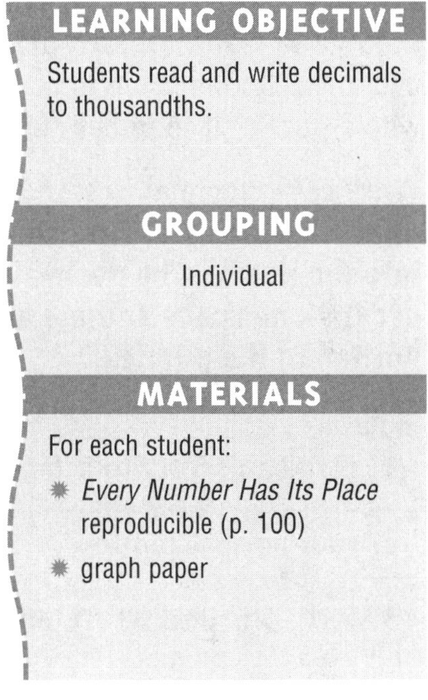

LEARNING OBJECTIVE

Students read and write decimals to thousandths.

GROUPING

Individual

MATERIALS

For each student:

- *Every Number Has Its Place* reproducible (p. 100)
- graph paper

Directions

1. Review place value to the thousandth place with the class.
2. To familiarize students with the puzzle, present the following sample:
   a. *Use the following decimals to complete the puzzle: 7.7, 40.8, 1.3, 38.18, 137.01, 1.6, 36.7.*
   b. *Decimal points occupy one space and are already written in.*
   c. *Sort and classify the decimals before you begin to solve the puzzle.* (Students may classify the decimals in different ways. One possibility is shown below.)

2 digits	3 digits	4 digits	5 digits
7.7	40.8	38.18	137.01
1.3	36.7		
1.6			

3. As the solution shows, by classifying and using the process of elimination, it's easy to solve the puzzle.
4. Distribute a copy of the reproducible to each student.

3	6	.	7			
			.		4	
	1	3	7	.	0	1
	.				.	
	3	8	.	1	8	
				.		
				6		

Taking It Further

Give students graph paper and have them make their own decimal puzzles.

Assessing Skills

Are students sorting and classifying the decimals before they begin solving the puzzle?

Name ______________________ Date ____________

Every Number Has Its Place

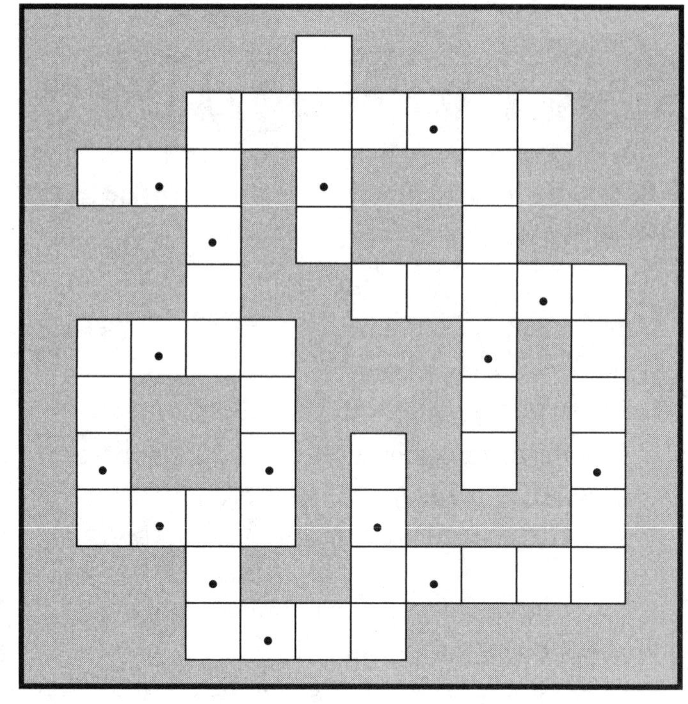

Approach this activity with caution—it's been known to produce high levels of fun and learning! Each digit can occupy only one place to make the whole puzzle fit together perfectly.

Write each decimal in standard form on the lines below. Fit the number into the puzzle. The decimal points occupy one space and are already written in the puzzle.

1. three and forty-four hundredths ____________
2. four and six tenths ____________
3. forty-one and seven tenths ____________
4. four thousand sixteen and thirty-two hundredths ____________
5. nine hundred forty-seven and thirty-six hundredths ____________
6. six and five tenths ____________
7. fifty-six and four tenths ____________
8. one and thirty-five hundredths ____________
9. one and six thousandths ____________
10. forty-five and sixty-three hundredths ____________
11. fifteen and three tenths ____________
12. three hundred seventeen and nine tenths ____________
13. three thousand seven and fifty-five hundredths ____________
14. six and nineteen hundredths ____________
15. six and ninety-nine hundredths ____________

"Weighty" Problems

Students compare and order decimals and find what we'd weigh on different planets!

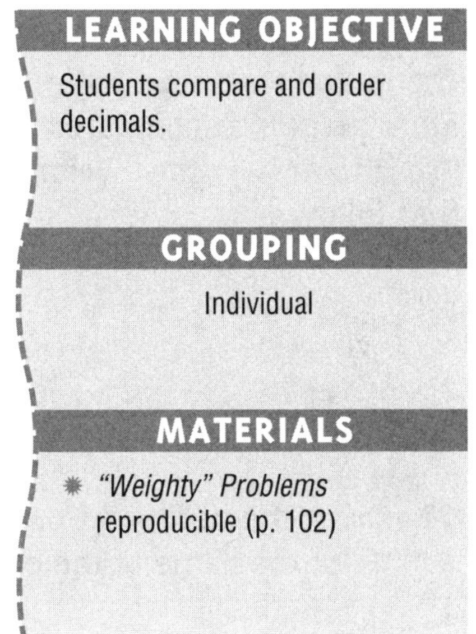

LEARNING OBJECTIVE

Students compare and order decimals.

GROUPING

Individual

MATERIALS

- *"Weighty" Problems* reproducible (p. 102)

Directions

1. Duplicate the reproducible for each student and distribute.
2. Review comparing and ordering decimals as follows:
   a. Compare 3.67 and 3.69.
   b. Begin with the digits on the left. The ones and tenths are the same.
   c. Compare the hundredths: 9 hundredths > 7 hundredths. So 3.69 > 3.67.
3. Let students complete the reproducible on their own.

Taking It Further

Obtain several books on the planets. Have students research the planets and compare the diameters, distance from the sun, and temperatures.

Assessing Skills

Are students looking at all the numbers to the left first? Some students may reason that 4,321.9 is larger than 4,322.7 because the digit in the tenths place is greater in the first number. They may fail to see that the 2 is greater than the 1 in the ones place.

Name ______________________ Date ______________

"Weighty" Problems

When you weigh yourself, you're really measuring how much gravity pulls on you. If you weigh 100 pounds on Earth, you'd only weigh 38 pounds on Mars. That's because the pull of gravity is less on Mars.

The table lists the pull of gravity on the other planets as compared to Earth's. Use it to answer the "weighty" problems that follow.

Planet	Gravitational Pull
Mercury	0.38 times Earth's
Venus	0.91 times Earth's
Earth	1.00 times Earth's
Mars	0.38 times Earth's
Jupiter	2.34 times Earth's
Saturn	0.93 times Earth's
Uranus	0.93 times Earth's
Neptune	1.14 times Earth's

1. Order the decimals from least to greatest. Write the name of the planet next to the decimal.

   a. ____________ ____________________
   b. ____________ ____________________
   c. ____________ ____________________
   d. ____________ ____________________
   e. ____________ ____________________
   f. ____________ ____________________
   g. ____________ ____________________
   h. ____________ ____________________

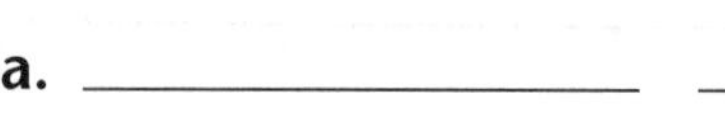

2. On which planet would you weigh the most? ____________________
3. On which planets would you weigh the least? ____________________
4. On which planets would you weigh the same? ____________________

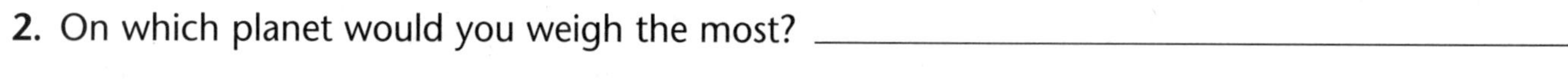

5. The pull of gravity on the sun is 2,800 times Earth's. A person who weighs 100 pounds on Earth would weigh ____________ pounds on the sun.

Wacky Presidential Firsts

Ordering decimals can be an adventure when the first decimal in the group reveals the name of the president who had a pet raccoon he walked on a leash!

Directions

1. Duplicate the reproducible for each student and distribute.
2. Review comparing decimals by asking students to look at place value.
   a. To compare 0.45 and 0.47, begin by lining up the decimal points.

      0.45
      0.47

   b. Compare tenths. If they are equal, compare hundredths.

      0.**4**5
      0.**4**7

   c. Compare hundredths.

      0.4**5**
      0.4**7**

   Since 7 > 5, 0.47 > 0.45.

Taking It Farther

Let students poll classmates and find out who was the first student to eat sushi or do any other zany action. Encourage them to create their own math problems based on these actions.

Assessing Skills

How do students approach problems with an uneven number of digits? Do they understand that 0.7 = 0.70?

LEARNING OBJECTIVE

Students compare and order decimals to the hundredths place.

GROUPING

Individual

MATERIALS

- *Wacky Presidential Firsts* reproducible (p. 104)

 Name ______________________ Date ______________

Wacky Presidential Firsts

These presidents go down in history not only as statesmen or for resolving international conflicts. They're also known for their offbeat actions.

Read each fact. Order the decimals under it from greatest to least. The greatest decimal reveals the name of the notorious president who did it!

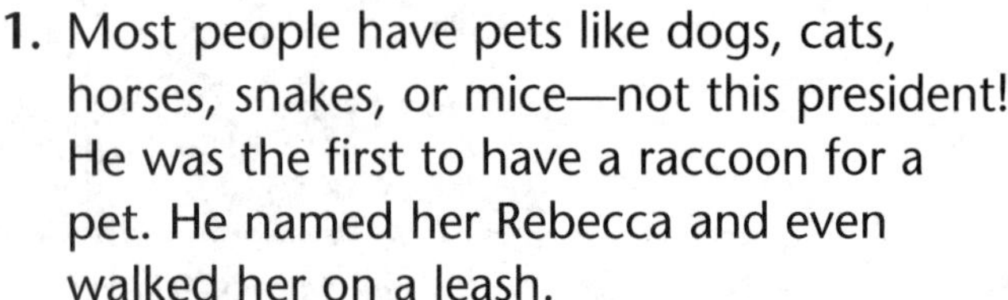

1. Most people have pets like dogs, cats, horses, snakes, or mice—not this president! He was the first to have a raccoon for a pet. He named her Rebecca and even walked her on a leash.

   128.8 (Abraham Lincoln)
   129.00 (Calvin Coolidge)
   128.87 (Herbert Hoover)

   ____

2. This president could write in Greek with one hand and in Latin with the other—at the same time!

   42.05 (James Garfield)
   42.01 (Rutherford Hayes)
   41.07 (Jimmy Carter)

   ____

3. Can you imagine getting a speeding ticket for riding a horse too fast? He was the first president to achieve such a feat!

   1.39 (Andrew Jackson)
   0.95 (Abraham Lincoln)
   1.7 (Ulysses S. Grant)

   ____

4. This president not only rode into battle on a horse, he was the first to ride a horse sidesaddle.

   143.99 (George Washington)
   143.9 (Ulysses S. Grant)
   144.00 (Zachary Taylor)

   ____

5. This president liked his horse so much that he brought her to live at the White House. The horse ate the grass on the White House lawn!

   2.08 (Richard Nixon)
   2.78 (Jimmy Carter)
   2.80 (Zachary Taylor)

   ____

6. This president was a very small man. He was the first to stand on a table to deliver a speech.

   3.00 (Martin Van Buren)
   2.00 (William Harrison)
   2.99 (John Quincy Adams)

   ____

Who's First?

This activity fosters cooperation and builds skills in reading, writing, and ordering decimals.

Directions

1. Divide the class evenly into groups of 4 or 5 students.
2. Tape a decimal number to each student's back.
3. Each person in the group asks yes or no questions of other group members to determine the decimal number that is on his or her back. Students may use paper and pencil to record the responses.
4. After each person has guessed his or her number, students arrange themselves so that they are standing in order from the least to the greatest decimal. At that time, they yell, "We're first!"
5. The other groups stop working, and the teacher determines if the group has met all the criteria. If not, the groups continue working until a winner is announced.

Taking It Farther

Play *We're Buddies,* a decimal place-value game that uses the same materials as *Who's First?* Write decimal numbers on half of the sheets of notebook paper. The number may have any number of digits. Write equivalent decimals on the remaining sheets of notebook paper; for example 13.1 and 13.10, 3.50 and 3.500. Attach a sheet to each student's back. The student asks yes or no questions to determine the decimal number on his or her back. Then that student finds the student who has the equivalent decimal on his or her back. The first pair to find each other is the winner.

Assessing Skills

- Do students identify each place by its appropriate name?
- Are students asking yes or no questions that eliminate large groups of numbers?

LEARNING OBJECTIVE

Students read decimals to hundredths. They also compare and order decimals.

GROUPING

Cooperative groups of 4 or 5

MATERIALS

- masking tape
- notebook paper (1 piece per student)
- black marker
- paper and pencil

ADVANCE PREPARATION

Write a decimal number on each piece of notebook paper. The numbers should have four digits with the decimal written to the hundredths place; for example, 23.98, 44.04, 16.22, 80.02.

Decimal Roundup

Students combine their knowledge, speed, and perseverance for an unforgettable decimal roundup.

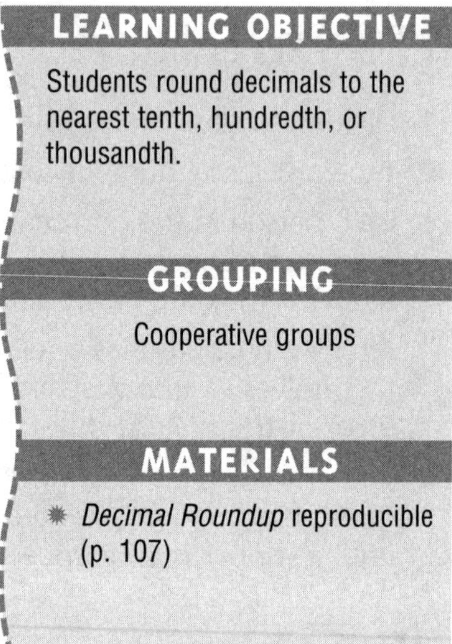
LEARNING OBJECTIVE

Students round decimals to the nearest tenth, hundredth, or thousandth.

GROUPING

Cooperative groups

MATERIALS

- *Decimal Roundup* reproducible (p. 107)

Directions

1. Remind students that to round a decimal to a specific place, they look at the number to the right of that place. If it is 5 or more, the number rounds up. If it is less than 5, the number remains the same.
2. Write the following table and examples on the board.

Original number is	Round it to the nearest	Digit to the right is	Is it 5 or more?	Rounded number is
97.6453	whole number	6	yes	98
97.6453	tenth	4	no	97.6
97.6453	hundredth	5	yes	97.65
97.6453	thousandth	3	no	97.645

3. Duplicate the reproducible for each group and distribute.
4. Tell students that you are looking for accuracy and speed. The first group with all the right answers wins.
5. Give the start signal and watch the learning begin!

Taking It Farther

Give students a number such as 4.78 and ask them to tell you all the numbers that could have been rounded to get this number and how they arrived at each number. [4.780, 4.781, 4.782, 4.783, 4.784, 4.775, 4.776, 4.777, 4.778, and 4.779]

Assessing Skills

Are students able to talk about the numbers using their correct place-value names?

Name ______________________ Date ______________

Decimal Roundup

Hold on to your hat, this roundup is guaranteed to have your head spinning in circles.

Use the digits 6, 7, 1, 4, and 9 to make each sentence true. Use all five digits in each number. Place the decimal point in one of the answer boxes.

1. ☐☐☐☐☐☐ rounded to the nearest hundredth is 6.19.

2. ☐☐☐☐☐☐ rounded to the nearest tenth is 679.1.

3. ☐☐☐☐☐☐ rounded to the nearest tenth is 97.4.

4. ☐☐☐☐☐☐ rounded to the nearest thousandth is 6.917.

5. ☐☐☐☐☐☐ rounded to the nearest thousandth is 9.615.

6. ☐☐☐☐☐☐ rounded to the nearest hundredth is 9.72.

7. There are two possible answers to this question. Can you find them both?

   ☐☐☐☐☐☐ and

   ☐☐☐☐☐☐ rounded to the nearest tenth are 67.9.

Top Secret Numbers

Students will become master detectives as they unravel clues to discover some top secret numbers.

Directions

1. Explain to groups that their goal is to be the first group to unravel the clues to discover the mystery number.
2. Distribute one clue card to each group member. Allow time for students to read their cards silently, then give the start signal.
3. Students share information about their clue with the group, but they *cannot* read the card aloud. The goal of this activity is to get students to communicate and work cooperatively to solve a problem.
4. The first team with the correct number [5555.5553] wins the game.

Taking It Further

Follow the directions above for this problem.

Card One My number has eleven digits. Four of my digits are decimals.

Card Two One of my digits is 8. The rest of my digits are a different number, but they are all the same.

Card Three When you round me to the thousandths place, my final digit becomes a 5.

Card Four All of my eleven digits are even.

[4,444,444.4448]

As an additional challenge, have each group write its own set of number clues. Groups trade sets of clues and solve.

Assessing Skills

* Are students able to talk about the numbers using their correct place-value names?
* Do students understand rounding decimals well enough to get clues from the information?

LEARNING OBJECTIVE

Students read decimals to ten-thousandths and round decimals to thousandths.

GROUPING

Cooperative groups of 4

MATERIALS

* set of 4 large index cards per group
* marker

ADVANCE PREPARATION

Write the information below on each set of cards.

Card One
All of my eight digits are 5 except for one digit. Four of my digits are decimals.

Card Two
All of my digits are odd.

Card Three
When you round me to thousandths, all of my digits are 5.

Card Four
None of my digits are 1.

Bag Math

This game requires speed, cooperation, and a sense of humor. Learning about decimals has never been this much fun!

Directions

1. Tell groups that the goal of this game is to be the first team to have all equivalent numbers in each bag.
2. Distribute the sets of bags to each group. Each group member takes one bag. Students need to face each other so they can work cooperatively.
3. Ask students to look at the contents of their paper bags. They can easily see that the decimals or fractions are not equivalent; however, if they could trade with other members of the group, they could have four equivalent numbers in each bag.
4. When you give the start signal, each student passes his or her paper bag clockwise. That person may either take a piece of paper out of the bag or put one in. After performing this task, the student passes the bag clockwise again. Students may talk during the activity, and they may look at the contents of the bag at any time. The team continues passing the bags around until one team wins the game.

Taking It Further

For a real challenge, place an improper fraction, a mixed number, a decimal, and a percent in each bag, for example, $\frac{11}{10}$, $1\frac{1}{10}$, 1.1, and 110%.

Assessing Skills

Are students developing a cooperative strategy?

LEARNING OBJECTIVE

Students pair equivalent decimals and mixed numbers.

GROUPING

Cooperative groups of 4

MATERIALS

- marker
- 1 sheet of paper cut into 16 pieces

For each group:

- 4 paper bags containing four decimals or fractions (see below)

ADVANCE PREPARATION

1. Label each set of bags 1, 2, 3, and 4.
2. Write the decimals or fractions listed below on separate pieces of paper and place them in the bag.

Bag 1: 1.3, 7.9, 90.07, 5.1

Bag 2: 1.30, 7.90, 90.070, 5.10

Bag 3: 1.300, 7.900, 90.0700, 5.100

Bag 4: $1\frac{3}{10}$, $7\frac{9}{10}$, $90\frac{7}{100}$, $5\frac{1}{10}$

Guarded Treasure

Decimal knights guard the crown jewels while opponent knights scramble to uncover the treasure. This game is full of intrigue, suspense, and action.

Directions

1. Explain to students that the goal of this game is to break through their opponent's decimal guards and uncover the crown jewels.
2. Direct students to put all 12 cards, or knights, in different sections in the egg cartons. As they learn to play the game, they'll develop a strategy for card placement.
3. Tell students to place the long sides of the egg cartons together so neither player can see the other's cards. Then they decide who will go first.
4. Player 1 may move one of her or his knights into the opponent's court. If the section is empty, the knight may freely occupy the section. If the cup is occupied, the players must compare the value of the two knights. The knight with the greater value occupies the section and the other knight is taken from the game. If the knights are equal in value, both knights are removed. Any knight can overtake the crown jewels.
5. All the knights may move freely about the board, but the crown jewels must remain in one spot throughout the game.
6. For each turn, every player must make a move. A player may make only one move per turn.
7. The first player to uncover the opponent's crown jewels wins.

Taking It Further

Play a similar game with fractions and decimals. To make the knights, write one of the following decimals or fractions on each card: 0.25, $\frac{25}{100}$, 0.5, 0.50, $\frac{50}{100}$, 0.75, $\frac{75}{100}$, 0.80, $\frac{80}{100}$, 0.99, and $\frac{99}{100}$. As they play the game, students compare the values of decimals and fractions.

Assessing Skills

- Do students understand that 0.8 is equivalent to 0.80 and 0.800?
- Are students able to develop strategies to protect the crown jewels, or are they placing the knights randomly?

LEARNING OBJECTIVE

Students order decimals written to the thousandths place, and identify equivalent decimals.

GROUPING

Pairs

MATERIALS

For each pair:

- 2 egg cartons
- 24 tagboard cards measuring 1 inch by 2 inches

ADVANCE PREPARATION

1. Cut the lids off of both egg cartons.
2. Make two identical sets of 12 cards. You may also want to let students make their own cards. To make the decimal knights, write one of the following decimals on each card: 0.250, 0.25, 0.50, 0.5, 0.75, 0.750, 0.8, 0.80, 0.800, 0.99, and 0.990. Write "Crown Jewels" on the remaining card.

Absolutely Magical

Watch the excitement build as students order and subtract decimals and wait for the magical number 61.74 to appear.

Directions

1. Duplicate the reproducible for each student and distribute.
2. To familiarize students with the formula, go over the problem on the reproducible.
3. Direct students to try two or three problems on their own.
4. Allow time for everyone to share their problems with others.

Taking It Farther

- Have students predict if this formula would work without the decimal points. For instance, would the number 6,174 appear?
- Introduce palindromes. A *palindrome* is a number or word that is the same backward and forward. For instance, the number *373* and the word *dad* are palindromes. You can make a palindrome by continually adding the reverse digits. Sometimes it takes many steps.

```
   82
+  28   Add the reverse.
  110
+ 011   Add the reverse.
  121   A palindrome results!
```

Assessing Skills

Are students placing decimal points in a straight line before subtracting?

LEARNING OBJECTIVE

Students order digits to create the largest and smallest possible numbers. They also subtract decimals.

GROUPING

Whole class or individual

MATERIALS

- *Absolutely Magical* reproducible (p. 112)
- paper and pencil

Name ______________________ Date ____________

Absolutely Magical

I'm sixty-one and seventy-four hundredths (61.74), and I am guaranteed to appear like magic whenever you follow an easy formula. Baffle your teachers, amaze your friends, and stump your families.

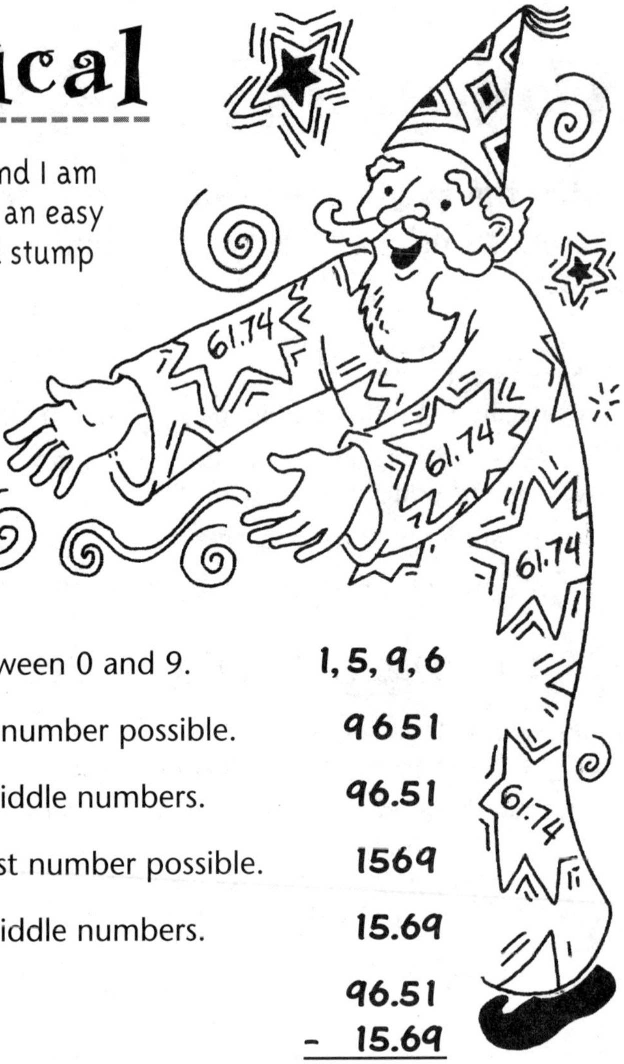

1. Pick any four different numbers between 0 and 9. **1, 5, 9, 6**
2. Arrange them to make the greatest number possible. **9651**

   Place a decimal between the two middle numbers. **96.51**
3. Then arrange them to make the least number possible. **1569**

   Place a decimal between the two middle numbers. **15.69**
4. Subtract the numbers.

   96.51
   − 15.69
   80.82
5. Use the four numbers in the difference.
   Repeat steps 2 through 4.

   (greatest number) **88.20**
   (least number) **− 02.88**
   (difference) **85.32**
6. Repeat the steps.

   (greatest number) **85.32**
   (least number) **− 23.58**
   (difference) **61.74**

**I told you so! I always appear sooner or later.
It doesn't matter what numbers you choose.
Try different numbers and amaze a friend or two!**

Shopping in the "Good Old Days"

What's more fun than spending money on toys? Spending money on toys at 1902 prices! This activity combines logical reasoning, adding decimals, and shopping.

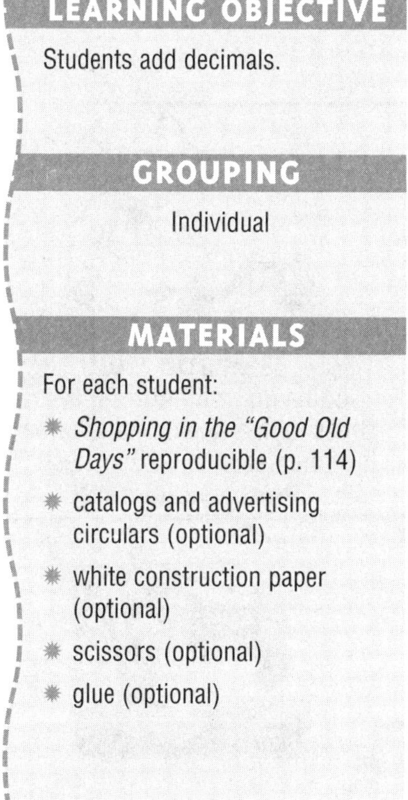

LEARNING OBJECTIVE

Students add decimals.

GROUPING

Individual

MATERIALS

For each student:

- *Shopping in the "Good Old Days"* reproducible (p. 114)
- catalogs and advertising circulars (optional)
- white construction paper (optional)
- scissors (optional)
- glue (optional)

Directions

1. Duplicate the reproducible for each student.
2. Review adding decimals, as follows:
   a. Write the problem with the decimal points in a line.
   ```
   $  2.13
      0.89
   + 11.99
   ```
   b. Add hundredths. Regroup if necessary
   ```
        2
   $  2.13
      0.89
   + 11.99
   -------
         1
   ```
   c. Add tenths. Regroup if necessary
   ```
       2 2
   $  2.13
      0.89
   + 11.99
   -------
       .01
   ```
   d. Add whole numbers.
   ```
       2 2
   $  2.13
      0.89
   + 11.99
   -------
   $ 15.01
   ```
3. Students should be able to complete the activity on their own.

Taking It Further

Have students bring catalogs and advertisements from home. Give each student a piece of white construction paper, scissors, and glue. They cut out pictures of toys that equal about $5.00 and glue them to the construction paper. Ask that they record the mathematics on the paper. Compare prices and products from 1902 and the present.

Assessing Skills

Are students adding randomly or developing strategies? Are they rounding numbers and making predictions? Are they determining sums and working backward?

Name ______________________ Date ______________

Shopping in the "Good Old Days"

It's hard to find a gift for $6.00 today. In 1902, that kind of money could buy four gifts or more. Look at the items in the Sears, Roebuck & Company catalog from 1902.

Find four items that when added equal exactly $6.00. Circle the items.

Did you know... a good monthly income in 1902 was $35.00!

Majestic Doll
China doll with moving eyes. Dressed in a fine lace and ribbon-trimmed chemise. 23 inches tall.
Price: $2.95 each

Toy Sewing Machine
This machine really sews and is beautifully decorated.
Price: $2.25 each

Laughing Camera
Look through this lens and stout people look thin and thin people look stout. More fun than going to the circus.
Price: $0.32 each

Mechanical Warship
This ship runs in a circle with two detachable masts. It has a lifeboat and four cannons.
Price: $0.43 each

Folding Checkerboard
14- by 14-inch board.
Price: $0.10 each

Dominoes
Set of 28 pieces.
Price: $0.05 each set

Rubber Bat Balls
2½-inch diameter.
Price $0.08 each

Boys' Farm Wagon
18-by-36-inch wagon. Has a seat, handle, and pair of hardwood shafts for a goat. Handsomely ornamented.
Price: $5.00 each

Chess Game
Chess pieces in black and yellow.
Price: $0.50 each set

China Tea Set
15 pieces with handsome filigree design.
Price: $0.75 each set

Now, can you find six items that equal exactly $5.00?

Running for the Gold

Students will understand decimals on a concrete level by playing this simple game.

Directions

1. Duplicate the reproducible for each student.
2. Distribute the number cubes and reproducibles to the groups.
3. Ask group members to decide on the order of play.
4. Go over the rules of the game, as follows:
   a. A player rolls the number cubes. Example: 6, 2
   b. The player chooses the order of digits and writes the decimal in the Record Rolls column. Example: 0.62 is a better choice than 0.26.
   c. The player shades 62 boxes in MILE ONE to represent the decimal 0.62.

Taking It Further

This game can easily be converted to a decimal subtraction game. Students start with three shaded boxes and subtract with each roll. The student who "unshades" all the boxes wins.

Assessing Skills

What strategies do students use for adding decimals—mentally grouping ones and tens, mentally rounding and working backward, or calculating with paper and pencil?

LEARNING OBJECTIVE

Students add and subtract decimals.

GROUPING

Cooperative groups

MATERIALS

For each student:

- *Running for the Gold* reproducible (p. 116)

For each group:

- 2 number cubes labeled 1–6

Name ______________________ Date ____________

Running for the Gold

Roll the number cubes to make the greatest decimal you can. Record it in the table below, shade the boxes to represent the decimal, and you're off and running! The first player to mark off three miles is the winner.

RECORD ROLLS		
0.___ ___	0.___ ___	**Mile One**
0.___ ___	0.___ ___	
0.___ ___	0.___ ___	
0.___ ___	0.___ ___	
0.___ ___	0.___ ___	

RECORD ROLLS		
0.___ ___	0.___ ___	**Mile Two**
0.___ ___	0.___ ___	
0.___ ___	0.___ ___	
0.___ ___	0.___ ___	
0.___ ___	0.___ ___	

RECORD ROLLS		
0.___ ___	0.___ ___	**Mile Three**
0.___ ___	0.___ ___	
0.___ ___	0.___ ___	
0.___ ___	0.___ ___	
0.___ ___	0.___ ___	

Decimal Points Everywhere

This crossword puzzle points students to success with the multiplication and division of decimals.

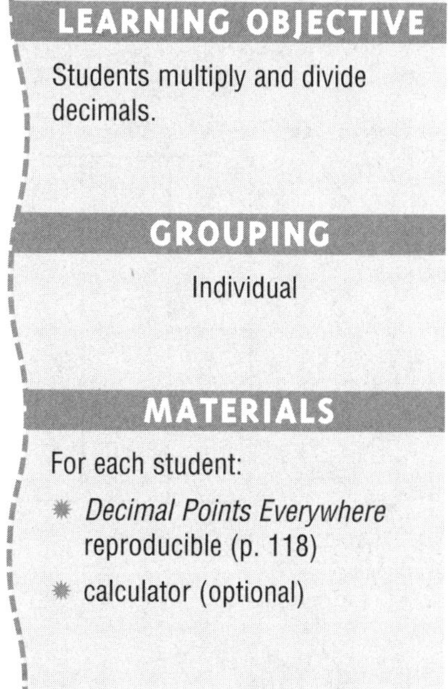

Directions

1. Duplicate the reproducible for each student.
2. Review the multiplication of decimals as follows.

   a. Multiply as you would with whole numbers.

   ```
      8.2
   x  1.3
      246
      82
     1066
   ```

   b. Put as many decimal places in the product as there are in the factors combined.

   ```
      8.2    ← 1 place
   x  1.3    ← 1 place
      246
      82
    10.66    ← 2 places
   ```

3. Review the division of decimals as follows.

   a. Place the decimal point in the quotient directly above decimal point in dividend.

   ```
        .
   7) 6.23
   ```

   b. Divide as you would with whole numbers.

   ```
      0.89
   7) 6.23
      5 6
        63
        63
   ```

4. Distribute the reproducible and allow students to complete it on their own. You may wish to let them use calculators.

Taking It Further

Encourage students to make their own decimal puzzles for classmates to solve. Use the crossword squares on the reproducible and have students write their own problems. Require them to make a key for checking.

Assessing Skills

- Are students counting decimal places from the left or the right?
- Encourage students to estimate to see that the answers are reasonable.

Name ______________________ Date ______________

Decimal Points Everywhere

Can you find the decimal point in each of these answers? This crossword puzzle is sure to sharpen your skills and point you toward success with multiplication and division of decimals.

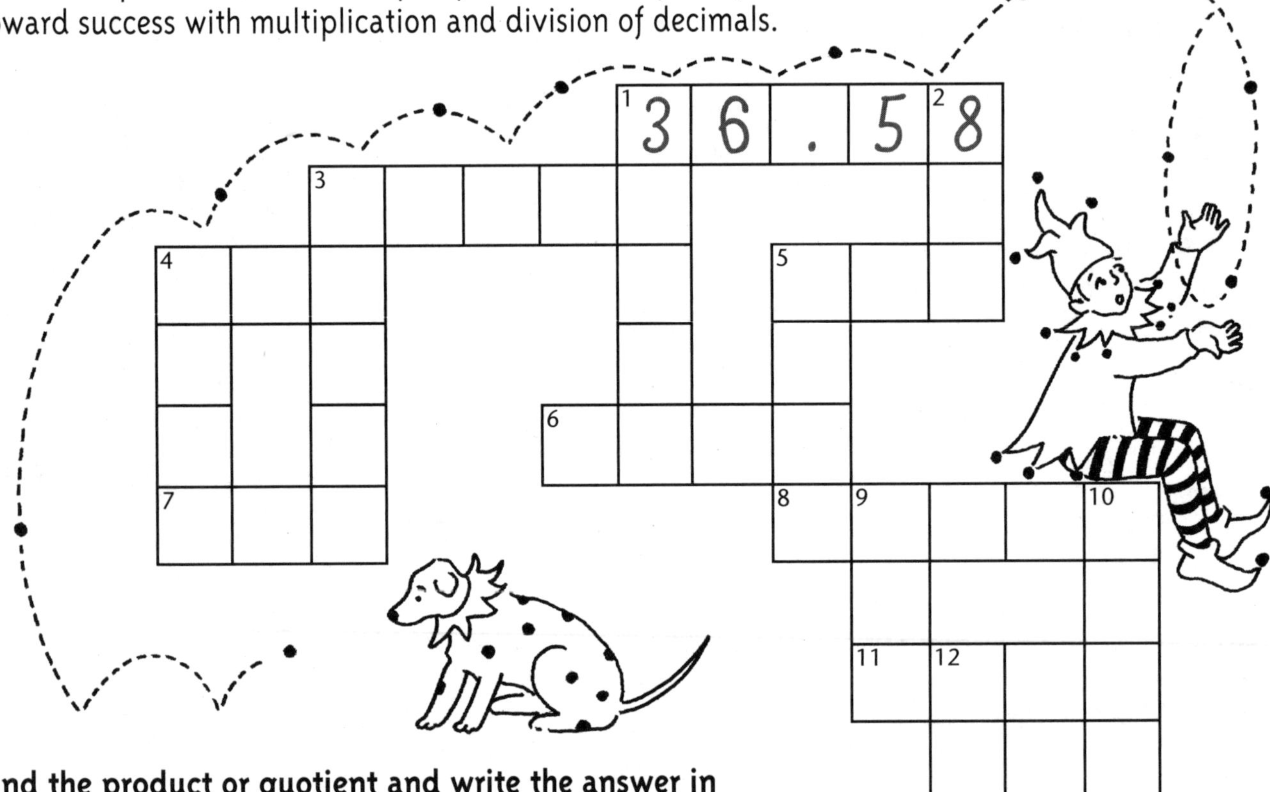

Find the product or quotient and write the answer in the crossword puzzle. The decimal point will occupy a square. The first one has been done for you.

ACROSS

1. 5.9 × 6.2 = 36.58
3. 3.3 × 3.8 = ________
4. 28.2 ÷ 6 = ________
5. 19.6 ÷ 2 = ________
6. 162.6 ÷ 6 = ________
7. 49.2 ÷ 6 = ________
8. 87.03 ÷ 3 = ________
11. 27.2 ÷ 2 = ________

DOWN

1. 6.7 × 5.1 = ________
2. 26.4 ÷ 3 = ________
3. 8.1 × 2.2 = ________
4. 2.14 × 2 = ________
5. 4.8 × 1.9 = ________
9. 36.4 ÷ 4 = ________
10. 1.4 × 1.2 = ________
12. 22.2 ÷ 6 = ________

Decimal Puzzlers

Students use their favorite pictures to make decimal puzzles for classmates to solve.

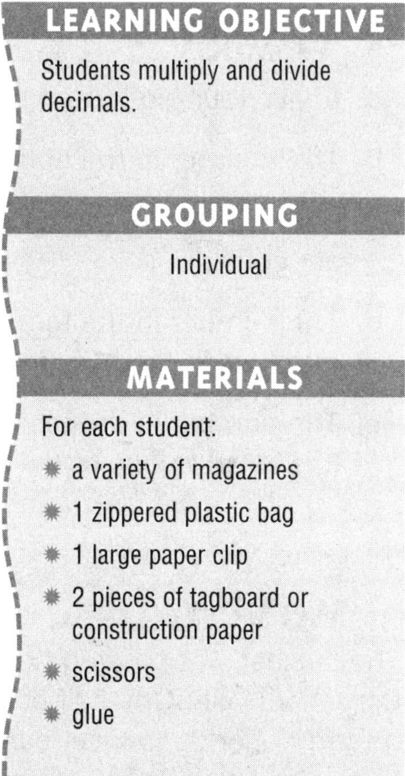

LEARNING OBJECTIVE

Students multiply and divide decimals.

GROUPING

Individual

MATERIALS

For each student:

- a variety of magazines
- 1 zippered plastic bag
- 1 large paper clip
- 2 pieces of tagboard or construction paper
- scissors
- glue

Directions

1. Distribute materials. Instruct students to cut out large color pictures from the magazines and glue them to the tagboard or paper.
2. When the glue has dried thoroughly, students trim the pictures into 6-inch by 8-inch rectangles. Then they cut the pictures into 2-inch by 2-inch puzzle squares. You may want to draw the puzzle diagram on the board for reference.
3. Tell students to write multiplication or division decimal problems on the back of each square. If possible, laminate the puzzle pieces so they will last longer.
4. To make the puzzle base, students draw 6-inch by 8-inch rectangles in the center of pieces of tagboard. Then they draw lines to divide the rectangles into 2-inch by 2-inch squares.
5. Tell students to assemble their puzzles on the base. Ask them to lift each piece and write the answer to the multiplication or division problem on the puzzle base below. When the puzzle is constructed, the pieces will be placed on the corresponding answers.
6. Have students place the puzzle pieces in zippered plastic bags and attach to the puzzle bases with large paper clips.
7. Encourage students to trade decimal puzzles and let the fun begin!

Taking It Further

Make a bulletin board entitled "Decimal Puzzlers." Display several puzzles that have been put together. Post several other puzzles for students to work on when they have available independent time.

Assessing Skills

- When multiplying decimals, do students count the decimal places in both factors before placing the decimal point in the product?
- When dividing decimals, do students place the decimal point in the quotient directly above the decimal point in the dividend?

$3\frac{1}{2} + 8\frac{1}{6} + \frac{1}{8} = ?$ ✱ $\frac{1}{2} = \frac{2}{4} = \frac{4}{8}$ ✱ $0.5 = 0.50 = 0.500$ ✱ $123.456789 + 9876.54321 = ?$

Fractions & Decimals Problem Bank

Use these quick skill-builders as self-starters, homework, or just for a fun break from the textbook.

1. WHO AM I?

a. I have four digits, and they are all odd.

b. The number in the hundredths place is 3.

c. The numbers in the hundredths place and ones place are equal.

d. The number in the tens place is the product of the numbers in the hundredths place and the ones place.

e. The number in the tenths place is greater than 4, and it is equal to one of the other digits.

2. MOVING DAY

The teacher was packing her books in boxes at the end of the school year. One-half of the books went in a large box on top of her desk. One-fourth of the books went into two small boxes in her cabinet. Twelve of the books were put into drawers, 15 of the books were given away to the students, and the other 3 were taken home for the summer. How many books did she have in all?

3. DART THROWER

A dart thrower made exactly $3\frac{1}{7}$ points after throwing five darts. Where did the darts land?

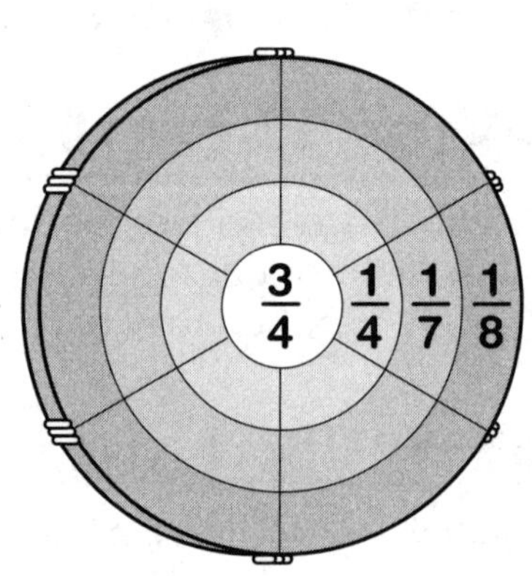

4. WHAT'S NEXT?

Complete the patterns.

$\frac{1}{2}$, 1, $1\frac{1}{2}$, 2, $2\frac{1}{2}$, _____, _____, _____, _____

$\frac{3}{4}$, $1\frac{1}{4}$, $1\frac{3}{4}$, $2\frac{1}{4}$, $2\frac{3}{4}$, _____, _____, _____, _____

12, $11\frac{1}{4}$, $10\frac{1}{2}$, $9\frac{3}{4}$, 9, _____, _____, _____, _____

$\frac{1}{2}$, $1\frac{3}{4}$, 3, $4\frac{1}{4}$, $5\frac{1}{2}$, _____, _____, _____, _____

5. MAGIC SQUARE

Combine the fractions in the adjacent cells to equal 1. Use each cell only once.

$\frac{2}{3}$	$\frac{1}{6}$	$\frac{7}{10}$
$\frac{1}{6}$	$\frac{1}{5}$	$\frac{1}{10}$
$\frac{1}{7}$	$\frac{3}{7}$	$\frac{3}{7}$

You may not connect cells like this:

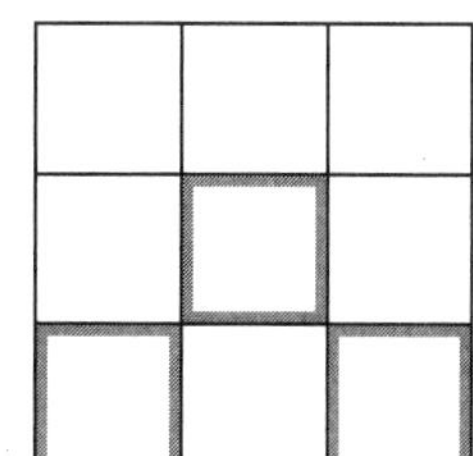

You may connect cells like this:

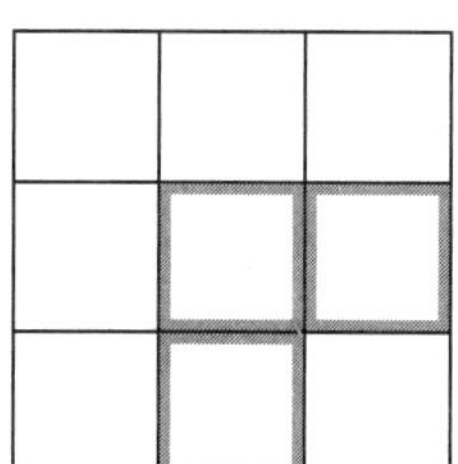

6. PIGGY BANK TROUBLES

Steven wanted $0.25 to put into a gum ball machine. He emptied coins from his piggy bank on the bed and discovered that he didn't have any quarters. If he added his eight coins together, he had enough change to make exactly $0.25. How many pennies, nickels, and dimes did he have?

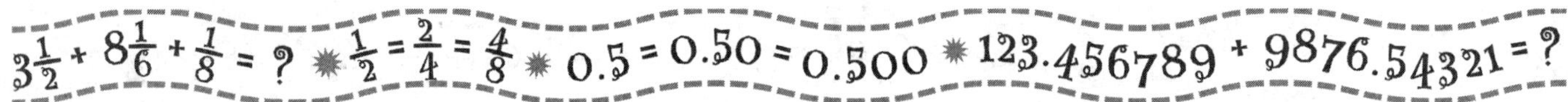

7. GARDENING FUN

Cecil, Patrick, and Amos were planting a garden at school and wanted to share expenses. Cecil spent $13.00 on fertilizers and soil mix, and Patrick spent $15.00 on plants and seeds. Amos bought a shovel for $11.00. Who paid exactly one-third the total amount? Who paid less than one-third and by how much? Who paid more than one-third and by how much?

8. MYSTERY NUMBERS

Shade the numbers described in the questions below.

21	15	100	9	16	30	8

How many thirds are in 3?

How many thirds are in 5?

How many thirds are in 7?

How many fourths are in 2?

How many fourths are in 4?

How many fifths are in 6?

What mystery number remains? ____

9. LETTER ADDITION

Each letter stands for a number from 0 to 9, but no two letters have the same number. Find the number expressed by each letter. (Hint: X = 2, R = 7, and P = 9)

```
    P T.M X K
+   O L.T X Z
-------------
  M R O.V V Z
```

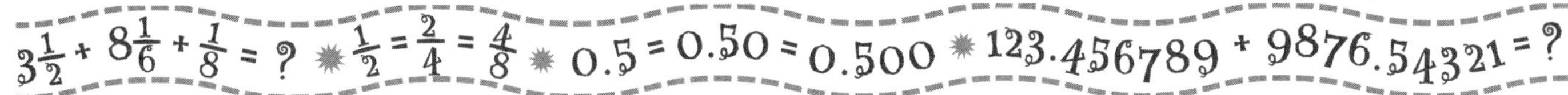

10. CIRCLE MATH

Where some circles overlap, there is a number. This number is the sum of the value of the two circles. Each circle has one of these fraction values: $\frac{5}{4}$, $\frac{1}{4}$, $\frac{1}{2}$, $\frac{1}{8}$, $\frac{3}{4}$, and $\frac{1}{16}$. No two circles have the same number. Can you find the fraction value for each circle?

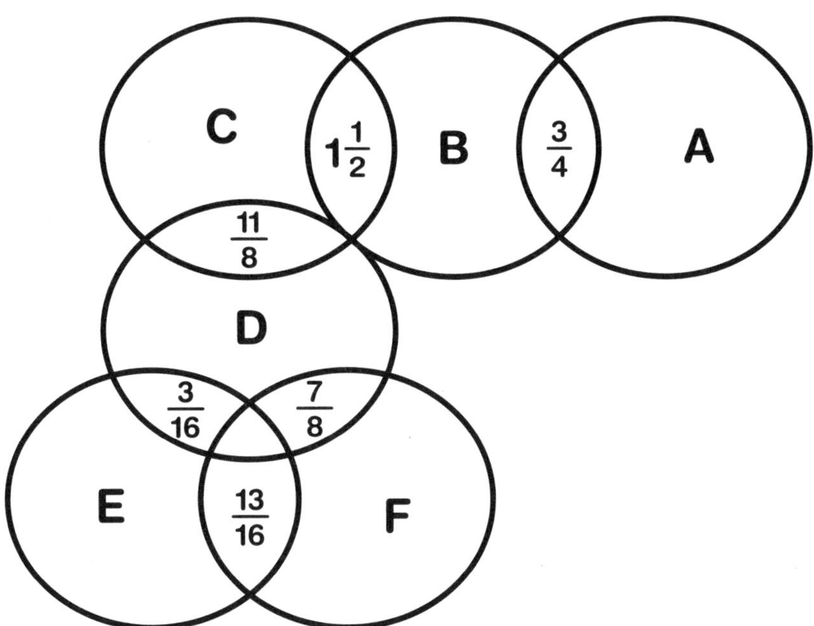

11. WHO AM I?

a. I have 4 digits.

b. The numbers in the tenths and hundredths places are the same.

c. The numbers in the ones place and tens place are the same.

d. The number in the tenths place when added to 4 and subtracted from 10 is 0.

e. The number in the ones place is 4.

Inside Out

It's easy to tell whether your canary is outside or inside its cage. It's not always so easy to tell whether a point is outside or inside a geometric figure.

Directions

1. Duplicate and distribute the reproducible.
2. Review with students what a simple closed figure is. Draw examples like the ones below to display. Ask volunteers to describe what they see.

Simple Open Figures	Simple Closed Figures

3. Present this plan to help students determine whether a point is outside or inside the figure. Invite discussion and clarification of the steps as necessary.
   a. Plot a new point well outside the figure.
   b. Using a straightedge, connect the outside point with the point in question.
   c. Count all intersections of the line segment and the figure. Repeat with other points and other figures. Ask: *What conclusions can you draw?* [An odd number of intersections means a point is inside the figure; an even number of intersections means it's outside.]
4. Have students complete the reproducible and verbalize their discoveries.

LEARNING OBJECTIVE

Students determine whether a point lies outside or inside a simple closed figure.

GROUPING

Individual or pairs

MATERIALS

For each student or pair:

- *Inside Out* reproducible (p. 125)
- straightedge

Taking It Farther

Let students create new Inside Out figures for classmates to analyze. Some students might explore whether the Inside Out rule applies to complex figures.

Assessing Skills

- Do students adequately test initial conclusions to see that they always work?
- What generalizations do students make?
- Can they apply their generalizations to new figures?

Name ______________________ Date ____________

Inside Out

Where is the point in each figure—inside or outside? Use the intersection method. Record your findings in the table.

A

B

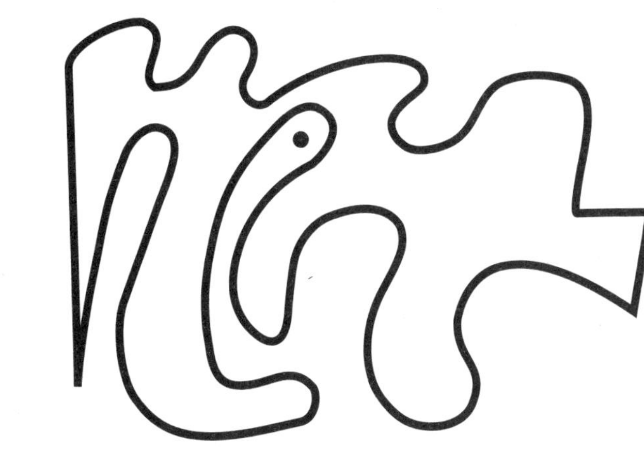

C

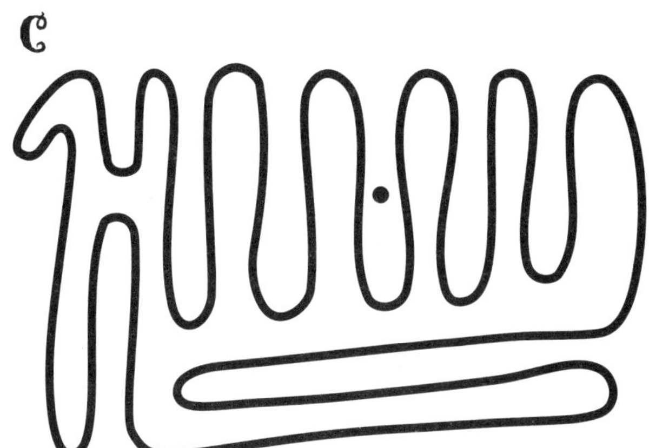

D

FIGURE	INTERSECTIONS	INSIDE?	OUTSIDE?
A			
B			
C			
D			

What's the Angle?

Just about everybody likes a good puzzle. To solve the one in this activity, students use what they know about angle measures.

Directions

1. Duplicate the reproducible for each student and distribute.
2. Review the concept of angle measurement and the use of a protractor. If necessary, review the meaning of *ray, endpoint, vertex,* and *angle.*
3. Draw a horizontal ray to display. Label its endpoint *V*. Ask a volunteer to turn the ray into angle *V*, which measures 90°.
4. Have students complete the reproducible on their own. If necessary, demonstrate how to crack the code by doing one example with the class.
5. After students complete the page, you may wish to tell them that Jorge Ojeda-Guzman's tightrope was 36 feet long. He positioned it 35 feet above the ground. As curious spectators gathered, he would walk, dance, or balance himself on a chair.

V

Taking It Further

Challenge students to create angle riddles for classmates to solve. Or have them use protractors to measure the angles formed by classroom objects, such as a stapler, open book, closet door, and so on.

Assessing Skills

- Do students complete each angle from the endpoint of the given ray?
- Do they use protractors correctly to draw the specified angles?
- Can students use visual estimation to predict which letter each new ray will (or will not) pass through?

LEARNING OBJECTIVE

Students use protractors and straightedge to complete angles of certain measure to decode an answer.

GROUPING

Individual

MATERIALS

For each student:

- *What's the Angle?* reproducible (p. 127)
- protractor
- straightedge

Name ____________________ Date ____________

What's the Angle?

Jorge Ojeda-Guzman of Orlando, Florida, set a world record. He spent 205 straight days—from January 1 to July 25, 1993—on a piece of equipment. On what did he set his unusual endurance record?

The answer is in code at the bottom on the page. To crack it, follow these steps:

1. From the endpoint of each given ray, draw an angle to the specified measure. Use a protractor for accuracy.
2. The angle will intersect a number. Find this number in the code. Write the vertex letter above it.
3. Draw all the angles to find the answer.

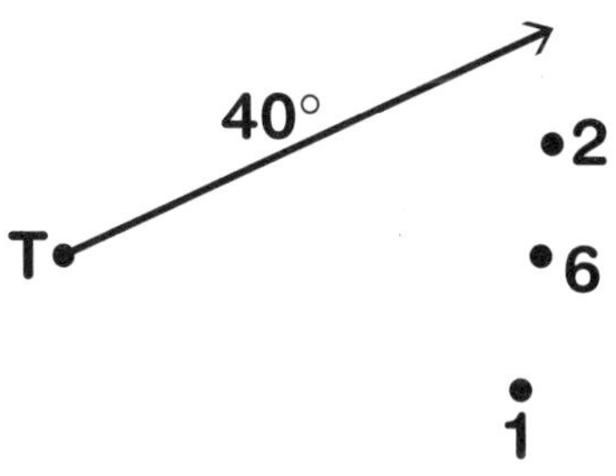

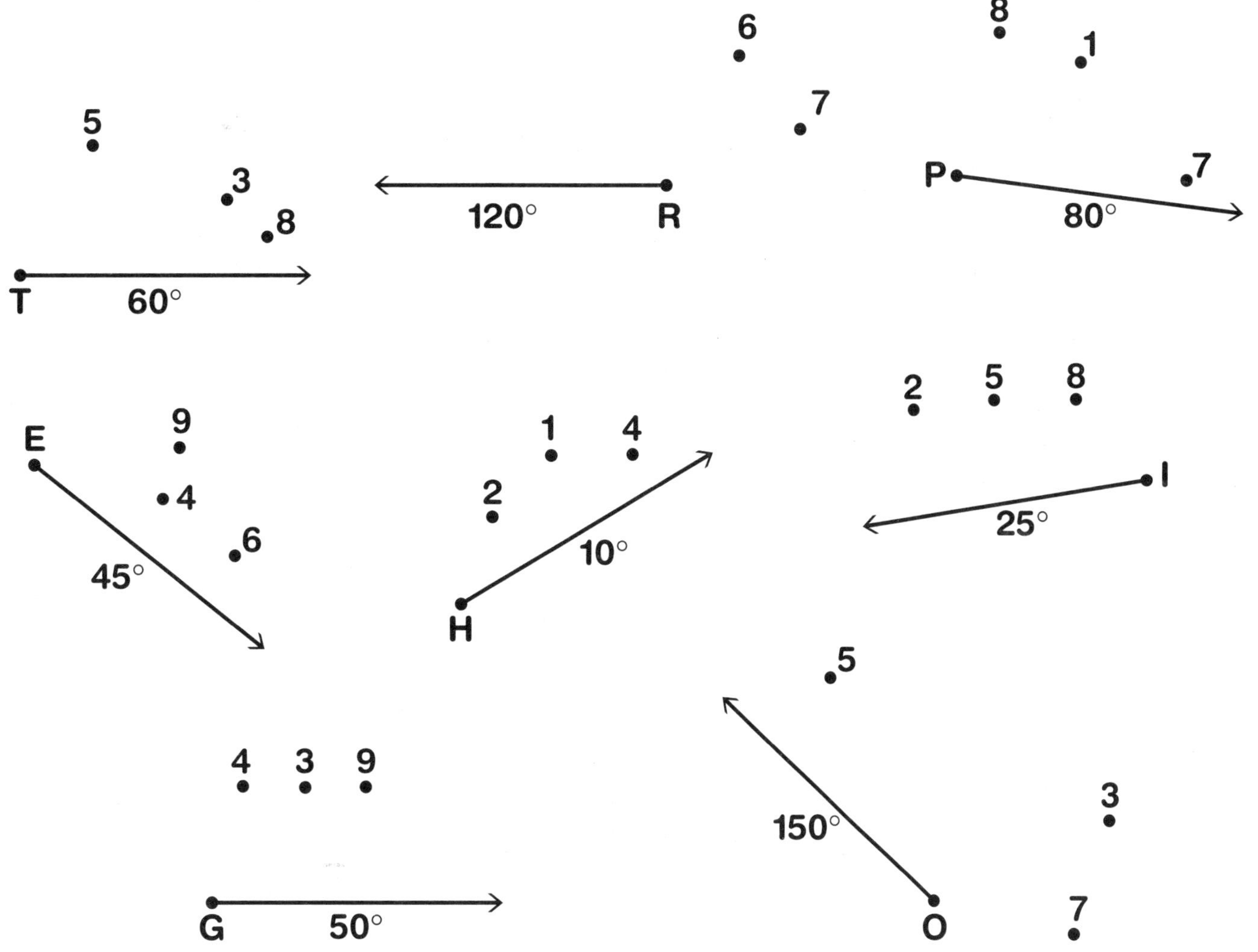

6 8 1 7

5 3 8 120° R P 7 80°

2 5 8

E 9 4 6 45° 1 4 2 10° H I 25°

5

4 3 9 150° 3

G 50° O 7

___ ___ ___ ___ ___ ___ ___ ___ ___
1 2 3 4 5 6 7 8 9

Musical Math

Musicians and monotones alike can practice mathematical communication by investigating the properties of instruments.

Directions

1. Obtain one or more triangles (the percussion instrument) from your school's music department or from a set of basic rhythm instruments. Show the triangle to students. You might have a volunteer play it for the class.
2. Challenge students to describe the triangle using as many mathematical terms as they can. For instance, they can give its geometric name, find the measures of its angles, the lengths of its sides, its perimeter, the area it encloses, its weight, the diameter of the tubing used to form it, the length of the striker, and so on.
3. Have students work in pairs or cooperative groups to describe, measure, analyze, sketch, and label drawings of the triangle or other musical instruments. Encourage them to discover as many mathematical ways to describe the instruments as they can. Make a variety of measuring tools available, such as tape measures, scales, calipers, stopwatches, and so on.
4. Students may present their analyses in any way they wish. Their presentations should be concise, precise, and easy for someone else to follow.

LEARNING OBJECTIVE

Students use mathematical terms to describe, analyze, quantify, and evaluate various musical instruments.

GROUPING

Pairs or cooperative groups

MATERIALS

- various musical instruments
- assorted measuring tools (tape measures, scales, calipers, stopwatches)
- drawing paper
- markers

Taking It Farther

Help students explore the physics of music by analyzing an instrument in terms of its fundamental frequencies and overtones, pitch range, range of volume, average length of the decay of a tone, and so on. Guide them in describing, measuring, and presenting this information to add to their analyses.

Assessing Skills

- Do students find a wide variety of ways to describe their instruments?
- How accurately and clearly do they present their findings?

Eye Spy

Visual/spatial problem solving is a key part of mathematical thinking. What strategies do students apply to solve "shapes-in-a-shape" puzzles?

Directions

1. Draw a 3 × 3 grid to display. Discuss with the class how to identify all the squares in the figure. [14] Some students will say that they see nine squares, which is only the number of its 1 × 1 squares. Guide them to see that the figure also contains 2 × 2 and 3 × 3 squares.

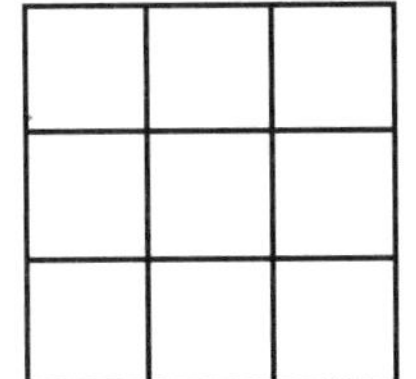

2. Model how to make an organized list to count all sizes of squares. You can use colored markers to trace or shade different size squares to help students better visualize them.
3. Draw 4 × 4 and 5 × 5 squares. Have students find the number of squares in each. [30; 55] Then guide them in identifying a pattern to find the total number of squares in any size square grid.
   [**Pattern:**
   3 × 3 square—number of 1 × 1 squares, 9; number of 2 × 2 squares, 4; number of 3 × 3 squares, 1; 9 + 4 + 1 = 14
   4 × 4 square—number of 1 × 1 squares, 16; number of 2 × 2 squares, 9; number of 3 × 3 squares, 4; number of 4 × 4 squares, 1; 16 + 9 + 4 + 1 = 30
   5 × 5 square—number of 1 × 1 squares, 25; number of 2 × 2 squares, 16; number of 3 × 3 squares, 9; number of 4 × 4 squares, 4; number of 5 × 5 squares, 1; 25 + 16 + 9 + 4 + 1 = 55]

Taking It Farther

Present similar problems using triangles-within-triangles.

Assessing Skills

- Can students visualize squares of different sizes in a figure?
- What techniques do students use to identify and count the squares?
- Do they record their information in an organized way?

LEARNING OBJECTIVE

Students develop and apply strategies to identify and count all the squares in a figure.

GROUPING

Individuals or pairs

MATERIALS

- colored markers or pencils

Tangram Investigations

Tangrams, the Chinese puzzles, are centuries old. Students examine the geometric relationships among the seven pieces as they create their own sets.

Directions

1. Duplicate the reproducible for each student and distribute.
2. As needed, help students work through the steps for making the pieces of the set. Guide them in looking at the diagrams carefully.
3. Encourage students to experiment with their tangram pieces to form various figures. Challenge them to form letters of the alphabet, numerals, animals, people, tools, vehicles, and so on.

4. Display students' creations. Or have them trace around the outside of each completed figure to form a template other students can fill in.

Taking It Further

Ask students to fill in some of the tangram templates classmates have made. You can also let students combine sets of tangrams to make larger figures.

Assessing Skills

- Do students follow the directions to create the seven tangram pieces?
- Are students' creations clear representations?
- Are students able to complete their classmates' puzzles?

LEARNING OBJECTIVE

Students make a set of tangrams and form several shapes and representations of different objects.

GROUPING

Individuals, pairs, or whole class

MATERIALS

Fore each student:

- *Tangram Investigations* reproducible (p. 131)
- square sheet of paper (6 to 8 inches on a side)
- scissors
- markers

Date

Tangram Investigations

You've seen a tangram—the seven-piece geometric puzzle. Here, you'll create a set of tangram pieces and then use them to form shapes and figures.

Start with a square sheet of paper. Follow the steps below and the diagrams to create your set of tangram pieces.

1. Fold your paper in half along the diagonal.
   Cut along the fold.
   Fold each triangle in half.
   Then cut along the fold of one of these triangles.
   Label the two small triangles.
   These are your first two tangram pieces.

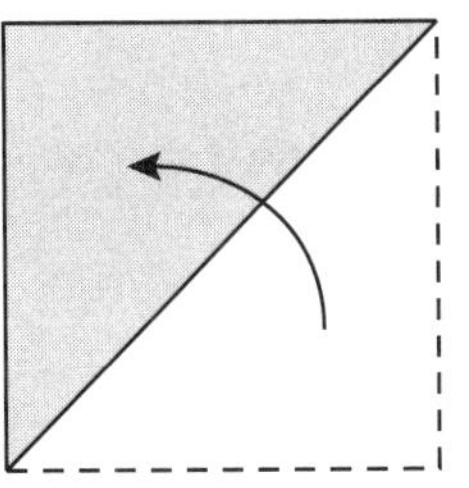

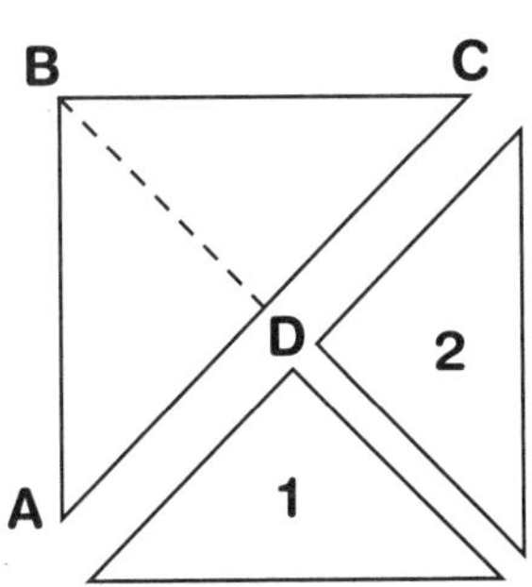

2. Fold the large triangle so that B meets D.
   Cut along fold EF.
   Label this triangle.
   It's your third tangram piece.

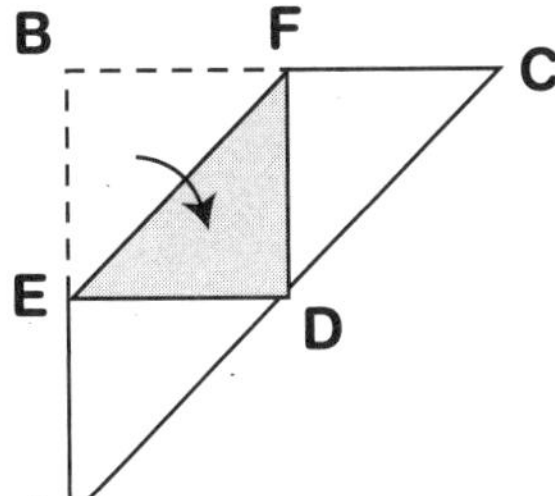

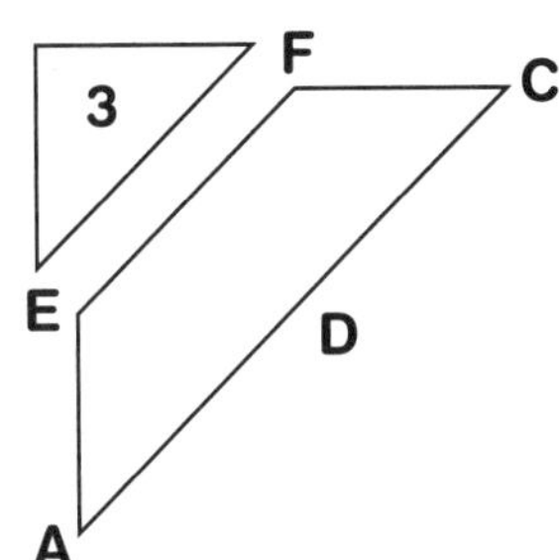

3. Fold C so that it meets D.
   Draw line GD parallel to FH.
   Cut along GD and FH.
   Label the triangle and the square.
   They're the fourth and fifth pieces.

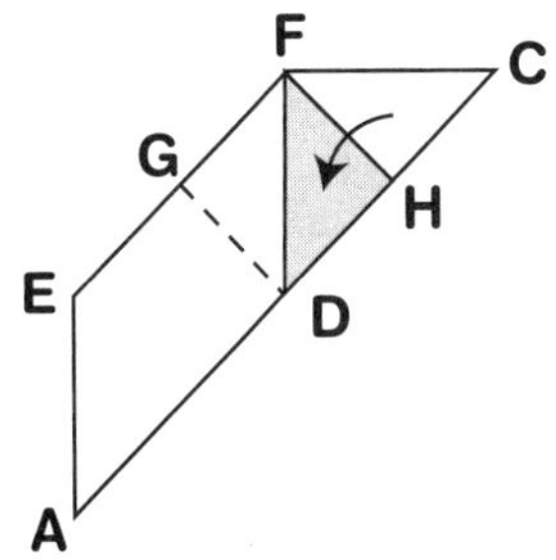

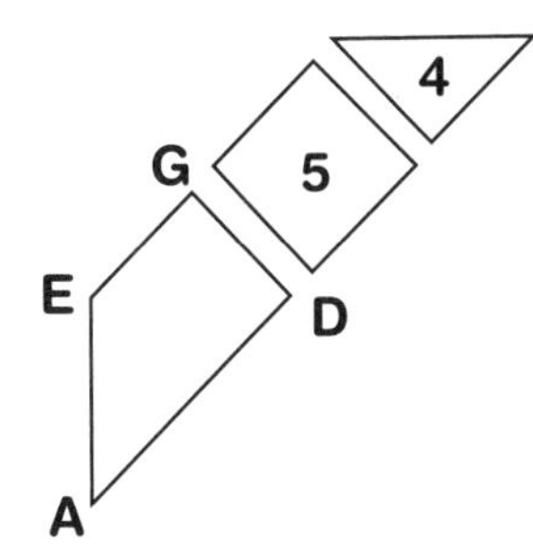

4. Fold D to meet E.
   Cut along the fold.
   Label the triangle and the parallelogram—your last two tangram pieces.

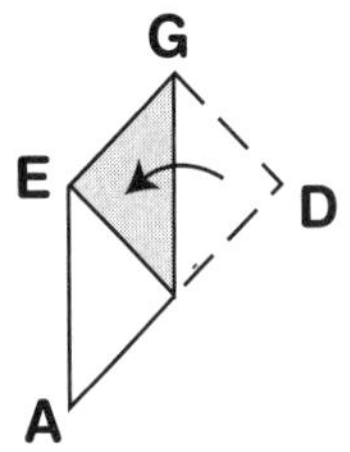

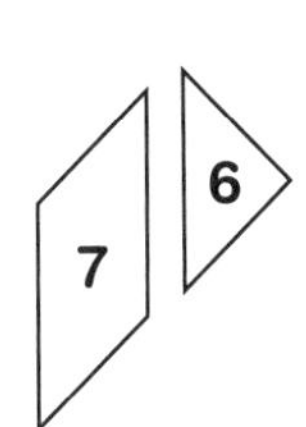

5. Now make a square with your seven tangram pieces.

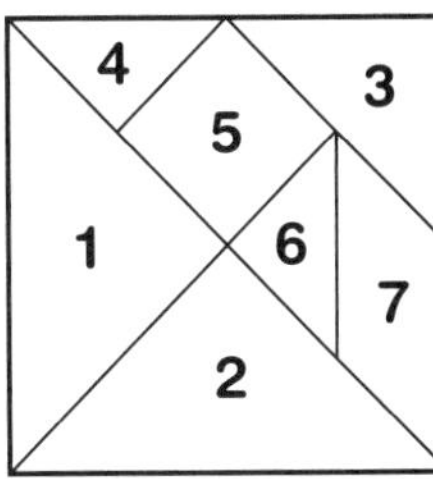

Bulletin Board Logic

Want to stimulate students' creativity, humor, and inductive reasoning skills? Then set up this interactive bulletin board.

Directions

1. Set aside bulletin board space for this activity. Give it a title, such as "What's My Rule?" or "Property Room."
2. Display a set of figures that go together because they share geometric attributes. Also give some counterexamples to help students isolate the common attribute(s) in the first set. Give each set a silly name, for example:

These are blorguls.	These are not blorguls.

3. Help students identify the attributes blorguls share. Discuss why the figures in the second group are not blorguls. [Blorguls are closed figures with a curve and a right angle.]
4. Each day, post a new set of examples, counterexamples, and "unknowns," all on index cards or self-stick notes. Invite students to discover the rule and then sort the "unknowns" into the correct sets. You might provide a blank space in which students write the rule in their own words.
5. Encourage students to add other examples to the display. Have them tell how they form generalizations and apply their reasoning to test unknowns.

LEARNING OBJECTIVE

Students use logical reasoning to make generalizations about geometric properties and apply their generalizations to new situations.

GROUPING

Whole class

MATERIALS

* index cards or self-stick notes

Taking It Farther

Provide examples only, without counterexamples. Ask students to draw other figures that fit the rule. Or have students create their own examples and counterexamples for classmates to analyze.

Assessing Skills

* How do students form their generalizations?
* Do their original examples always observe the rule?

Models in Space

Students handle solid figures to sharpen their ability to visualize geometry in three dimensions.

Directions

1. Display assorted materials. Students pick the materials they want to use to construct space figures. Or present different materials on different occasions to provide a variety of construction experiences.
2. Have individual students or pairs make six different space figures. For example, they can tightly roll and tape sheets of newspaper into long tubes, which they can cut to desired lengths and tape together at the ends to form cubes, pyramids, or prisms. They can also make these figures with straws and clay or toothpicks and marshmallows. They can use construction paper or oak tag to form cylinders or cones.

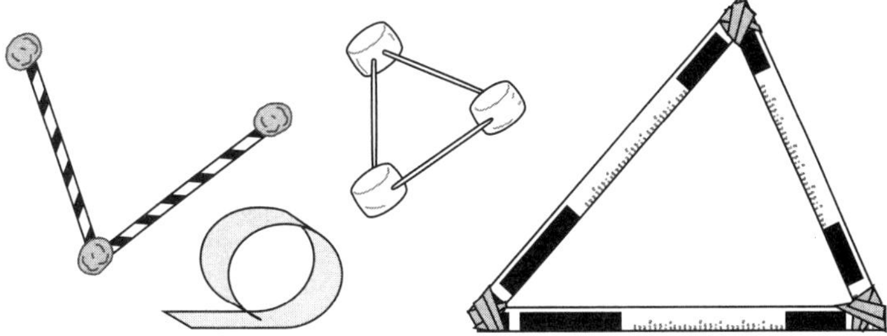

3. Allow time for students to display their models and refer to them to answer questions such as: *How many faces in a pyramid? How many vertices in a hexagonal prism? How many edges in a cone?* Students can make tables to list the number of faces, edges, and vertices for each type of figure. Ask them to describe similarities and differences among the solid shapes.

Taking It Further

Let students experiment with their space figures to determine which is the strongest, the weakest, or the most versatile as a building module.

Assessing Skills

- How many different space figures do students make?
- What generalizations can they make about space figures?

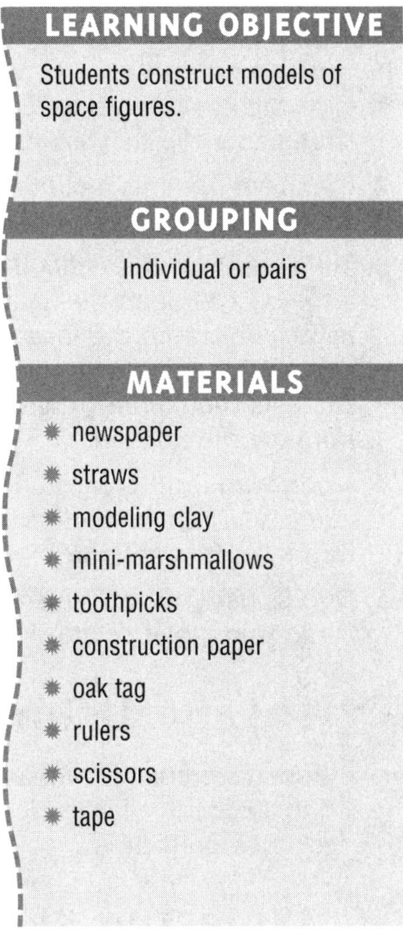

LEARNING OBJECTIVE

Students construct models of space figures.

GROUPING

Individual or pairs

MATERIALS

- newspaper
- straws
- modeling clay
- mini-marshmallows
- toothpicks
- construction paper
- oak tag
- rulers
- scissors
- tape

Any Way You Slice It

When you slice an apple pie, you know what you expect to see. But when you slice a clay figure, it's not always so clear what you'll find inside.

Directions

1. Give each pair or group some modeling clay and a plastic knife or large paper clip they can unbend and use as a cutting wire.
2. First have students mold the clay into solid figures—cones, cubes, spheres, cylinders, prisms, and pyramids.
3. Then ask them to predict the shapes of faces that would be exposed if they cut through the figures at various angles. Tell them first to name and sketch the shape of each face they visualize. Then they should slice the clay to verify their predictions. After each cut, students should draw the actual shape of the exposed face if it differs from their prediction.
4. Along with instructing students to make different cuts in the same figure, you can have them make cuts in the same orientation through different figures.
5. Discuss patterns that emerge. Encourage students to present their findings in tables or drawings.

LEARNING OBJECTIVE

Students explore the shapes of faces that have been cut into solid figures.

GROUPING

Pairs or cooperative groups

MATERIALS

- modeling clay
- plastic knives or large paper clips
- drawing paper
- pencils

Taking It Farther

Have students predict how many different polygonal faces they can form by slicing a cube in all possible ways. They can make a cube and slice it to check their predictions.

Assessing Skills

- Observe students as they form the solid figures. Check that the figures embody the required properties.
- How well do students visualize the shapes of faces before they cut? Does their ability to predict the shapes improve as they work?

Mapping Up

Anyone can build a tower of blocks, but it takes practice in spatial and visual reasoning to create a map that matches the structure.

Directions

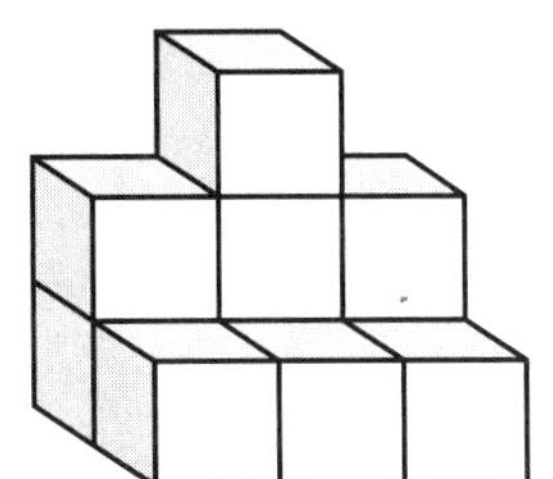

2	3	2
1	1	1

1. Build or draw the 10-cube structure (at right) to display.
2. Then draw the accompanying map.
3. Guide students to see that the map and the cube structure contain the same information. Have them verbalize the relationship between the structure and its map. [Each square on the map tells how many cubes rise above it.] You may want to point out that a map like this is called a base drawing.
4. To provide practice at this, have pairs of students use cubes to make some simple towers and then make a map to go with each one.
5. Duplicate the reproducible for each pair and distribute. Also give each pair several sheets of grid paper and drawing paper.

Taking It Further

Invite students to work with partners. One creates an elaborate cube skyscraper that contains several wings and towers of different heights. The other makes a map that matches the structure. Students can exchange roles.

Assessing Skills

- Do students see the relationship between each structure and its map?
- Can students make a cube structure given its map?
- Can they make a map given a picture or model of a structure?

LEARNING OBJECTIVE

Students explore the relationship between a 3-dimensional structure and a 2-dimensional map of it.

GROUPING

Pairs

MATERIALS

- *Mapping Up* reproducible (p. 136)
- centimeter cubes or snap cubes
- grid paper
- drawing paper
- markers

Name ______________________ Date ____________

Mapping Up

Build a cube structure for each map shown.

1.

2	2	2	2
3	4	4	3
2	2	2	2

2.

2	3	4		
3	4	5		
	5	6	5	
		4	3	2
			2	1

3.

7	4	4	3		4	4	4	
4	6	4	3		5	5		
3	6		3	4	5		4	
3					4			3

Draw a map for each cube structure shown.

4.

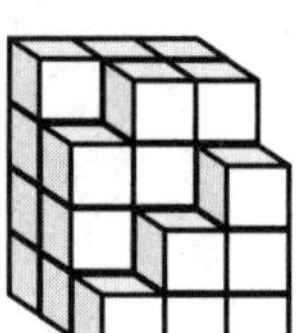

5.

Are You Sure?

Do your students complain that you ask them to do the impossible? Well, with this activity, they may be right!

Directions

1. Set aside bulletin board space for this activity. Give it a title, such as "Is This Possible?" or "Are You Sure?"
2. Display descriptions of geometric figures with specific attributes, such as a scalene right triangle or a regular pentagon. Include some descriptions of figures that are impossible to draw, such as an equilateral right triangle or a quadrilateral with three right angles.
3. Invite students to draw an example of each figure on an index card or self-stick note, which they post beneath each description. Accept as many different examples of each figure as students can draw. As an alternative to using index cards or self-stick notes, students can draw right on a large sheet of chart paper or butcher paper that has the descriptions written on it.
4. If students think a particular figure is impossible, they can write this on a card with an illustration or explanation of why they think so.
5. Every day or so, post new descriptions. Resolve conflicts among drawings. Take time to discuss with students why they cannot draw the impossible examples.

Taking It Further

On one side of a bulletin board, post descriptions of geometric figures. On the other side, post, in scrambled order, examples of these figures cut from magazines, catalogs, or newspapers. Challenge students to match each description with its example.

Assessing Skills

- How do students determine whether it is possible for them to draw a figure?
- Are students able to explain why a figure is impossible to draw?

LEARNING OBJECTIVE

Students use an interactive bulletin board to explore geometric possibilities by trying to draw figures with certain characteristics.

GROUPING

Whole class

MATERIALS

- index cards or self-stick notes
- thumbtacks
- chart paper or butcher paper (optional)

Icosa-Questions

An *icosahedron* is a solid figure with 20 faces. Get students to do some solid problem solving by playing this variation of Twenty Questions.

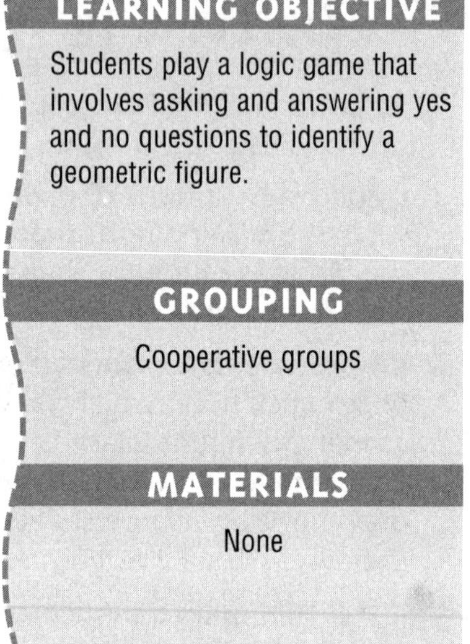

LEARNING OBJECTIVE

Students play a logic game that involves asking and answering yes and no questions to identify a geometric figure.

GROUPING

Cooperative groups

MATERIALS

None

Directions

1. Review the game Twenty Questions: Someone is "It." "It" picks an unknown object without telling the group what it is. To identify the object, players take turns asking questions that can be answered only by yes or no. Players may have up to 20 guesses to figure out the answer.
2. Play Icosa-Questions the same way. The player who is "It" picks a plane or solid geometric figure as the unknown object. Suppose "It" picks an isosceles right triangle. Here's how the questioning might begin:

   Question 1: Is it a space figure? [no]
   Question 2: Is it a polygon? [yes]
   Question 3: Does it have more than four sides? [no]
   Question 4: Does it have four sides? [no]

   By this point, most players will know that the figure is a kind of triangle.
3. Play a demonstration game with the class. Model how to formulate useful questions. Help students interpret answers by asking, "What do you now know for sure?" "What figure can you eliminate now?" or "What would you like to know?"
4. Form cooperative groups. Each group needs someone to be "It" and someone to keep track of the number of questions asked. Everyone else guesses.
5. Remind groups to listen carefully to each other's questions and answers so they can accumulate enough information to identify the geometric object in 20 guesses or fewer. Students should trade tasks in subsequent rounds.

Taking It Farther

Broaden Icosa-Questions to include geometric concepts, such as *parallel, area, perimeter, volume,* and so on. Encourage students to ask an early question to learn whether the unknown object is a figure or a concept.

Assessing Skills

- How well do players formulate their questions?
- Does "It" answer accurately and objectively?
- How do groups collaborate to identify the unknown object?

Figure With Figures

Students use mental math as they play a game about geometric properties.

Directions

1. In a brainstorming session with the class, list geometric properties students can count. For instance:
   - number of faces a rectangular pyramid has (or hexagonal prism, triangular pyramid, cube, and so on)
   - number of angles an octagon contains (or hexagon, decagon, and so on)
   - number of vertices a cube has (or triangular prism, pentagonal pyramid, and so on)
   - number of diagonals a hexagon has (or octagon, heptagon, and so on)
   - number of edges a cylinder has (or cone, cube, and so on)
2. Divide the class into pairs or groups. Have each pair or group prepare a set of 20 to 25 cards, each of which gives one property, such as the number of faces a cube has, from the class list. Pairs or groups should prepare an answer key on a separate sheet of paper to refer to as they play.
3. One student shuffles the cards. In turn, each player draws a card and determines the number of the property described. That number becomes the player's score. If the player gives an incorrect answer, he or she earns no points that round. The first player to accumulate 25 or more points wins. Pairs may take turns keeping score, and groups may designate a scorekeeper.

LEARNING OBJECTIVE

Students determine the number of faces, edges, and vertices for geometric figures.

GROUPING

Pairs or cooperative groups

MATERIALS

- 20–25 index cards per group or pair
- markers
- paper

Taking It Further

Vary the game by including statements with larger numbers, such as the number of degrees in a right angle, the sum of the interior angles of a triangle, and so on. Change the target score to reflect the new data.

Assessing Skills

- How do students verify whether an answer is right or wrong?
- Which properties are most challenging for students to figure out?

Geometry Jumble

Students can apply their critical-thinking and problem-solving skills to solve a puzzle that combines geometric terms with spelling.

Directions

1. Duplicate the reproducible for each student or pair and distribute.
2. Tell students to unscramble each word, the letters of which they write in the given spaces. When the puzzle is completed, the highlighted letters in each word will spell the answer to the question.
3. You may want to provide a word list students can consult as they work. The words, in alphabetical order, are *angle, cone, perpendicular, point, prism, pyramid, ray, segment, sphere, vertex,* and *volume.*
4. When students finish the puzzle, you may tell them that the original castle at Gomdan, Yemen, had 20 stories and was built sometime prior to A.D. 100. Allow time for students to find Yemen on a world map or globe.

Taking It Further

Invite students to make up their own Geometry Jumble puzzles for classmates to solve. They can hide a fun fact in the words. Or highlighted letters can, when they are unscrambled, reveal a bonus geometry word.

Assessing Skills

- Do students know what each geometry term means? If not, what do they do to find out the meaning?
- How do students use the word list, if it is available to them?

LEARNING OBJECTIVE

Students unscramble geometry terms to solve a riddle.

GROUPING

Individual or pairs

MATERIALS

- *Geometry Jumble* reproducible (p. 141)
- world map or globe
- word list (optional)

Name ______________________ Date ______________

Geometry Jumble

Where is the world's oldest castle found?

To find out, unscramble each geometry word. Write the correctly spelled word in the spaces provided—one letter per space. When you finish, read the highlighted letters from top to bottom for the location.

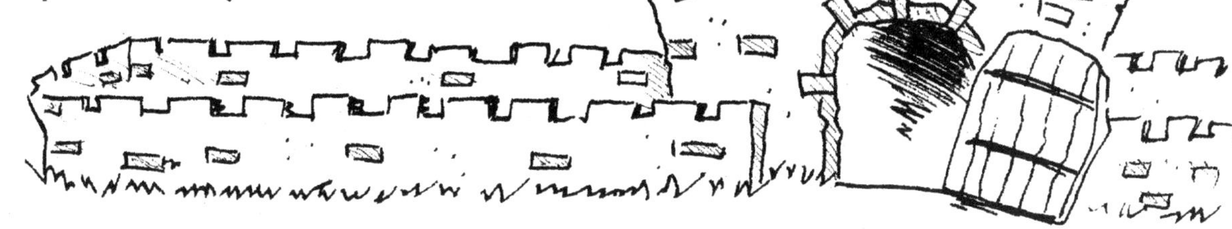

1. NESTMEG ___ ___ [ ] ___ ___ ___ ___
2. NECO ___ [ ] ___ ___
3. ELMOVU ___ ___ ___ ___ [ ] ___
4. CRINAPPLERUDE ___ ___ ___ ___ ___ ___ [ ] ___ ___ ___ ___ ___ ___
5. AYR ___ [ ] ___
6. GLEAN ___ [ ] ___ ___ ___
7. YAMDRIP ___ [ ] ___ ___ ___ ___ ___
8. PESHER ___ ___ ___ [ ] ___ ___
9. MIRPS ___ ___ ___ ___ [ ]
10. REXVET ___ ___ ___ ___ [ ] ___
11. PINTO ___ ___ ___ [ ] ___

Right Angle Tic-Tac-Toe

The plotting will surely thicken as students play this graphing game.

LEARNING OBJECTIVE

Students use visual/spatial reasoning and coordinate geometry to play a game in which they try to plot five adjacent points that form a right angle.

GROUPING

Cooperative groups or pairs

MATERIALS

- centimeter grid paper
- markers

Directions

1. Have students make a first-quadrant coordinate grid whose axes number from 0 to 10. You may also prepare the grids in advance.
2. Tell students that the object of the game is for a team to plot five adjacent Xs or Os to form a right angle, for example, (2,2), (3,2), (4,2), (4,1), and (4,0).
3. To play, divide the class into groups or pairs. Then divide each group or pair into two teams—Team X and Team O. Team X names the coordinates of a point they want to plot and then plots it. Then Team O names and plots its desired point. Play continues in turn this way.
4. Each team judges the accuracy of the other team's plotting. If a team names a point already taken, or a point off the graph, the turn is lost.
5. Encourage teams to play defensively as well as offensively.
6. The first team to plot five adjacent Xs or Os that form a right angle wins the game.

Taking It Further

Play using other quadrants of the coordinate grid. Or change the rules so that teams form a seven-point right angle, a square, or another shape they agree on.

Assessing Skills

- Do students correctly name and plot points on the coordinate grid?
- What strategies do teams use to win or to defend?

Finger Twister

Students who are "all thumbs" needn't worry. This game's for the other four fingers!

Directions

1. Ask students who know the party game Twister to describe it. Review the rules if needed. This game is like Twister, but the mat is a coordinate grid.
2. Divide the class into groups of 4. Each group needs three things—a coordinate grid labeled from 0 to 5 on each axis, a cardboard spinner in fourths labeled to indicate fingers: I (index), M (middle), R (ring), and P (pinkie), and a number cube or number cards labeled 0 to 5. Help students as needed to make the spinners and coordinate grids. If number cubes are used, instruct students to cover the 6 on the cube with tape and write a zero on the face.
3. Discuss the object of the game—to put the specified finger of one hand only (NO thumbs!) on a point on the grid. Once a finger is placed, it must stay there unless, in a future turn, the spinner calls for the use of that finger again.
4. To play, the first player spins to see which finger to place, then rolls the number cube twice (or picks two number cards) to form an ordered pair. The player places that finger on that point and keeps it there as other players move. A player is out if his or her finger slips off its point, or if the player uses his or her thumb. Play continues in turn until no one can move or until all but one player is out. The last player left "standing" wins. All fingers go on the same grid, so entanglements will arise!
5. If a player can't place the finger on a point because another finger already occupies it, he or she may reverse the order of the number pair to create another point. If that doesn't work, the player may roll (or pick) once more.

LEARNING OBJECTIVE

Students play a game to locate points on a coordinate grid.

GROUPING

Cooperative groups of 4

MATERIALS

- inch (or larger) grid paper
- cardboard
- markers
- paper clips and pencils to make spinner divided into fourths
- number cards or number cube labeled 0–5
- masking tape
- plastic shower curtain (optional)

Taking It Further

Have students play with larger coordinate grids. Or they can make a floor mat with a plastic shower curtain and masking tape to play with right and left hands and feet.

Assessing Skills

- Do students accurately locate points on the coordinate grid?
- What tricks do students use to help them hold their positions on the grid?

Rectangle Hunt

Knowing a rectangle's area doesn't mean knowing its dimensions. In this game, students use logic and geometry to find a rectangle on a coordinate grid.

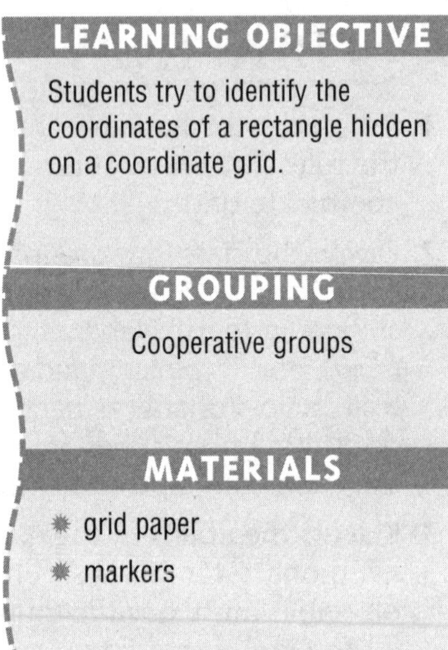

LEARNING OBJECTIVE

Students try to identify the coordinates of a rectangle hidden on a coordinate grid.

GROUPING

Cooperative groups

MATERIALS

- grid paper
- markers

Directions

1. Review the definition of rectangle. Remind students that a square is a kind of rectangle.
2. Divide the class into cooperative groups. Each group makes a coordinate grid with axes labeled from 0 to 10 on grid paper.
3. One person "hides" a rectangle on the coordinate grid so that the sides follow grid lines and the corners fall on intersections. That player shields the grid from the others' view and finds the area in square units of the hidden rectangle. Its area is given as the opening hint.
4. The rest of the group then tries to identify the corners of the hidden rectangle. To do so, they take turns naming coordinate pairs. The person who has drawn the rectangle tells whether each named point is outside, inside, or on the rectangle. Players keep track of points named and responses given.
5. Play continues until the group locates the four corners of the rectangle. Their score is the number of guesses it took to find all the corners. Players switch tasks and play again. The lower score wins.

Taking It Further

Make the game more difficult by not giving the area of the rectangle. Or let players hide a parallelogram or a rhombus.

Assessing Skills

- What strategies do students use to keep track of the information they learn with each guess?
- How logically do subsequent guesses follow from information learned?

Shark Stretch

It's knowledge of coordinate geometry and functions, not skill at aquatic aerobics, that's the key to success in this activity.

Directions

1. Tell students to imagine a rectangle plotted on a grid. Ask them to predict what would happen to the appearance of that rectangle if they doubled its *x* coordinates. [It will be twice as long.] Then ask them to predict what the figure would look like if both its *x* and *y* coordinates were doubled. [It would be a similar shape twice as long and twice as tall.] Discuss students' responses. Invite them to sketch rectangles on grid paper to test their guesses. Alternatively, you might show the changes with a computer graphing program or graphing calculator.
2. Duplicate the reproducible for individuals or pairs and distribute.
3. Circulate and observe students as they plot and analyze their drawings. Guide them to list each new set of ordered pairs. When students finish, have them compare their findings and generalizations.

Taking It Further

Challenge students to design and plot their own animals or objects and compare how changing the coordinates in each ordered pair in the same way affects the figures' shapes and areas. Ask them to determine how the changes affect the perimeters of the figures.

Assessing Skills

* What do students notice about the functional relationships among the shark drawings?
* What generalizations can they make based on the drawings they've plotted?

LEARNING OBJECTIVE

Students explore how changing *x* and *y* values of ordered pairs affects the appearance of a figure on a coordinate grid.

GROUPING

Individual or pairs

MATERIALS

* *Shark Stretch* reproducible (p. 146)
* straightedge
* colored pencils
* grid paper
* computer graphing program or graphing calculator (optional)

Name ______________________ Date ____________

Shark Stretch

Grab your pencil and straightedge. You're going to change the shape of a shark without relying on brute strength—just a little "coordination."

On the grid, plot and connect in order the following points:

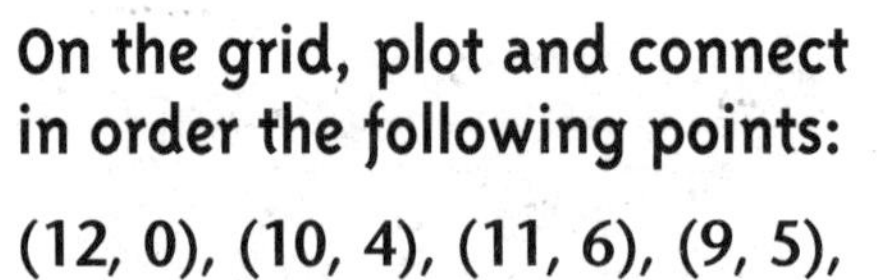

(12, 0), (10, 4), (11, 6), (9, 5), (6, 5), (6, 7), (4, 5), (0, 5), (2, 3), (1, 2), (10, 2), (12, 0).

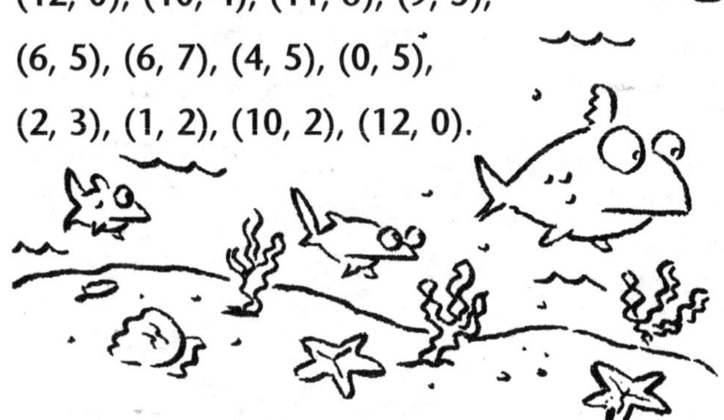

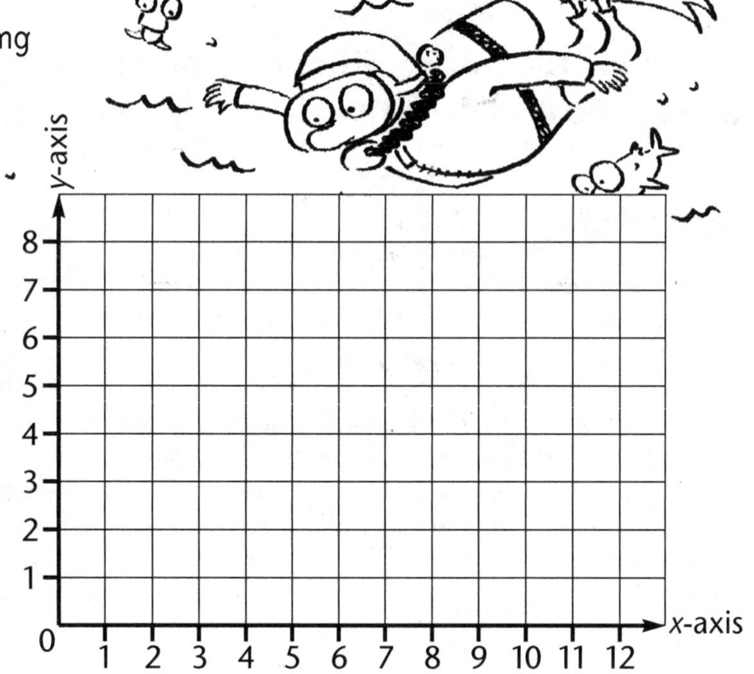

1. What is the area of your shark? ______________________

Draw another grid. Double each x value in the first grid and plot the new shark.

2. In what ways is it like the original shark? How is it different?

____

____

3. What is the area of the new shark? ______________________

Draw another grid. Double each y value in the first grid and plot this new shark.

4. How is this shark like the original? How is it different? What is its area?

____

____

Draw yet another grid. Double each x and y value from the first grid and plot this new shark.

5. What do you discover?

____

____

6. What is this shark's area? ______________________

Art Explosion

Before machines made easy enlargements and reductions possible, artists applied proportional thinking and visual reasoning to make copies of different sizes.

Directions

1. Display a grid. Invite a volunteer to draw a simple geometric figure on it.
2. Display a grid of another size. Discuss with students how to "copy" the drawing onto the second grid, where it will be either larger or smaller. Guide students to examine the figure box by box and copy what they see on one grid into the analogous boxes on the other. This procedure will produce a pair of similar drawings.
3. Now have students make their own copies. Provide assorted line drawings or cartoons from which they can pick. Or let them select their own drawings or cartoons to copy. Provide two sizes of grid paper. If necessary, model how to superimpose a grid onto the drawing to facilitate the copying process (refer to item 2).
4. Display the originals with students' copies. Talk about the process with the class. Encourage students to share their strategies and impressions.

Taking It Further

Try a similar activity using maps, photographs, works of art, or product logos. Encourage students to make both an enlarged and a "shrunken" version of the same picture to compare and contrast the process.

Assessing Skills

- What organizational techniques do students employ in this process?
- How accurately does the copy reflect the original?

LEARNING OBJECTIVE

Students apply the concepts of ratio, proportion, and similarity to make similar drawings.

GROUPING

Individual

MATERIALS

- grids in two sizes (for example, inch and half inch)
- line drawings or cartoons
- grid paper in several sizes

Partner Symmetry

Double students' creativity by having partners form symmetrical designs.

Directions

1. Divide the class into pairs. Hand out the manipulatives with which they can form designs. Choose from the materials listed, or use whatever is at hand.
2. Give each person a piece of yarn or string to use as a line of symmetry, which can be placed horizontally or vertically on the work area of the grid or dot paper. Each person makes a design on only one side of the line. Encourage students to create complex and inventive designs. Designs should also be 3-dimensional.
3. At a signal, partners switch seats. Each person now tries to complete the other person's design by creating the symmetrical missing half on the other side of the line of symmetry.
4. Partners then return to their original designs to see whether their partner's design forms an exact symmetrical duplicate.
5. Discuss the process with the class. Invite students to describe any difficulties they encountered.

Taking It Farther

Try the same activity, but have pairs use grid or dot paper and colored markers or crayons. Or students may prepare half of a drawing on plain paper around a line of symmetry, to be completed by a partner.

Assessing Skills

- Are the completed designs symmetrical?
- Are students more adept at beginning or at completing a design?

LEARNING OBJECTIVE

Students apply concepts of symmetry to complete a 3-dimensional figure around a given line of symmetry.

GROUPING

Pairs

MATERIALS

- pattern blocks, color tiles, snap cubes, or other manipulatives
- yarn or string
- grid paper or dot paper
- colored markers or crayons
- drawing paper

Pentominetris

Students play a low-tech variation of the computer game Tetris.

Directions

1. Duplicate the reproducible for each student and distribute. Identify the 12 figures as a set of pentominoes, each formed by five centimeter cubes joined in different ways.
2. Provide students with envelopes, colored markers or crayons, and scissors. Have each one prepare two sets of pentominoes for the game. Students shade or color each pentomino and then carefully cut it out and place it in the envelope.
3. Form game groups. Each group needs a piece of centimeter grid paper as a game board and the prepared sets of pentominoes. Players in a group may combine all their pentominoes into one envelope.
4. To play, each player in turn randomly draws a pentomino from the envelope and puts it, colored side up, anywhere on the grid. All outer edges of the pentomino must align with grid lines. A player may slide or turn a pentomino into any orientation to fit the available space. Pentominoes may interlock but may not overlap or extend beyond the borders of the grid. Pentominoes may not be flipped to the unshaded side.
5. If a pentomino can't fit anywhere on the grid, the player who picked it is out. The last player who can place a piece wins.

LEARNING OBJECTIVE

Students explore transformational geometry in a game that involves recognizing and manipulating pentominoes.

GROUPING

Cooperative groups

MATERIALS

- *Pentominetris* reproducible (p. 150)
- envelopes
- colored markers or crayons
- scissors
- centimeter grid paper

Taking It Further

Vary the rules to allow students to pick once more before they're out. Or use a smaller portion of the centimeter grid paper, such as an 8 by 12 area, for a more challenging game.

Assessing Skills

- Observe how students place the pentominoes. What strategies do they use?
- How well do students visualize the pieces in different orientations?

Name ______________________ Date ______________

Pentominetris

Here are two sets of 12 different pentominoes. Color and cut them out to play Pentominetris. Use a piece of centimeter grid paper as your game board.

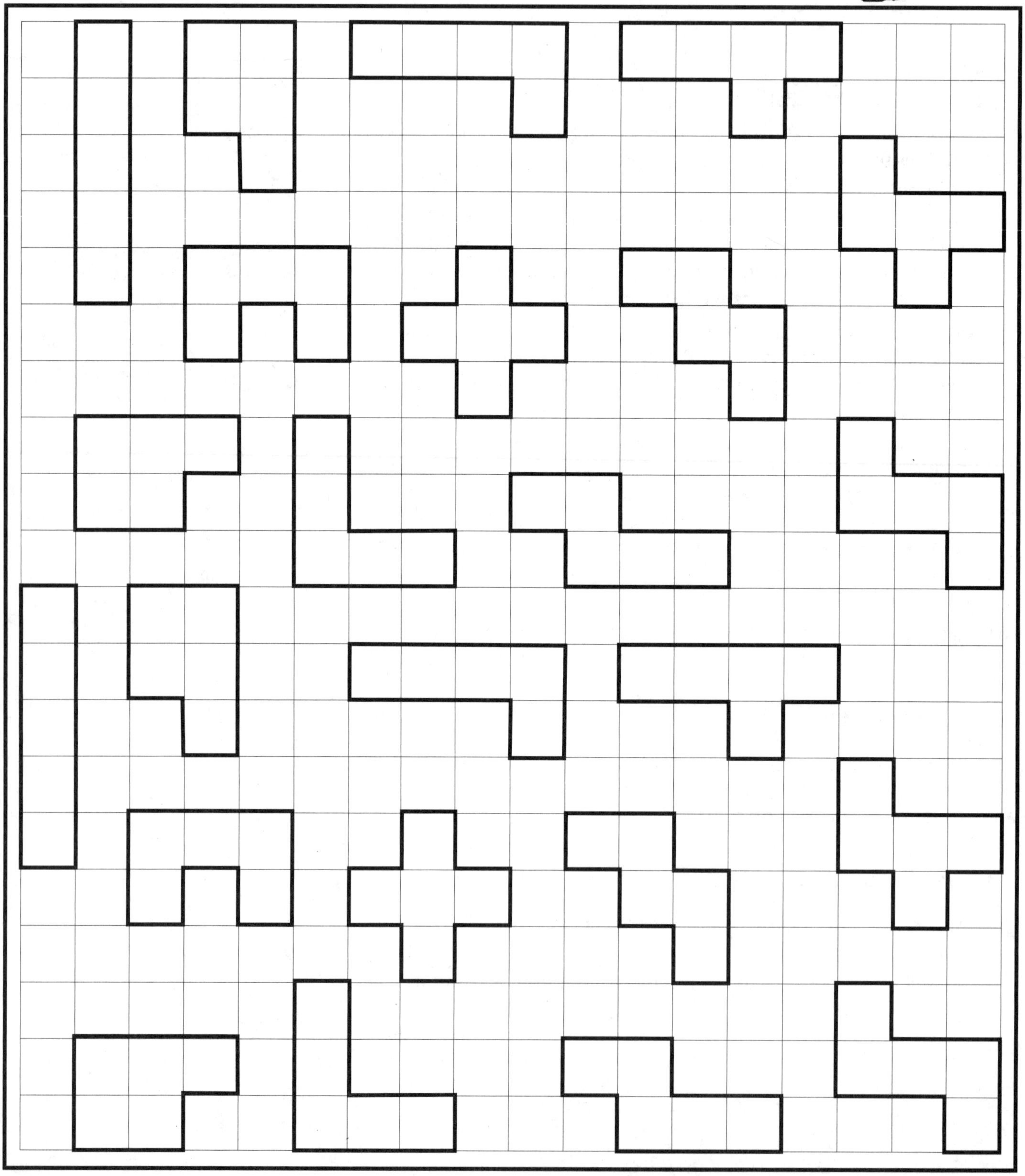

Creative Compass Constructions

A compass and colored pencils become powerful tools that students can use to explore geometric patterns involving circles, points, radii, and arcs.

Directions

1. Duplicate the reproducible for each student and distribute. Also give each student a compass, colored pencils, several sheets of white paper, and an eraser.
2. Tell students that all figures on the reproducible were created from combinations of arcs and circles only. Have them use a compass to replicate the circle designs they see on the page.
3. Then instruct students to create their own circle and arc designs. Display all completed designs on a geometry bulletin board.
4. Challenge students to replicate each other's original designs.

Taking It Farther

Ask students to design a class, team, or school logo based on circles and arcs.

Assessing Skills

- How do students go about trying to replicate a given design?
- What observations do students make about arcs, circles, radii, and points?

LEARNING OBJECTIVE

Students use compasses and colored pencils to create interesting designs.

GROUPING

Individual

MATERIALS

- *Creative Compass Constructions* reproducible (p. 152)
- compass
- unlined white paper
- colored pencils
- erasers

Name ______________________ Date ______________

Creative Compass Constructions

Each of these designs was made with a compass and a pencil . . . and sometimes an eraser. Can you figure out how to reconstruct them?

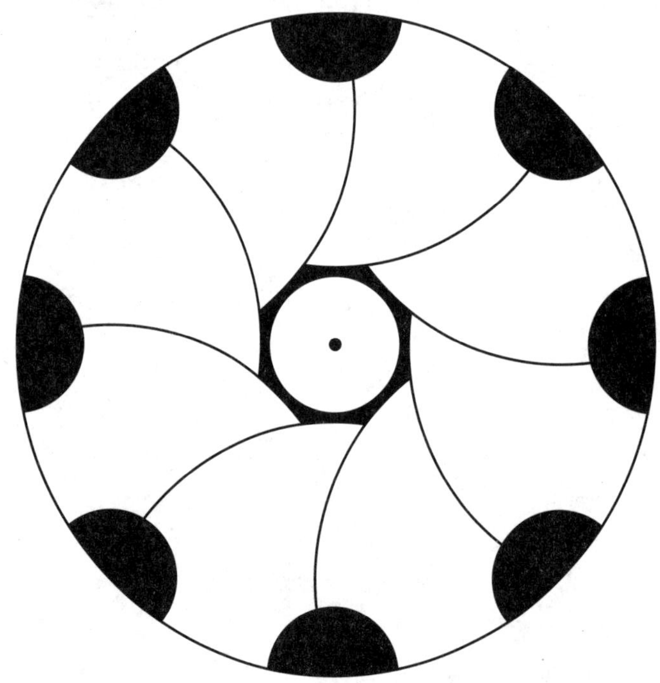

Measurement Scavenger Hunt

Students can sharpen their skills in estimating and visual/spatial reasoning by holding a classroom scavenger hunt.

Directions

1. Prepare a checklist of items students must find in the classroom. Describe each item in terms of some kind of measurement—metric, customary, or both. Include length, width, height, weight, perimeter, area, and volume. Here are some examples:
   - a book that weighs between 500 and 750 grams
   - a pencil less than 5 inches long
   - a student taller than 175 centimeters
   - a picture whose perimeter is about 20 inches
   - a container whose volume is about 36 cubic inches
   - a circle whose diameter is 8 to 10 centimeters
   - a coin whose circumference is about 7 centimeters
2. Discuss the scavenger hunt rules with students. For instance, do they collect each item, or is it enough for them to identify and describe it? Who verifies measurements, and when? What time limit, if any, should be set?
3. Conduct the scavenger hunt according to the rules you establish. Give each individual hunter or pairs or groups of hunters a checklist of items and access to measurement tools.
4. After the hunt is completed, allow time for students to share how they found, estimated, and measured one item.

Taking It Further

Have students try a similar activity at home with family members. They can use the same checklist or make up their own. Or have students make up their own checklist of items for an outdoor measurement scavenger hunt.

Assessing Skills

- Observe as students work on the measurement scavenger hunt. What estimation skills or benchmarks do they employ?
- Do students' estimation skills improve as they work?
- With which kinds of measuring skills do students need more practice?

LEARNING OBJECTIVE

Students locate classroom objects of given length, weight, volume, area, or perimeter.

GROUPING

Individual, pairs, or cooperative groups

MATERIALS

- scavenger hunt checklist (see examples, at left)
- assorted measuring tools

Measuring Across and Down

What's the abbreviation for pound? What 7-letter word means ten decades?

Directions

1. Duplicate a set of the reproducibles for each student or pair and distribute. Page 155 has the puzzle grid and page 156 provides the clues.
2. If necessary, review how to solve a crossword puzzle. Remind students that each word they use in the puzzle grid must fit its clue exactly.
3. Have students work on the puzzle independently or in pairs. Allow them to consult a dictionary for correct spelling or refer to their math books to verify clues.

Taking It Farther

Challenge students to create their own crossword puzzles using units of metric measure, geometry terms, or other categories of math words.

Assessing Skills

- How do students figure out the answers to the clues?
- What do students do when they're stuck?

LEARNING OBJECTIVE

Students review and reinforce relationships and definitions of customary units of measure by solving a crossword puzzle.

GROUPING

Individual or pairs

MATERIALS

- *Measuring Across and Down* reproducibles (pp. 155–156)
- dictionary (optional)

Name ______________________ Date ______________

Measuring Across and Down

All the clues in this puzzle are about units of customary measure. Along with the puzzle grid, you'll also need the clues, which are on the next page.

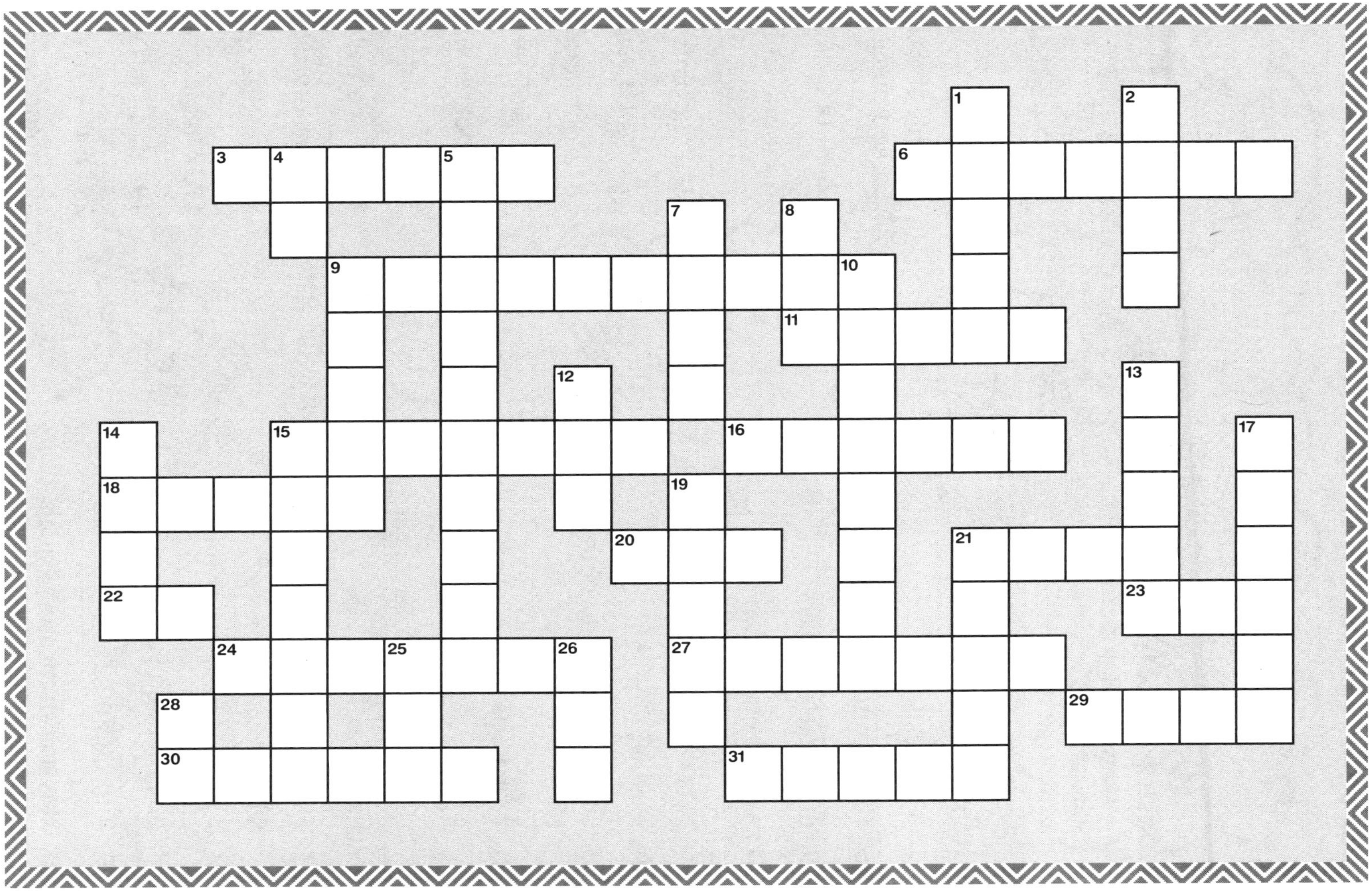

Name ________________________ Date ______________

Measuring Across and Down

ACROSS

3. A year has 12 ______.
6. These contain four quarts.
9. one thousand years
11. A quart equals two ______.
15. groups of ten years
16. $\frac{1}{60}$ of an hour
18. One hundred sixty of these equal one square mile.
20. $\frac{1}{4}$ of a quart
21. 52 weeks
22. abbreviation for the unit that has 12 inches
23. A small car might weigh about 1 ______.
24. A minute has sixty of these.
27. one hundred years
29. A fortnight has 14 ______.
30. This unit of measure equals 4 pecks or 32 dry quarts.
31. A non-leap-year February has exactly four of them.

DOWN

1. unit of weight for gems and precious stones
2. $\frac{1}{24}$ of a day
4. abbreviation for the unit that is $\frac{1}{8}$ of a cup
5. Four pints is one of these.
7. $\frac{1}{36}$ of a yard
8. eight fluid ounces
9. 10,560 feet = 2 ______
10. another way to say 12:00 A.M.
12. years in a decade
13. $\frac{1}{4}$ of a gallon
14. Twenty-six weeks is this part of a year.
15. units for measuring temperature
17. A typical cat might weigh 10 ______.
19. $\frac{1}{128}$ of a gallon
21. A mile has 1,760 ______.
25. 3,600 seconds = ______ hour
26. half a dozen
28. abbreviation for weight equivalent to 16 ounces

Hidden Meters

It's easy to recognize a meter on a meterstick. But what if a meter is broken into different units and scattered on a puzzle?

Directions

1. Review the relationships among metric prefixes as well as how to convert from one metric unit to another.
2. Duplicate the reproducible for each student and distribute. Tell them that the grid has 16 trios of measurements that combine to make 1 meter. The hidden meters can be found by identifying three measures in a row vertically, horizontally, or diagonally whose sum is 1 meter; for example, 40 cm + 2 dm + 400 mm = 1 m. Students ring the sets of three boxes. Some rings overlap.
3. You may let students use calculators. Alert them to enter numbers with the decimal point in the correct position in order for the calculator to be useful.

Taking It Further

Make up similar game grids in which you vary the units to present measurement sums of 1 gram or 1 liter.

Assessing Skills

What techniques do students use to make conversions among units?

LEARNING OBJECTIVE

Students reinforce their understanding of metric prefixes, practice metric conversions, and add decimals and whole numbers.

GROUPING

Individual

MATERIALS

- *Hidden Meters* reproducible (p. 158)
- calculators (optional)

Name ____________________ Date ____________

Hidden Meters

Find three boxes horizontally, vertically, or diagonally whose sum is 1 meter. There are 16 such trios. Ring each trio you see. You may use a calculator.

90 mm	11 cm	0.8 m	500 mm	40 cm	25 cm	0.5 m	0.25 m
200 mm	50 dm	60 cm	1 dm	30 cm	9 mm	1 cm	0.8 m
40 cm	1 cm	700 mm	8 cm	5 cm	4 dm	550 mm	50 cm
400 mm	0.3 m	300 mm	3 dm	40 cm	0.3 m	0.4 cm	300 cm
2 dm	3 dm	40 mm	15 mm	1.1 m	300 mm	9 m	0.5 m
0.3 cm	1 m	30 cm	600 mm	1 dm	8 dm	20 cm	350 mm
50 cm	0.45 m	1 dm	45 cm	2.5 cm	0.1 m	9 dm	15 cm
200 mm	3 dm	50 cm	0.95 m	4 cm	3 cm	0.80 m	40 dm
10 mm	250 mm	600 dm	4.5 dm	0.07 m	600 mm	70 cm	300 mm

Lengthy Words

At times, students may think that words carry little weight. But this activity will prove that words carry length!

Directions

1. Duplicate the reproducible for each student or pair and distribute.
2. Review measuring to the nearest half centimeter (5 millimeters).
3. Present this code for the alphabet letters: A = 0.5 cm, B = 1.0 cm, C = 1.5 cm, D = 2.0 cm, and so on, through Z = 13.0 cm. Tell students that if a line segment measures 5.5 cm, for instance, then its letter value would be K.
4. For a group of line segments, students measure to find the letter value for each segment. Then they arrange those letters into one or more words.
5. You may want to do one example with the class. Then have students complete the activity on their own or in pairs.

Taking It Farther

Encourage students to make their own sets of segments for classmates to measure and decode. Or, challenge students to try the reverse: to draw a set of segments to represent given words.

Assessing Skills

- Do students measure accurately?
- How well do students form words from the letters they find? Can they find more than one word for a given set of letters?

LEARNING OBJECTIVE

Students measure line segments to the nearest half centimeter, assign letter values to the lengths, and use the measurements to form words.

GROUPING

Individual or pairs

MATERIALS

- *Lengthy Words* reproducible (p. 160)
- centimeter ruler

Name ______________________ Date ____________

Lengthy Words

Measure the segments in each open figure. Determine the letter values, based on the code A = 0.5 cm, B = 1.0 cm, C = 1.5 cm, and so on. Make as many words as you can from each set of letters.

1.

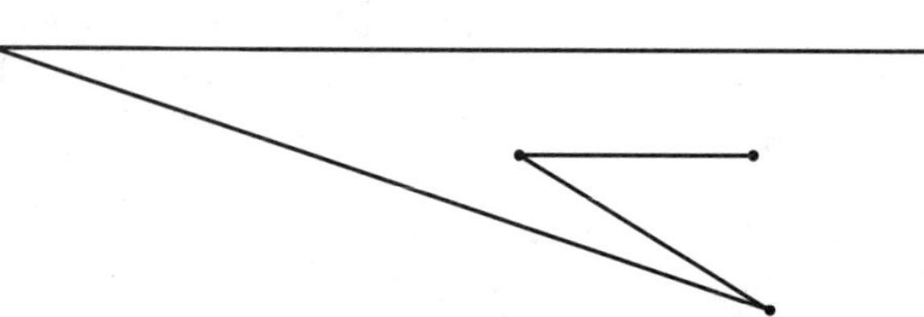

2.

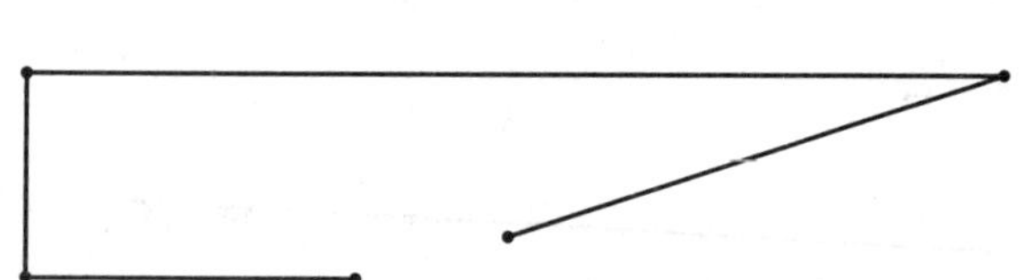

3.

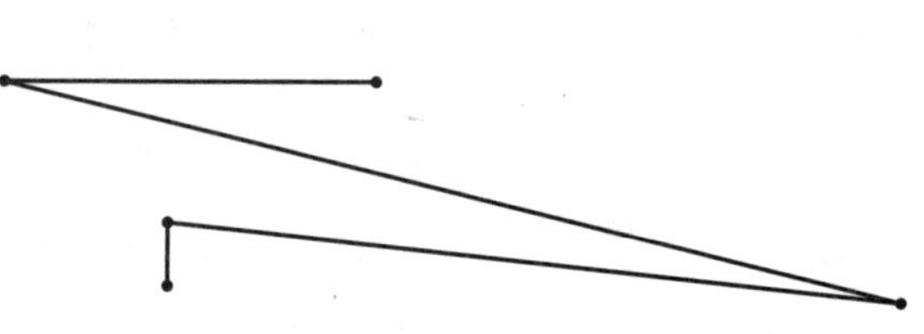

4.

5.

6.

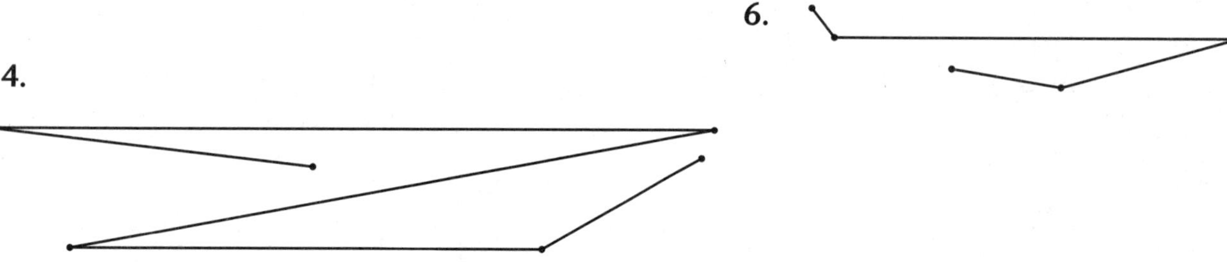

7.

Pin That Area

Geoboards or dot paper and the trusty old alphabet can provide new ways for students to explore perimeter and area.

Directions

1. Tell students that it is possible to use one or two rubber bands on a geoboard to form every uppercase letter of the alphabet. Some letters require a little imagination to create, but each is possible, some in several ways.
2. Have students predict a range of areas and perimeters for the letters. For example, they might guess that E has a greater perimeter than V or that the area of Q is greater than the area of I. Suggest that they sort their predictions into two lists: least/middle/greatest perimeter; least/middle/greatest area.
3. Provide geoboards and rubber bands or dot paper to pairs or groups. Students form block letters on the geoboards or dot paper and then calculate their perimeters to the nearest linear unit and their areas to the nearest square unit.
4. When students finish, instruct them to compare their estimates with the measured areas and perimeters they found. Encourage groups to share and compare their discoveries.

Taking It Further

Encourage students to perform a similar activity with the numerals 0 to 9.

Assessing Skills

- Can students form every letter of the alphabet?
- What methods do they use to calculate the perimeters? the areas?
- How closely do predictions match measured dimensions?

LEARNING OBJECTIVE

Students form block letters on geoboards or dot paper to explore area and perimeter.

GROUPING

Pairs or cooperative groups

MATERIALS

- geoboards and rubber bands or dot paper
- colored pencils

Area Irregulars

Students don't have to cry over spilled milk. They can figure out how to measure it instead!

Directions

1. Draw the figure at right to display. Ask students for suggestions on how to determine the area it encloses. Discuss their ideas.
2. Distribute grid paper. Ask students to draw an irregular shape, similar to the one you've shown, on their grids. Guide them to understand that the area of the shape is the total of all the full and partial squares it encloses.
3. Then present the following method for approximating the area:
   a. Count all squares that lie completely within the outline.
   b. Count all squares through which the outline passes; these lie only partially within the outline. Divide this number by 2.
   c. Add the sum from **a** and **b**. This gives a reasonable estimate of the area of the irregular figure.
4. Have students use this method to estimate the area of the figure they drew on their grid paper. Then have them try it again, using another shape.
5. Duplicate the reproducible for individuals or pairs and distribute. Allow time for students to compare answers.

Taking It Further

Challenge students to describe methods for getting an even closer approximation of the area within an irregular figure. Invite them to demonstrate their methods for improving accuracy. [Sample answers: Use smaller squares; subdivide all the squares into fourths, even sixteenths.]

Assessing Skills

- Do students understand the method presented for approximating the area of an irregular figure? Can they apply this method correctly?
- Can students come up with ways to improve the estimates? Can they explain their methods in a comprehensible way?

LEARNING OBJECTIVE

Students estimate the area of irregular figures.

GROUPING

Individual or pairs

MATERIALS

- *Area Irregulars* reproducible (p. 163)
- grid paper (ideally, 4 squares/inch)

Name ______________________ Date ______________

Area Irregulars

Estimate the area enclosed by each outline.

1.

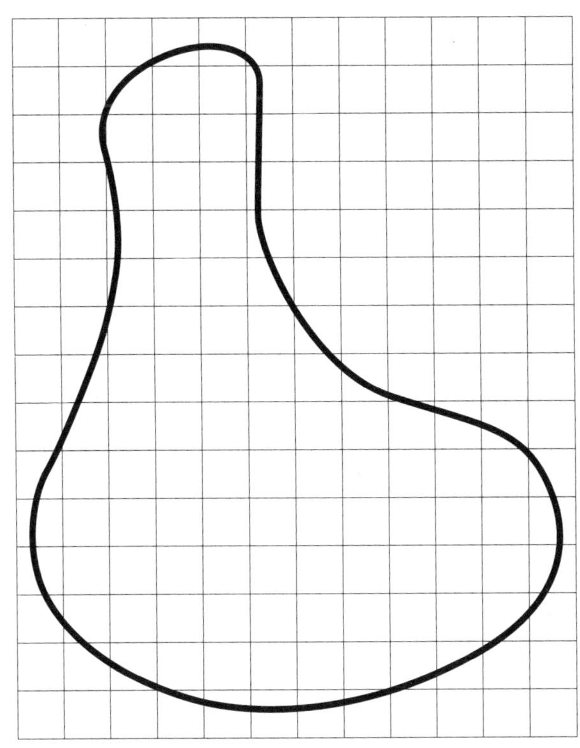

2.

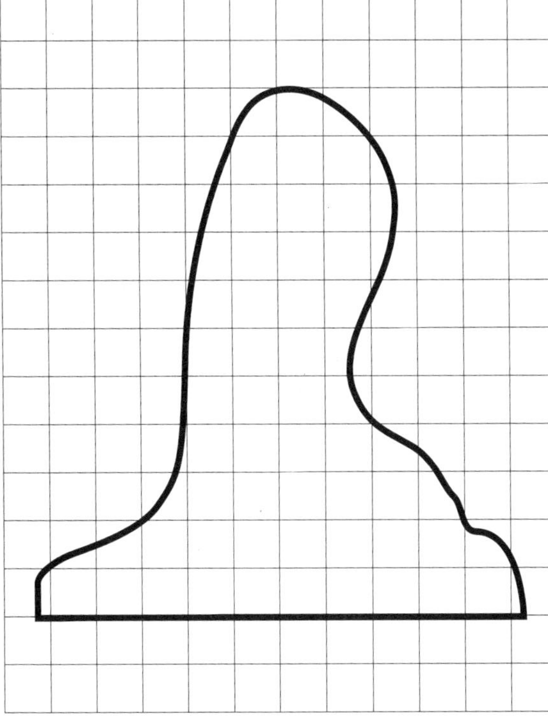

3.

4.

Have a Ball!

Here's an investigation of volume that should keep students bouncing!

Directions

1. Have students describe the "ball rooms" at children's play facilities. A ball room is a contained area—a room or fenced-off part of a room—full of colorful plastic balls, in which young children roll and romp.
2. Divide the class into cooperative groups. Challenge each group to estimate how many balls it would take to create a children's ball room for playing.
3. Guide groups to determine a reasonable size for the ball room. It must be big enough for many children to play in safely. Encourage students to use proportional reasoning to break down the task to make it manageable. Have grid paper and markers available if students want to make floor plans of their rooms.
4. Ask groups to repeat the investigation for three different sizes of balls. Provide an assortment of balls.
5. When groups finish, have them share their estimates and strategies.

Taking It Further

Tell students to estimate the cost to fill the play space they plan. Or they can contact a local play facility that has a ball room to find out its dimensions and how many balls it takes to fill the space.

Assessing Skills

- Observe groups during this investigation to see that all members participate actively.
- How do students approach the question, and what strategies do they use?
- Do their estimates make sense?

LEARNING OBJECTIVE

Students estimate and calculate the volumes of rooms and spheres; they apply proportional reasoning and geometric formulas for volume.

GROUPING

Cooperative groups

MATERIALS

- spherical balls of different sizes, such as tennis balls, soccer balls, table tennis balls, softballs, marbles, squash balls, beach balls, and so on
- grid paper and markers (optional)

Gourmet Pet Problems

There's no getting around it: using proportional reasoning can speak volumes for smart shoppers.

Directions

1. Ask students to figure out which is the better buy: a 14-inch-diameter pizza that costs $12, or an 8-inch pizza that costs $6. Challenge them to use mental math.
2. Have students explain their answers and methods. Discuss that the 14-inch pie is the better buy, since it's more than 3 times as large as the 8-inch pie but costs only twice as much. You can ask a volunteer to demonstrate how to use the area formula for circles to show that the larger pie has an area, in square inches, of 153.86 and the smaller one has an area of 50.24.
3. As needed, review the formulas for finding area and volume.

   Area of a circle: $A = \pi \times r^2$

   Volume of a cylinder: $V = \pi \times r^2 \times h$
4. Discuss the concept of unit pricing, and that when comparing two items, the one with the lower unit price is the better buy.
5. Duplicate the reproducible for each student or pair and distribute. Guide students to use the computation method that makes the most sense—paper and pencil, calculator, or mental math—to solve the problems on the page.

Taking It Further

Ask students to formulate "geometric better buy" problems of their own for classmates to solve. Challenge them, for example, to create pizza problems in which one pie is a circle and the other is a rectangle, or packaged food problems in which one container is a can and the other is a box.

Assessing Skills

- Do students apply the correct formulas and use proportional reasoning to solve the better buy problems?
- Do they use a computation method that makes good sense?

LEARNING OBJECTIVE

Students use the formulas for finding the area of a circle and the volume of a cylinder to determine which product is the better buy.

GROUPING

Individual or pairs

MATERIALS

- *Gourmet Pet Problems* reproducible (p. 166)
- calculator (optional)

Name ______________________ Date ____________

Gourmet Pet Problems

Imagine that you're shopping for pet food. For each item, you need to choose between similar products. Unfortunately, the labels don't contain unit prices.

Use your knowledge of finding area and volume and of proportions to choose the better buy. Use the computation method that makes sense.

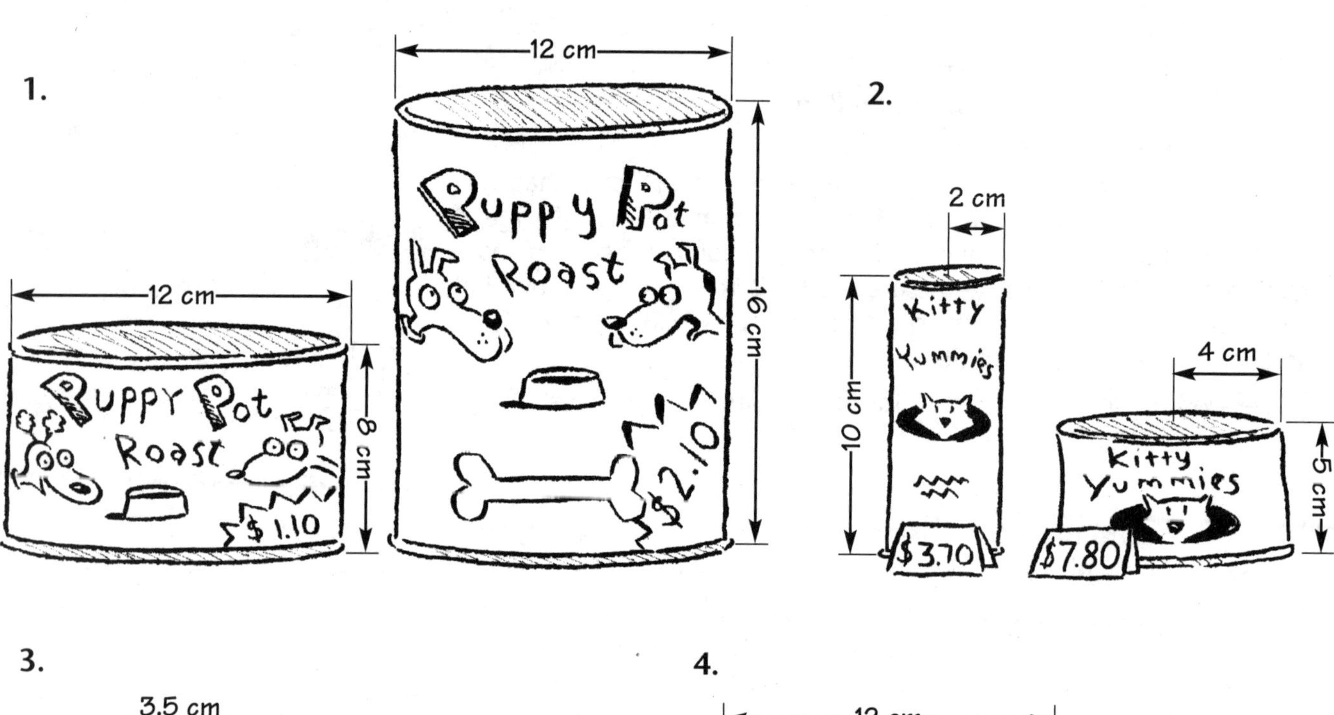

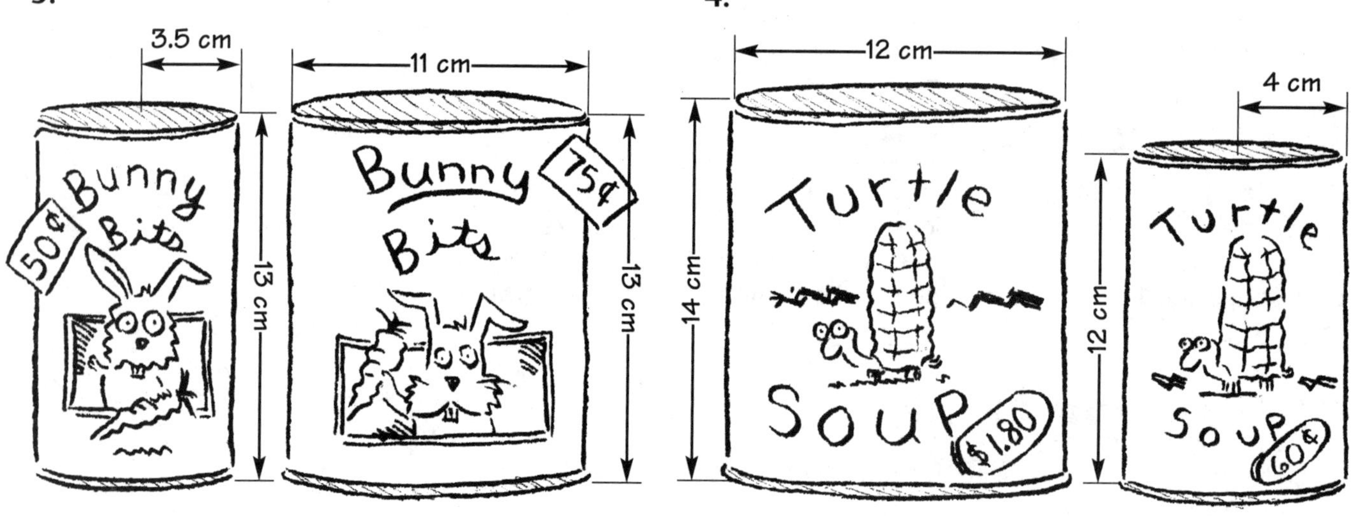

Design a Wall Unit

Furniture designers use geometry and measurement to create wall units that are functional and attractive. Students try their hand at this creative task.

Directions

1. If possible, obtain some furniture catalogs that show different kinds of wall units. Some are open. Others have doors and closed compartments that hold video and stereo equipment. Some have book or display shelves, media storage areas, drawers, and pull-out desk surfaces.
2. Divide the class into design groups. Challenge each group to design a wall unit for the classroom. Discuss some of the features designers always keep in mind, such as height, width, and depth of available space, adequate storage area for the kinds of things the unit will hold, air circulation space around electronic equipment, interesting and practical design, thickness of wood, and so on.
3. Have groups make labeled scale drawings on grid paper of their wall units. Drawings should include all dimensions and measurements so that someone could use the drawing to build the wall unit.
4. Hold a design showcase where groups can share their designs and explain the unique features. You may also want to conduct a group critique of designs and let all the groups collaborate on an ideal wall unit that includes the best features of all the plans.

LEARNING OBJECTIVE

Students measure, estimate, and draw to scale wall units to fit a space in their homes.

GROUPING

Cooperative groups

MATERIALS

- measuring tools
- grid paper
- furniture catalogs (optional)

Taking It Further

Invite students to design their ideal room. They can design an area of any shape with an area of 600 square feet of floor space. Have them include any kind of furniture, windows, built-ins, or other features.

Assessing Skills

- How thoroughly do students undertake the task?
- Do drawings include sufficient details to serve as a preliminary plan?
- What observations do students make about each other's plans?

Geometry Jeopardy

Students expect to answer questions in school. In this activity, however, students do the asking.

Directions

1. Have a volunteer explain the idea behind the TV game show *Jeopardy.* (Players ask questions which match given answers.) Point out that in Geometry Jeopardy, all questions are in the category of Geometry and Measurement. Students will formulate a question to fit data in the space that player lands on. For instance, if a space says 18 square feet, a good question might be: *What's the area of a rectangle 6 feet long and 3 feet wide?*
2. Give each player a marker, such as a colored cube or counter. Players flip a coin to determine moves: heads = 2 spaces forward, tails = 1 space forward.
3. Divide the class into groups of 3 to 5. Duplicate the reproducible for each group and distribute.
4. In each group, one person acts as judge, the others as players. The judge decides if a question is correct. If not, that player moves back 1 space and awaits his or her next turn. If the question is acceptable, the next player goes. The first player to reach the END wins.
5. Before groups play, formulate other rules they may need, such as: If two players land on the same space, can the second person give the same question the first person gave? What happens if the judge makes an error?

Taking It Further

Have groups create a new board with other answers. Or they can create a game that more closely resembles the television game show, with answers in order of difficulty in geometry and measurement subcategories, such as 2-dimensional shapes, 3-dimensional figures, metric measures, and so on.

Assessing Skills

- What strategies do students use to formulate their questions?
- How does the judge evaluate the questions?

LEARNING OBJECTIVE

Applying their knowledge of geometry and measurement concepts, students work backward to form questions that fit given answers.

GROUPING

Cooperative groups

MATERIALS

- *Geometry Jeopardy* reproducible (p. 169)
- centimeter cubes or counters
- coins
- calculator (optional)

Name ____________________ Date ____________

Geometry Jeopardy

The category for all questions is Geometry and Measurement. Each player needs a play marker. Use this game board and a coin to determine moves: heads = move 2 spaces, tails = move 1 space. Ask a question that fits the answer in the space you land on. The judge decides whether to accept your answer. The first player to reach END wins.

Here's an example: The answer is **12 mm**. What's the question?
How about: **What's the radius of a circle whose diameter is 24 mm?**

START

36 square feet

10 cubic inches

30 centimeters

about 78.5 square inches

60 cubic feet

12 square yards

14 miles

90 square meters

12 cubic inches

9 square yards

216 meters

about 56.5 square feet

27 cubic centimeters

1 square foot

26 yards

7.5 square feet

6 cubic yards

120 cubic inches

about 28 square miles

600 square centimeters

END

Analog Angles

Digital clocks may be accurate and easy to read, but analog clocks display lots of geometric possibilities.

Directions

1. Display an analog clock. Point out the angles of different measures that form as the hands move around the clockface.
2. Use a protractor to find the angle measure of the current time.
3. Post these angle questions. Challenge students to determine an answer for each one.
   - morning times in three different hours when the hands form obtuse angles
   - afternoon times in three different hours when the hands form straight angles
   - a mealtime when the hands form a right angle
   - times in three different hours when the hands form angles of less than 15°
   - times in three different hours when the hands form angles of about 150°
   - three times during the school day when the hands form a right angle
4. To facilitate solving the problems, students can use a real or play clock with movable hands. They can also make or draw clocks as they work.

Taking It Farther

Ask students to write riddles about times and angle measures; for instance, "What right angle time sounds like consecutive multiples of the hour?" [5:10]

Assessing Skills

- Observe students as they solve the problems. In what ways do they use analog clockfaces?
- How do students verify their answers?

LEARNING OBJECTIVE

Students visualize angles formed by the hands of an analog clock to solve problems.

GROUPING

Individual or pairs

MATERIALS

- analog clocks
- protractors
- real or play clocks with movable hands

Cuckoo Clocks

In this activity, the clock becomes a puzzle that takes visual and spatial reasoning to unravel.

Directions

1. Duplicate the reproducible for each individual or pair and distribute.
2. Tell students that the clock puzzles require visual/spatial reasoning and geometric thinking to solve.
3. Do one demonstration problem from each kind of clock puzzle. Then have students complete the page on their own or in pairs. You may want to have a mirror available for students to use for questions 1–6.

Taking It Further

Inspire students to create other puzzles like the ones on the reproducible to share with classmates.

Assessing Skills

- What strategies do students use to solve the problems?
- Which type of puzzles were more challenging to them? Can they explain why?

LEARNING OBJECTIVE

Students use visual/spatial and geometric reasoning to solve puzzles based on analog and digital clockfaces.

GROUPING

Individual or pairs

MATERIALS

- *Cuckoo Clocks* reproducible (p. 172)
- mirror (optional)

Name ______________________ Date ______________

Cuckoo Clocks

Here are mirror images of analog clocks without numbers. What time is it?

1. ______________ 2. ______________ 3. ______________

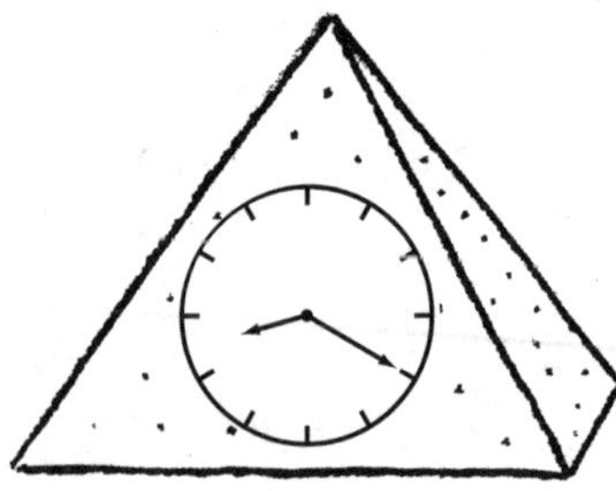

4. ______________ 5. ______________ 6. ______________

These digital clocks have part of their numerals blocked. What time is it?

7.

8.

9.

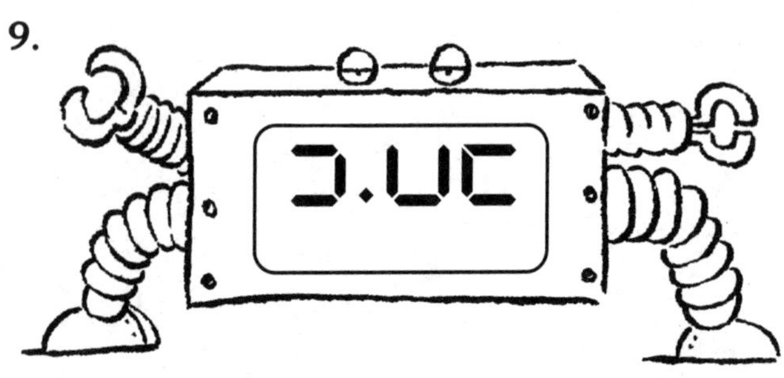

10.

Warmth War

Which is warmer, 35°F or 15°C? If students can figure this out, they have all it takes to win a round of Warmth War.

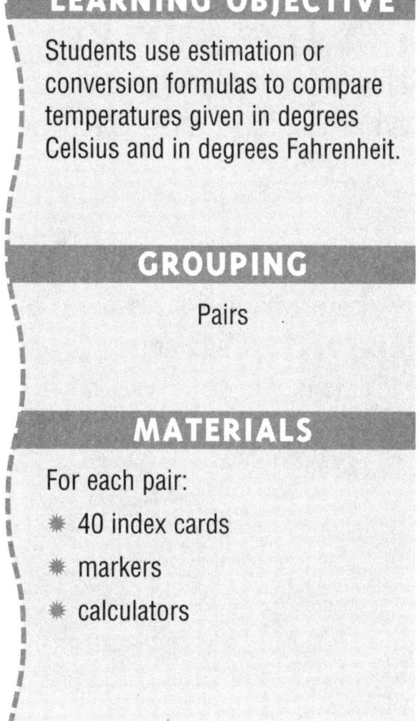

LEARNING OBJECTIVE

Students use estimation or conversion formulas to compare temperatures given in degrees Celsius and in degrees Fahrenheit.

GROUPING

Pairs

MATERIALS

For each pair:

- 40 index cards
- markers
- calculators

Directions

1. Review the formulas commonly used to convert temperatures between Fahrenheit and Celsius.

   Fahrenheit to Celsius: $\frac{5}{9}F - 32 = C$

   Celsius to Fahrenheit: $\frac{9}{5}C + 32 = F$

2. Also review the traditional card game War, in which opponents try to capture cards by turning over a card with a greater value.
3. Divide the class into pairs. Give each pair 40 index cards. One student makes 20 cards with temperatures between 0° and 100° Celsius. The partner makes 20 cards with temperatures between 32° and 212° Fahrenheit. Encourage pairs to prepare cards with a wide range of temperatures.
4. When all cards are ready, students mix them together, then divide the deck into equal piles—one for each player. To play, opponents turn over their top cards. The player whose card gives a warmer temperature wins both cards. If both cards give Fahrenheit or Celsius temperatures, the comparison will be easy. If temperatures are given in different scales, players use estimation or conversion formulas to determine which card is the winner.
5. In case of "war," in which both cards give the same temperature, players use the rules of the traditional game: turn over three more cards. Players compare only the third cards; the winner gets all cards used in that turn.
6. Play continues until one player has captured all the cards.

Taking It Further

Prepare decks in advance so that the given temperatures fall within a closer range, requiring more frequent use of conversion formulas.

Assessing Skills

- Can students use estimation skills to determine the winner of some rounds?
- Do students apply the correct formula to convert temperatures?

Geometry & Measurement Problem Bank

Use these quick skill-builders for self-starters, homework, or just for a fun break from the textbook!

1. A DAY'S DAZE

The day before yesterday was Monday, September 30.
What day and date will it be the day after the day after tomorrow?

2. WHICH WAY IS UP?

Make a Möbius strip from a strip of paper approximately 16 inches long and 1 inch wide. Give it one twist and tape the ends together. Which is the top? Which is the bottom? What's going on here?!

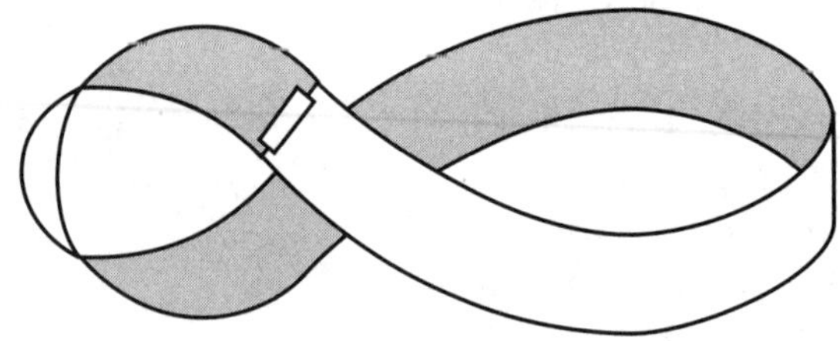

3. A TRAVEL CLOCK

A clock has a diameter of 17 inches. Its minute hand is 8 inches long. About how far does the point of that minute hand travel over 24 hours?

4. THE 1,000,000TH SECOND

Suppose you want to celebrate the one millionth second of the year. That's a great idea, but when will you celebrate? How can you figure it out?

5. GAME'S OVER

The Boston Red Sox are playing the Seattle Mariners on Monday night in Seattle. Larry watches the game on television in Boston. The game starts at 7:40 P.M. Seattle time and lasts for 3 hours and 10 minutes. Larry shuts off the TV as soon as the game ends. When does Larry turn off his TV in Boston?

6. PIECE OF CAKE

Janet bakes a round cake. She wants to cut it into 11 pieces, but she doesn't care if they are different sizes. She figures out how to do this with only 4 straight cuts. What does she do?

7. WHAT'S THE POINT?

Avery wrote a paragraph about his classroom, but he left out all the decimal points. Add a decimal point to each measurement so that the statements make sense.

My classroom is big. The ceiling is about 571 m high, and the room is about 148937 cm long. My chair is a good fit for me—it's about 6500 cm high. Out the window I can see train tracks across a field, about 9875 m away.

8. 10 TOOTHPICKS

Use ten toothpicks. Form two squares.

9. SETTING YOUR SITES

The map shows where Mayan artifacts were found. Four archaeologists who study the area want to divide the site so each person can examine the same number of artifacts. Draw two straight lines to show how they can do this.

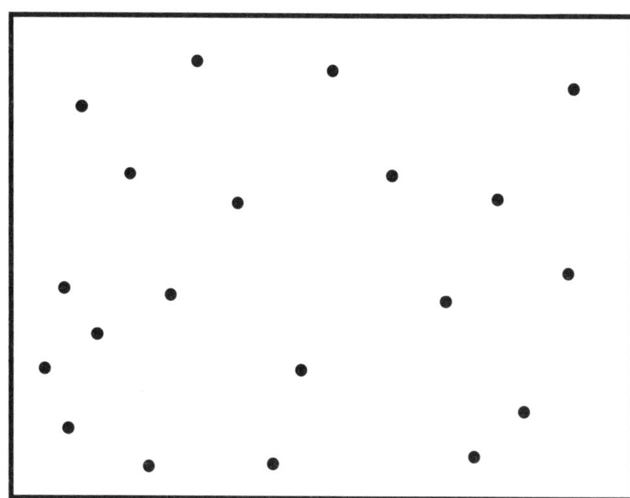

10. STEP UP

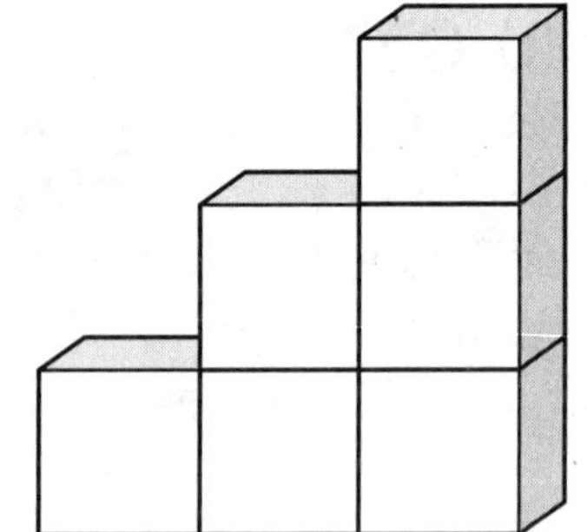

Maris builds a block staircase with 3 steps. How many blocks does she need to build a block staircase with 20 steps?

11. WHAT TIME IS IT?

Picture the smallest 4-digit time you'd see on a digital clock. How much later will the greatest 3-digit time appear?

12. SQUARES EVERYWHERE

Find the total number of squares on a standard chessboard.

13. TANGRAM SHAPES

Use your tangram set to make a variety of shapes and figures. Use all seven pieces each time. Draw a diagram to show how you made the following:

a. a right triangle
b. a rectangle that is not a square
c. a parallelogram that is neither a square nor a rectangle
d. a trapezoid
e. a boat
f. an animal
g. a candle
h. a figure of your choice

14. GOURMET PET PROBLEMS

Doggie scrapple-and-bone pizzas come in three sizes and two shapes. There are two round pies: a 6-inch one that costs $2.50 and an 18-inch one that costs $12. There's a 12-inch by 19-inch rectangular pie for $6. Which pizza is the best buy?

15. ANALOG ANGLES

Look at an analog clock to answer the following questions.

- What is the earliest time in a typical day when the hands form a 60° angle?
- What is an afternoon time when the hands form a 135° angle?
- What is the latest time in a typical day when the hands form an 11° angle?
- What is the angle the hands form when your favorite TV show starts?

16. MAPPING UP

Build a cube structure for each map.

a.

3	3	3	3
4	5	5	4
2	1	1	2

b.

2	4	6		
	5	6	5	
		4	3	4
			2	1

c.

5	4	2		6	6
4	4	2		5	5
3		2	3	5	
3				4	

17. MAPPING UP

Draw a map for each cube structure.

a.

b.

Toy Joy

Toy Joy will hit students when they design a spinner game to win their favorite toys.

Directions

1. Duplicate a copy of the reproducible for each student.
2. Display a replica of the spinner on the board. Color two of the spinner sections red and two of the spinner sections yellow. Ask students: *If you spin the spinner, which color would you most likely spin? Why?* [red or yellow because each color takes up an equal amount of the spinner] Discuss students' responses.
3. Distribute the reproducible. Tell students that they will be designing a spinner game. The object of the game is to spin to win a toy. They begin by writing down their favorite toy, and then three other toys. Ask students to create a spinner that will give them the most likely chance of spinning their favorite toys. They must use at least two different toys and two different colors in their spinners.
4. Show students how to cut out and assemble their spinners. Let students spin their spinners 10 times and record their results. Discuss the results. Did they design a winning spinner?

Taking It Further

Have students draw spinners with five, six, or eight sections and use them in the experiment. How do their strategies and results change?

Assessing Skills

Observe whether students understand that using fewer toys in their spinners increases the likelihood of winning their favorite toys.

LEARNING OBJECTIVE

Students explore the meaning of probability.

GROUPING

Individual

MATERIALS

* *Toy Joy* reproducible (p. 179)
* crayons
* scissors
* paper clip and pencil (to make the spinner)

Name ________________________________ Date ______________

Toy Joy

What is the likelihood of winning your favorite toy? Design a winning spinner and find out!

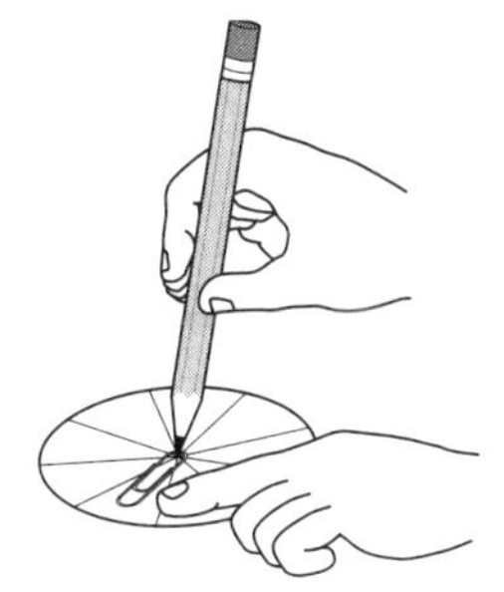

Write down your favorite toy on a sheet of paper. Then write down three other toys. Use at least two toys in the spinner below. Write a toy in each section. Color the sections. Cut out your spinner and spin it 10 times. Record your results.

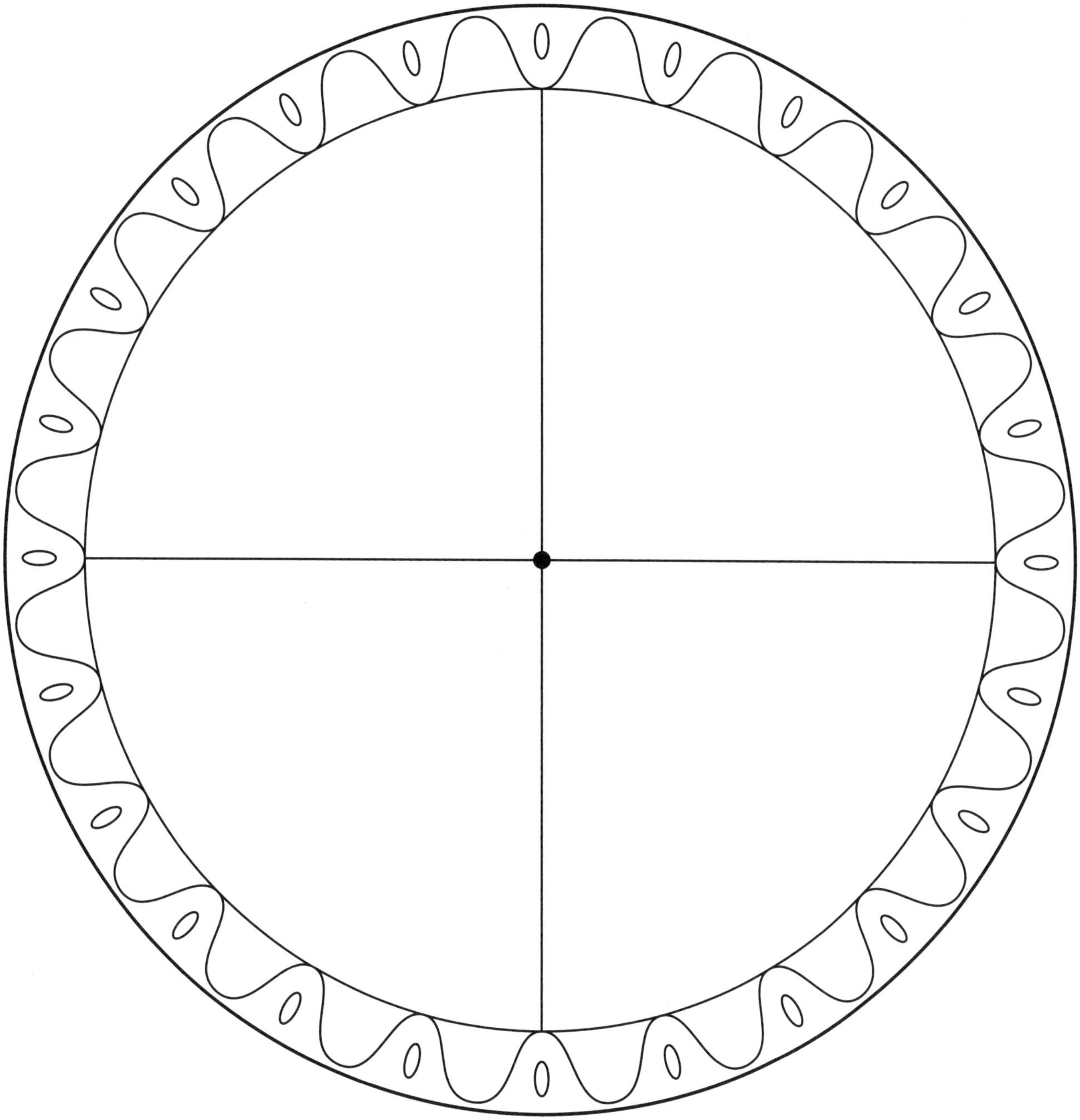

Guess 'n' Go

In this probability game, students guess which color counter they will draw.

Directions

1. Pair students and then pass out the game bags and copies of the reproducible. Explain that they will be playing a guessing game.
2. The partners take turns. Each guesses whether she or he will draw a red counter or a yellow counter from the bag. If the guess is incorrect, the player moves 1 space. If the guess is correct, the player moves 3 spaces for a red counter and 2 spaces for a yellow counter. Players set counters aside—do not return counters to the bag. Whoever reaches the finish space first is the winner.
3. Remind players to keep a record of their guesses and the colors of the counters they draw. Draw the following table on the board with the example. Have each player copy the blank table.

I Guessed	I Drew	I Moved
Red	Yellow	1 space

Taking It Farther

At the end of the game, there will be counters remaining in the bag. Tell students that each bag contained 20 counters at the beginning of the game. Challenge them to guess how many counters of each color are still in the bag. Ask them to discuss their reasoning.

Assessing Skills

Question students about how they made their decisions about which color to choose.

LEARNING OBJECTIVE

Students try to predict the number of red and yellow counters inside a bag.

GROUPING

Pairs

MATERIALS

For each pair:

* *Guess 'n' Go* reproducible (p. 181)
* 20 red and yellow counters
* paper bag
* game markers

ADVANCE PREPARATION

Prepare bags of counters for each pair. Each bag should contain a total of 20 counters. Vary the ratio of red to yellow counters in each bag. Duplicate the reproducible.

 Name ______________________ Date ____________

Guess 'n' Go

This game is in the bag—all you have to do is guess and draw the right color counter!

Decide which player will go first. Each player guesses whether he or she will draw a red or a yellow counter out of the bag. Here's how you can move on the game board:

An incorrect guess . . . . Move 1 space.

A correct guess (Yellow) . . . . Move 2 spaces.

A correct guess (Red). . . . . . . Move 3 spaces.

PLAYER 1 START →

← PLAYER 2 START

Oops! Lose a turn!

Take 1 more turn.

Oops! Lose a turn!

Go back 1 space.

Go ahead 1 space.

Go back 1 space.

Go ahead 1 space.

FINISH

Flip for Probability

How many times will the coin come up heads? Your class will flip over this chance to test how probability works.

Directions

1. Write the following definition on the board:

   Probability of event = *P*(event) = $\frac{\text{Number of Favorable Outcomes}}{\text{Number of Possible Outcomes}}$

2. Discuss the definition of probability with the class. Talk about the terms *event, experiment,* and *outcome.* In probability, an *experiment* is a trial, such as flipping a coin. The *outcome* is the result.
3. In the experiment of flipping a coin, one outcome is heads. Ask: *What is the probability of getting heads?* The answer is:

   $P(\text{heads}) = \frac{1 \text{ (Number of Favorable Outcomes: heads)}}{2 \text{ (Number of Possible Outcomes: heads or tails)}}$

   Explain that this can be expressed as an equivalent decimal or percent: 0.5, or 50%.
4. Then ask: *If you flip a coin 10 times, how many times would you predict that you would get heads?* [$\frac{1}{2}$ of 10, or 5 times] Direct each group to flip a coin 10 times and record how many times heads comes up.
5. Have students predict how many times they will get heads if they flip the coin 30 times. [$\frac{1}{2}$ of 30, or 15 times] Each group conducts the experiment, flipping the coin and recording the results.
6. Let students repeat the experiment, this time flipping 100 times.
7. Allow time for each group to share their results with the class. What trends do they notice in the results? [Answers will vary; however, the general trend should be that the more times the coin is flipped, the closer the outcome gets to the prediction.]

Taking It Farther

Ask students: *What if you flipped two coins at once? What is the probability of both coins landing on heads?* [$\frac{1}{4}$, or 25%; the possible outcomes for the two coins are: (heads, heads), (heads, tails), (tails, heads), (tails, tails).] Have students repeat the experiments, this time flipping two coins to see if (heads, heads) comes up $\frac{1}{4}$ of the time.

Assessing Skills

To determine if students understand the ratio at work in probability, note whether they are able to convert the fractions from their experiments to the equivalent percents.

LEARNING OBJECTIVE

Students find the probability of a simple event and use an experiment to test their conclusions.

GROUPING

Cooperative groups

MATERIALS

- pencil and paper
- coins

Odds and Evens

Are these games fair or unfair? Students use probability to decide and then play the games to see if they're right.

Directions

1. Remind students that an *event* is the outcome of something that happens. For instance, in rolling a number cube, rolling a specific number is an event. Review the ratio that is used to express the probability of an event:

   $$\text{Probability of event} = P(\text{event}) = \frac{\text{Number of Favorable Outcomes}}{\text{Number of Possible Outcomes}}$$

2. Divide the class into pairs and distribute copies of the reproducible.
3. Partners work together to complete the table in the reproducible, answer the questions, and then test their answers by playing the game. The table may be completed by the entire class if students are unsure of how to complete it on their own.
4. Have pairs play the game again, but instead of adding the two numbers, they multiply. Compare the results of the two games. The outcomes are the same. Tailor questions 2a–6 on the worksheet to fit the new game. [**2a.** 27 **b.** $\frac{27}{36}$, or $\frac{3}{4}$, or 75% **3a.** 9 **b.** $\frac{9}{36}$, or $\frac{1}{4}$, or 25%. 4–**6.** Answers will vary. The game is unfair because there are many more ways to get an even number than to get an odd number.]

LEARNING OBJECTIVE

Students find the probability of simple events and experiment to test their conclusions.

GROUPING

Pairs

MATERIALS

For each pair:

- *Odds and Evens* reproducible (p. 184)
- 2 number cubes
- pencil and scrap paper

Taking It Further

Ask students to make up games or think of existing games where the probability of winning can be calculated. For example, suppose you must pick an ace from a deck of cards. The probability is $\frac{4}{52}$, or $\frac{1}{13}$. Have them test each game many times to see if the predicted probability works. (Note: In the case of picking from a deck of cards, the card must be returned to the deck before the next card is picked to keep the same probability of picking an ace.)

Assessing Skills

Observe whether students understand the importance of the order of the number cubes. For example, throwing (3, 4) is a separate outcome from (4, 3). Thus, there are two ways to throw a combination of a 3 and a 4.

Name ________________ Date ________________

Odds and Evens

What are your chances of winning this game?
Probability will help you find out!

Toss two number cubes 25 times. Each time the two numbers add up to an even number, Player 1 gets one point. Each time they add up to an odd number, Player 2 gets one point. Whoever has more points after 25 tosses wins.

BEFORE YOU PLAY:

1. List the possible outcomes for each toss in the table.

1,1	2,1		4,1	5,1	
1,2	2,2		4,2		6,2
1,3		3,3		5,3	
1,4	2,4			5,4	
1,5		3,5			
1,6	2,6		4,6		6,6

2a. How many of the outcomes in the table add up to an even number? ________________

2b. For each toss, what is the probability of getting an even number? ________________

3a. How many of the outcomes in the table add up to an odd number? ________________

3b. For each toss, what is the probability of getting an odd number? ________________

AFTER YOU PLAY:

4. How many tosses added up to an even number? ________________

5. How many tosses added up to an odd number? ________________

6. Play the game two more times. Record your results on a separate piece of paper. Do you think the game is fair? Explain why or why not.

____

____

____

Probability at Play

Students learn how probability is used in their favorite video games and practice writing probability as a fraction, decimal, and percent.

Directions

1. Duplicate the reproducible for each student.
2. Review with students the process for converting a fraction to a decimal and a percent. Give a few examples of fractions and have volunteers give the equivalent decimals and percents. Use an example such as $\frac{5}{8} = \frac{62.5}{100} = 63\%$ so students can become familiar with rounding percents.
3. Discuss reasons why it might be convenient to look at probability as a decimal or a percent, rather than as a fraction. For example, it may be easier to compare probabilities when they are written as percents rather than as fractions with different denominators.
4. Distribute the reproducible and let students complete it on their own. You may want to let them use calculators.

Taking It Farther

Ask students to look for other everyday areas in which probability is used, such as weather prediction. They may do research and then present their findings to the class.

Assessing Skills

Observe whether students can successfully convert fractions to decimals and percents, and whether they use mental estimation to determine if their answers make sense. Some students, for example, may write $\frac{1}{2}$ as 2% or as 0.5%.

LEARNING OBJECTIVE

Students write probability as a fraction, decimal, and percent.

GROUPING

Individual

MATERIALS

- *Probability at Play* reproducible (p. 186)
- calculators (optional)

Name ______________________ Date ______________

Probability at Play

Flip on your favorite video game, and chances are you're also turning on a game of probability! Game designers program random chance into their games to keep them interesting. That way, you'll never know exactly how many bad guys you'll have to battle, or just where that secret power source is hidden.

To help Luis get a high score in the video game below, use your math smarts to find the equivalent probability at each fork in the maze. Turn down the path of the correct probability to reach FINISH.

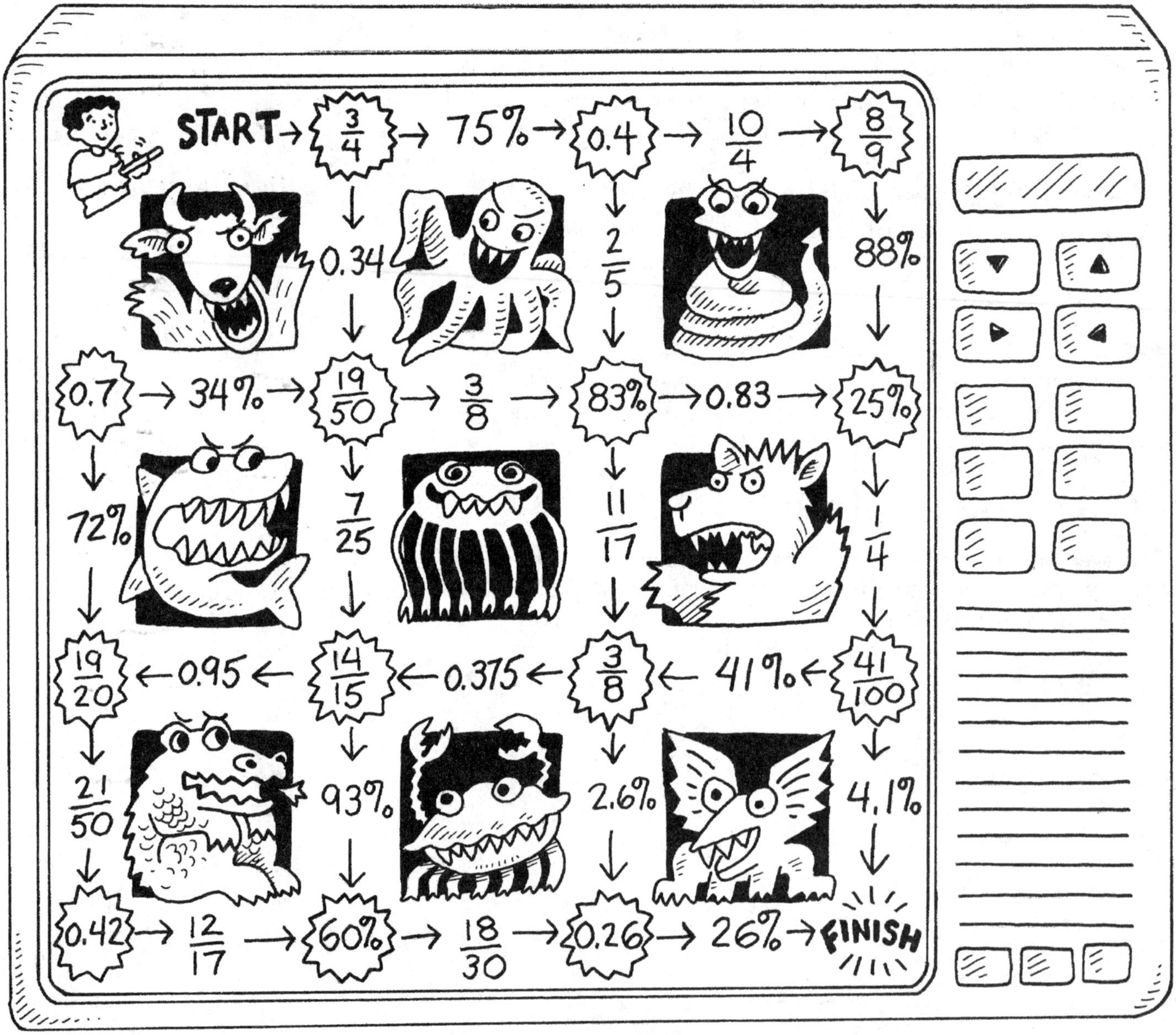

START → $\frac{3}{4}$ → 75% → 0.4 → $\frac{10}{4}$ → $\frac{8}{9}$

↓ 0.34 ↓   ↓ $\frac{2}{5}$ ↓   ↓ 88% ↓

0.7 → 34% → $\frac{19}{50}$ → $\frac{3}{8}$ → 83% → 0.83 → 25%

↓ 72% ↓   ↓ $\frac{7}{25}$ ↓   ↓ $\frac{11}{17}$ ↓   ↓ $\frac{1}{4}$ ↓

$\frac{19}{20}$ ← 0.95 ← $\frac{14}{15}$ ← 0.375 ← $\frac{3}{8}$ ← 41% ← $\frac{41}{100}$

↓ $\frac{21}{50}$ ↓   ↓ 93% ↓   ↓ 2.6% ↓   ↓ 4.1% ↓

0.42 → $\frac{12}{17}$ → 60% → $\frac{18}{30}$ → 0.26 → 26% → FINISH

Go for a Spin

Vrooom! Students practice finding the probability of a simple event as they motor around the track in a sports car board game.

Directions

1. Review the formula for finding the probability of an outcome:

   Probability of event = $P(\text{event}) = \dfrac{\text{Number of Favorable Outcomes}}{\text{Number of Possible Outcomes}}$

2. If necessary, go over an example such as the following with the class:

   There are 5 slices of pizza in a box—2 pepperoni, 1 mushroom, and 2 eggplant. If you reach into the box without looking and take a slice, what is the probability you will get a pepperoni slice? [$\frac{2}{5}$]

3. Divide the class into groups of 3 or 4 and distribute one copy of the reproducible to each group.

4. Explain the rules of the game on the reproducible. Each student cuts out and colors a game marker from the reproducible. To play, students begin at the Start square. Each space tells which letter or pattern is needed to move ahead. At each turn, a player must decide which of the two spinners available provides the greater probability of landing on the desired outcome. First, the player writes each probability as a fraction. Then, the player compares the probability for Spinner A versus Spinner B, using scrap paper if necessary. Finally, the player spins, using the spinner that provides the greater probability. The first player to cross the finish line wins.

LEARNING OBJECTIVE

Students find the probability of a simple event and write it as a fraction.

GROUPING

Cooperative groups

MATERIALS

For each group:

* *Go for a Spin* reproducible (p. 188)
* scissors
* colored markers or pencils
* paper
* pencil and paper clip (to make the spinner)

Taking It Further

Have students use colored markers to draw their own spinners, filling in the sections with different patterns and colors. Divide students into pairs, and have each partner write the probability (in fraction form) of spinning a specific pattern or color on his or her partner's spinner. Students may then experiment by spinning the spinner 10 or 25 times, recording the outcomes, and writing a fraction to show how many times the desired outcome occurred. Students then compare the probability fraction and the outcome fraction.

Assessing Skills

Note whether students are able to compare the values of two fractions with different denominators. You may review this skill by showing how to rewrite fractions with common denominators. Manipulatives and fractional diagrams can also help reinforce this skill.

Name ______________________ Date ______________

Go for a Spin

Rev up your probability skills as you race around the track below. Cut out the sports car game pieces and get ready to start your engines!

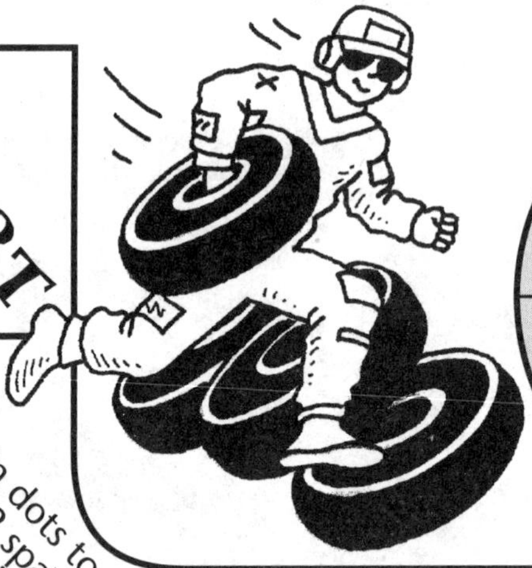

Spinner A — Z, R, R, X, X, R, Z, R

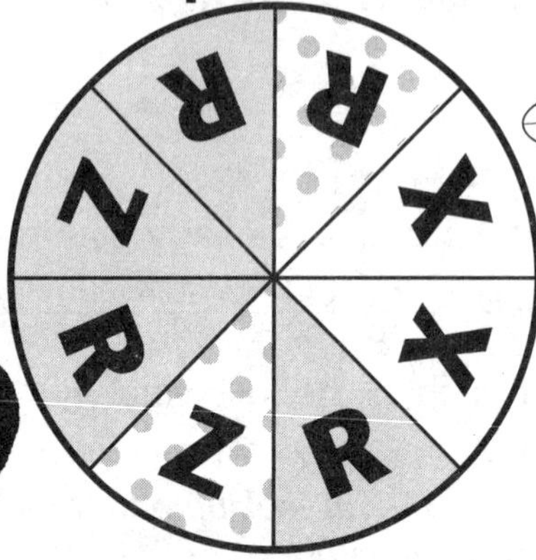

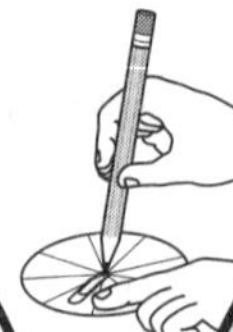

Spinner B — X, R, R, X, Z

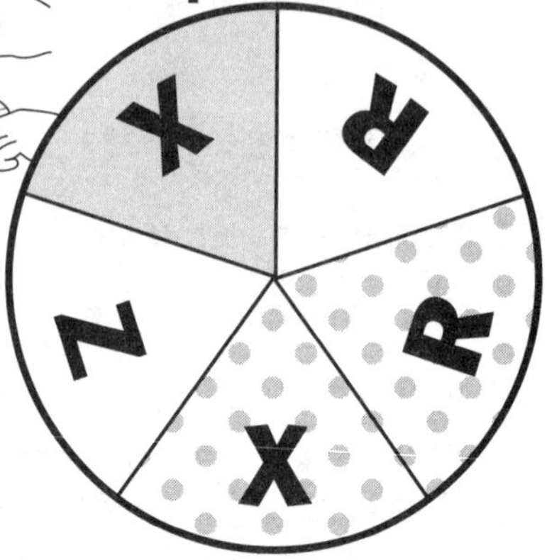

START

Spin dots to move ahead 2 spaces. If you spin white or gray, move ahead 1.

Spin gray to move ahead 3. Otherwise, stay put.

Flat tire! Spin an X to zip ahead 2 spaces and get a new tire. If you spin another letter, roll ahead 1.

Full tank of gas! Spin Z and race ahead 3. Otherwise, go back 2 spaces to avoid a crash.

Put your pedal to the metal, spin dots, and move up 3 spaces. Otherwise, move up 1.

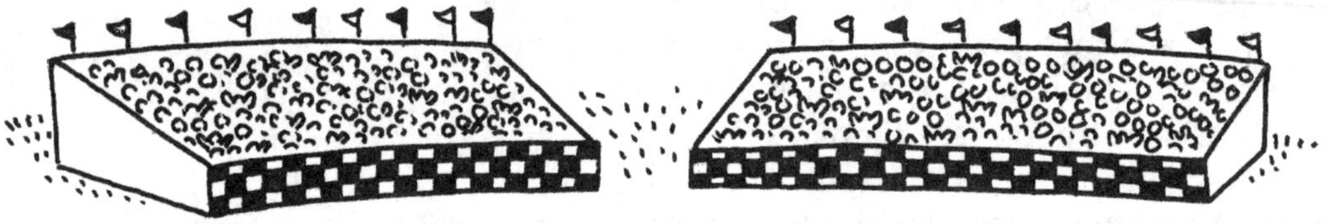

Full tank of gas! Turbo boost! Spin gray to blast up 4 spaces. Otherwise, stay put.

Spin white to move ahead 2. If not, go back 1.

Flat tire! Spin an X to pit stop! Spin an R to gas up and move ahead 4 spaces. If you spin Z, go back 2.

Move ahead 3 spaces if you spin dots. Otherwise, fall back 1.

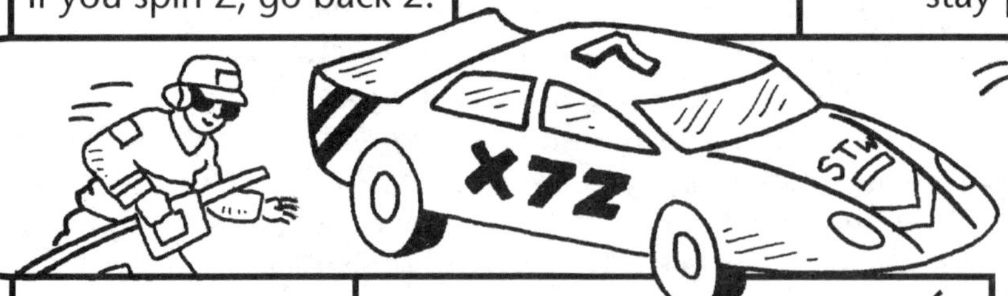

Spin X to zip ahead 2. If you spin another letter, move up 1.

Spin R to race ahead 1. If not, go back 2.

Home stretch! Spin gray to cross the finish line. Otherwise, wait here.

FINISH

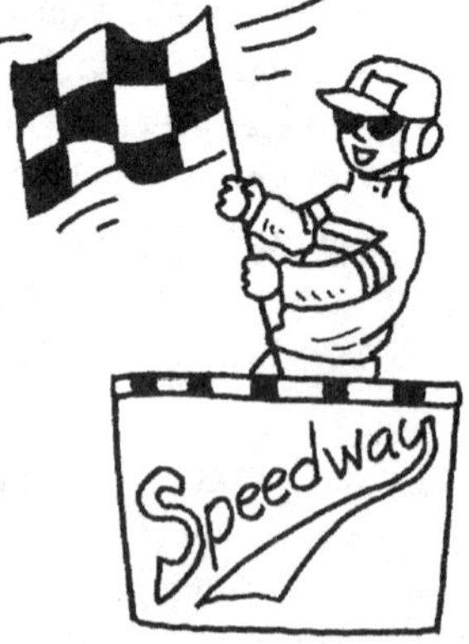

Speedway

GAME PIECES

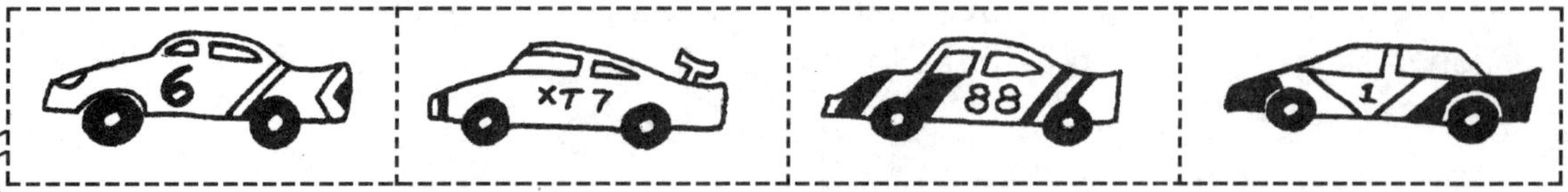

Sweet Experiments

Probability—how sweet it is! Students use tasty candy manipulatives to compare theoretical and experimental probability.

Directions

1. Distribute one paper bag to each pair or group of students, along with a handful of small, different-colored candies.
2. Have students place several candies in the bag. There should be at least three colors represented, but they may use different numbers of candies for each color; for example, students may choose 5 green, 2 yellow, and 3 red candies.
3. Then they write down the probability of randomly picking each color from the bag, writing the probability as a fraction, decimal, and percent. In this case, the probability of picking green is $\frac{1}{2}$, or 0.5, or 50%.
4. One student holds the bag while another student reaches in without looking, picks out a candy, notes the color, and returns it to the bag. Students repeat this process over and over, keeping a tally of how many times each color is chosen. After 50 trials, students may use their tallies to figure out what fraction of the time each color was chosen, then write this experimental probability as a decimal and percent as well. (Students can round decimals to the nearest hundredth and percents to the nearest whole number.)
5. After comparing the theoretical and experimental probability, have students continue the process of picking candy until they have tallied 100 trials. They again compare the theoretical and experimental probabilities, and share results with the class.

LEARNING OBJECTIVE

Students do hands-on experiments and write probability as a fraction, decimal, and percent.

GROUPING

Pairs or cooperative groups

MATERIALS

For each pair or group:

* class-size bag of small, different-colored candies (Substitute another manipulative, if necessary.)
* small paper bags
* paper and pencil

Taking It Further

Repeat the experiment with odd numbers of candies (such as 9 or 11) so that students can practice working with more difficult fractions.

Assessing Skills

Ask students: *When might it be an advantage to look at probability as a decimal or a percent?* [One possible answer: When you want to compare probabilities at a glance; for example, comparing a probability of $\frac{7}{9}$ and $\frac{24}{29}$ is more difficult than comparing the equivalent probabilities 78% and 83%.]

Take a Sample

Students take a sample of sample space.

Directions

1. The *sample space* is the set of all possible outcomes for an experiment. In the case of flipping a coin, the sample space is heads, tails.Tell students that an *event* is always a subset of the sample space. For example, if they roll a number cube and want to roll a number greater than 3, the event is 4, 5, 6. The sample space is 1, 2, 3, 4, 5, 6. The ratio is:

$$P(\text{number} > 3) = \frac{3}{6} \quad \frac{(4, 5, 6)}{(1, 2, 3, 4, 5, 6)}$$

2. Take out your props and call on students to describe the sample space for tossing a number cube, picking a number from the bag, ordering a lunch or dinner entree at a restaurant, and sports teams playing against each other.
3. Then let students use the yellow pages to look up various listings such as "Locksmith." Ask: *What would be the sample space for calling a locksmith from the phone book?*
4. Finally, have students describe the sample space of all the math classes they might be assigned to next year (for example, Ms. Smith's class, Mr. Jones's class, and Mrs. Garcia's class).

Taking It Farther

Challenge students to choose a career such as astronaut or doctor and do research to find experiments that might occur while performing that job. They should do research to write a sample space for each experiment.

Assessing Skills

Do students understand the difference among event, outcome, and sample space? To help visual learners, have them act out an experiment such as picking a number from the bag. Ask them to identify the event, outcome, and sample space.

LEARNING OBJECTIVE

Students are introduced to the concept of sample space.

GROUPING

Whole class

MATERIALS

- coin
- number cube
- paper bag containing strips of paper numbered from 1 to 10
- one or more of the following: takeout menus from local restaurants (lunch and dinner menus, if possible), the sports section of a newspaper, a telephone book yellow pages, a list of math teachers in your school for the grade following that of your class

Lost in Sample Space

Students begin to see probability all around them as they find the sample space for occurrences in their everyday lives.

Directions

1. Duplicate the reproducible for each student.
2. Review the terms *experiment, outcome,* and *sample space.* Ask students to name some experiments in their daily lives and some possible outcomes. Start them off with the example of dialing a phone number. They may hear a ring, a busy signal, or an answering machine message, or someone may answer the phone. With students' directions, make complete lists describing the sample space for each experiment.
3. If necessary, review a few examples of an experiment, an outcome, and a sample space, such as tossing a number cube. The experiment is tossing the cube; the outcome is that the cube turns up 3; the sample space is 1, 2, 3, 4, 5, 6.
4. Distribute the reproducible. You can call on volunteers to read the story at the top of the page out loud. Or have students silently read the story to themselves.
5. Let students complete the reproducible on their own. If they experience trouble, complete the first question as a class.

LEARNING OBJECTIVE

Students practice applying the concept of sample space.

GROUPING

Individual

MATERIALS

* *Lost in Sample Space* reproducible (p. 192)
* paper and pencils
* number cube (optional)

Taking It Further

Ask students to write their own short stories that involve various experiments. The stories may be about whatever students choose, or you may ask them to write stories about real or fictional trips. Classmates may read each other's stories and write out the sample space for each experiment in the stories they read.

Assessing Skills

Watch for students who write an incomplete list of possible outcomes to describe the sample space.

 Name ______________________ Date ______________

Lost in Sample Space

Astronaut Andrea's space ship is malfunctioning! She's adrift somewhere in our solar system. Before she makes it back to Earth, she must deal with some weird random events on her ship.

Read about one of Andrea's days in space. Then answer the questions about sample space on a separate sheet of paper.

BRRRRRIIING! Andrea awoke with a start as her space alarm went off at 2:00 A.M., Eastern Standard Time. Oh, well, she thought, slapping down the snooze button. At least it was morning. She never knew what time the alarm would go off—just that it would be exactly on the hour, like 7:00 or 8:00. Yesterday, the alarm didn't go off until 5:00 P.M., and she missed the whole day!

Andrea floated over to the food console and pushed a button marked "breakfast." She wasn't too surprised when pork chops appeared. Ever since the ship started malfunctioning, breakfast had been a random selection of macaroni and cheese, pork chops, or cotton candy. Andrea sighed and wished for a banana muffin.

Cheering up, Andrea prepared for the best part of her day. Every afternoon, the ship would choose one of the 8 planets in the solar system and come in for a landing. Would today be Earth? The ship drew closer and closer . . . and shot off toward Mars. Arggh!

When she reached Mars, Andrea decided to pick up some rock samples for scientific research. She sent the ship's robot out to pick up 5 rocks. Unfortunately, the robot decided to bring any number of rocks that was a *multiple* of 5. Later, as Andrea tried to squeeze past the 85 rocks in her living quarters, she thanked her lucky stars that the machine couldn't carry more than 100 rocks. Falling asleep on a large boulder, Andrea decided to give up on her research until she got a better spaceship.

1. Experiment: The ship's alarm clock randomly picks a time to ring.
   a. What was the outcome for this experiment in the story?
   b. What is the sample space for this experiment?

2. Experiment: Andrea orders breakfast.
   a. What was the outcome for this experiment in the story?
   b. What is the sample space for this experiment?

3. Sample space: Mercury, Venus, Earth, Mars, Jupiter, Saturn, Uranus, Neptune
   a. What was the experiment for this sample space in the story?
   b. What was the outcome in the story?

4. Outcome: 85
   a. What was the experiment for this outcome in the story?
   b. What is the sample space for this outcome?

Clothes Combos

How many outfits can students make from a pile of clothes? With tree diagrams, they'll always dress for success!

Directions

1. Duplicate the reproducible for each student.
2. At the start of class, bring out your items of clothing. Make sure the different types of items are all mixed together. Ask volunteers to come up and make as many different outfits as possible using one hat, one shirt, and one pair of pants for each outfit. Choose another volunteer to record all the different outfits on the board.
3. When students are confident they have come up with every possibility, distribute the reproducible. Let students complete it on their own.
4. After students have finished, have them compare answers.
5. Ask volunteers to draw tree diagrams on the board showing how many outfits can be made with the items of clothing they looked at earlier. Students may draw each item or describe it in words. When the volunteers are finished, determine whether they have come up with the same number of outfits as before.
6. Ask students to describe the benefits of using a tree diagram versus making a list. In this case, a tree diagram makes it easier to keep track of every possible outcome, and every outcome is clearly shown in order.

LEARNING OBJECTIVE

Students draw tree diagrams to count possible outcomes.

GROUPING

Whole class/Individual

MATERIALS

- *Clothes Combos* reproducible (p. 194)
- a number of different items of clothing: hats, shirts, and pants, for example (These may be funny/silly items if you want.)

Taking It Farther

Repeat the activity several times using new groups of clothes. You may also ask students to make a list of several of their favorite clothing items and draw tree diagrams to count how many outfits they can make.

Assessing Skills

Observe whether students are able to correctly describe all the outcomes from their tree diagrams. If they are having difficulty, try having them trace the "limbs" of a tree diagram with their finger. For example, they may start at "green hat," and follow the branch to "yellow shirt" and then "blue pants."

Name ______________________ Date ______________

Clothes Combos

How many combinations can you make with your favorite clothes? A tree diagram can show you. For example, Doug has one baseball cap, three shirts, and two pairs of pants. If he chooses one hat, one shirt and one pair of pants for each outfit, how many outfits can he make?

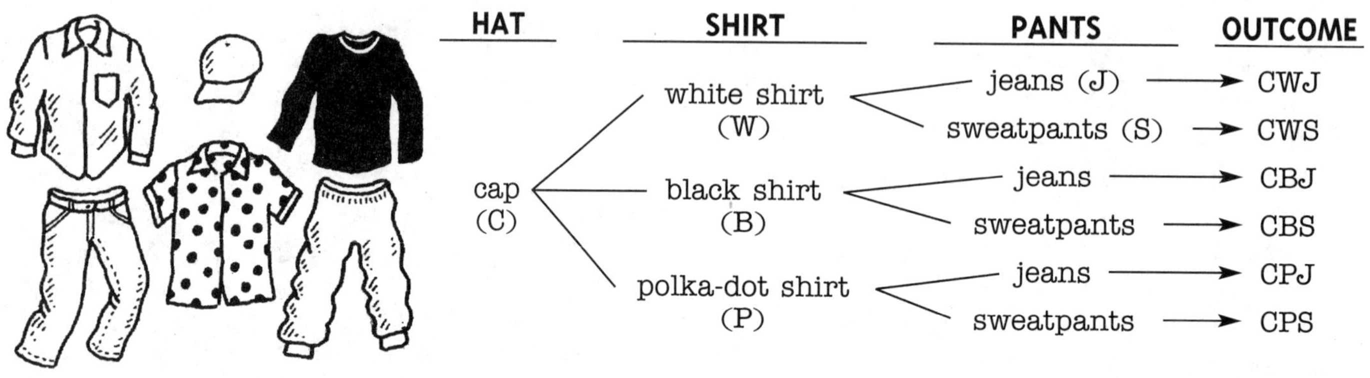

1. How many of Doug's outfits include a baseball cap? ______________
2. How many outfits include a white shirt? ______________
3. How many outfits include jeans? ______________

Fill in this tree diagram to find out which different outfits Stella can make with *her* clothes. She can pick one shirt, one skirt, and one pair of shoes for each outfit. Here's what she's got: polka-dot shirt, striped shirt, long skirt, short skirt, sneakers, and sandals.

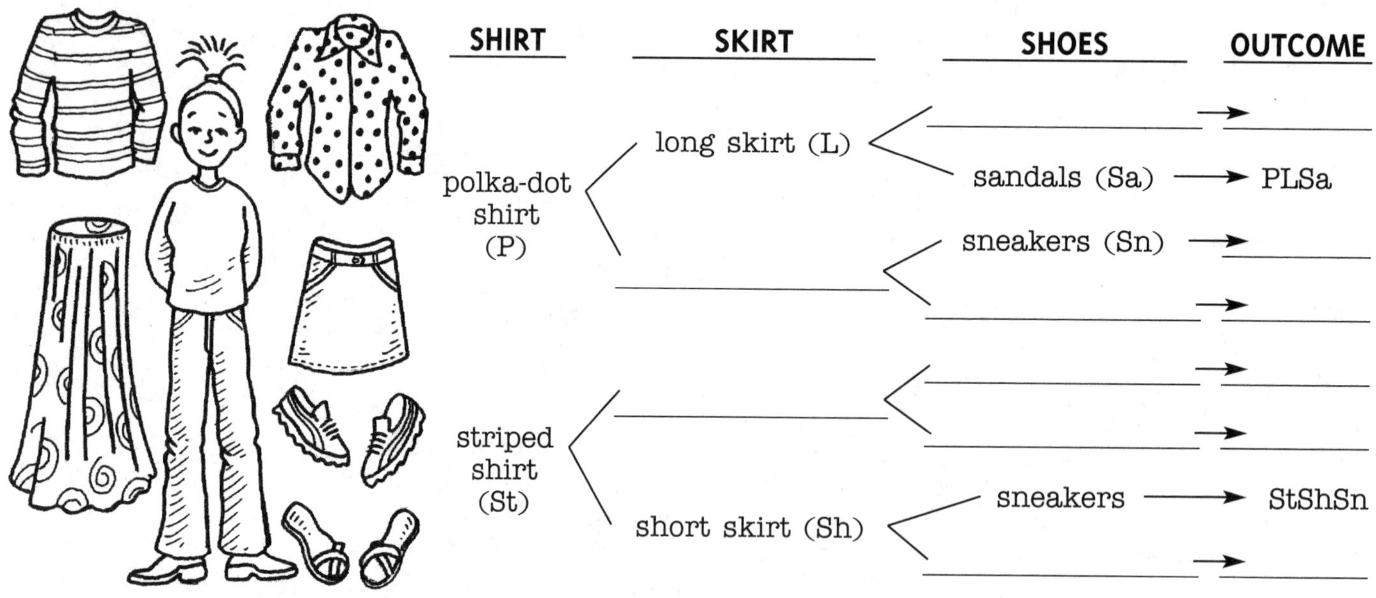

4. How many of Stella's outfits include a striped shirt? ______________
5. How many outfits include a long skirt? ______________
6. How many outfits include sneakers? ______________

Tree-Licious Diagrams

Students use tree diagrams to find funky food combinations in your school cafeteria, a deli, or even an ice cream store.

Directions

1. Review tree diagrams with the class.
2. Using the menus, pick out different food items and have students figure out how many combinations could be created with the options listed. Here are some possible examples:
   - At a pizzeria: If you have 5 toppings to choose from and 3 pizza sizes to choose from, how many different pizzas could you make if each pizza has one topping?
   - At a deli: How many different sandwiches could be made using 1 kind of bread, 3 meats, and 2 cheeses?
   - At the school cafeteria: Find all the possible combinations that contain 1 drink, 1 sandwich or entree, and 1 dessert.
   - At a restaurant: Pick a few appetizers, entrees, beverages, and desserts. How many combinations can be made with these choices?

LEARNING OBJECTIVE

Students draw tree diagrams to count possible combinations of food.

GROUPING

Whole class

MATERIALS

- menus from the school cafeteria, a local deli, ice cream store, pizzeria, or any other food store (You may invent food choices for this activity if menus are not available.)

Taking It Farther

To prepare students to learn the Fundamental Counting Principle, challenge them with the following problem: *You work at an ice cream store that offers 31 flavors of ice cream, 25 kinds of flavored syrup, and 18 different toppings. A customer asks how many different types of sundaes could be made using one kind of ice cream, one syrup, and one topping. Could this problem be solved with a tree diagram?* [yes] *Would this approach be practical?* [Probably not, because the problem would take a long time and would require a *very large* piece of paper.]

Assessing Skills

Note whether students completely draw every section of a tree diagram, especially if there are two choices in the first column.

Count on Sports Schedules

Probability theory makes a touchdown in students' minds as they learn how the Fundamental Counting Principle can help simplify a school's sports schedule.

Directions

1. Start with an example from the WNBA (Women's National Basketball Association). Tell students that in its first season, there were 8 teams in the WNBA. Ask students: *If each team must play one away game at each of the other 7 teams' stadiums, how many games must be played?*
2. Explain that they could use tree diagrams to find out this information, but it would take a long time since there are so many outcomes. Tell students that an easier way is to use the Fundamental Counting Principle. Write the following definition on the board and discuss it with the class:

   Fundamental Counting Principle
   If one choice can be made in x ways, and for each of these choices a following choice can be made in y ways, then the choices can be made in xy ways (that is, x times y ways).
3. In the example above, there are 8 teams, and each team must play at 7 other teams' stadiums. Therefore, there will be 8×7, or 56, games played in all.
4. Students may check the answer by drawing tree diagrams for each team's away games and adding the results. Then use your own school's sports teams for additional examples. For instance, if there are 6 schools in your soccer league, and each soccer team must play an away game at every other school, how many games will be played?

LEARNING OBJECTIVE

Students use the Fundamental Counting Principle to count outcomes.

GROUPING

Whole class

MATERIALS

- sports schedules for different varsity sports in your school or a sports schedule from a professional league
- calculators (optional)

Taking It Further

Challenge students to use the Fundamental Counting Principle to find the following: the total number of possible area codes; the total number of possible 7-digit telephone numbers; the total number of possible car license plates, where each plate has two letters followed by three numbers. (Students may use calculators to do the arithmetic.)

Assessing Skills

Ask students to use the Fundamental Counting Principle to find the number of possible sundaes in Taking It Further on page 195.
[$31 \times 25 \times 18 = 13{,}950$ sundaes]

Pet Peeves

Some wild and woolly manipulatives will help students model and understand the Fundamental Counting Principle.

Directions

1. Duplicate the reproducible for each student and distribute. Direct students to cut along the dotted lines to separate each animal card.
2. Pose the following problem to students: *Wally loves animals. Today he brought home 3 dogs, 2 cats, and 1 cow! But Wally's mom says he can keep only 1 of each type of animal for a pet. How many different ways can Wally choose 1 dog, 1 cat, and 1 cow?*
3. To answer the question, ask students to pick out 3 dog cards, 2 cat cards, and 1 cow card. Have them move around the cards to model the answer to the question. Write down the combinations they discover. Then ask them to sort the cards into one vertical dog column, one cat column, and one cow column.
4. Remind students that to use the Fundamental Counting Principle, they multiply the number of items in each column: $3 \times 2 \times 1 = 6$ possible combinations. This answer should be the same as the number of combinations you wrote on the board.
5. Next, have students turn all their cards facedown. After they mix the cards, ask students to pick out 8 different cards. On separate sheets of paper, students write down which cards they picked and use the Fundamental Counting Principle to figure out how many different combinations could be made that contain one animal from each type picked. For example, of the 8 cards picked, there could be 2 dogs, 3 cats, 1 fish, 2 gerbils. To determine the number of combinations that could be made, multiply $2 \times 3 \times 1 \times 2$ for 12 combinations. Repeat this exercise several times, asking students to pick a different number of cards each time.

Taking It Further

Let students go back and use the Fundamental Counting Principle to check their work for the tree diagram activities on pages 193–195. The outcomes should be the same. Ask students: *Which method of counting outcomes do you prefer? Why?*

Assessing Skills

Ask students: *Say you pick 8 animal cards. If you pick 3 gerbil cards and 5 fish cards, will you have the same number of possible combinations as if you pick 1 gerbil card and 7 fish cards? Why or why not?*

LEARNING OBJECTIVE

Students use manipulatives to model the Fundamental Counting Principle.

GROUPING

Individual

MATERIALS

- *Pet Peeves* reproducible (p. 198)
- paper and pencil
- scissors

Name ______________________ Date ____________

Pet Peeves

Cut out the animal cards.
Group the same types of animals together.

Bowser	Katrina	Jaws	Lance	Gertrude
Dotty	Santa Claws	Bubbles	Harry	Moo-ria
Wags	Snaggles	Rover	Jane	Daisy
Lula	Tiger	Glub-Glub	Nibbles	Henrietta
Rex	Snowball	Fluffy	Farley	Babs

School Daze

Students choose whether to use tree diagrams or the Fundamental Counting Principle to help a girl make choices during her school day.

Directions

1. Duplicate the reproducible for each student and distribute.
2. Review tree diagrams and the Fundamental Counting Principle as necessary.
3. Explain to students that they may use either tree diagrams or the Fundamental Counting Principle to solve each problem on the reproducible. There is no right or wrong method to choose, but students should be aware that tree diagrams may take up a lot of space and time where many choices are involved.
4. Allow students to complete the reproducible on their own. Remind them to answer the questions and show their solutions on separate sheets of paper.
5. Have students share their answers with the class and explain why they chose each method to solve the problems.

Taking It Further

Encourage students to write their own problems based on choices they make during their school day. The problems can be based on real choices, or students may invent situations.

Assessing Skills

Observe students who choose to use just one method (tree diagrams or the Fundamental Counting Principle) to solve the problems. To determine whether they understand how to use the other method, suggest that they check a few of the answers using the other method.

LEARNING OBJECTIVE

Students compare the merits of using tree diagrams and the Fundamental Counting Principle to count outcomes.

GROUPING

Individual

MATERIALS

- *School Daze* reproducible (p. 200)
- paper and pencil

Name ______________________ Date ______________

School Daze

Wendy always likes to make an informed decision. But she has many choices as she goes through her school day.

Help Wendy decide by drawing a tree diagram or using the Fundamental Counting Principle. Choose whichever method you like!

1. Wendy plans to travel to school with her friend Jennifer. First, Wendy needs to get to Jennifer's house. To get there, she can ride her bike, in-line skate, or walk. From there, the girls can get to school by taking the bus, getting a ride in Jennifer's dad's car, or riding on Jennifer's scooter.

   a. How many different ways can Wendy get to school in all?

   ____

   b. Which method did you use to solve this problem? Why?

   ____

   ____

   ____

   c. Show your solution on a separate sheet of paper.

2. Lunchtime! Wendy eats a sandwich in the cafeteria and decides to go to the ice cream parlor across the street. Wendy has 7 favorite ice cream flavors: chocolate, strawberry, cookies 'n' cream, vanilla, mint, peanut butter swirl, and peach.

   a. If Wendy gets a triple-scoop cone, how many combinations can she make using her favorite flavors?

   ____

   b. Which method did you use to solve this problem? Why?

   ____

   ____

   ____

   c. Show your solution on a separate sheet of paper.

Gold, Silver, Bronze

How many different ways can athletes place in races or other competitions? Students find out by working with permutations!

Directions

1. Go over the concept of permutation with the class. A *permutation* is an arrangement or list of choices in a particular order. (In combinations, which can be found with tree diagrams or the Fundamental Counting Principle, order is not important.)
2. Pose this problem to the class: *There are 4 runners in a race. How many different ways can the runners place first, second, and third?*
3. Explain that to answer this question, you would write the following permutation problem: $P(4, 3)$. This means that you are finding the permutation of 4 things (in this case, runners) taken 3 at a time (in this case, first, second, and third place).

   To find the answer, you multiply as follows: $4 \times 3 \times 2$. Any of 4 runners may get first place; any of the remaining 3 runners may get second place (because 1 runner has already won first place), and any of the remaining 2 runners may get third place (because 2 runners have already won first and second place).

   Therefore, there are 24 ways for the runners to place first, second, and third. Point out to students that the number of choices decreases by 1 each time.
4. Now have students use the lists of athletes to write and solve more permutation problems. For example, if there are 10 figure skaters in the Olympics, how many ways can they win the gold, silver, and bronze medals? [$P(10, 3)$; $10 \times 9 \times 8 = 720$]

LEARNING OBJECTIVE

Students are introduced to permutations and use this concept to solve problems.

GROUPING

Whole class

MATERIALS

* scrap paper and pencil

ADVANCE PREPARATION

Compile lists of athletes who compete in popular sporting events such as the Olympics or tennis or golf tournaments. Otherwise, fictional athletes may be used.

Taking It Further

Challenge students to use the lists of athletes to find the total number of ways athletes could place in a competition. For example, to find out how many different ways 10 skaters could place in the Olympics, you would solve the problem $P(10, 10)$. The symbol 10! can also be used to express this problem. The notation 10! is read "ten factorial." It means $10 \bullet 9 \bullet 8 \bullet 7 \bullet 6 \bullet 5 \bullet 4 \bullet 3 \bullet 2 \bullet 1$.

Assessing Skills

To see whether students understand permutations, have them use manipulatives (such as scraps of paper with athletes' names) to model problems. For instance, ask: *How many ways can 3 runners place first and second in a race?* [$P(3, 2) = 3 \times 2 = 6$]

Career Day Conundrums

Students get up close and personal with permutations as they figure out how many career presentations can be seen at Mathville Middle School's Career Day.

Directions

1. Duplicate the reproducible for each student and distribute.
2. Review permutations with the class if necessary. Here is an example you can use: *A radio disc jockey (DJ) wants to pick 3 songs from a list of 5 songs to play on the air. He doesn't want to repeat any songs. How many ways can he play 3 songs from the list?*
3. The problem would be written as follows: $P(5, 3)$. In other words, you are finding the permutation of 5 things taken 3 at a time. For the first song, the DJ has 5 choices. For the second song, he has 4 choices, since he has played 1 song from the list already. For the third song, he has 3 choices, since he has played 2 songs from the list already. So to find the answer, you would multiply 5 • 4 • 3. There are 60 ways the DJ could play 3 songs from the list.
4. Let students complete the problems on their own. When students are finished, you may want to have them work in pairs to check and discuss their answers.

LEARNING OBJECTIVE

Students practice using permutations to find arrangements where order is important.

GROUPING

Individual

MATERIALS

- *Career Day Conundrums* reproducible (p. 203)
- pencil and scrap paper

Taking It Further

Have students use their own class schedule to find the number of permutations of ways they could take their classes. For instance, if there are 8 class periods in a day, and they take 7 classes, how many different ways could they arrange their schedules? Tell students to assume that they can take any class at any time of day.

Assessing Skills

Note whether students understand how many numbers to multiply to find the correct permutation. For example, in trying to find the number of ways to play 3 songs from a 5-song list, some students may multiply 5 • 4 • 3 • 2 • 1. This would be incorrect, since the DJ wants to play only 3 songs at a time.

Name ______________________ Date ______________

Career Day Conundrums

It's Career Day at Mathville Middle School! Kids at the school will participate in workshops about many exciting jobs. Unfortunately, they can't attend every workshop. Help the students find out how many ways they can choose to attend different career workshops.

Use the tables and your knowledge of permutations to answer the questions. Remember, none of the students wants to attend the same workshop more than once.

Table One: CAREER DAY WORKSHOPS	
Firefighter	Interior Decorator
Engineer	Politician
Doctor	Lifeguard
Hotel Manager	Telephone Repairer
Journalist	Photographer

Table Two: WORKSHOP TIMES
All presentations are offered at each time listed.
9:30 A.M.
10:30 A.M.
1:30 P.M.
2:30 P.M.

1. Victor is interested in the following workshops: Politician, Journalist, Engineer, Doctor, and Hotel Manager. If he attends one workshop at each of the four times they are offered, how many different ways can he arrange his schedule?

   a. Write this as a permutation problem.

   ____

   b. How many ways can Victor arrange his schedule?

   ____

2. Lydia is interested in all of the workshops, but she is available to attend workshops only in the morning. How many ways can she arrange her schedule?

   a. Write this as a permutation problem.

   ____

   b. How many ways can Lydia arrange her schedule?

   ____

3. Alex has chosen 4 workshops: Lifeguard, Firefighter, Photographer, and Engineer.

   a. If Alex is available for all 4 workshop times, how many ways can he arrange his schedule?

   ____

   b. If he is available at only 3 of the times, how many ways can Alex arrange his schedule?

   ____

4. a. Which of the workshops interest you?

   ____

   b. If you could attend all 4 workshop times, how many ways could you arrange your schedule?

   ____

   c. Suppose you could attend only afternoon workshops. How many ways could you arrange your schedule?

   ____

Turnover Turns

Fractions and an area model will help students understand the twists and turns in these pastry probability problems.

Directions

1. Duplicate and distribute the reproducible. To familiarize students with how to use an area model, go over the first problem with the class. You may want to draw the maze and the area model on the board so that you can refer to it during the class discussion.
2. Start by tracing each path from the left. Ask students:
   - *At the first fork in the path, what is the probability that Terence will choose each path?* [$\frac{1}{3}$]
   - *When the upper path divides into two more paths, what is the probability for each of these new paths?* [half the probability of the previous path, or $\frac{1}{6}$ each]
3. Ask a volunteer to color in the fractions in the area model, using a different color for each destination. This shows even more clearly how the fractions represent the destinations.
4. Have students add the fractions to find the probability that Terence will end up at each destination on the maze. Write in the answers to questions 1 and 2.
5. Divide the class into cooperative groups and have them draw area models to answer the remaining questions, using crayons or colored pencils to color in their models.

LEARNING OBJECTIVE

Students use fractions and area models to understand the probability of compound events.

GROUPING

Cooperative groups

MATERIALS

- *Turnover Turns* reproducible (p. 205)
- crayons or colored pencils

Taking It Further

When the groups have completed the reproducibles, challenge them to draw their own mazes on separate paper. Then, groups switch mazes and draw area models to find the probabilities of randomly choosing each path and of ending up at each finishing location. Students may invent funny or interesting scenarios to go along with their problems.

Assessing Skills

Some students may try to calculate the probability of reaching each destination by counting the number of path endings that reach that destination. Point out that this approach will not work, since the probability of reaching a path ending depends on how many times the path has forked along the way.

Name ______________________________ Date ______________

Turnover Turns

Every Tuesday, Terence delivers his tasty turnovers. Today's deliveries will take him through some long, winding forest roads to Carla's Campground. Unfortunately, Terence lost the directions to the campground! If he just guesses which way to turn at each fork in the road, what is the probability he will wind up in the right place?

Use the area model to help you find out!

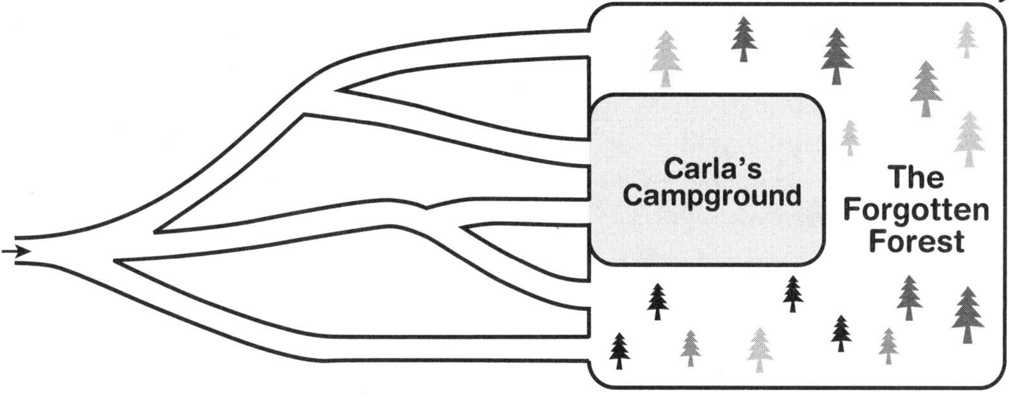

Upper Path	Forest
	Carla's
Middle Path	Forest
	Carla's
Lower Path	Forest

Area Model of MAZE 1

MAZE 1: Terence needs to get to Carla's Campground.

1. What is the probability Terence will end up at Carla's Campground if he randomly chooses which way to turn at each path? ______________

2. What is the probability he will wind up in the Forgotten Forest? ______________

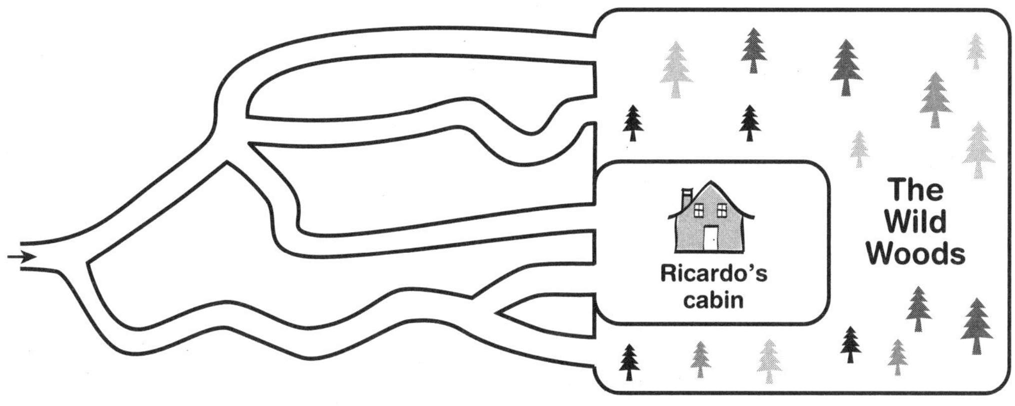

MAZE 2: Terence needs to get to Ricardo's cabin.

3. If he randomly chooses which paths to turn down, what is the probability Terence will make it to the cabin? ______________

4. What is the probability he will end up in the Wild Woods? ______________

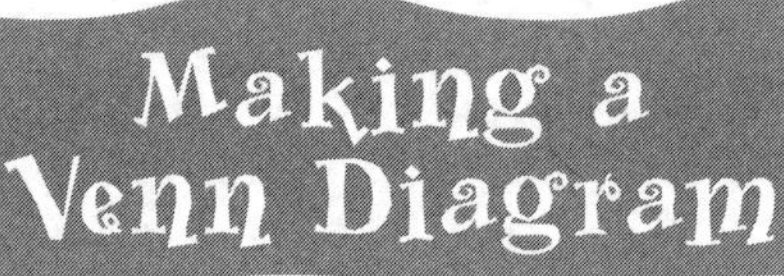

Join the Club

When looking at a group of kids and their extracurricular activities, Venn diagrams make visualizing probability extra clear.

Directions

1. Distribute a copy of the reproducible to each student. Start by reviewing Venn diagrams. If necessary, go over the first problem with the class. Before you answer the questions, ask volunteers to point out the total number of students in each activity, the number of students in more than one activity, and so on, to reinforce an understanding of how Venn diagrams work.
2. Let students complete the rest of the reproducible on their own, drawing Venn diagrams on separate paper for each problem.

Taking It Further

Have your class survey a large group of students in your school. They can ask several questions, such as what extracurricular activities each person participates in, favorite cafeteria lunches, and so on. Students can then draw Venn diagrams based on their research and use the diagrams to make probability statements about the student body; for example, "If I picked a student at random, the probability that pizza is that person's favorite lunch would be 20 percent."

Assessing Skills

Note whether students check their Venn diagrams by adding up all the numbers in each circle to make sure the sum equals the total number of students in that club.

LEARNING OBJECTIVE

Students draw Venn diagrams to find probabilities.

GROUPING

Individual

MATERIALS

- *Join the Club* reproducible (p. 207)
- pencil and paper

Name ______________________ Date ____________

Join the Club

The kids at A.K. Tivitee Junior High love after-school clubs. Which clubs are they most likely to join? Check out some Venn diagrams to get a closer look.

1. In one group of 100 students, there are lots of members of the Harmonica Club and the Tiddleywinks Society. Some students even belong to both clubs!

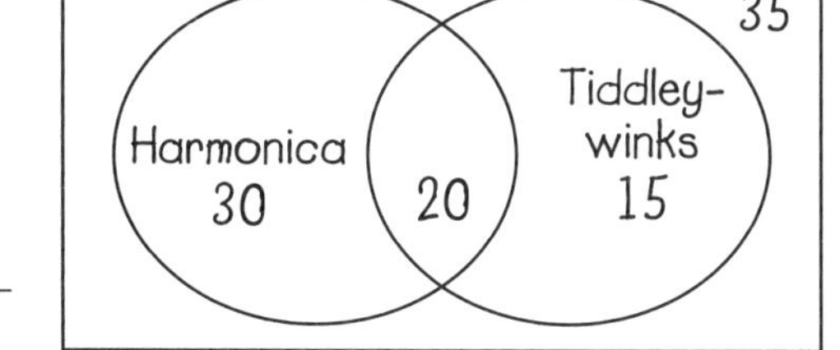

   a. According to the Venn diagram, how many students are in the Tiddleywinks Society? ________

   b. How many students are in both clubs? ________

   c. How many students are not members of either club? ________

   d. If you pick one of the 100 students randomly, what is the probability that he or she is a member of the Harmonica Club? ________

   e. What is the probability that the student is a member of both clubs? ________

   f. What is the probability that the student isn't in either club? ________

2. It was discovered that many of the same students also play on the varsity Foosball team. Many students enjoy Cheese Sculpture Classes as well.

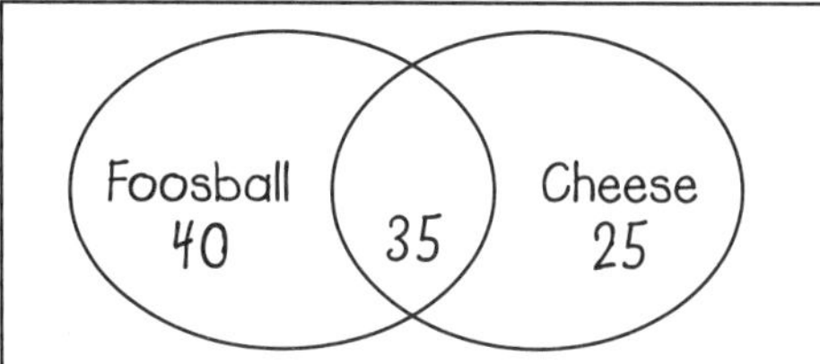

   a. How many students play foosball? ________

   b. If you pick a student at random, what is the probability that he or she takes cheese sculpture classes? ________

   c. What is the probability that you will pick a student who takes cheese sculpture classes but does not play foosball? ________

   d. What is the probability that you will pick a student who plays foosball or takes cheese sculpture classes but does not do both activities? ________

   e. What is the probability you will pick a student who doesn't participate in either foosball or cheese sculpture? ________

Stamp to It!

How many different ways could you tear off four attached stamps from a sheet? Don't look to your mail carrier for the answer—make a model!

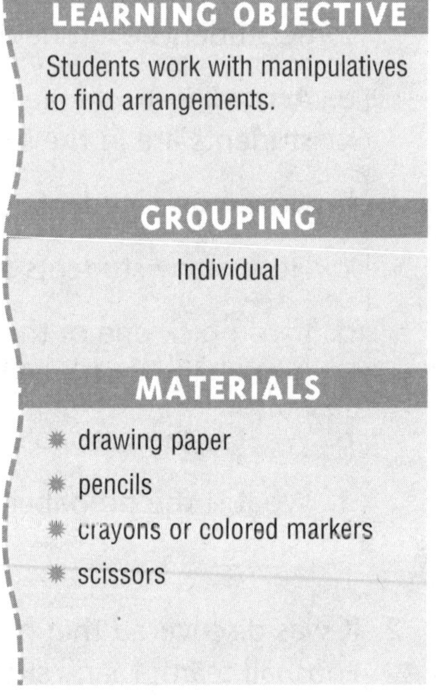
LEARNING OBJECTIVE

Students work with manipulatives to find arrangements.

GROUPING

Individual

MATERIALS

- drawing paper
- pencils
- crayons or colored markers
- scissors

Directions

1. Have students cut out four paper squares of identical size so they can be arranged in groups of four later. They should create a stamp design for the squares. The design can be simple, as long the top and bottom of it are clear. Students should draw their designs on all four squares.
2. Draw the following shape on the board:

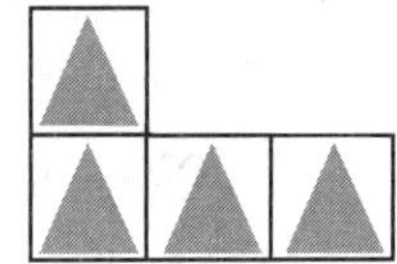

   Explain to students that the drawing shows one arrangement in which four stamps could be torn from a sheet of stamps so that they remain attached.
3. Ask the class how many different arrangements for the four stamps they can find. Tell them that each stamp must be attached to at least one other stamp along an entire side—diagonal attachments don't count. To find the answer, students move around the stamps they made on their desks to make different arrangements. When new arrangements have been found, students sketch them on separate sheets of paper. (See the possible arrangements, at right.)

Possible Arrangements

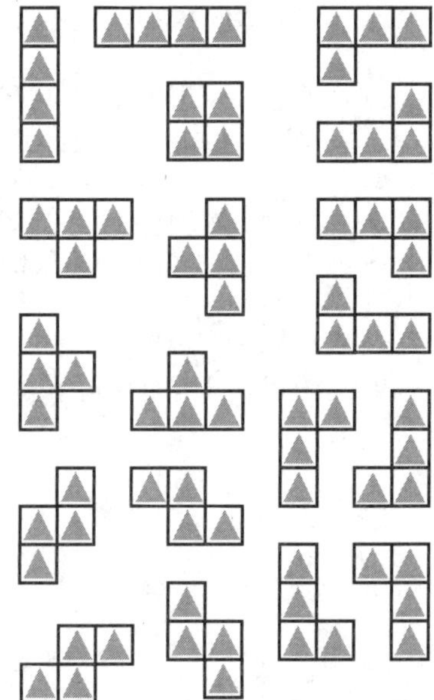

Taking It Farther

Add a fifth stamp to the activity. Challenge students to see who can come up with the most arrangements.

Assessing Skills

Note whether students realize that most of the shapes can be arranged in more than one way by rotating the shape 90°.

Spin to Win

It's the bottom of the ninth—and a simulation experiment can show students how likely it is that they'll win the game.

Directions

1. Divide the class into groups and distribute a copy of the reproducible to each group. Briefly review fractions and circle graphs with students. Show how fractional probabilities are translated into slices of the circle graphs to make the spinners in the activity.
2. Let each group conduct the simulations independently, spinning a paper clip around a pencil point on each spinner. Before spinning, the group predicts whether each player will score for the win. Each member of the group can take turns spinning.
3. When all the groups are finished, have the class share and discuss their answers.

Taking It Further

* Let students create their own sports scenarios and draw circle graphs to illustrate the scenarios. They may even research their favorite sports players (to find out a basketball player's free throw shooting percentage, for example) and use that information to make their own circle graphs to use in simulations.
* For the basketball problem where the player must make two shots, ask students to multiply the probabilities to find the mathematical probability that the player will score on both shots. Then have them compare that probability to the result of their simulations. Tell students to repeat the simulation several more times and note whether the predicted probability is now more accurate.

Assessing Skills

Ask students to look at the first spinner to answer these questions:

* *For Lefty's next 12 times at bat, how many times can she expect to make an out?* [3]
* *How do you know?* [She makes an out $\frac{1}{4}$ of the time, and 3 is $\frac{1}{4}$ of 12.]

LEARNING OBJECTIVE

Students conduct simulations to gain a concrete understanding of fractional probability.

GROUPING

Cooperative groups

MATERIALS

For each group:

* *Spin to Win* reproducible (p. 210)
* pencil and paper clip (to make the spinner)

Name ______________________ Date ______________

Spin to Win

This athlete is in a tough spot. At the end of a game, it's up to her to make the winning score!

Based on her previous scoring record, we know the probability that she will score. What does that mean for the team? Make a prediction based on the circle graph. Then, spin the spinner to see what happens. Repeat the simulation 10 times. Mark your results in the Score Box.

It's the bottom of the ninth inning, and Lefty is up at bat. For her team to win the game, Lefty must hit a home run or a triple to drive in other runners on the bases. What are her chances? Over the past season, she's hit a home run $\frac{1}{16}$ of her times at bat. She's hit a triple $\frac{1}{8}$ of the time, a double $\frac{3}{16}$ of the time, a single $\frac{3}{8}$ of the time, and has made an out $\frac{1}{4}$ of the time. To see what Lefty does this time, spin the spinner. Record your result in the Score Box.

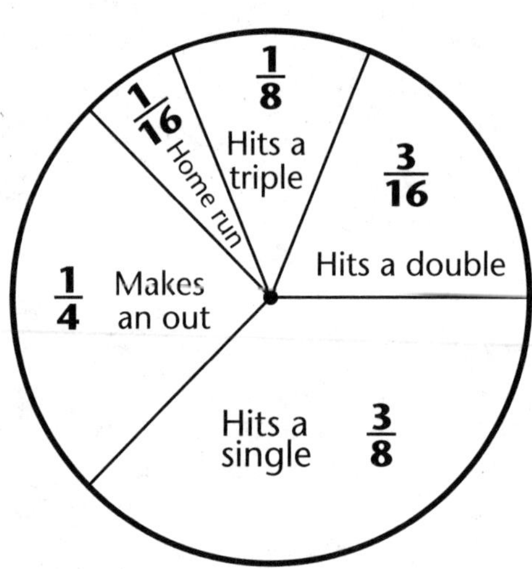

SCORE BOX

Trial	Out, Single, or Double	Triple or Home Run
1		
2		
3		
4		
5		
6		
7		
8		
9		
10		

False Hopes

Should students study for that true or false quiz, or just try to guess the answers? After completing this simulation, they'll run to hit the books!

Directions

1. On the board, write the following, in vertical columns:

1. T	6. F	11. F	16. T	21. T
2. T	7. F	12. T	17. F	22. F
3. T	8. F	13. F	18. F	23. T
4. T	9. F	14. T	19. T	24. F
5. T	10. F	15. F	20. F	25. T

2. Ask students to copy the list of numbers and T or F answers in one column down the left-hand side of a piece of paper. While they complete this task, hand out the coins.
3. Now have students flip their coins to see if they would guess correctly on each of the questions. Explain that flipping heads will represent True, while flipping tails will represent False. As they flip their coins, they mark a check next to each answer that the coin flip matches and an X next to each answer that the coin flip does not match.
4. When they are finished, students may score 4 points for each answer they matched with a coin flip. Have students determine their "grade" and compare their results.

LEARNING OBJECTIVE

Students use a simulation experiment to get a hands-on understanding of probability of compound events.

GROUPING

Individual

MATERIALS

For each student:

* coin
* pencil and paper
* number cube (for Taking It Further)

Taking It Further

Repeat the simulation, this time using multiple-choice questions with A, B, and C as possible answers. Write a list of 10 or 20 numbers with A, B, and C answers on the board. Have each student conduct the simulation by rolling a number cube; 1 and 2 can represent A, 3 and 4 can represent B, and 5 and 6 can represent C. What difference do students see in their results this time?

Assessing Skills

Ask students: *Does the chance of getting 100 percent by guessing on the quiz increase or decrease as more questions are added? Why?*

The Real Meal Deal

How many meals will students have to buy to collect all six toys from a fast-food chicken restaurant promotion? A simulation will give them a good idea.

Directions

1. Duplicate the reproducible and distribute a copy, along with a number cube, to each pair or group.
2. Explain to students that they will be testing to see how many meals they must buy to collect all six toys from a fast-food promotion. Before they begin, ask pairs or groups to predict how many meals they think it will probably take. Have them discuss the reasoning behind their answers.
3. Let students conduct the simulation on their own, rolling the number cube to represent each fast-food meal purchased. For each roll of the number cube, they make a tally mark next to the toy indicated by the number on the cube. For example, a 1 on the cube indicates Chaka the Chicken figure, and so on. Students keep rolling until they have collected every toy available. They repeat the simulation two more times and record the results in the columns.
4. When everyone is finished, allow time for students to compare answers to see how many rolls of the number cube it took to collect all the toys.

Taking It Further

Encourage students to look for real promotions where more than one item can be collected; for example, cereal boxes with promotional giveaways inside or soda bottle caps with special codes printed on them. Assuming there is an equal number of each item distributed, how long might it take to collect all of the items? Challenge students to design and conduct a simulation to find out.

Assessing Skills

To make sure students understand the principle at work behind their simulations, have them do mathematical calculations to check the probability of collecting all six toys in the activity in only six tries. To do this, they should multiply: $\frac{1}{6} \times \frac{1}{6} \times \frac{1}{6} \times \frac{1}{6} \times \frac{1}{6} \times \frac{1}{6} = \frac{1}{46,656}$.

LEARNING OBJECTIVE

Students use a simulation experiment to see how long it might take to collect all the toys from a fast-food restaurant promotion.

GROUPING

Pairs or cooperative groups

MATERIALS

For each pair or group:

* *The Real Meal Deal* reproducible (p. 213)
* number cube

Name ______________________ Date ______________

The Real Meal Deal

Jack's Chicken Shack is offering a special toy with each Chipper Chicken Meal. There are six different toys, which are distributed into the meal boxes at random. How many meals will you have to buy to collect all six toys?

Roll your number cube to see which toy you get. Match the number you roll with number of the toy. Make a tally mark in the Simulation A column next to that toy. Keep rolling the cube and making tally marks until you have collected each toy. Repeat the simulation for columns B and C.

CHIPPER MEAL TOY	SIMULATION A	SIMULATION B	SIMULATION C
1. Chaka the Chicken toy			
2. Chipper Chicken mobile			
3. Drumstick squeak toy			
4. Giblet Giggles joke book			
5. Peepers the Baby Chick wind-up toy			
6. Jack's Shack bouncing rubber egg			

What's Behind Door Number 2?

This problem was posed by Marilyn vos Savant, who was once listed in the *Guinness Book of World Records* as having the world's highest IQ.

LEARNING OBJECTIVE

Students conduct a simulation to understand a deceptively difficult probability problem.

GROUPING

Pairs

MATERIALS

For each pair:

- *What's Behind Door Number 2?* reproducible (p. 215)
- scissors
- 3 paper cups numbered 1, 2, 3

Directions

1. Write the problem on the board.

   You're on a game show, and you're given a choice of three doors. Behind one door is a car; behind the other two are goats. You pick a door, say, door number 1. The host, who knows what's behind the doors, opens another door, say, number 3, which has a goat. He then asks you if you want to switch to door number 2. Would switching increase your chances of winning the car?

2. Have students discuss the question. Intuitively, most students will probably say that there is no point in switching doors, since there are now two doors, one with a car and one with a goat. The probabilities appear to be equal.

3. The intuitive answer is incorrect, says vos Savant. Switching doors will increase your probability of winning the car. The reason? The host knows which door has the car. Use the following explanation:

   - You pick door number 1. The probability that you have chosen the door with the car is $\frac{1}{3}$. The probability that the car is behind one of the other two doors is $\frac{2}{3}$.
   - The host shows you what is behind door number 3. If you didn't pick the car, he will *never* show you the door with the car. Instead, he will always show you the door with the goat.
   - The probability that the car is behind one of the doors you *didn't* pick is still $\frac{2}{3}$—but you know that one of them has a goat. If you switch to door number 2, you have a $\frac{2}{3}$ chance of winning the car. If you don't switch, the chance is $\frac{1}{3}$.

4. Many students will still be skeptical. Divide the class into pairs, with one student playing the part of the host and the other playing the contestant. Students model the problem 50 times, switching choices each time. Discuss the results as a class.

Taking It Farther

Let students play the game again, this time always keeping their original door choice instead of switching. What is the outcome?

Assessing Skills

When they have completed the experiments, ask students to explain in their own words how the problem works.

Name ______________________ Date ______________

What's Behind Door Number 2?

Get ready to win a brand-new car . . . or maybe a brand-new goat!

Here's how to play the game:

1. Cut out the pictures of the goats and car below.
2. Decide who will be the game show host and who will be the contestant.
3. While the contestant looks away, the host puts one picture under each of three paper cups. The cups are the "doors." Only the host knows which door has the car.
4. The contestant picks a door. Then the host opens one of the other two doors—one that does not have a car behind it.
5. Now the contestant switches to the other unopened door.

Play the game 50 times, alternating roles. Each time, make a tally mark to show whether you won the car or a goat.

CONTESTANT'S NAME:	
WON CAR!	
WON GOAT!	

CONTESTANT'S NAME:	
WON CAR!	
WON GOAT!	

Elective Detective

Who is most likely to win the school election? Students use sampling to get a good estimate.

Directions

1. This activity is most appropriate for a time close to a school election. Begin by discussing polls conducted during city, state, and national elections. Have students noticed reports of these polls in the past? Discuss how polls are taken and how they work.
2. Now prepare for a small-scale sampling activity in your classroom. Write the names of the candidates for student council president on the board. Have each student write his or her vote for president on a slip of paper. Place all the slips of paper into a bag and call on a volunteer to randomly pick out 10 slips. Ask the volunteer to tally the votes on the board next to the candidates' names.
3. Ask students: *Based on these responses, how many total votes do you estimate the class has cast for each candidate? How would you make an estimate?* [One way is to use proportions to find an answer.] When you have discussed this, have another volunteer tally the remaining votes. How close were students' estimates?
4. Use all of the votes to have students predict how many votes will be cast for each candidate in the schoolwide election. How accurate might this estimate be? Discuss reasons why a student might be more likely to vote for one candidate instead of another, such as sharing a class with the candidate.
5. If possible, have students do a more randomized sample by randomly picking names of students in all the classes in your grade and interviewing them to find out their voting plans. Compare the resulting predictions to the predictions from the class poll. Then wait for the real election and see how close your predictions were!

Taking It Farther

Ask students to come up with other ideas for ways of taking a sample. Have them try their methods by surveying students about an issue such as voting age or a topic such as favorite television show.

Assessing Skills

Note whether students are able to use ratios and proportions correctly when trying to predict voting based on the sample.

LEARNING OBJECTIVE

Students conduct a survey to learn about sampling.

GROUPING

Whole class

MATERIALS

- pencil and paper
- paper bag
- list of all students in grade (if possible)

Picky, Picky

How many marbles of each color are in the bag? Students pick marbles and record their results to make predictions based on relative frequency.

Directions

1. Divide the class into pairs and give each pair a paper bag.
2. Explain that one student will reach into the bag without looking, mix up the marbles, and pick one marble from the bag. The partner will write the color on a sheet of paper.
3. The first student now returns the marble to the bag, mixes up the marbles again, and picks another marble. This process is repeated until it has been done 5 times, with the second student tallying the results.
4. At this point, students should try to guess how many marbles of each color are in the bag.
5. Students continue the activity until they have completed 10 draws from the bag and then guess the bag's contents again. Encourage them to revise their predictions as they continue to work.
6. Students repeat this process for 30 draws and 50 draws.
7. Finally, students look into the bag to check their predictions.

Taking It Further

Repeat the activity, this time placing 10 or more marbles in each bag and having students conduct more trials.

Assessing Skills

Ask students:

- *Which predictions were most accurate?*
- *Why were they most accurate?*
- *What are some ways to check if a prediction will probably be correct or close to correct?*

LEARNING OBJECTIVE

Students find relative frequency and make predictions.

GROUPING

Pairs

MATERIALS

For each pair:

- brown paper bag
- 8 marbles of three different colors or other uniformly shaped items of different colors, such as colored paper clips
- pencil and paper

ADVANCE PREPARATION

Prepare brown paper bags by putting 8 colored marbles or other items in each bag. There should be three colors represented in each bag, with different proportions of colors.

Trick-or-Treat Numbers

At Halloween or any time of year, students will have a frightfully good time as they use candy to model the probability of independent events.

Directions

1. Start by reviewing the probability of independent events. To find the probability of two independent events occurring, multiply the probabilities.
2. Bring out the bag of candy and explain its contents. Ask students:
   - *If you pick one candy at random, what is the sample space?* [0, 1, 2, 3, 4, 5, 6, 7, 8, 9]
   - *What is the probability you will pick a number greater than 5?* [$\frac{4}{10}$, or $\frac{2}{5}$]
   - *What is the probability you will pick a number less than 3?* [$\frac{3}{10}$]
   - *Say you pick one candy, return it to the bag, then pick another candy. What is the probability you will pick first a number greater than 5, and then a number less than 3?* [$\frac{2}{5} \bullet \frac{3}{10} = \frac{6}{50}$, or $\frac{3}{25}$]
3. Ask several more questions, such as, *What is the probability of drawing first an even number, and then and odd number?* or *What is the probability of drawing a number greater than 3 and then a number less than 7?* [$\frac{2}{5} \bullet \frac{1}{2} = \frac{2}{10}$, or $\frac{1}{5}$; $\frac{3}{5} \bullet \frac{7}{10} = \frac{21}{50}$]
4. For each question, have volunteers use the bag of candy to model the question several times. The class keeps track of the results of these experiments and discusses the outcomes.

Taking It Farther

Ask students: *How do these problems change if the candy is not returned to the bag after the first pick?* [They become problems of probability of dependent events, since the outcome of the first pick changes the sample space for the second pick.] Repeat the problems using this new method, and have students figure out the new probabilities. How do they compare?

Assessing Skills

Note whether students understand that the probability for an event such as "greater than 7" is different from the probability for the event "7 or greater." Ask students to explain this in their own words.

LEARNING OBJECTIVE

Students find the probability of independent events and use models to investigate their answers.

GROUPING

Whole class

MATERIALS

- Halloween trick-or-treat bag or plastic trick-or-treat pumpkin
- 10 pieces of identically wrapped candy
- pencil or marker

ADVANCE PREPARATION

Use a pencil or marker to number the candies 0 through 9. Place them in the Halloween bag.

Game Show Showdown

Students take a new spin on the number 10 as they experiment with independent events.

Directions

1. Duplicate the reproducible for each group and distribute.
2. Describe the Go for a Spin! game to students. In the game, a wheel is divided into eight spaces labeled 1–8. Three players take turns spinning the wheel and can spin either once or twice. The object is to have the sum of the spins come as close to 10 as possible without exceeding 10.
3. To find the probability of getting two specific spins, you can multiply the probability of each spin. For example, to find the probability of spinning a 2 or lower on the first spin and a 2 or higher on the second spin, you'd multiply: $\frac{2}{8} \bullet \frac{7}{8} = \frac{14}{64} = \frac{7}{32}$.
4. Divide students into groups of three and let them play the game on their own. Students should develop their own strategies for winning. When all groups have played the game several times, let them share their strategies with the class. The class tries to decide which strategies work best and why.

Taking It Further

Repeat the activity, but this time have students construct a large spinner with 20 spaces labeled in increments of 5¢ from 5¢ to $1.00. Challenge students to devise their own strategies for spinning close to $1.00 without going over.

Share with students that in 1993, a college math student named Steve Goodman used this information to develop a winning strategy for the showdown round of the TV game show *The Price Is Right*. For example, Goodman found that if the first player spins a 65¢ or lower on the first spin, he or she should spin again.

Assessing Skills

Note whether students use their knowledge of the probability of independent events as they develop winning strategies.

LEARNING OBJECTIVE

Students develop strategies to win a game by finding the probability of independent events.

GROUPING

Cooperative groups of 3

MATERIALS

For each group:

- *Game Show Showdown* reproducible (p. 220)
- pencil and paper clip (to make the spinner)

Name ______________________ Date ______________

Game Show Showdown

Hello! I'm Will S. Pinnen. Welcome to *Go for a Spin!* How do you get close to 10 without going over? Try a few different strategies and see. Use your knowledge of probability of independent events to help you. Good luck!

The object is to spin as close to 10 as possible, without going over. Players take turns spinning. After a player's first turn, he or she can decide to spin again, or decide to stay at one spin. Then it's the next player's turn.

SCORE SHEET

Game	Player	Score	Game	Player	Score
Game A	Player 1		Game D	Player 1	
	Player 2			Player 2	
	Player 3			Player 3	
Game B	Player 1		Game E	Player 1	
	Player 2			Player 2	
	Player 3			Player 3	
Game C	Player 1		Game F	Player 1	
	Player 2			Player 2	
	Player 3			Player 3	

Bon Voyage

In this hands-on activity, students jet around the world with the probability of dependent events.

Directions

1. With dependent events, the outcome for one event depends on the outcome of a previous event. To find the probability, find the probability of the first event. Then use the new sample space to find the probability of the second event. If you want to find the probability that the two events will both happen, multiply the probabilities.
2. Ask volunteers to describe faraway places in the world they'd like to visit. Write the names of several destinations on the board. Direct each student to draw and cut out a picture of a plane ticket to one of the destinations. Each student may draw more than one ticket. Collect the tickets and make sure there are several tickets for each destination.
3. Place several tickets in a bag. Start with two destinations; for example, 6 tickets to China and 4 tickets to Morocco.
4. Have two volunteers say which of the two destination they'd like to visit. (Students may select the same destination.) Ask the class: *Picking at random from the bag, what is the probability that the first student will pick the destination of his or her choice?* Let the student pick and reveal her or his ticket. Now ask: *What is the probability that the second student will pick his or her choice? What is the probability that both students will pick the tickets of their choice?*
5. Continue modeling additional problems using more destinations and students. For each simulation, write the theoretical probability on the board before conducting the experiment.

Taking It Further

Have cooperative groups of students use the plane tickets to model their own problems. Each group should conduct its experiments repeatedly and share results with the class.

Assessing Skills

Ask students: *If the probability that an event will happen is $\frac{1}{6}$, and you conduct the same experiment 6 times, is it certain that the event will happen?* [No. The results of a previous experiment do not affect the experiments that follow. The event could occur any number of times from 1 to 6, or not at all.]

LEARNING OBJECTIVE

Students conduct a simulation to test the theoretical probability of dependent events.

GROUPING

Whole class

MATERIALS

- drawing paper
- pencils
- crayons or colored markers
- scissors
- paper bag

Critter Cards

Which animal is on the card? As students guess and turn over each card, the probability they will guess right on the next card increases.

Directions

1. Review dependent events as necessary and distribute copies of the reproducible. Each student cuts out the two sets of five animal pictures, placing one set in a row across his or her desk. Then he or she tapes or glues each of the matching pictures to the back of an index card, turns the cards facedown, and mixes them.
2. On a piece of graph paper, each student marks off five columns, labeling them Guess 1, Guess 2, and so on. Students then mark off 30 rows, labeling them Round 1, Round 2, Round 3, and so on to 30.
3. Begin by conducting Round 1 as a class, using one student's set of cards. Students guess which of the five animals is on the first card. Then turn over the card. If the guess was correct, students make a check under Guess 1 in the first row, Round 1. If the guess was incorrect, they make an X.
4. Now, place the card you picked over its matching animal cutout. For Guess 2, students guess which of the four remaining animals will appear on the second card. Repeat for all five cards.
5. To continue, students turn over the cards, mix them up, and make five more guesses. They should repeat this process 30 times.

LEARNING OBJECTIVE

Students conduct a hands-on activity to gain an understanding of the probability of dependent events.

GROUPING

Individual

MATERIALS

For each student:

- *Critter Cards* reproducible (p. 223)
- 5 index cards
- scissors
- tape or glue
- graph paper

Taking It Further

Ask students:

- *What is the probability that you will guess correctly on the first guess?* [$\frac{1}{5}$]
- *What is the probability that you will guess correctly on the fifth guess?* [1]

Have students look at the proportion of correct guesses they made in each column. Ask: *How does the proportion compare with the theoretical probability? What is the probability that on one round of five guesses you will guess each animal correctly?* [$\frac{1}{5} \bullet \frac{1}{4} \bullet \frac{1}{3} \bullet \frac{1}{2} \bullet 1 = \frac{1}{120}$]

Assessing Skills

To see if students understand the term *dependent*, challenge them to think of events in their own lives that are dependent on other events.

Name ______________________ Date ______________

Critter Cards

Cut out the animals. Tape or glue one set of animals to the back of index cards.

Card Tricks

An explanation for the probability of mutually exclusive events is in the cards!

Directions

1. Mutually exclusive events are two events that cannot happen at the same time. For example, when rolling a number cube, rolling an even number or rolling a 5 are mutually exclusive events. To find the probability of two mutually exclusive events occurring, add the probabilities. The probability of rolling either an even number or a 5 is $\frac{1}{2} + \frac{1}{6}$, or $\frac{2}{3}$.
2. Display the deck of cards. Pose the probability questions below, asking students to describe the probability of the mutually exclusive events. Then have pairs model one of the problems at least 25 times to test the theoretical probability.
3. Note that in some problems, students must distinguish between mutually exclusive and non–mutually exclusive events. If an event is not mutually exclusive, it must be subtracted from the probability. For example, the probability of rolling an even number or a number less than 3 on a number cube is: $\frac{1}{2}$ (even numbers: 2, 4, 6) + $\frac{1}{3}$ (numbers less than 3: 1, 2) – $\frac{1}{6}$ (2, which appeared in both sets) = $\frac{2}{3}$.

Probability questions:

- *What is the probability of picking an ace, king, queen, or jack?* [mutually exclusive: $\frac{4}{52} + \frac{4}{52} + \frac{4}{52} + \frac{4}{52} = \frac{16}{52}$, or $\frac{4}{13}$]
- *What is the probability of picking a club or a red face card (jack, queen, king, ace)?* [mutually exclusive: $\frac{13}{52} + \frac{8}{52} = \frac{21}{52}$]
- *What is the probability of picking a number card greater than 7 or a jack?* [mutually exclusive: $\frac{12}{52} + \frac{4}{52} = \frac{16}{52}$, or $\frac{4}{13}$]
- *What is the probability of picking a number card less than 8 or a diamond?* [non–mutually exclusive: $\frac{28}{52} + \frac{13}{52} - \frac{7}{52} = \frac{34}{52}$, or $\frac{17}{26}$]
- *What is the probability of picking an odd number card or a black card?* [non–mutually exclusive: $\frac{16}{52} + \frac{26}{52} - \frac{8}{52} = \frac{34}{52}$, or $\frac{17}{26}$]

Taking It Farther

Have students write a list of mutually exclusive events from their own lives. Hold a class contest to see who can think of the most examples.

Assessing Skills

Observe whether students are able to distinguish between mutually exclusive and non–mutually exclusive events.

LEARNING OBJECTIVE

Students find the probability of mutually exclusive events.

GROUPING

Whole class/pairs

MATERIALS

- deck of playing cards
- scrap paper and pencil

Wheel of Fortune

Students step right up and learn how odds come into play at a county fair!

Directions

1. Duplicate the reproducible for each student.
2. Discuss the concept of *odds* with students. When have they heard the term before? Students may not realize that the odds of an event are different from the probability of an event. On the board, write this definition of odds as related to winning a game:

   $$\text{Odds of winning} = \frac{\text{Number of winning outcomes}}{\text{Number of losing outcomes}}$$

   The *probability* of winning compares the following:

   $$\text{Probability of winning} = \frac{\text{Number of winning outcomes}}{\text{Number of all possible outcomes}}$$

3. Distribute the reproducible. Have students color in alternating sections of the spinner in light blue and yellow, so that half of the sections are yellow and half are blue. Make sure that the colors do not obscure the spinner numbers.
4. Students complete the reproducible on their own.

Taking It Farther

Let students go back to questions 2–5 on the reproducible and determine the probability of the outcomes.

Assessing Skills

Observe whether students compute the odds of winning or losing, as opposed to the probability.

LEARNING OBJECTIVE

Students learn about odds and practice applying the concept in a game.

GROUPING

Individual

MATERIALS

- *Wheel of Fortune* reproducible (p. 226)
- light blue and yellow crayons or colored pencils
- pencil and paper clip (to make the spinner)

Name ______________________ Date ______________

Wheel of Fortune

Note: Before playing the game, color in alternating sections of the spinner with light blue and yellow crayons or pencils.

Poor Louie! Here at the County Fair, he's placed ten bets in a row on 12—his lucky number. But the number hasn't been so lucky for Louie today. He's lost every time!

Help Louie understand why by using the Wheel of Fortune to answer the questions about odds and test your answers. Remember, in this game you can bet that the spinner will land on any number, shape, or color. Good luck!

1. How many chances does Louie have to win if he bets on
   a. one number? ____________
   b. one shape? ____________
   c. one color? ____________

2. What are Louie's *odds* of winning if he bets on
   a. one number? ____________
   b. one shape? ____________
   c. one color? ____________

3. Choose a number for Louie to bet on. Spin the spinner 25 times.
   a. How many times did Louie win?
   ____
   b. How many times did Louie lose?
   ____

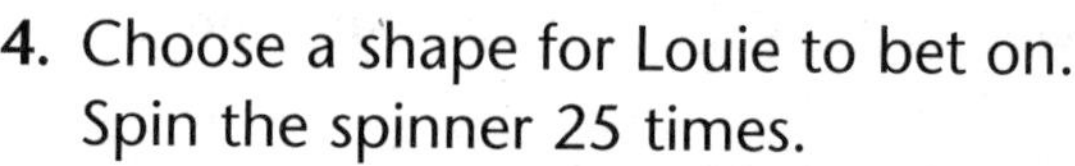

4. Choose a shape for Louie to bet on. Spin the spinner 25 times.
   a. How many times did Louie win?
   ____
   b. How many times did Louie lose?
   ____

5. Choose a color for Louie to bet on. Spin the spinner 25 times.
   a. How many times did Louie win?
   ____
   b. How many times did Louie lose?
   ____

Above Average

Mean, median, or mode? Student statisticians decide!

Directions

1. Usually, an average refers to a mean. But statisticians sometimes use the median or mode of a group to make the most accurate predictions. It all depends on what is appropriate for the data collected and what type of prediction you want to make.
2. For example, consider the shoe sizes of a group of people.
   - The *mean* is the sum of all the sizes divided by the number of people in the group.
   - The *median* is the number exactly in the middle of the group—an equal number of people have a smaller shoe size and an equal number have a larger shoe size. If one or two people have a much smaller or a larger size than the rest of the group, the median may give you a better idea of the size of the group's feet.
   - The *mode* is the shoe size that occurs most often in the group. To find out which size you would be most likely to get if you picked a person at random, you would use the mode. A mode can also be used as the average when many of the measurements in a group are the same or similar.
3. Have students provide some or all of the following information:
   - how far the student travels to get to school each day
   - shoe size or length of foot in centimeters
   - height in inches
4. Tally the results and let students use the information to make predictions about the rest of the students in their grade. For example, what would be the most likely height for a randomly selected student? Discuss whether mean, median, or mode is the most effective way to represent each result.

Taking It Farther

Ask students to come up with fictional scenarios in which it would be most useful to make predictions based on a mean, median or mode.

Assessing Skills

Observe how students differentiate among *mean*, *median*, *mode*, and *average*. Can they clearly explain their reasoning about which to use?

LEARNING OBJECTIVE

Students explore why statisticians might choose to use mean, median, or mode when making different kinds of predictions.

GROUPING

Whole class

MATERIALS

- rulers and other measuring tools (optional)

Rain, Rain, Go Away

What does "a 40 percent chance of rain" really mean? Students get an idea as they keep track of weather forecasts and compare them to the actual weather.

Directions

1. Discuss weather forecasting with the class. Ask students if they have heard forecasts that included a percent chance of showers, snow, and so on. Can they explain what the forecast meant? How would they write "a 40 percent chance" as a fraction?
2. Each day for several weeks, have students check the same source (a cable TV weather channel, a newspaper, or a radio station) for the weather forecast for the following day.
3. On days when a specific weather condition such as snow or rain is forecast, ask students to record the percent chance of the condition in their notebooks.
4. The next day, students record the actual weather that occurred beside the forecast.
5. After two or more weeks, let students read through the notebooks to analyze the results. Do the predictions seem accurate? What are some reasons why the forecasts might or might not have been accurate?

Taking It Further

On a day when a percent chance of rain, snow, or another weather condition is forecast, have students use fractions to create a circle graph spinner. The percent chance of rain or snow should be colored in and the rest of the graph left blank. If there was the same chance of rain or snow for 15 days in a row, on how many of those days might it actually rain or snow? Have students spin repeatedly to get an idea of what could happen.

Assessing Skills

Ask students: *If there is a 40 percent chance of rain on one day, and a 60 percent chance of rain on a second day, what is the probability that it will rain on both days?* [Since these are independent events, multiply $\frac{2}{5} \bullet \frac{3}{5} = \frac{6}{25}$.]

LEARNING OBJECTIVE

Students follow weather reports to gain an understanding of probability and chance.

GROUPING

Whole class

MATERIALS

- daily weather reports from newspapers, radio, or television
- notebook for recording forecasts and weather observations
- scissors
- cardboard
- colored pencils or markers
- pencil and paper clip (to make the spinner)

Collect All Six

"Six NBA glasses—collect the whole set!" Probability shows students why that's easier said than done.

Directions

1. Duplicate the reproducible for each student and distribute. Then pose this situation to the class:

   Suppose a fast-food restaurant is giving away a free NBA All-Star glass with the purchase of a large soft drink. There are six glasses in the collection. When you buy your drink, you never know which glass you're going to receive.

   Ask students to predict how many soft drinks they'd have to buy to get all six glasses. Have them record their prediction.

2. Explain that the six numbers on the number cube will represent the six different NBA All-Star glasses. Each toss of the number cube represents the glass the student would receive. If a student rolls a two, for example, he or she would receive glass number two.
3. Have students toss the number cube and make a tally mark in the table in the Trial 1 row under the number rolled. Students should keep tossing the number cube and marking the results in the table. Trial 1 is over when every number on the cube has been rolled at least once. When students have finished Trial 1, have them record the total number of rolls in the trial.
4. Have students do nine more trials. When they've finished, have them compute and record the average of the total number of rolls for all ten trials.
5. As a class, find the average of all the individual averages. Have students record that number where indicated. Ask students to discuss what they learned. When they get glasses randomly, what can they say about their chances of getting a complete set?

Taking It Further

Ask students to compare the final class average to the prediction they made at the beginning of the activity. Were there differences in the two numbers? Why or why not?

Assessing Skills

Students should understand that the final average represents a good idea of the number of soft drinks they'd have to buy to get all six NBA All-Star glasses, assuming all are equally available.

LEARNING OBJECTIVE

Students calculate averages and, similar to the activity on pages 212–213, see how difficult it might be to collect a "complete set" from a fast-food restaurant promotion.

GROUPING

Individual

MATERIALS

For each group:

* *Collect All Six* reproducible (p. 230)
* number cube
* pencil

Name ______________________ Date ______________

Collect All Six

How many soft drinks would you have to buy to get all six glasses?

My prediction: ______________________

Now roll your number cube. Make a tally mark under the number you get. For each Trial, keep rolling until you get all six numbers. Then count up the total number of rolls for that Trial. Complete all 10 Trials.

Number Rolled	1	2	3	4	5	6	Total Number of Rolls
Trial 1							
Trial 2							
Trial 3							
Trial 4							
Trial 5							
Trial 6							
Trial 7							
Trial 8							
Trial 9							
Trial 10							

Average number of times rolled in one trial—ME: __________

Average number of times rolled in one trial—MY CLASS: ______

Probability Problem Bank

Use these quick skill-builders as self-starters, homework, or just for a fun break from the textbook!

1. 7-11 BIRTHDAY

Who wants a happy birthday Slurpee? You pick a person at random out of a crowd. What is the probability that the person's birthday falls on either the seventh or eleventh day of a month? Write the answer as a fraction, a decimal rounded to the nearest thousandth, and a percent rounded to the nearest tenth. When answering, disregard February 29, which occurs once every four years at leap year.

2. SPIN CITY

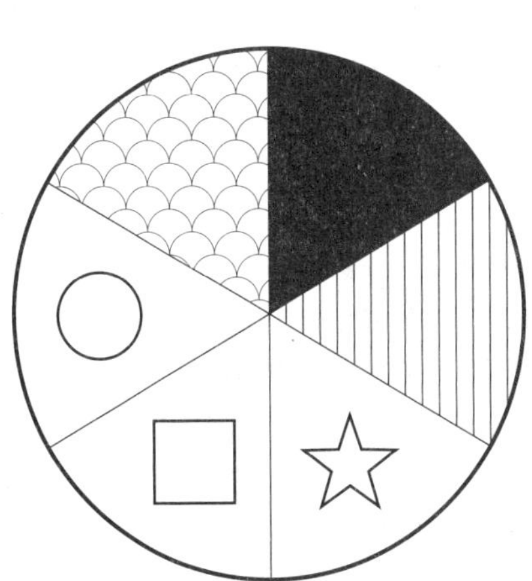

The spinner is spun three times. How many combinations of spins are possible? (Hint: Remember to use the Fundamental Counting Principle to find an answer.)

3. COOKIE CONUNDRUM

Suppose you are making a batch of six cookies. You drop ten chocolate chips into the batter and mix it up. If the chips are randomly distributed among the cookies, how likely do you think it is that you will get a cookie with three or more chocolate chips? Come up with a theory and test it by rolling a number cube ten times.

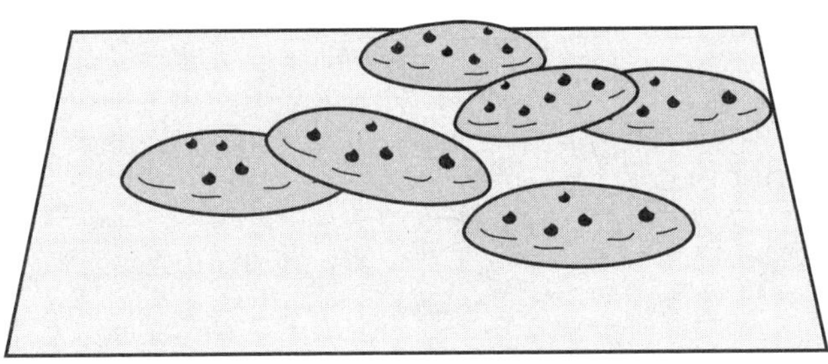

4. WHAT'S THE NUMBER?

You're having trouble remembering a friend's phone number. You know the first three digits, but you can remember only that the last four digits consist of a 2, 4, 7, and 8 in some order. How many ways could you arrange the four numbers to finish the phone number? (Hint: Use a tree diagram to help you find out.) What if the last four numbers were 2, 4, 4, and 7? How many different arrangements could you make then?

5. HAT TRICK

There are strips of paper numbered 1 to 10 in a hat.

* If you pick a strip of paper without looking, what is the probability you will pick an even number?
* What is the probability you will pick a prime number?
* What are the odds you will pick a prime number?

6. SCHOOL DAZE

For English homework, Trevor has 4 lists of poems. He must pick a poem from each list and read it. The first list contains 12 poems. The second list has 4 poems, the third list has 8 poems, and the fourth list has 5 poems. (Hint: Remember to use the Fundamental Counting Principle to find an answer.)

a. How many different combinations of poems could Trevor choose to read?

____

b. Which method did you use to solve this problem? Why?

____

____

____

c. Show your solution on a separate sheet of paper.

7. JOIN THE CLUB

In a different group of 50 students, there are 30 members of the Dandelion Conservation Organization, and 25 members of Students for the Promotion of Plaid. Of those students, 15 belong to both groups. On a piece of paper, draw a Venn diagram to illustrate this group of students.

a. If you pick a student at random, what is the probability he or she belongs to Students for the Promotion of Plaid?

____

b. What is the probability he or she doesn't belong to either club?

____

8. SPIN TO WIN

Rhonda's basketball team is counting on her. It's the end of the game, and Rhonda is at the freethrow line. She has two shots, and she must make both of them to win the game. Will Rhonda do it? In the past, she has made $\frac{2}{3}$ of her free throw shots and missed $\frac{1}{3}$. Spin the spinner once to find out if Rhonda makes her first shot, then spin again to see if she makes the second shot. Repeat the simulation 10 times and make a check for each basket she makes in the Score Box. If she misses, leave the box blank.

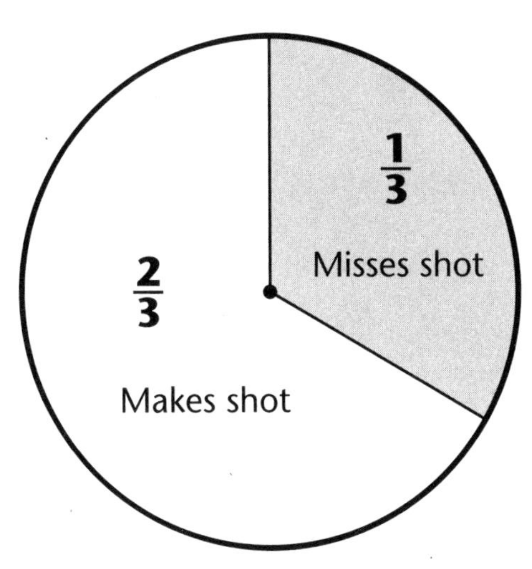

SCORE BOX

Trial	First Shot	Second Shot
1		
2		
3		
4		
5		
6		
7		
8		
9		
10		

Tasty Properties

Students get a flavorful look at U.S. cities named after foods as they find out about the properties of addition and multiplication.

Directions

1. Duplicate the reproducible for each student and distribute.
2. Review the properties of addition and multiplication. Write the following definitions and examples on the board and discuss them with the class.

Commutative Properties

Addition: You can change the order of addends without changing the sum. EXAMPLE: $8 + 3 = 11$, $3 + 8 = 11$, $8 + 3 = 3 + 8$

Multiplication: You can change the order of factors without changing the product. EXAMPLE: $7 \times 5 = 35$, $5 \times 7 = 35$, $7 \times 5 = 5 \times 7$

Associative Properties

Addition: You can change the way addends are grouped without changing the sum. EXAMPLE: $7 + (12 + 3) = 22$, $(7 + 12) + 3 = 22$, $7 + (12 + 3) = (7 + 12) + 3$

Multiplication: You can change the way factors are grouped without changing the product. EXAMPLE: $(9 \times 5) \times 8 = 360$, $5 \times (9 \times 8) = 360$, $(9 \times 5) \times 8 = 5 \times (9 \times 8)$

Identity Properties

Addition: The sum of any addend and zero is the addend. EXAMPLE: $2 + 0 = 2$

Multiplication: The product of any factor and 1 is the factor. EXAMPLE: $6 \times 1 = 6$

Taking It Farther

- Ask students to explain whether subtraction is commutative. Also query them about whether subtraction is associative.
- Have students look up the words *commute, associate,* and *identity* in the dictionary. How do the words relate to the properties of addition and multiplication?

Assessing Skills

A common error is always to identify a property as associative if there are more than two numbers. Check to see if students can correctly identify cases of the commutative property that use three or more numbers.

LEARNING OBJECTIVE

Students use and identify the Commutative, Associative, and Identity Properties of addition and multiplication.

GROUPING

Individual

MATERIALS

- *Tasty Properties* reproducible (p. 235)

Name ______________________ Date ______________

Tasty Properties

How would you like to own property in Cookietown, Oklahoma? All across the United States, you can find cities named after food. To find out where the mouthwatering towns below are located, use the commutative, associative, and identity properties of addition and multiplication.

For each problem, circle the statement that completes the equation correctly. Next to it is the state where the town is located. Write the state. Then write the property you used to find the answer. The first one is done for you.

1. Noodle, Texas ______ $(4 \times 2) \times 3 = ?$ 2(4 + 3) Idaho (2(4 • 3) Texas)

   What property is shown? Associative property of multiplication

2. Beanville, ______ $5 + 0 = ?$ 5×0 Hawaii 5 Vermont

   What property is shown? ______

3. Olive, ______ $4 \times 15 = ?$ 15×4 Montana 14×5 Washington

   What property is shown? ______

4. Spuds, ______ $7 + (8 + 3) = ?$ (7 + 8)3 Michigan 8 + (3 + 7) Florida

   What property is shown? ______

5. Walnut, ______ $(x + 4) \times 1 = ?$ $4x$ New York $(x + 4)$ Iowa

   What property is shown? ______

6. Jelly, ______ $12xy = ?$ $y12x$ California $24y$ North Carolina

   What property is shown? ______

7. Mustard, ______ $v + 5 = ?$ $5v$ Colorado $5 + v$ Pennsylvania

   What property is shown? ______

8. Eggville, ______ $cd + 0 = ?$ cd Mississippi $c + d$ Delaware

   What property is shown? ______

9. Sandwich, ______ $(7 + j) + 4 = ?$ $(j \bullet 11)$ Georgia $j + 11$ Illinois

   What property is shown? ______

Opposites Subtract

And sometimes, opposites add, multiply, or divide! Students learn about inverse operations by finding inverses to actions from their daily lives.

Directions

1. Remind students that inverse operations are operations that "undo" each other. (See answers, bottom right, for the following problems.)
2. Write the following statements on the board:

   a. 17 + 5 = 22 **b.** 11 – 7 = 4 **c.** 6 • 2 = 12 **d.** 15 ÷ 5 = 3

   Have students "undo" the math by using inverse operations. Call on volunteers to share their answers.
3. Write the following list of everyday actions on the board:

   a. gaining 10 yards in football
   b. taking 3 steps backward
   c. withdrawing $20 from a bank account
   d. breaking a plate into 5 equal pieces

   Ask students to give an example of an inverse of each action.
4. Challenge students to find the math operations that were done and then undone by their inverses in each example.
5. Direct pairs to come up with their own lists of inverses for real-life actions. One student writes an action on a sheet of paper, and the other student supplies the inverse action. Then partners switch roles. They continue until they have at least five examples of actions and inverses.

LEARNING OBJECTIVE

Students conceptualize and use inverse operations.

GROUPING

Pairs

MATERIALS

✱ paper and pencil for each student

Taking It Farther

Do the following example on the board to show that inverse operations can be used to solve equations:

$$n \div 4 = 7$$
$$n = 7 \times 4$$
$$n = 28$$

Let students use inverse operations to solve equations such as:

$r - 12 = 14$ $k \bullet 3 = 27$ $h + 7 = 25$ $x \div 6 = 4$

Assessing Skills

✱ When solving problems, students may use the operation in the problem instead of its inverse.

✱ Also note whether students check their answers using estimation or by plugging the variable value into the original equation.

ANSWERS

2 a. 22 – 5 = 17
b. 4 + 7 = 11
c. 12 ÷ 2 = 6
d. 3 • 5 = 15

3 a. losing 10 yards
b. taking 3 steps forward
c. depositing $20 in a bank account
d. gluing the 5 pieces back together

4 a. addition, subtraction
b. subtraction, addition
c. subtraction, addition
d. division (1 ÷ 5), multiplication ($\frac{1}{5} \times 5$)

Olympic Flips

As they practice finding reciprocals, students will flip for this fun maze!

LEARNING OBJECTIVE

Students find the reciprocals of integers, fractions, and mixed numbers.

GROUPING

Individual

MATERIALS

- *Olympic Flips* reproducible (p. 238)

Directions

1. Duplicate the reproducible for each student and distribute.
2. Review the term *reciprocal* or *multiplicative inverse.* Remind students that if they multiply a number by its reciprocal, the product is always 1. One way to find a reciprocal is to write the number as a fraction and switch the numerator and the denominator. Write the following examples on the board:

$$\frac{1}{3} \times \frac{3}{1} = 1$$

$$-\frac{4}{7} \times -\frac{7}{4} = 1$$

$$\frac{a}{b} \bullet \frac{b}{a} = 1$$

3. Note that a mixed number must be changed to a fraction before finding the reciprocal. Explain, too, that reciprocals may be written in lowest terms. Write the following examples on the board:

What is the reciprocal of $5\frac{2}{3}$?

$$5\frac{2}{3} = \frac{17}{3}$$

$$\frac{17}{3} \times \frac{3}{17} = 1$$

The reciprocal is $\frac{3}{17}$.

What is the reciprocal of $\frac{4}{9}$?

$$\frac{4}{9} \times \frac{9}{4} = 1$$

$$\frac{9}{4} = 2\frac{1}{4}$$

The reciprocal of $\frac{4}{9}$ is $2\frac{1}{4}$.

4. Have students complete the reproducible on their own.

Taking It Further

Encourage students to calculate the reciprocals for numbers in the maze that were not part of the path to the finish line.

Assessing Skills

- Observe whether students make the error of inverting just the fractional part of a mixed number, leaving the whole number alone.
- Note whether students check their work by multiplying the number and its reciprocal.

Name ______________________ Date ______________

Olympic Flips

Help gymnast Airy Shrugg flip across the mat and score a perfect **10**!

Begin at Start. Find the reciprocal of $\frac{14}{9}$. The reciprocal will always be in the top circle of a pair of circles. Trace the line to that circle. Then find the reciprocal of the fraction in the bottom circle. Trace a line to the circle with its reciprocal. You can move in any direction, as long as the circles are connected by a line. Keep moving until you reach Finish.

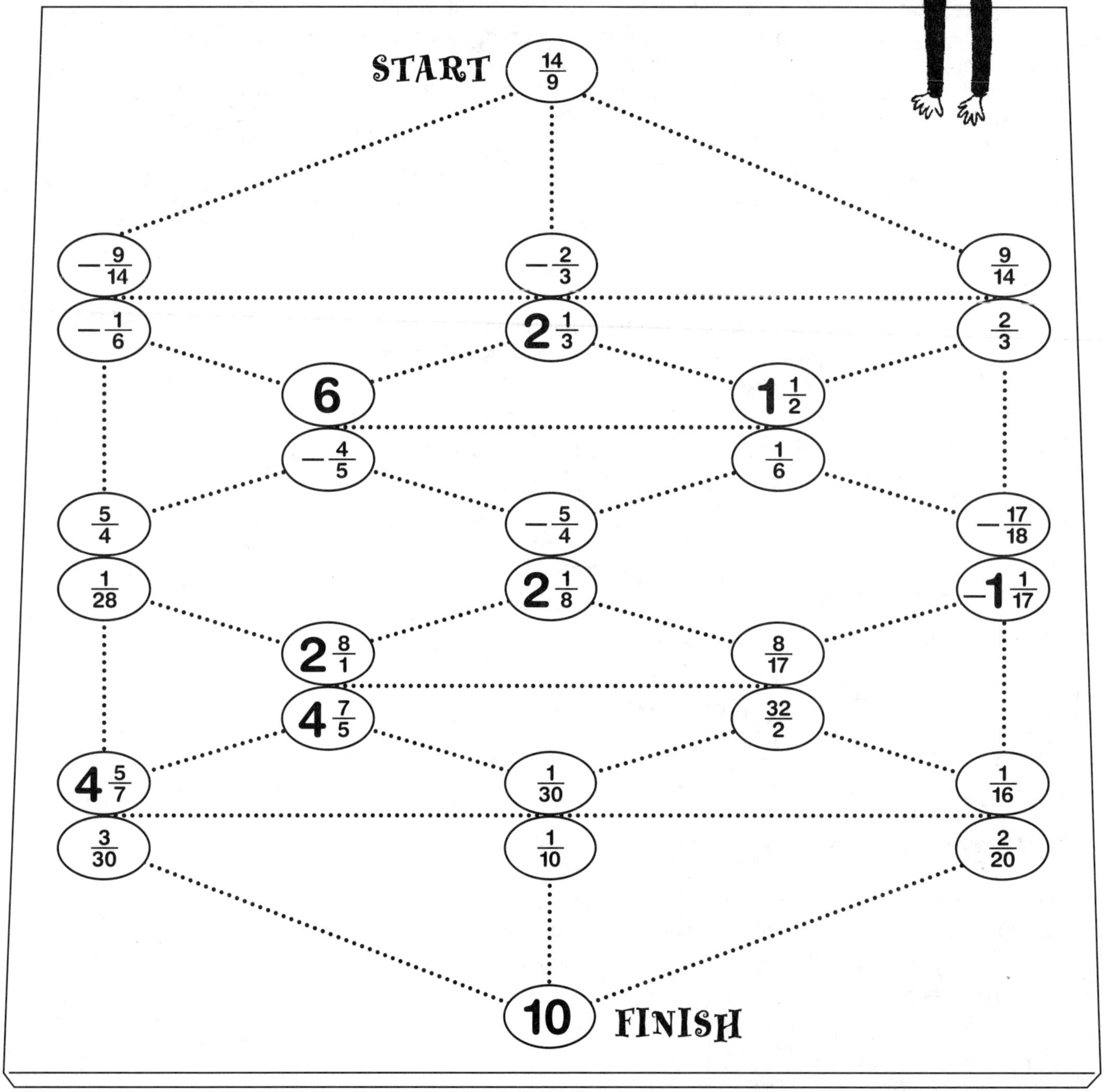

START $\frac{14}{9}$

$-\frac{9}{14}$ $-\frac{2}{3}$ $\frac{9}{14}$

$-\frac{1}{6}$ $2\frac{1}{3}$ $\frac{2}{3}$

6 $1\frac{1}{2}$

$-\frac{4}{5}$ $\frac{1}{6}$

$\frac{5}{4}$ $-\frac{5}{4}$ $-\frac{17}{18}$

$\frac{1}{28}$ $2\frac{1}{8}$ $-1\frac{1}{17}$

$2\frac{8}{1}$ $\frac{8}{17}$

$4\frac{7}{5}$ $\frac{32}{2}$

$4\frac{5}{7}$ $\frac{1}{30}$ $\frac{1}{16}$

$\frac{3}{30}$ $\frac{1}{10}$ $\frac{2}{20}$

10 FINISH

Have No Fear

Does your class suffer from algebraphobia? Students practice using the distributive property and learn about some common phobias.

Directions

1. Duplicate the reproducible for each student.
2. Review the distributive property with students. You may want to write the following definition on the board:

   For any numbers x, y, and z, $x(y + z) = xy + xz$.

3. Write the following expressions on the board. Have volunteers use the distributive property to rewrite the expressions. (Answers are given in brackets.) Note: Students should not compute the value of the expression.

4(3 + 7)	[4 • 3 + 4 • 7]
5k + 5y	[5(k + y)]
6(x + 3)	[6x + 18]

4. Explain to students that an expression in simplest form should have no like terms and no parentheses. Ask: *Which expressions written on the board are in simplest form?* [the last expression]
5. Finally, distribute the reproducible and have students complete it on their own. Note that in some cases they will have to use other properties, such as the commutative property of addition, as well as the distributive property.

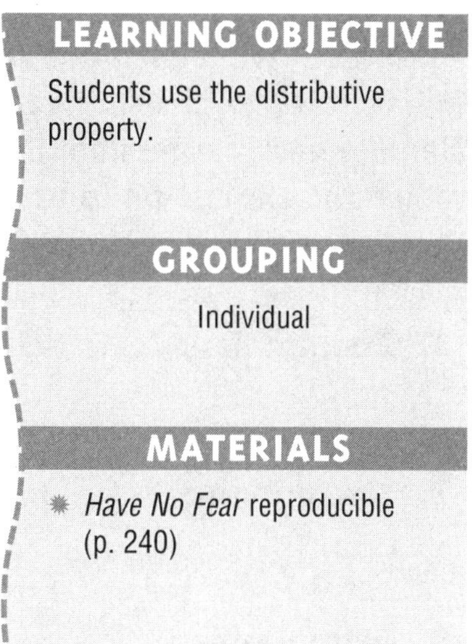

LEARNING OBJECTIVE

Students use the distributive property.

GROUPING

Individual

MATERIALS

- *Have No Fear* reproducible (p. 240)

Taking It Further

Have students use properties to rewrite each expression in the activity in as many ways as they can. For example, 4(x + 3) can also be written as 2(2x + 6), 4x + 12, (x + 3)4, or 2x • 2 + 12.

Assessing Skills

Observe whether students are completing the distribution. For example, some students may rewrite 8(4 + 6) as 32 + 6, instead of as 32 + 48.

Name ______________________ Date ______________

Have No Fear

Don't worry—algebra is nothing to fear! But some people do fear specific things, like heights, snakes, or fire. These strong fears are called *phobias*.

To find out what each phobia below means, use the distributive property to simplify each expression. Draw a line to match the expression to its simplest form.

	Phobia	Expression	Simplest form	Meaning
1.	**Zoophobia**	$4n + 2n$	$6n + 36$	**Fear of Water**
2.	**Nyctophobia**	$x + 3x$	$6n + 3$	**Fear of Snakes**
3.	**Astraphobia**	$p + 8 + 7p$	$8x + 28$	**Fear of Light**
4.	**Ophidiophobia**	$8n + 3 - 2n$	$6n$	**Fear of Animals**
5.	**Pyrophobia**	$4(x + 3)$	$9n + 12$	**Fear of Dirt**
6.	**Acrophobia**	$6p + 17 - 8 - 2p$	$12p + 30$	**Fear of Infinity**
7.	**Hydrophobia**	$3(n + 6) + 3(n + 6)$	$4p + 9$	**Fear of Heights**
8.	**Photophobia**	$7(2x + 4) - 6x$	$4x + 12$	**Fear of Fire**
9.	**Apeirophobia**	$5(2p + 6) + 2p$	$4x$	**Fear of Darkness**
10.	**Mysophobia**	$n(6 + 3) + 12$	$8p + 8$	**Fear of Lightning**

Order Up!

Waiter! We'll have a large order of operations, with a helping of diner slang on the side.

Directions

1. Duplicate the reproducible for each student.
2. Review the rules for order of operations with students:
   a. First, do the math that's inside parentheses.
   b. Next, do the multiplication and division.
   c. Finally, do the addition and subtraction.

   Remember: Do each step from left to right. If there is more than one case of multiplication or division, do the problem on the left first, then move to the next problem on the right, and so on.
3. Distribute the reproducible and go over the example with students. Have them redo the problem on paper, but this time do the operations in a different order. How many different answers can they find? Ask a volunteer to demonstrate his or her alternative answers on the board. Encourage students to discuss why order of operations is useful to ensure that everyone gets the same answer for a math problem.
4. Instruct students to complete the page on their own. If you like, they may use calculators to do the computation.

Taking It Farther

- Have each student pick his or her favorite food from the list and make up a new series of operations that will yield that number. A classmate can do the math to find out which food was picked.
- Students may also use current teen expressions to make up their own order of operations puzzle. Or they may research jargon used by other groups such as surfers, snowboarders, or workers in a parent's or a relative's profession.

Assessing Skills

If there is more than one operation contained within parentheses, do students still follow order of operations?

LEARNING OBJECTIVE

Students solve problems using order of operations.

GROUPING

Individual

MATERIALS

- *Order Up!* reproducible (p. 242)
- paper and pencil
- calculators (optional)

Name ______________________ Date ____________

Order Up!

"Hey Louie—give me a British!" a waiter yells to the cook in a restaurant. He's using "diner slang" to say he needs an English muffin. Diner slang is a fast way to describe food orders. Plus, it's funny! To find out what other diner slang means, place your order for order of operations! The example below will show you how.

Diner Slang

52	Poached eggs on an English muffin
79	Corned beef hash
61	Orange juice
4	Crackers
18	Hot dogs
38	Water
208	Chili

EXAMPLE: 27 + 5 – (4 ÷ 2) × 7 ***"I need three bun pups!"***

- First, do the math in parentheses: 27 + 5 – 2 × 7
- Then, do the multiplication: 27 + 5 – 14
- Finally, do the addition and subtraction, from left to right: 32 – 14
- Answer: 18

Find your answer in the Diner Slang box. The food listed next to the correct number tells you what the order was for: Hot dogs.

Now, take a bite out of these unusual-sounding food orders!

1. 72 × 3 – 8 ***"Give me two bowls of red!"***

   This order is for ______________________.

2. 288 ÷ 12 × 3 + 7 ***"Clean up the kitchen!"***

   This order is for ______________________.

3. 42 – (2 × 6) ÷ 3 ***"Pour out three glasses of city juice!"***

   This order is for ______________________.

4. 20 × (7 – 2) – (8 × 6) ***"Give me an Adam and Eve on a raft!"***

   This order is for ______________________.

5. (12 – 32 ÷ 8) ÷ 2 ***"Where are those dog biscuits?"***

   This order is for ______________________.

6. (2 + 12 × 10) ÷ (11 – 9) ***"I need a squeeze!"***

   This order is for ______________________.

Numbers of Invention

Which came first, calculators or frozen food? This number line will get students plugged in to some of the world's greatest inventions!

Directions

1. Duplicate the reproducible for each student.
2. Review number lines and positive and negative numbers. Remind students that the greater a number is, the further to the right it is on the number line.
3. Draw the following number line on the board:

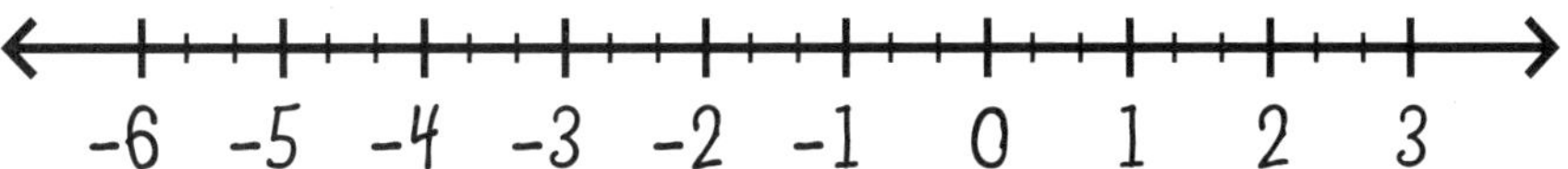

4. Call on volunteers to plot the points $1\frac{2}{3}$, –3, and $-5\frac{1}{3}$ on the number line.
5. Ask students: *Which number is the greatest? Which number is the least? How do you know?*
6. Distribute the reproducible and have students complete it on their own.

Taking It Further

Challenge each student to create a number line similar to the one in the activity but based on events in his or her own life. Partners can then trade puzzles and solve them to find the order of events.

Assessing Skills

- Do students understand that –3 is greater than –5?
- Note whether students plot negative fractions correctly, to the left of the negative whole number.

LEARNING OBJECTIVE

Students plot points on a number line.

GROUPING

Individual

MATERIALS

- *Numbers of Invention* reproducible (p. 244)

Name ____________________ Date ____________

Numbers of Invention

Over the years, scientists have come up with some terrific ideas. Today, it's pretty hard to imagine life without such wonders as computers, video games, or even Velcro.

Which of these inventions came first? Plot some points on a number line to find out! After you mark each point, write the name of the invention underneath. One is done for you. The inventions will go from earliest to most recent, from left to right along the number line.

Inventions

$-3\frac{3}{4}$	Car	$2\frac{7}{8}$	Velcro
-2	Frozen Food	$-\frac{5}{8}$	Television
$4\frac{1}{2}$	Audiocassette	$-3\frac{1}{8}$	Toaster
$-4\frac{1}{2}$	Telephone	$1\frac{1}{8}$	Tupperware
$5\frac{5}{8}$	Video Game	$-5\frac{3}{8}$	Calculator
$\frac{1}{4}$	Computer		

−6 −5 −4 −3 −2 −1 0 1 2 3 4 5 6

Car

Year each invention appeared, in order on the number line from least to greatest:
1833, 1876, 1889, 1918, 1924, 1927, 1944, 1945, 1948, 1963, 1972

Write the name of each invention and the year it appeared.

Inequality Mix-Up

When half the students in your class search for the student whose graph matches their inequality, the result equals fun!

Directions

1. Review the symbols >, ≥, <, and ≤. Remind students that inequalities using these symbols can be solved much the same as an equation.
2. Write the following inequality on the board:

$$-5x - 4 < 11$$
$$-5x - 4 + 4 < 11 + 4$$
$$-5x < 15$$
$$-5x/-5 < 15/-5$$
$$x > -3$$

   Ask volunteers to go though each step to solve it, or write and explain each step yourself. Note that when you divide by a negative number, you must reverse the inequality symbol.
3. On the board, graph the solution on a number line:

4. If the plotted point is filled in, it represents a number. If the solution to the inequality were $x \geq -3$, the graph would be as follows:

–5 –4 –3 –2 –1 0 1 2 3 4 5

5. Distribute one index card to each student. Half the cards should have an inequality written on them. The other half should show the graph of the solution.
6. Have each student with an inequality card find the student who has the matching graphed solution.

Taking It Further

Ask each student to create and graph his or her own inequality on two index cards. You now have enough inequality cards to play the game two more times!

Assessing Skills

Do students understand the difference between graphing > and ≥, and the difference between graphing < and ≤?

LEARNING OBJECTIVE

Students solve and graph inequalities.

GROUPING

Whole class

MATERIALS

✸ index card for each student

ADVANCE PREPARATION

Write inequalities and their corresponding graphed solutions on different index cards. Each student should receive one card. Here are examples of some inequalities you may want to use:

$x + 2 \geq 7$

$3n < -9$

$15y + 8 > 9y + 20$

$4b - 7 < 9$

$2(c - 3) > -2$

$5j \leq 3j + 10$

$-3m \geq 6$

$-4h - 3 > 17$

$t + 3 < 5$

$4 + 7r - 6 > 5$

$p - 21 \leq -21$

$8w + 7 \geq 55$

Amazing Animal Inequalities

Get ready for some animal facts that are really wild! Students work with inequalities to figure out which statements are true.

Directions

1. Duplicate the reproducible for each student.
2. Review the inequality symbols >, <, ≥, and ≤ with students. Emphasize that for an inequality statement to be true, the smaller end of the symbol must point to the smaller number.
3. Write the following inequality statements on the board:

$$x + 5 < 8$$

$$2y - 3 \geq 12$$

   For each inequality, ask volunteers to find values for *x* and *y* that make the statement true. Then have them identify values for *x* and *y* that make the statement false.
4. Distribute the reproducible and let students complete it on their own. If you like, they may use calculators to do the computation.

LEARNING OBJECTIVE

Students evaluate inequalities.

GROUPING

Individual

MATERIALS

- *Amazing Animal Inequalities* reproducible (p. 247)
- calculators (optional)

Taking It Further

Ask each student to do library research on a favorite animal, making a list of interesting facts about the animal. Then they use their imaginations to come up with false statements about the animals. To accompany their statements, they can write true and false inequalities for classmates to solve.

Assessing Skills

Note whether students reverse the greater than and less than signs when evaluating the inequalities.

Name ______________________ Date ______________

Amazing Animal Inequalities

Below you'll find some incredible facts about animals. But only some of them are true! To find out which statements are just hogwash, look at each inequality. If the inequality is true, so is the fact. Circle True. If the inequality is false, the statement is too. Circle False.

1. Some types of bats measure just one inch long.

   True or False?

   $2x - 14 \leq 8,\ x = 11$

2. Ostriches spend 10 hours per day hiding their heads in holes in the ground.

   True or False?

   $12 < 5r + 4,\ r = 2$

3. A giant South American species of rabbit can weigh up to 275 pounds.

   True or False?

   $o + 14 - 2o \leq 12,\ o = 1$

4. Blue whales weigh as much as 260,000 pounds.

   True or False?

   $20 > 7 + 4j,\ j = 2$

5. Koalas are the laziest animals in the world. They snooze 22 hours per day.

   True or False?

   $4y + 6 + 3y < 50,\ y = 6$

6. There are at least 1,000,000 insects for every human being on Earth!

   True or False?

   $16 < 3t + 8,\ t = 3$

7. In England, "Beano" is one of the top ten names for pet dogs.

   True or False?

   $4c + c - 6 \geq 15,\ c = 5$

8. One of the top ten names for pet goldfish in the U.S. is "Fluffy."

   True or False?

   $u \div 12 \geq 3,\ u = 24$

9. Some clams live up to 200 years.

   True or False?

   $15 \geq 18 - 3z,\ z = 1$

10. The amazing cheetah can run 120 miles per hour.

    True or False?

    $3p - 12 > 0,\ p = 4$

Happy Birth Day!

On which day of the week were you born? Using this handy formula, students will find out in less time than it takes to sing "Happy Birthday to Me!"

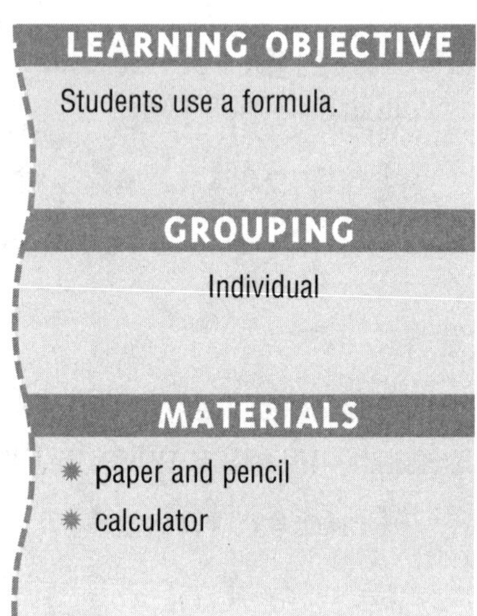

Directions

1. Explain to students that they will use a formula to find out on which day of the week they were born. Write this formula on the board:

$$\text{Birth Day } (b) = \frac{y + d + f}{7}$$

Let y equal the year that you were born.
Let d equal the day of the year you were born, from 1 to 366.
Let f equal $\frac{y-1}{4}$. Ignore the remainder and just use the whole number for f.

2. You may want to go over the following example first and work through each step as a class.

Juana was born on April 15, 1984, which is a leap year. (Remember that February has 29 days in a leap year. Any year that is evenly divisible by 4 is a leap year.)

a. Add 31 (days in January) + 29 (days in February) + 31 (days in March) + 15 (days in April) = 106.

b. Plug in the values for y, d, and f into the formula for b. Do the division without a calculator to find the remainder.

$$\frac{1984 + 106 + 495}{7} = 369 \text{ R2}$$

c. Use the remainder to find out on which day you were born. Write the following on the board as a reference:

0 = Friday	1 = Saturday	2 = Sunday	3 = Monday
4 = Tuesday	5 = Wednesday	6 = Thursday	

d. Since Juana's remainder is 2, April 15, 1984, was a Sunday.

3. Have each student use his or her birthday to work through the steps.

Taking It Farther

Have students find the birth day for members of their families. Also, encourage them to research the birthdays of their favorite sports and media celebrities and use the formula to find their birth days.

Assessing Skills

Ask students to explain the formula in their own words. Are they able to describe what each variable stands for?

The Shadow Knows

How tall is your school building? Students don't have to climb it to find out. Just wait for a sunny day, head outside, and use this formula!

LEARNING OBJECTIVE

Students practice using a formula.

GROUPING

Whole class

MATERIALS

* paper and pencil
* yardstick or meterstick
* measuring tape (or another yardstick)
* calculators (optional)

Directions

1. Make sure it is a sunny day. Explain to students that they will be using shadows to find the heights of tall objects. Have them write the following formula at the top of their papers:

$$\frac{\text{Stick Length} \times \text{Object Shadow}}{\text{Stick Shadow}} = \text{Object Height}$$

2. Take the class outside. Instruct students to hold the yardstick or meter stick straight up, touching the ground. Using the measuring tape or the other yardstick, have them measure the shadow cast along the ground by the upright yardstick.
3. Next, ask students to use the measuring tape or yardstick to measure the shadows cast by several tall objects, such as your school building, a flagpole, or a tree.
4. Students should use their measurements and the formula to find the heights of the objects. You may want to let them use calculators to do the computation.

Taking It Further

* Have students check that the formula works by measuring their own shadows and using the formula to find their own heights.
* Ask students: *Why would you get an inaccurate answer if you measured the yardstick's shadow at 9:00 A.M. and then measured a tree's shadow at 11:30 A.M.?* [Because the sun would be higher in the sky at 11:30 A.M., shortening the length of the tree's shadow. This formula is based on the following ratio: $\frac{\text{Stick Length}}{\text{Stick Shadow}} = \frac{\text{Object Height}}{\text{Object Shadow}}$.]

Assessing Skills

Do students convert all measurements into the same units (such as inches or centimeters) before they plug the numbers into the formula?

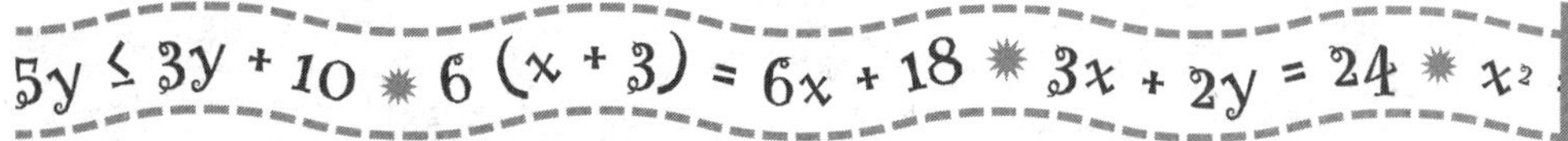

Bone Up on Formulas

Make no bones about it—students will get a thrill out of finding out how forensic scientists use formulas to do their jobs!

Directions

1. Duplicate the reproducible for each student and distribute.
2. If necessary, review the terms *variable* and *formula* with the class.
3. Explain to students that they will be using formulas that are part of a forensic scientist's job. Scientists use these formulas to find out more about old bones or bones related to crimes.
4. Let students complete the activity on their own. If they are not yet comfortable using formulas, you may want to go over the first one or two questions with the entire class first.

Taking It Farther

- Remind students that all measurements in the activity are in centimeters. To get an idea of how tall each person mentioned in the activity really is, have them convert measurements into meters or feet and inches.
- Challenge students to find other jobs in which formulas are used. They may interview family members or do research in a library. Examples include retail sales (in which sale prices and stock needs may be calculated with a formula), accounting (tax rates), and truck driving (using the formula for rate to estimate how long it will take to drive a given distance). Then ask each student to interview an adult who uses formulas on the job. Students can present their findings in class, and even invite the adult to visit the class and answer questions about his or her job.

Assessing Skills

Note whether students understand the difference among the variables r, h, and t, and employ the correct formula for each question.

LEARNING OBJECTIVE

Students practice using a formula.

GROUPING

Whole class

MATERIALS

- *Bone Up on Formulas* reproducible (p. 251)
- calculators (optional)

Name ______________________ Date ______________

Bone Up on Formulas

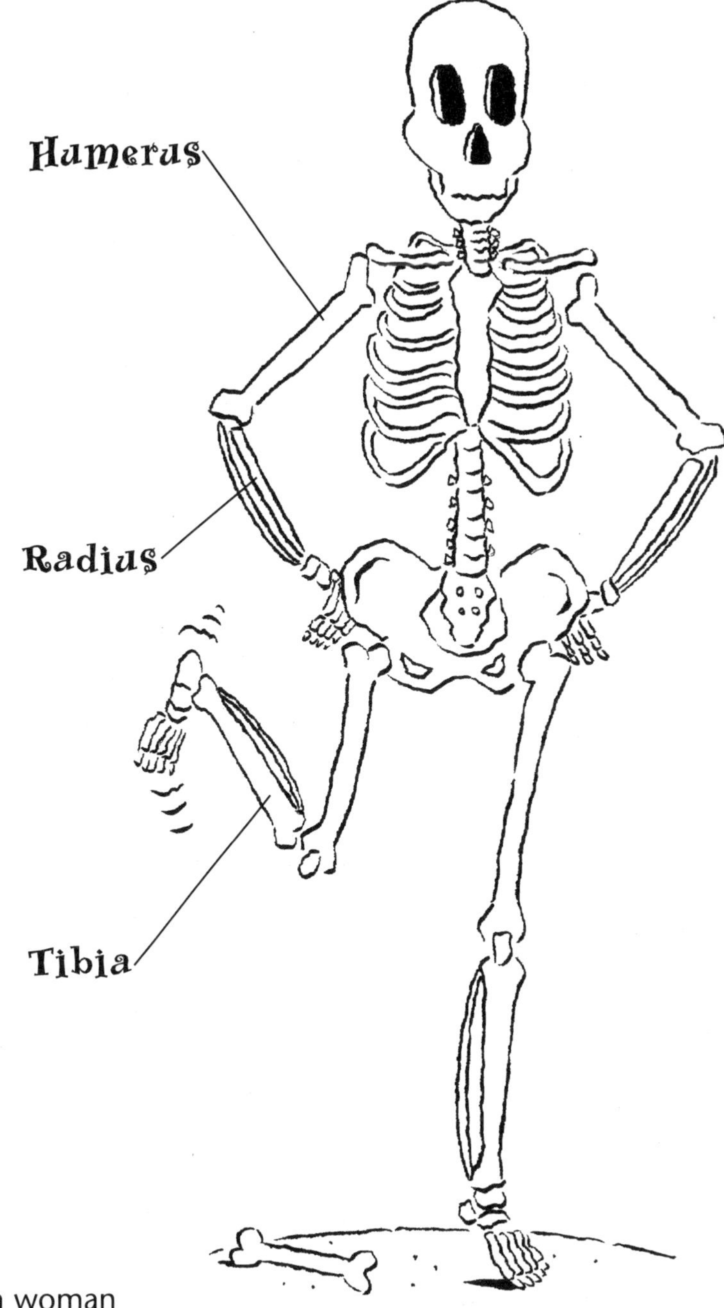

To a forensic scientist, a skeleton isn't just a pile of old bones. It's a clue! Sometimes, a scientist may have only one bone to study. But thanks to formulas, even that can be enough to find out information such as how tall the person was when he or she was alive.

Take a look at the real-life forensic formulas below. Then use them to answer the questions.

Forensic Formulas for Height

In these formulas, r = radius, h = humerus, and t = tibia. All measurements are in centimeters (cm).

MALE:	$80.4 + 3.7r$ = height
	$73.6 + 3.0h$ = height
	$81.7 + 2.4t$ = height
FEMALE:	$73.5 + 3.9r$ = height
	$65.0 + 3.1h$ = height
	$72.6 + 2.5t$ = height

1. A forensic scientist is given the tibia of a woman who lived hundreds of years ago, found at an archaeological dig. What formula should the scientist use to find out how tall the woman was? ______________
2. If the tibia from question 1 was 37 cm long, how tall was the woman? ______________
3. Suppose police find a man's tibia that is 46 cm long. How tall was he? ______________
4. Say a woman's humerus, 28 cm long, is discovered. How tall was she? ______________
5. A forensic scientist finds a man's radius, 31 cm long. How tall was he? ______________

Party With Variables

Real-life math meets real-life fun as students use prealgebra skills to plan a party.

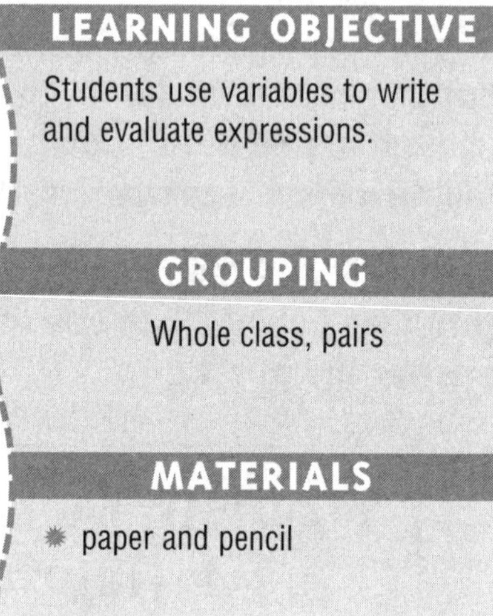

LEARNING OBJECTIVE

Students use variables to write and evaluate expressions.

GROUPING

Whole class, pairs

MATERIALS

✱ paper and pencil

Directions

1. Start by reviewing the term *variables* and tell students they'll be using variables to plan a fictional party. Discuss the many variables involved in party planning, including number of guests to invite, types of food and beverages, and decorations.
2. Have students suggest items to buy for the party. Write the list of items on the board, and assign a letter variable to each item. For example, p could be used to represent pizzas, and c to represent bags of chips.
3. Discuss the number of guests to invite. Once the class has decided, begin writing expressions on the board showing how many of each item will be needed. Say there will be 30 guests, and you want to have one bag of chips for every 3 guests. The expression for the number of bags of chips needed is $10c$. Ask volunteers to write expressions for the remaining items on the board.
4. Next, write an estimated cost for an item on the board, such as $c = \$1.69$. Explain that this means one bag of chips costs $1.69.
5. Have pairs estimate costs for the remaining items. Using these estimates, students evaluate the expressions. What will be the total cost of the party? Ask students to compare and discuss their answers.

Taking It Further

Let students research the actual prices of items for their party, finding prices for different brands of the same item, different types of foods, and so on. They may work in groups, where each group member is responsible for researching a different item. Then each group evaluates the expressions using the real-life prices and compares the total party costs if different brands are purchased. If possible, you may even have students use this method to plan a real holiday or end-of-the-year party.

Assessing Skills

- Observe whether students can explain the reasoning behind the expressions they write. Do they understand that $10c$ means $10 \times c$?
- Two items may begin with the same letter. Do students realize that they must then assign a different variable to the second item?

Variable Bingo

Students will invariably have a great time as they play this game. Plus they'll get lots of practice using variables.

LEARNING OBJECTIVE

Students substitute different values for variables.

GROUPING

Whole class

MATERIALS

- *Variable Bingo* reproducible (p. 254) (2 copies for each student)
- 24 slips of paper
- paper bag or other container

ADVANCE PREPARATION

On each of the 24 slips of paper, write one of the following: A1, A2, A3, A4, A5, A6, B1, B2, B3, B4, B5, B6, C1, C2, C3, C4, C5, C6, D1, D2, D3, D4, D5, D6.

Put the slips of paper in the paper bag.

Directions

1. Duplicate and distribute the reproducibles.
2. Ask students to randomly fill in each square on their bingo cards with one of the bingo numbers.
3. Draw a slip of paper out of the paper bag, calling out the letter and number that you drew. The letter tells students which expression to evaluate. The number tells them what value to substitute for the variable in that expression. For example, if you call B4, students should substitute the number 4 for n in Expression B: $n + 21$. The solution is 25.
4. Students look for that solution on their bingo cards. If the number is there, they draw an X over it.
5. Continue drawing slips of paper and have students solve the equations. The first student to get four across, down, or diagonally wins.
6. Play the game again, with students choosing different numbers for their bingo cards.

Taking It Further

As a more difficult way to play the game, have students randomly write A1, A2, A3, A4, A5, A6, B1, B2, and so on in their bingo squares. Then write the solution numbers (the bingo numbers listed on the reproducible) on 24 slips of paper, and draw those from the bag. When you call out a number, students must figure out which variable value was used with which expression to get that number.

Assessing Skills

- Do students use estimation to check the reasonableness of their solutions?
- If the solution is not on their cards, note whether students check the bingo number list to make sure it is one of the possible solutions.

Name ______________________ Date ____________

Variable Bingo

Write one of the bingo numbers in each square.
Use a different number in each square.

Bingo Numbers

0	3	4	6	7	9
10	12	13	15	16	19
22	23	24	25	26	27
29	31	33	35	37	39

EXPRESSION A: $3x - 3$
EXPRESSION B: $n + 21$
EXPRESSION C: $22 - 3k$
EXPRESSION D: $27 + 2p$

WORK SPACE

Magical Memorizing Math Teacher

Use this memory trick on students, and they'll be in for a treat when they use variables and the distributive property to see how it works!

Directions

1. When class begins, tell students that you have memorized an entire textbook. Tell them you will prove it, but that they will have to do some math first.
2. Ask students for a three-digit number. Write the number on the board. Reverse the three digits, and subtract the smaller number from the larger number.
3. The difference will be one of the following numbers: 0, 99, 198, 297, 396, 495, 594, 693, 792, or 891. If the number is within the range of your textbook's pages, tell students to turn to that page while you magically tell them, without looking, the last word on that page. If the answer is 0 or a number that is too high, try again.
4. Repeat the test until it becomes evident that the same numbers are coming up again and again. Then do the following proof to show how the trick works.
5. Tell the class you will use variable letters to represent the digits in the problem. Use x for the hundreds place, y for the tens place, and z for the ones place. Therefore, the first 3-digit number can be written: $100x + 10y + z$. (If students are confused, give them a concrete example, such as $327 = 300 + 20 + 7$.)
6. When the digits are reversed, you get $100z + 10y + x$. What happens now? Assume x is greater than z. When you take $100x + 10y + z$ and subtract $100z + 10y + x$, the answer is $99x - 99z$. With the distributive property, that becomes $99(x - z)$.
7. Since x and z are single-digit numbers, the difference between them will be 0, 1, 2, 3, 4, 5, 6, 7, 8, or 9. (This will be the same whether x or z is greater.) When you multiply these digits by 99, you will get the ten numbers listed above.

Taking It Farther

Have students research other algebra proofs and present an explanation of them to the class.

Assessing Skills

Challenge students to write step-by-step descriptions, in their own words, of how the above proof works.

LEARNING OBJECTIVE

Students use variables and the distributive property to understand an algebra proof.

GROUPING

Whole class

MATERIALS

* math textbook (or any other textbook)

ADVANCE PREPARATION

Before class, memorize the last word on the following pages of the textbook: 99, 198, 297, 396, 495, 594. (If your book is very long, also memorize the last word on the following pages: 693, 792, 891.) If you don't want to memorize the words, write out a small "cheat sheet" that can be hidden in your hand.

Train Trouble

Every stop on this train will give students more fun practice with variables!

Directions

1. Duplicate the reproducible for each group and distribute.
2. Divide the class into groups of 3 or 4. Instruct groups to cut out the spinners on the reproducible.
3. Players place their markers on Start and spin to see who goes first. To use the spinner, they spin the paper clip around the point of a pencil.
4. For their first turn, players spin to see how many spaces to move. On each succeeding turn, players spin and then evaluate the expression on the space by substituting the number spun for the variable. If the answer is a positive number, the player moves that many spaces forward. If it is a negative number, the player moves that many spaces backward.
5. Here is an example you may use to explain game play to students. *Say your marker is on the space* r – 3. *If you spin a 1, your answer will be –2, and you must move back 2 spaces. If you spin a 4, your answer will be 1, so you move forward 1 space.*
6. The first player to pass the Finish space wins. It is not necessary to reach Finish on an exact number.

Taking It Further

After playing the game a few times, ask students to predict what would happen if the spinner were changed to show the numbers 1–8. Students can trace the spinner on the reproducible and divide it into 8 equal sections. After labeling the sections from 1 to 8, they can cut out the spinner and use it to play the game again to test their theories.

Assessing Skills

Observe whether students have difficulty evaluating the expressions when the answer is a negative number.

LEARNING OBJECTIVE

Students substitute numeric values for variables.

GROUPING

Cooperative groups of 3 or 4

MATERIALS

- *Train Trouble* reproducible (p. 257)
- different-colored game markers for each student
- scrap paper
- scissors, pencil, and paper clip (to make the spinner)

Name ______________________________ Date ______________

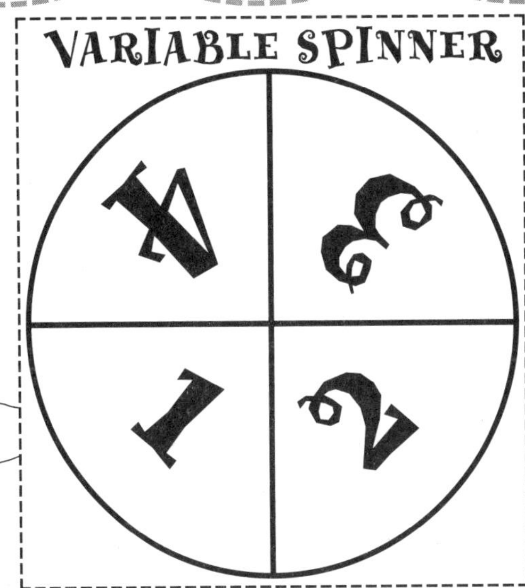

Train Trouble

All aboard! The *Algebra Express* train is about to depart. Unfortunately, the train is overdue for repairs. Sometimes it travels fast, sometimes it travels slowly, and sometimes it even travels backward! Better get that train to the repair shop . . . and step on it!

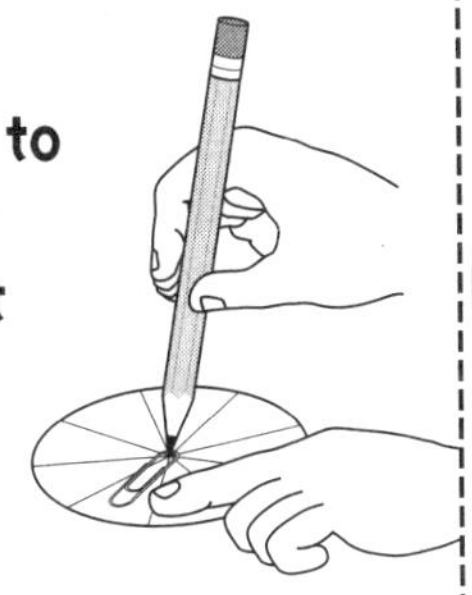

VARIABLE SPINNER
4
3
1
2

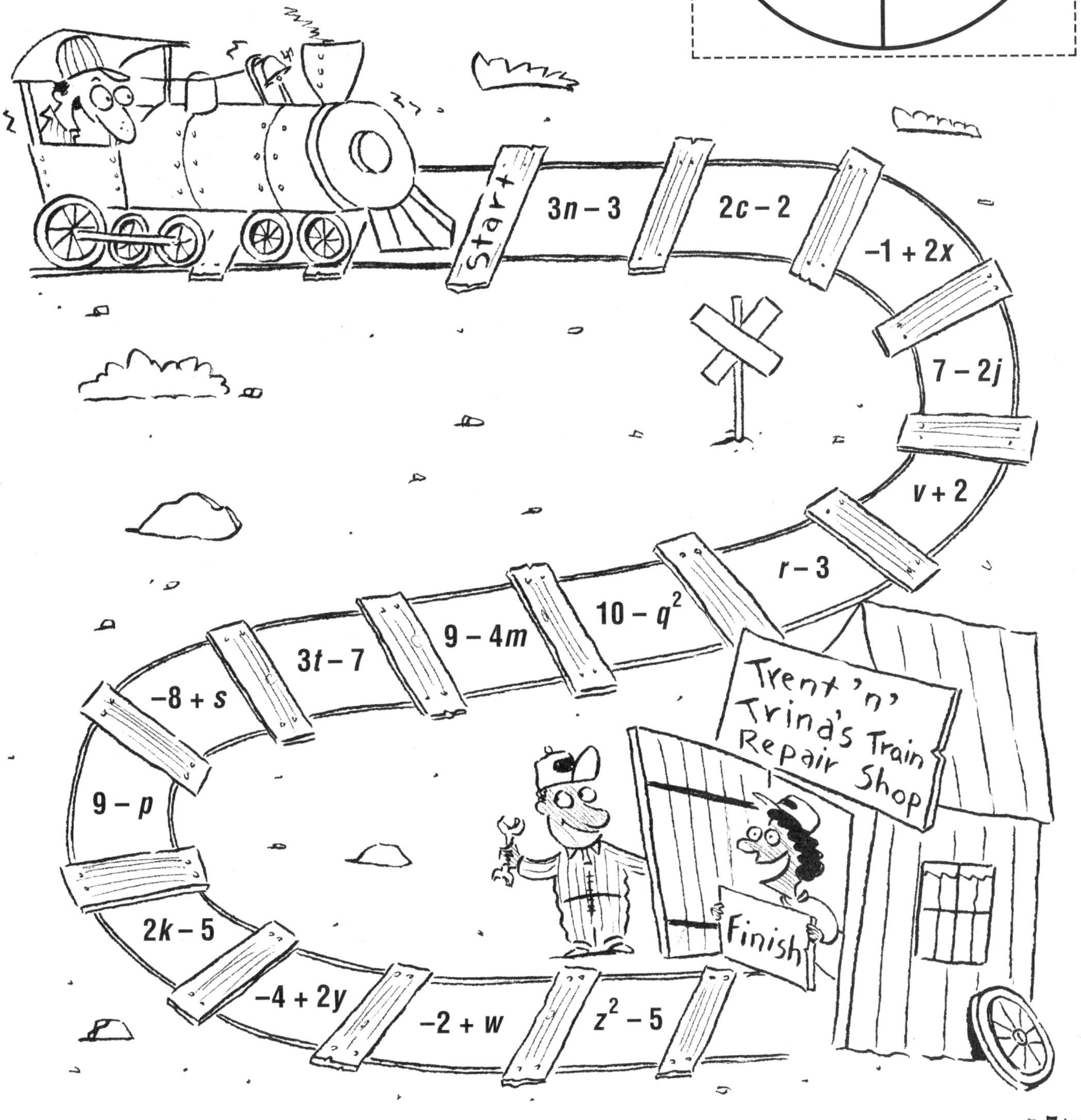
Start
$3n - 3$
$2c - 2$
$-1 + 2x$
$7 - 2j$
$v + 2$
$r - 3$
$10 - q^2$
$9 - 4m$
$3t - 7$
$-8 + s$
$9 - p$
$2k - 5$
$-4 + 2y$
$-2 + w$
$z^2 - 5$
Trent 'n' Trina's Train Repair Shop
Finish

Express Yourself

How do students' favorite stars of sports, music, and movies express themselves? Evaluate expressions to find out!

Directions

1. Duplicate the reproducible for each student and distribute.
2. Review the term *expression* with students and remind them that expressions are evaluated. The evaluation of an expression will change if you change the value of any of the variables in the expression. On the board, write the following expression from question 1 of the reproducible: $6m + 3$.
3. Go over the example using the value $m = 7$ from the reproducible. Ask a volunteer to evaluate the expression again, using a different value for m.
4. Let students complete the page on their own. You may want to have them use calculators to do the computation for each problem.

Taking It Farther

What happens when you substitute different values for the variables in the activity? Encourage students to pick one of the single-variable expressions on the reproducible and evaluate it where the variable = 1, 2, 3, and so on. (Students should round their answers to the nearest hundredth.) What pattern is evident? Students can compare their answers, explaining how they think different operations such as division and multiplication affected their results.

Assessing Skills

- In cases where there is more than one variable, note whether students substitute the correct value for the correct variable.
- Are students applying knowledge of order of operations to evaluate the expressions correctly?

LEARNING OBJECTIVE

Students evaluate expressions when given values for variables.

GROUPING

Individual

MATERIALS

- *Express Yourself* reproducible (p. 259)
- calculators (optional)

Name ______________________ Date ____________

Express Yourself

You probably have a lot on your mind. Well, so do the famous people listed on this page! Each of them made one of the statements in the box. Who said what?

To find out, evaluate the expression above each celebrity's name. Then find your answer next to a quote in the Answer Box. Write the quote in the blank. We did the first one for you.

Answer Box

10.68	"I always liked math."
54	"I'm not a couch potato."
20.55	"I used to eat mayonnaise sandwiches."
45	"I always wanted to go in the space shuttle."
24.18	"I'm such a mall rat."
30	"I think it's OK to be a movie star."
37.8	"I have a nervous stomach."
20	"I feel a little ridiculous."

1. Evaluate $6m + 3$, where $m = 7$.

   Substitute 7 for m: $6 \times 7 + 3 = 45$.

   Actor Will Smith said: "I always wanted to go in the space shuttle."

2. Evaluate $4p$, where $p = 5$.

   Actress Claire Danes said: ______________________

3. Evaluate $7i - 12$, where $i = 3.24$.

   Basketball star Scottie Pippen said: ______________________

4. Evaluate $r + 3t$, where $r = 0.9$ and $t = 12.3$.

   Actor Brad Pitt said: ______________________

5. Evaluate $25.75k - 12m$, where $k = 9$ and $m = 17.6$.

   Actress Jennifer Aniston said: ______________________

6. Evaluate $23 + 4.8z - y$, where $z = 7.5$ and $y = 5$.

   Football star Jerry Rice said: ______________________

7. Evaluate $6j \div 3.07$, where $j = 15.35$.

   Actress Winona Ryder said: ______________________

8. Evaluate $4.004 + 8g \div 0.5e$, where $g = 12.61$ and $e = 10$.

   Singer Darius Rucker of Hootie and the Blowfish said: ______________________

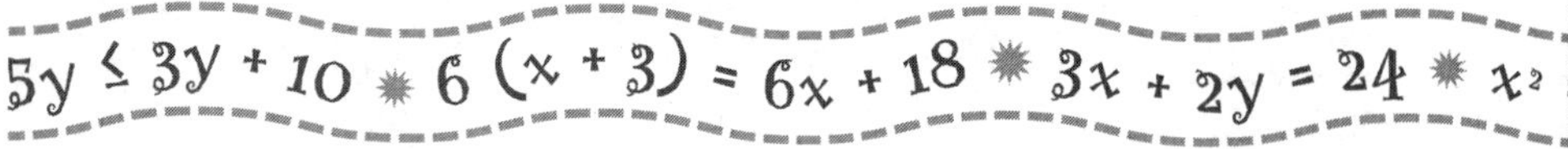

Equations Are the Name of the Game

Do students love basketball? Here's an equation that can help sports fans really know the score!

LEARNING OBJECTIVE

Students use equations to solve an everyday problem.

GROUPING

Whole class

MATERIALS

- sports section of a newspaper, showing box scores from basketball games (Note: This activity should be done during basketball season.)

Directions

1. Ask a student who is familiar with basketball to explain the sport's 2- and 3-point shot scoring system.
2. Many box scores list a player's total number of field goals scored (with both 2- and 3-point shots included), number of 3-point shots scored, and total points scored. They do not list 2-point shots scored. (Box score formats may vary. If your newspaper does itemize 2-point shots, leave out that number when you give the information for this activity to students.)
3. Ask students: *Using the numbers from the box score, how could you find out how many 2-point field goals a player scored in a game?* After some discussion, they should find that they can multiply the number of 3-point shots scored by 3, subtract the product from the total number of points scored, and divide the difference by 2.
4. Challenge students to make this process easier by writing an equation to describe the number of 2-point shots, 3-point shots, and total points scored. They should start by assigning a variable to describe 2-point shots and another variable to describe 3-point shots. After some discussion, they should come up with this equation or a variation of it:

   If t = total points, p = 2-point shots, and q = 3-point shots, then: $t = 2p + 3q$.
5. Allow time for students to plug numbers from several box scores into their equations.

Taking It Further

What other equations can be used in determining sports scores? Hold a class discussion, asking students who are sports fans to share their knowledge to help identify equations.

Assessing Skills

In the equation, do students understand why one variable is multiplied by 2, while one is multiplied by 3? Ask them to explain in their own words.

The Amazin' Equation Game

Get ready for do-it-yourself math, as students make up equations for classmates to solve.

Directions

1. Duplicate the reproducible for each student and distribute.
2. If necessary, review how to use inverse operations to solve simple equations of the form $x + a = b$ or $b = x + a$.
3. Divide the class into groups. One student will be the master of ceremonies (MC), while the other students are the players.
4. Direct students to cut out the spinners on the reproducible. To begin a round, the MC spins the number spinner four times and then spins the operations spinner two times. Each player writes the four digits and two operations (– or +) spun in the spaces for Round 1.
5. Each player now creates an equation using the four digits and the two operations. The equation should be of the form $x + a = b$ or $b = x + a$. For example, the following digits and operations are spun: 7, 3, 0, 8, –, +. Three possible equations that could be made are:

   $80 = x + (-37)$ $x - 8 = 70 + 3$ $-308 = x + 7$
6. Now, each player passes his or her reproducible to the player on the left. Players solve the equations they are given, with the player who wrote each equation checking the answer. Each player who solves an equation correctly gets one point. The MC keeps score.
7. For rounds 2 through 4, students alternate passing their equations to the right and to the left. Whoever has the most points after four rounds is the winner.

LEARNING OBJECTIVE

Students write and solve equations.

GROUPING

Cooperative groups of 3 to 5

MATERIALS

- *The Amazin' Equation Game* reproducible (p. 262)
- scrap paper and pencil
- scissors, a pencil, and a paper clip for each group (to make the spinner)
- calculators (optional)

Taking It Further

To make the game harder, white-out one + and one – on the operations spinner on a duplicate of the reproducible. Write × and ÷ in their place and duplicate the revised reproducible. Note: In this version of the game, some equations may yield long decimal answers. You may want to have students use calculators and round answers to the nearest hundredth or thousandth.

Assessing Skills

Note whether students are able to think of several different types of equations. Also, observe whether they have difficulty solving equations in which the variable is to the right of the equal sign.

Name ______________________ Date ______________

The Amazin' Equation Game

ROUND 1

Numbers: ☐ ☐ ☐ ☐

Operations: ☐ ☐

Equation: ______________________

Solution: $x =$ ______________________

ROUND 3

Numbers: ☐ ☐ ☐ ☐

Operations: ☐ ☐

Equation: ______________________

Solution: $x =$ ______________________

ROUND 2

Numbers: ☐ ☐ ☐ ☐

Operations: ☐ ☐

Equation: ______________________

Solution: $x =$ ______________________

ROUND 4

Numbers: ☐ ☐ ☐ ☐

Operations: ☐ ☐

Equation: ______________________

Solution: $x =$ ______________________

NUMBERS SPINNER

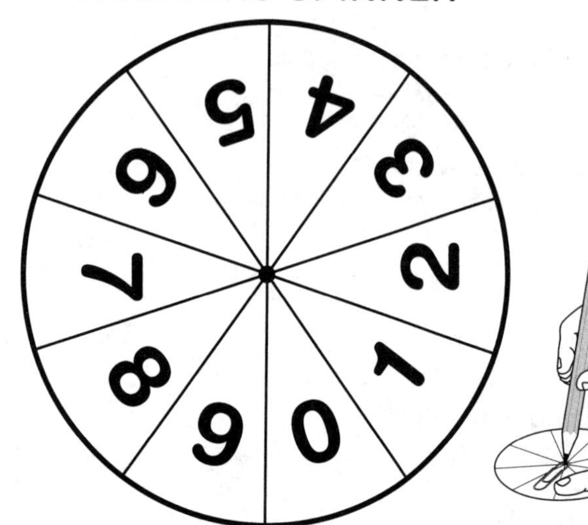

OPERATIONS SPINNER

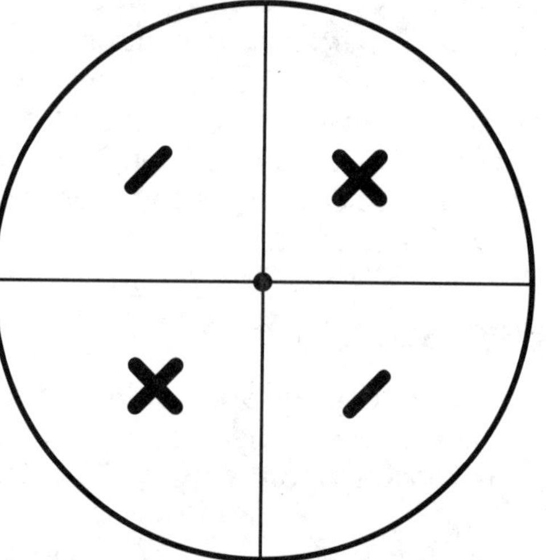

On Sale Now—Algebra!

In this real-life math activity, students use equations to discover how much they'd pay in finance charges if they bought a product on an installment plan.

LEARNING OBJECTIVE

Students solve equations and see how prealgebra can be used in everyday life.

GROUPING

Whole class

MATERIALS

* newspaper and magazine ads, store circulars, and so on, showing installment plan prices and cash prices for products such as stereo systems, cars, and kitchen appliances

Directions

1. A few weeks before doing the activity, ask students to look for ads for products that offer the option of full payment or payment by an installment plan. They may also write this information for products shown in television ads or infomercials. If students have an older sibling who has taken out a loan to pay for college, they can also use information from the student loan repayment plan.
2. Once you have collected a few advertisements, you're ready to do the activity.
3. Go over the term *finance charge*. Can students explain what a finance charge is?
4. Write the following equation on the board:

   Cash price (c) = Installment plan price (i) – Finance charge (f)
5. Write the information from an ad on the board. Ask a volunteer to come up and use the information to plug the cash price and the installment plan price into the equation. (The student will have to multiply the amount of one installment payment by the number of payments required.)
6. Next, call on another volunteer to solve the equation and determine the finance charge.
7. Repeat the activity for all the advertisements collected.

Taking It Farther

Ask students: *Would you ever consider buying something on an installment plan? Why or why not? What are some pros and cons to buying on an installment plan?* Have students write a paragraph that refers to the results of the class activity.

Assessing Skills

Observe to see if students use estimation to check whether their answers make sense.

Step "Two" It!

Students solve two-step equations to find out who stole Two-Step Tony's tap shoes!

Directions

1. Duplicate the reproducible for each student.
2. Review the process of solving two-step equations in class. Here is an example you can write on the board:

$$x + y = 14$$
$$3x - 2y = 2$$

3. Call on a volunteer to solve the equations for x and y, assuming that x and y have the same value in both equations. [$x = 6$, $y = 8$]
4. If students have trouble with the example, go through the steps on the board of one possible solution:
   a. Use inverse operations to rewrite the first equation:
   $$x = 14 - y$$
   b. Substitute for x in the second equation:
   $$3(14 - y) - 2y = 2$$
   c. Solve for y:
   $$42 - 3y - 2y = 2$$
   $$40 = 5y$$
   $$8 = y$$
   d. Use the value for y to solve for x:
   $$x + 8 = 14, \text{ so } x = 6$$
   e. Check that your answer is correct by plugging the values for x and y into both equations to see if they work.
5. Distribute the reproducible and let students complete it on their own. They should have plenty of scrap paper for doing the calculations. If you like, they may also use calculators to do the computation.

Taking It Further

Challenge students to write their own two-step equations for classmates to solve.

Assessing Skills

Observe whether students make correct use of the distributive property when substituting values for a variable. For example, in the problem above, $3(14 - y)$ becomes $42 - 3y$. Also, what do students do if the values they find for x and y do not work in the original equations?

LEARNING OBJECTIVE

Students solve two-step equations.

GROUPING

Individual

MATERIALS

* *Step "Two" It!* reproducible (p. 265)
* scrap paper and pencil
* calculators (optional)

Name ______________________ Date ______________

Step "Two" It!

Trouble in Tinsel Town! Someone has stolen the famous dancer Two-Step Tony's tap shoes! To taunt poor Tony, the thief left a clue—some two-step equations.

First, solve the two-step equations to find the values of x and y. Then, look for those numbers on the lineup of suspects below.

A. $x - y = 3$ ANSWER: $x =$ ______

$4y + x = 38$ $y =$ ______

B. $2x + 4y = 54$ ANSWER: $x =$ ______

$23 = 3y - 2x$ $y =$ ______

C. $y - 3x = -30$ ANSWER: $x =$ ______

$x + 2y = 94$ $y =$ ______

Circle the suspect who is carrying or wearing all six numbers. That person is the thief!

Factor Falls

Factors make a big splash as students try to find their way through a white-water rafting maze.

Directions

1. Duplicate the reproducible for each student and distribute.
2. Review the term *factor* with students.
3. Write the following list of numbers on the board: 5, 9, 3, 81, 25, 27, 150, 675. Call on volunteers to identify numbers on the list that are factors of other numbers on the list. Then ask them to write more factors of the listed numbers on the board.
4. Have students complete the reproducible on their own.

Taking It Further

Challenge students to find as many factors as possible for the numbers in the maze. Who can come up with the most factors?

Assessing Skills

Observe whether students use basic multiplication facts and divisibility tests to help them find the correct answers. For example, the number 432 does not end in a 0 or 5, so it is not divisible by 5. When students are trying to find a factor of 432, the number 15 can be automatically ruled out, since any multiple of 15 will also be divisible by 5. Therefore, the other choice listed (12) must be the correct answer.

LEARNING OBJECTIVE

Students identify factors of numbers.

GROUPING

Individual

MATERIALS

- *Factor Falls* reproducible (p. 267)
- markers or pencils
- calculators (optional)

Name ____________________ Date ____________

Factor Falls

Are you ready to brave the rapids of Factor Falls? It's a dangerous ride—and you'll need a strong knowledge of factors to make it down safely!

At each fork in the path, you'll come to a rock with a number. To avoid crashing into the rock, follow the path going down the falls that contains a factor of that number. If there is no path with a factor, you've made a wrong turn. Go back and try again. Trace your path with a marker or pencil.

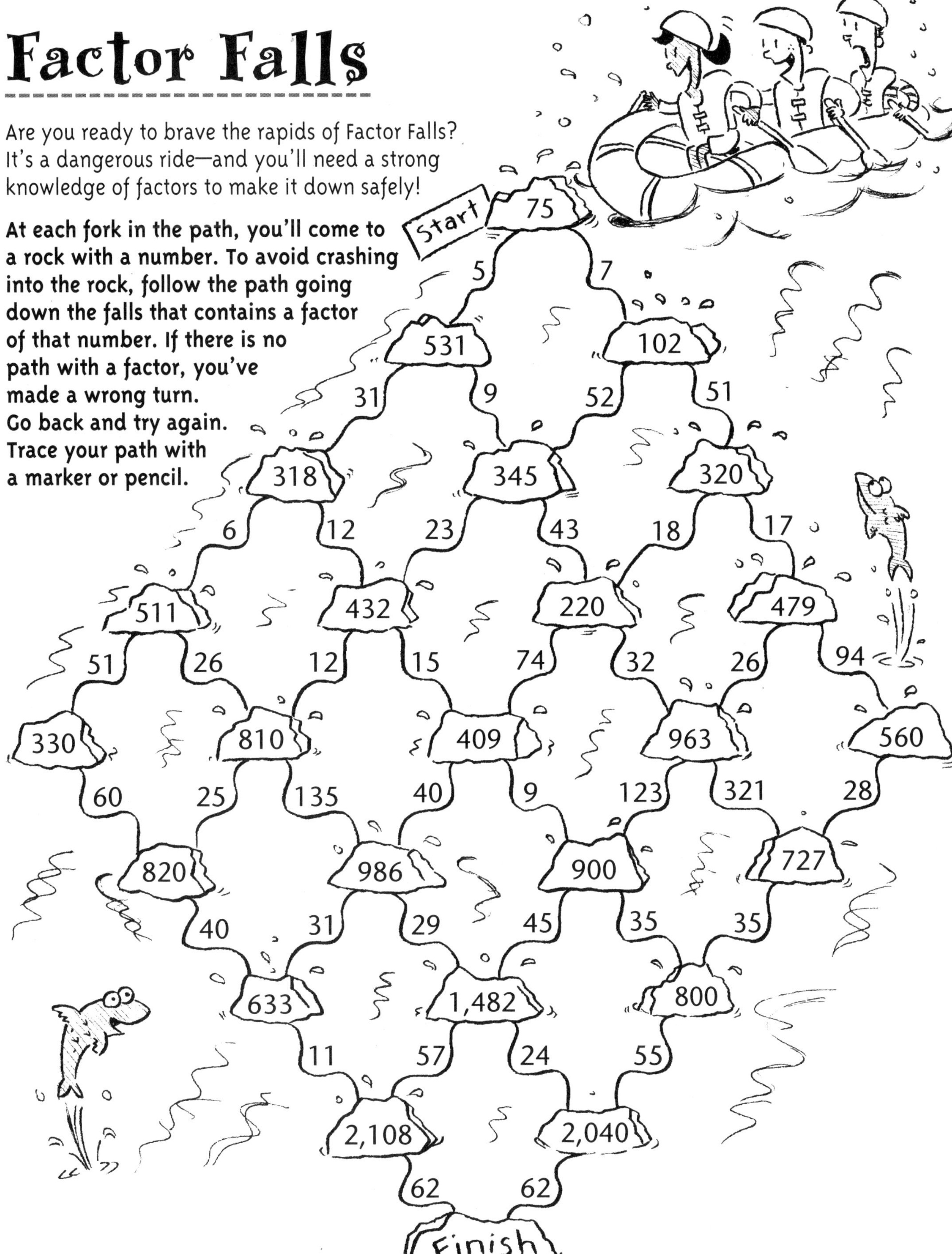

Let's Make a Factor!

Who knew factors could be so much fun? As they play this game, students may not even notice that they're practicing factoring and problem solving!

Directions

1. Duplicate the reproducible for each pair and distribute.
2. Review the term *factor* with students. You may also want to review common divisibility tests that can be used to easily find factors of numbers (for example, a number is divisible by 5 if it ends in 5 or 0).
3. Divide students into pairs. Direct them to use the spinner as shown on the reproducible. Pairs spin to decide who goes first.
4. Player 2 spins four numbers. Player 1 writes the numbers in the "Numbers Spun" spaces on the score sheet. Then, Player 1 uses three of those numbers in any order to make a 3-digit number. Player 1 writes his or her number in the "My 3-Digit Number" spaces on the score sheet. In the space below, Player 1 writes as many factors as he or she can find for the number. The object is to create a number that has as many factors as possible. If you like, students can use calculators to help them find and check factors. (If there is not enough space on the score sheet, scrap paper can be used to write out the factors.)
5. Now, Player 1 spins four numbers, and Player 2 makes a 3-digit number from them. Player 2 finds as many factors as possible for his or her number.
6. The player who has found more factors after three rounds wins.

LEARNING OBJECTIVE

Students find factors for 3-digit numbers.

GROUPING

Pairs

MATERIALS

* *Let's Make a Factor!* reproducible (p. 269)
* pencil and a paper clip for each pair of students (to make the spinner)
* calculators (optional)
* scrap paper (optional)

Taking It Farther

* Have students play the game, spinning only three numbers and making a 3-digit number. How does this change the game?
* After they play several times, encourage students to write journal entries explaining the strategies they used.

Assessing Skills

Observe whether students are able to find more complex factors of numbers, such as 2-digit factors.

Name ______________________________ Date ________________

Let's Make a Factor!

How many factors can you find? Start spinning, and find out!

ROUND 1

PLAYER 1

Numbers Spun: ☐ ☐ ☐ ☐

My 3-Digit Number: ☐ ☐ ☐

Factors:

Total Factors Found: __________

PLAYER 2

Numbers Spun: ☐ ☐ ☐ ☐

My 3-Digit Number: ☐ ☐ ☐

Factors:

Total Factors Found: __________

ROUND 2

PLAYER 1

Numbers Spun: ☐ ☐ ☐ ☐

My 3-Digit Number: ☐ ☐ ☐

Factors:

Total Factors Found: __________

PLAYER 2

Numbers Spun: ☐ ☐ ☐ ☐

My 3-Digit Number: ☐ ☐ ☐

Factors:

Total Factors Found: __________

ROUND 3

PLAYER 1

Numbers Spun: ☐ ☐ ☐ ☐

My 3-Digit Number: ☐ ☐ ☐

Factors:

Total Factors Found: __________

PLAYER 2

Numbers Spun: ☐ ☐ ☐ ☐

My 3-Digit Number: ☐ ☐ ☐

Factors:

Total Factors Found: __________

Cool Off With Coordinates

To keep tea from cooling off too fast, should you add milk right away or when you are ready to drink it? This hands-on activity reveals the answer!

Directions

1. Explain to students that they will be measuring the temperature of tea to find out if it cools off faster when milk is added at once, or if it stays hotter longer when the milk is added after 5 minutes.
2. On graph paper, have students draw *x*- and *y*-axes. On the *x*-axis, they should mark intervals of 30 seconds up to 10 minutes and label the *x*-axis "Time Elapsed." The *y*-axis should be marked off in intervals of 10 degrees Fahrenheit to 200 degrees Fahrenheit and labeled "Temperature."
3. Since students will be doing the experiment with two cups of tea, they should draw an identical *x*- and *y*-axis for the second experiment.
4. If you have two sugar thermometers and stopwatches, you may divide the class into two groups to do the experiment. The first group pours the tea and notes its temperature every 30 seconds, marking the coordinates on the graph. (One student may be in charge of working the stopwatch, while another measures the temperature, and still others write the coordinates and make the graph.) After 5 minutes, the group pours milk into the cup and keeps measuring the temperature for another 5 minutes. The second group pours the same amount of milk into the cup at the beginning and marks the tea's temperature every 30 seconds for 10 minutes. Afterward, the two groups compare their graphs to see which cup of tea was hotter after 10 minutes.
5. If you only have one stopwatch or thermometer, do the experiment as a class, adding milk after 5 minutes. Then repeat the experiment adding milk right at the beginning.
6. Students should discover that the beverage stays hotter if milk is added at once.

LEARNING OBJECTIVE

Students make graphs by plotting coordinates.

GROUPING

Cooperative groups or whole class

MATERIALS

- 2 sheets of graph paper
- straightedge
- 1 or 2 sugar thermometers
- 1 or 2 stopwatches
- 2 cups of hot tea
- milk

Taking It Farther

Have students repeat the experiment several times. How do results vary? Encourage students to write journal entries explaining the experiment and the results.

Assessing Skills

Do students understand that the first number in an ordered pair relates to the *x*-axis, while the second number relates to the *y*-axis? Look for students who mix up the numbers.

Grid Giggles

When students use ordered pairs to decipher the answer to a joke, they'll be laughing all the way to their next math test!

Directions

1. Duplicate the reproducible for each student and distribute.
2. Review ordered pairs. If students need practice before they try the activity, draw a grid on the board and call on volunteers to mark points on the grid based on ordered pairs that you call out.
3. To complete the puzzle on the reproducible, students use the ordered pairs under each blank to find a letter positioned at those coordinates on the grid. When the correct letters are written in each blank, the answer to a math riddle is spelled out.
4. Let students complete the reproducible on their own.

Taking It Further

Encourage students to write their own math jokes or riddles. Then give them graph paper and ask them to use the joke to create a puzzle like *Grid Giggles* for classmates to solve.

Assessing Skills

Observe whether students are confused by negative numbers in the ordered pairs.

LEARNING OBJECTIVE

Students use ordered pairs to locate points on a grid.

GROUPING

Individual

MATERIALS

- *Grid Giggles* reproducible (p. 272)
- graph paper

Name ______________________ Date ______________

Grid Giggles

Under each blank is an ordered pair. Use the ordered pair to find the correct point on the grid. Write the letter from that point in the blank. When you're done, you will have spelled out the answer to this riddle:

Why did the algebra teacher send back the box of peaches he got in the mail?

ANSWER:

(2, –3) (3, 3) (–5, –2) (1, 1) (–1, 1) (–2, 3) (3, 3)   (4, 1) (3, 3)

(4, 1) (1, 1) (3, –5)   (5, –3) (–3, –3) (3, –5) (3, 3) (–3, –3) (3, 3) (3, –5)

(–3, –5) (1, 1) (–4, 1) (–3, –3) (–2, 3)!   ((–3, –5) (3, 3) (1, 1) (–3, –3) (–2, 3))

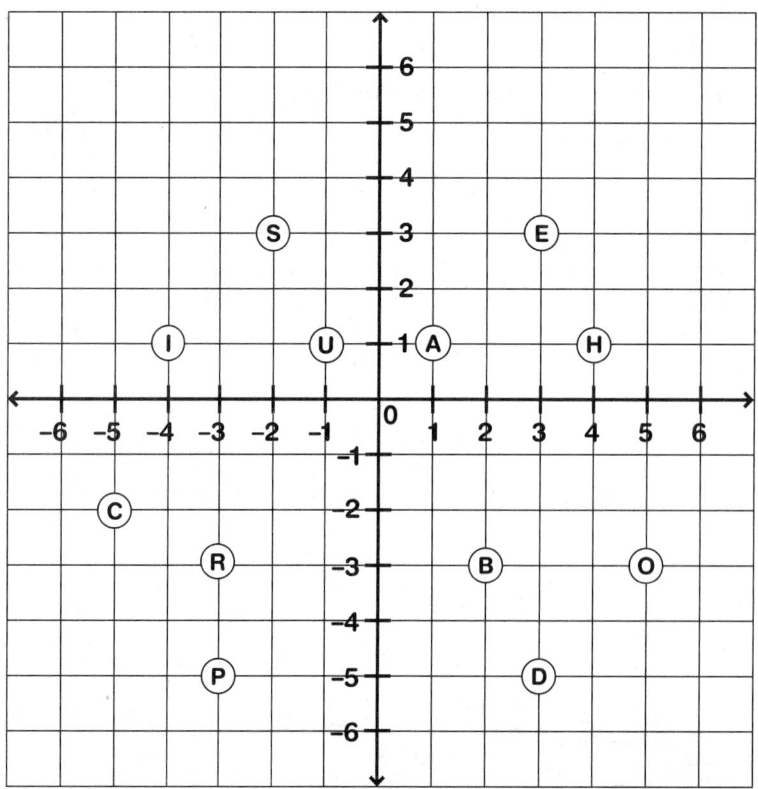

Scatterplot Scores

Students get the score on their favorite basketball players when they use coordinate graphing to make a scatterplot of sports scores.

Directions

1. Distribute one cut-out box score (or copy of a box score) to each pair, along with a piece of graph paper and scratch paper.
2. Students look at the statistics for the team that won the game. On paper, one student writes the number of minutes each athlete played during the game. The other student writes the number of points each athlete scored.
3. On the graph paper, students draw an *x*-axis and a *y*-axis. They label the *x*-axis "Minutes Played" and the *y*-axis "Points Scored."
4. The student who wrote the number of minutes each athlete played counts out how many spaces to move to the right on the graph. The student who wrote points scored counts how many spaces to move vertically on the graph.
5. Students mark a point on the graph for each athlete, labeling the point with the athlete's last name.
6. When the graphs are complete, tack them to a bulletin board to share with the class. Ask students who are familiar with basketball to help you analyze the scatterplots in a class discussion. For example, how does a player's team position influence his or her spot on the graph? [Due to their role on the court, defensive players may play for a long time and score few points.]

LEARNING OBJECTIVE

Students use coordinates to make a scatterplot graph.

GROUPING

Pairs

MATERIALS

- basketball box scores from the sports section of a newspaper (Activity should be done during basketball season if possible; otherwise, save sports sections of the paper from basketball season.)
- graph paper
- scratch paper and pencil

Taking It Further

Challenge students to keep track of statistics at school basketball games and make scatterplots from the results. If they make scatterplots from several games, can they see any trends?

Assessing Skills

Observe whether students label the graphs correctly. Are they able to explain what the points marked on the graphs represent?

Integer Football

Play this fun game and get ready for a kickoff of intensive integer computation practice. Students won't fumble positive and negative numbers again!

Directions

1. Duplicate the reproducible for each pair and distribute. Review the terms *integer, positive,* and *negative* with the class.
2. One player takes the side of the Touchdown Negatives, while the other takes the side of the Pigskin Positives. To start, each player's three counters are placed on the 0-yard line. The object is for players to get all three of their counters to their own 50-yard lines (positive or negative) first.
3. Players use a pencil and paper clip to make the spinner, spinning the clip around the pencil.
4. For each turn, a player spins the Yards spinner and moves a counter the number of positive or negative yards indicated. To clarify, draw the following number line on the board:

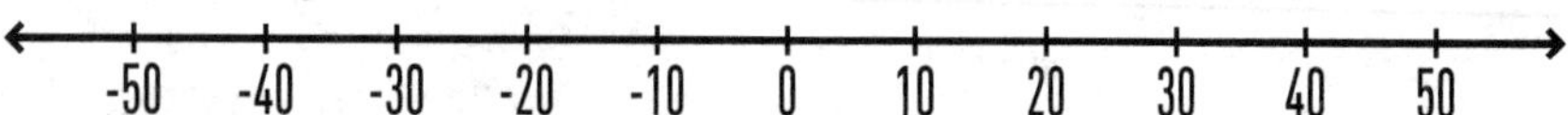

Suppose a player who had a counter on the 10-yard line spins a –30. Draw an arrow as below, or move a counter to show students that the player would move 30 yards to the left.

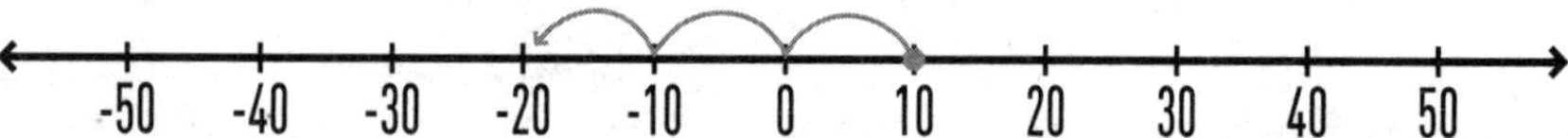

5. If all three of one player's counters land on the opposing side's 50-yard line, all those counters should be moved back to 0. A player does not need an exact spin to land on a 50-yard line. The first player to get all three counters on his or her own 50-yard line wins.

Taking It Further

To make the game harder, duplicate the reproducible. Change +10 and –10 to +5 and –5, change +20 and –20 to +15 and –15, and change +30 and –30 to +25 and –25. Use a ruler to draw 5-yard lines between the 10-yard lines. Make copies of the new reproducible for students to play the game again.

Assessing Skills

Observe whether students understand which direction to move a counter that is already on the negative side of the board. If they spin a –10, do they move 10 yards to the left? Students may be confused and move to the –10 yard line instead.

LEARNING OBJECTIVE

Students add positive and negative integers.

GROUPING

Pairs

MATERIALS

- *Integer Football* reproducible (p. 275)
- pencil and paper clip for each pair (to make the spinner)
- 3 different-colored counters for each student

Name ______________________ Date ______________

Integer Football

Attention sports fans—and math fans! Are you ready to tackle a fun new game? Your goal is to get all your players to your own team's 50-yard line. Don't fumble!

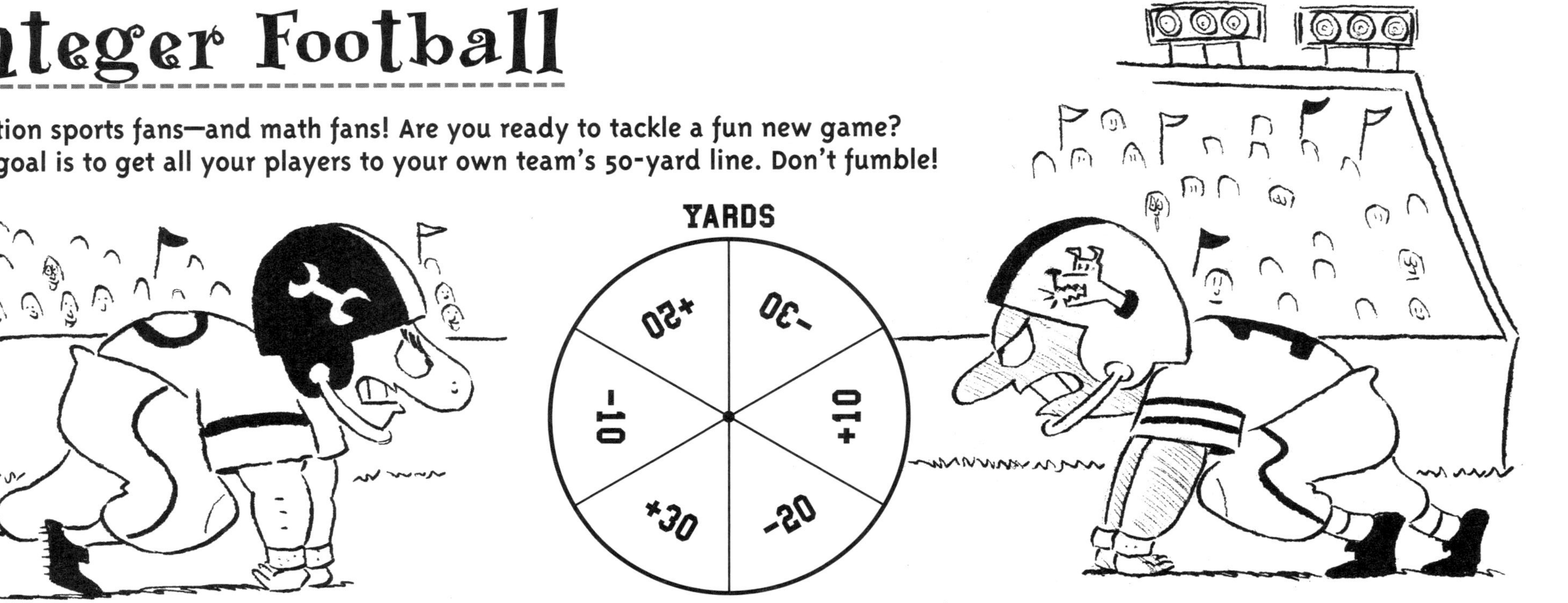

TOUCHDOWN NEGATIVES

-50 -40 -30 -20 -10 0 10 20 30 40 50

PIGSKIN POSITIVES

Mouthwatering Math

When students use candy manipulatives to add integers, they'll get some sweet computation and problem-solving practice. Algebra never tasted so good!

Directions

1. Separate the candy by color. Each pair of players gets two candy colors, ten of each. They decide which color will represent positive integers and which will represent negative integers.
2. Each pair arranges their three cups or bowls in a triangle.
3. Player 1 turns his or her back. Meanwhile, Player 2 puts candy in each cup, using only one color in each cup. For example, if yellow is positive and green is negative, three yellow candies represent +3. Five green candies represent –5. (Note: Player 2 does not have to use all the available candy.)
4. Player 2 finds the sum of the integers in two adjacent cups. She or he writes the sum on a piece of paper and places the paper between the two cups. Player 2 does this for each pair of integers so there is a piece of paper between each pair of cups.
5. Player 2 removes the candy from the cups and places it in front of Player 1.
6. Player 1 turns around. Using the candy and the sums on the paper between each pair of cups, Player 1 figures out how many candies—and which color—go in each cup.
7. Players switch roles and play again.

LEARNING OBJECTIVE

Students add positive and negative integers.

GROUPING

Pairs

MATERIALS

- large bag of round, colored candy (Substitute another manipulative, if necessary.)
- 3 bowls or cups for each pair of students
- paper and pencil for each pair

Taking It Farther

After a few rounds, have students try the game using subtraction instead of addition. To find the difference to write on the paper between two bowls, players first subtract the left number from the right number, then subtract the right number from the left number. The answers should be the positive and negative versions of an integer, such as ±5.

Assessing Skills

- What strategies do students use? Guess and check may be one method.
- Do they realize that one of the sums on the paper will be the total number of positive or negative candies they are handed (assuming both colors were used)?

Square Off

Students get squared away with squares and square roots as they complete a cross-number puzzle.

Directions

1. Duplicate the reproducible for each student and distribute.
2. Review the terms *square* (as in square of a number) and *square root.*
3. Write the following numbers on the board:

   25 [5^2, 5]

   49 [7^2, 7]

   64 [8^2, 8]

   169 [13^2, 13]

   Ask volunteers to identify the square and the square root for each number. Answers are given in brackets.
4. Let students complete the reproducible on their own. If you want, they may use calculators for computation and to check answers.

Taking It Further

Encourage students to create their own cross-number puzzles. If exponents have been covered in class, students may use exponents greater than 2 in their puzzles. They may also use cube roots. Each student then gives his or her puzzle to a classmate to solve.

Assessing Skills

* Do students use multiplication and division to check their answers?
* If an answer going down does not fit with an answer going across the same space, what do students do?

LEARNING OBJECTIVE

Students find squares and square roots of numbers.

GROUPING

Individual

MATERIALS

* *Square Off* reproducible (p. 278)
* calculators (optional)

Name ______________________ Date ____________

Square Off

You're no square! So go ahead—find squares and square roots of numbers to fill in the cross-number puzzle. The answer for Across A is done for you.

A 1	6	■	B	■	C	D
	■	F			■	
■	G	■		■	■	
H			■	I	J	
	■	■	K	■		■
	■	L			■	M
N		■		■	O	

ACROSS

A. 4^2

B. $\sqrt{81}$

C. 9^2

F. 20^2

H. 17^2

I. 18^2

L. 12^2

N. $\sqrt{196}$

O. $\sqrt{225}$

DOWN

A. $\sqrt{100}$

B. 30^2

D. 32^2

G. $\sqrt{324}$

H. 51^2

J. $\sqrt{484}$

K. 21^2

M. $\sqrt{625}$

Laboratory Labyrinth

As students wind their way through this maze to a mad scientist's lab, they find squares and square roots at every turn!

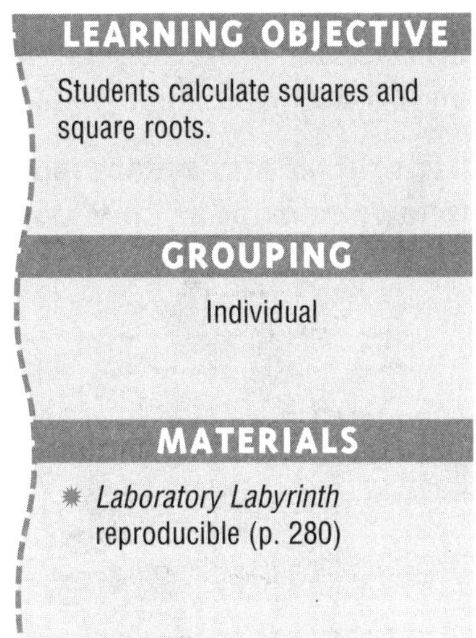

LEARNING OBJECTIVE

Students calculate squares and square roots.

GROUPING

Individual

MATERIALS

- *Laboratory Labyrinth* reproducible (p. 280)

Directions

1. Duplicate the reproducible for each student.
2. Review squares and square roots with the class. To complete your review, call on volunteers to write examples of some squares and square roots on the board.
3. Distribute the reproducible. Explain that to find the correct path through the castle, students must follow Maddy Seintyst's directions, located at the top of the maze. For each step, students find the square or square root of the number as indicated. Then they draw a line through the passage that contains the answer.
4. Let students complete the reproducible on their own.
5. When students have finished, allow time for them to compare answers. Was there more than one way to get through the maze?

Taking It Farther

Challenge students to create and illustrate their own mazes. To make the mazes more challenging, you can have them use exponents other than 2 and cube roots in the clues.

Assessing Skills

Note whether students confuse the operations of finding a square and finding a square root. Some students may also multiply a number by 2 instead of finding the square, or divide by 2 when they want to find the square root. In the maze, using the wrong method sometimes leads students down a wrong path.

Name ______________________ Date ____________

Laboratory Labyrinth

Directions to the lab.
• $\sqrt{9}$
• 16^2
• 10^2
• $\sqrt{144}$
• $\sqrt{49}$
• 36^2
• $\sqrt{121}$
• $\sqrt{64}$
• 12^2

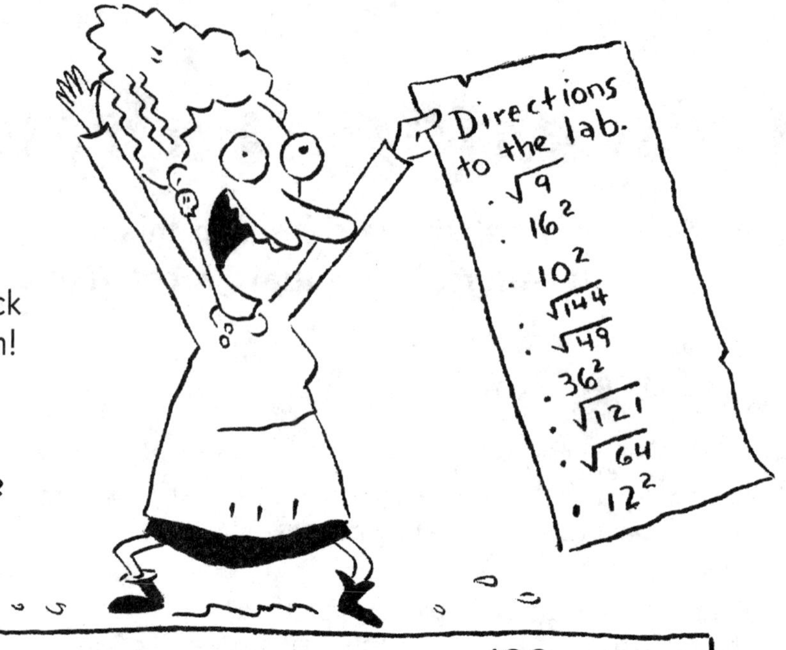

Hi! I'm Maddy Seintyst. I've got to get back to the lab. I think I left a Bunsen burner on! Unfortunately, the passages of my castle are filled with all kinds of danger.

Use squares and square roots to help me follow my map, or I'm a goner!

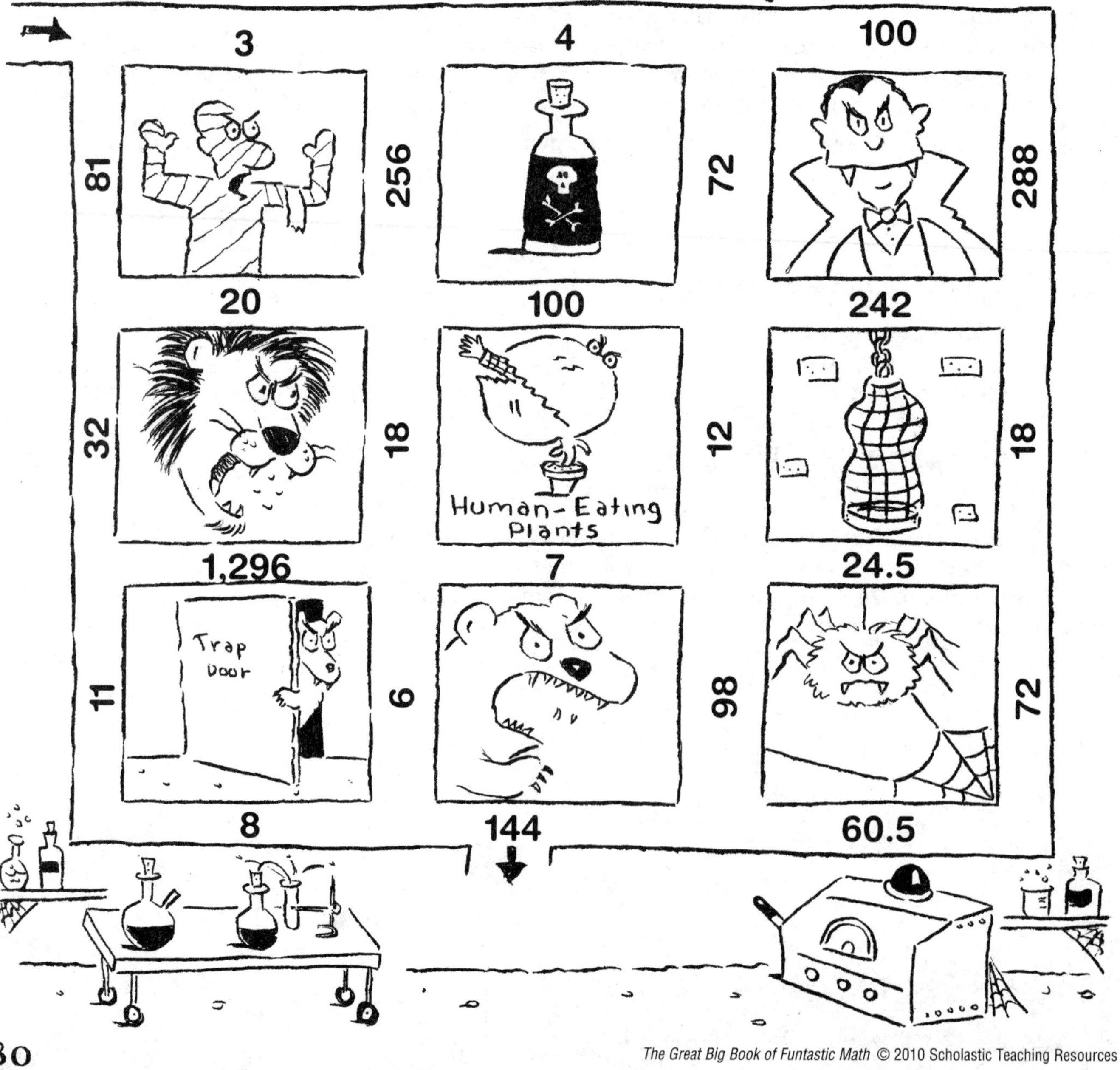

3
4
100
81
256
72
288
20
100
242
32
18
Human-Eating Plants
12
18
1,296
7
24.5
Trap Door
11
6
98
72
8
144
60.5

Paper Patterns

Students will "half" a great time figuring out the pattern that evolves when a piece of paper is folded again and again.

Directions

1. Start by discussing patterns. Tell students that to complete a pattern, they can decide what math was done to get each successive number in the pattern. Then they can test the idea to make sure it works.
2. Hold up a piece of paper and fold it in half, like this:

   Have each pair of students fold a piece of paper as well. Note to the class that with 1 fold, you have 2 sections of paper.
3. Now fold the paper again, like this:

   With 2 folds, there are now 4 sections.
4. On the board, write a table like the following:

PATTERN OF FOLDS

FOLDS	SECTIONS
1	2
2	4

Have students copy and continue the table on their own paper, looking for patterns. After 3 folds, each pair should try to predict how many sections there will be with 6 folds. Then they can test to see if their predictions were correct.

Taking It Further

A piece of paper can be folded only a few times. But say it could be folded 15, 20, or 25 times. Challenge students to find ways to figure out how many sections there would be. One way is to continue the table, doubling the number of sections each time. Another way is to express FOLDS as n, and SECTIONS as $2n$. So after 15 folds, you'd have 2×15, or 30 sections.

Assessing Skills

Observe how many folds it takes for students to discover the pattern. Are they able to correctly predict how many sections there will be after 6 folds?

LEARNING OBJECTIVE

Students make a table to find a pattern.

GROUPING

Pairs

MATERIALS

- paper and pencil

Function Detective

Students use math clues to get hot on the trail of a mystery function!

Directions

1. Review the term *function* with students.
2. Divide the class into groups of four students. Two students in each group should work together to write a simple function, such as $f(x) = 3x + 2$ on an index card. The other two students are the Function Detectives who figure out the function.
3. The Function Detectives turn their backs so they cannot see the function. The Function Detectives then write a number on a separate index card and hand it to the students who hold the function.
4. The students plug the number into the function and write the answer on the Function Detectives' card. For example, if a function is $f(x) = 3x - 2$, and the card reads 3, the students write $3 \rightarrow 7$ on the card. Then they hand it back to the Function Detectives.
5. The Function Detectives write another number on another card and repeat the process. After the Function Detectives have collected several cards, they try to guess what the function is.
6. When the Function Detectives have figured out the function, students switch roles. The former Function Detectives write a function. The other pair of students are now the Function Detectives.

LEARNING OBJECTIVE

Students find the functions that describe number patterns.

GROUPING

Cooperative groups of 4

MATERIALS

* several index cards or pieces of paper for each student

Taking It Further

As they play more rounds of the game, challenge students to find the functions with fewer and fewer tries.

Assessing Skills

Have each student write a journal entry describing the strategies he or she used to find the functions.

Crunchy Functions

Watch students sink their teeth into functions and problem solving (not to mention snack crackers) with this tasty hands-on activity!

Directions

1. Review the terms *function* and *perimeter* with students. Explain to groups that they will use crackers to find functions in shape patterns.
2. FUNCTION 1: On the board, draw one square. Note that if you call each side 1 unit, the square has a perimeter of 4 units.
3. Draw another square next to and touching to the first one. Ask students: *What is the perimeter now?* [6 units]

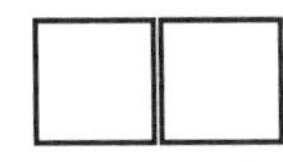

4. Next, have each group place crackers in a row to discover the perimeter for a row of 3, 4, 5, 6, or 7 crackers. Have them determine what function can be used to figure the perimeter for a row of 15 squares. [If s = the number of squares, the function is $2s + 2$. So a row of 15 squares has a perimeter of 32.]
5. FUNCTION 2: Tell students that in this activity, they will be building large squares from the small cracker squares. Draw squares on the board as shown. Point out that to make a square with a length of 1 unit, you need 1 cracker. To make a square with a length of 2 units, you need 4 crackers.

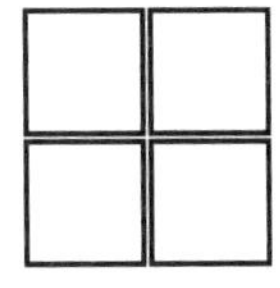

6. Have students use crackers to make squares with lengths of 3, 4, and 5 units. Let them determine how many crackers it will take. Ask: *What function could be used to find the number of crackers you would need to make a square with a length of 12 units?* [If ℓ = the length of the square, the function is $\ell \times \ell$, or ℓ^2. So for a 12-unit-long square, you need 144 crackers.]
7. FUNCTION 3: Have students build squares to find the function for the perimeter. Ask: *What is the perimeter of a square with a length of 12 units?* [Where ℓ = length, the perimeter is 4ℓ. For the 12-unit square, the perimeter is 48 units.]

Taking It Further

Let students use sugar cubes to find functions for the surface area of a stack of cubes, and for large cubes made out of smaller cubes.

Assessing Skills

Observe whether students test their functions to see if they work.

LEARNING OBJECTIVE

Students use manipulatives to find and test functions.

GROUPING

Cooperative groups

MATERIALS

- one or two boxes of square-shaped crackers, at least 25 per group. (Square counters may be used instead of crackers.)
- pencil and paper for each group
- sugar cubes (optional)

Missing Museums

Students find the missing number that completes each pattern and learn where some of the wildest and wackiest museums are located!

Directions

1. Duplicate the reproducible for each student.
2. Discuss number patterns with the class. Ask students: *What is the difference between a pattern and a group of random numbers?*
3. Talk about how students can find the missing number in a pattern. One way is to hypothesize about what was done to each number in order to reach the next number in the pattern. Then test the theory to see if it works.
4. Write the following examples on the board:
   2, 5, 8, 11, 14, ...
   2, 5, 11, 23, 47, ...

   Ask volunteers to find the number that comes next in each pattern and explain how they found the answer. [In the first example, 3 is added to each succeeding number, so the next number in the pattern is 17. In the second example, each number is multiplied by 2, and 1 is added to the product. So the next number in the pattern is 95.]
5. Note that in the examples, the first two numbers are the same. Can students think of any other ways to complete a pattern that begins with 2, 5, ... ? [One possible answer: Take each number squared and then add 1. So the pattern would be: 2, 5, 26, 677, and so on. Another possible answer: Multiply each number by 3 and subtract 1. So the pattern would be: 2, 5, 14, 41, 122, and so on.]
6. Distribute the reproducible and let students complete it on their own.

LEARNING OBJECTIVE

Students complete number patterns.

GROUPING

Individual

MATERIALS

- *Missing Museums* reproducible (p. 285)
- pencils
- scrap paper

Taking It Further

Have students write journal entries explaining the strategies and tests they used to discover the number patterns in the activity. Challenge each student to come up with a number pattern for the rest of the class to solve. Can students find more than one way to complete some of the patterns?

Assessing Skills

Ask students to explain verbally the reasoning behind their answers to the problems on the reproducible. Ask: *What numbers would continue the sequences even further?*

Name ______________________ Date ______________

Missing Museums

Meet Anne DeSplay. She just loves museums! Anne was planning a trip to see some of her favorite museums in the U.S., but she got them all mixed up. Now, Anne needs your help!

To find out where each real museum is located, figure out what number completes each number pattern in the left column. Draw a line to your answer in the right column.

MUSEUM NAMES

A. Tupperware Historic Food Container Museum
224, 112, 56, 28,...

B. Museum of Bad Art
11, 24, 37, 50,...

C. Hall of Flame (Fire Fighting Museum)
5, 9, 17, 33, 65,...

D. Leroy's Motorcycle Museum
2, 5, 0, 0, 8, 11, 0, 0, 14, 17, 0, 0,...

E. National Museum of Roller Skating
48, 47, 45, 42, 38, 33,...

F. Tolbert's Chili Parlor and Museum of Chili
1, 1, 2, 3, 5, 8, 13, 21,...

G. The Potato Museum
60.75, 40.5, 27, 18,...

H. The Museum of Pez (candy) Memorabilia
2, 3, 5, 7, 11, 13, 17,...

MUSEUM LOCATIONS

27 Lincoln, Nebraska

19 Burlingame, California

63 Boston, Massachusetts

14 Orlando, Florida

34 Dallas, Texas

12 Albuquerque, New Mexico

20 Wichita, Kansas

129 Phoenix, Arizona

$5y \leq 3y + 10$ ✱ $6(x + 3) = 6x + 18$ ✱ $3x + 2y = 24$ ✱ $x^2 = 25$ ✱ $4c + 6 + 3c < 50$

Algebra Readiness Problem Bank

Use these quick skill-builders as self-starters, for homework, or just for a fun break from the textbook!

1. STORMY WEATHER

How do meteorologists predict how long a thunderstorm will last? One way they find an estimate is by using the following formula:

$$t^2 = \frac{d^3}{216}$$

In this formula, t = the length of time the storm will last (in hours), and d = the diameter of the storm. If the diameter of a storm is 6 miles, about how long will the storm last?

2. WE'RE TELLING THE TOOTH!

Bite into variables to find out some amazing facts about teeth! For each problem, plug in these variable values: $t = 4$, $k = 500{,}000$, $m = 72.3$. Write your answer in the blank space to complete the tooth fact.

a. $t^2 \div 2$	The teeth of a Tyrannosaurus rex dinosaur were as long as ____ inches!
b. $80k$	About _____ Americans never go to a dentist.
c. $32m - 2{,}213.6$	Crocodiles have up to ____ teeth.
d. $1{,}500{,}008 - 3k$	One out of every ____ people has no teeth.

3. AGE-OLD PROBLEM

Right now, Jamal's mother is 3 times older than Jamal. But in 12 years, her age will be exactly 2 times greater than Jamal's. How old are Jamal and his mother today?

4. HEADS UP

Rachel's uncle Rupert invited her to visit his llama and ostrich farm. Today he asked her to help out by counting all the llamas and ostriches in the barn. The animals are running around so fast, Rachel just can't keep track. But she's sure she counted 35 heads and 94 feet. How many llamas are there? How many ostriches are there? (Remember: Llamas have 4 feet; ostriches are birds that have 2 feet.)

5. SWEET DIVISION

Larissa has a bag full of gumdrops. She knows there are fewer than 75 pieces of candy in all. When she divides them into groups of 3, 4, 5, or 6, there is always 1 gumdrop left over. How many gumdrops does Larissa have?

6. PICTURE THIS!

Mark off the following points. As you mark each point, draw a line to connect it to the previous point. When you're done, the connected dots will make a picture. What is it?

a. (4, 4)
b. (7, 3)
c. (16, 2)
d. (25, 3)
e. (29, 5)
f. (32, 2)
g. (31, 6)
h. (33, 12)
i. (29, 8)
j. (25, 10)
k. (19, 12)
l. (18, 18)
m. (11, 12)
n. (4, 10)
o. (0, 8)
p. (3, 5)
q. (6, 5)
r. (4, 4)

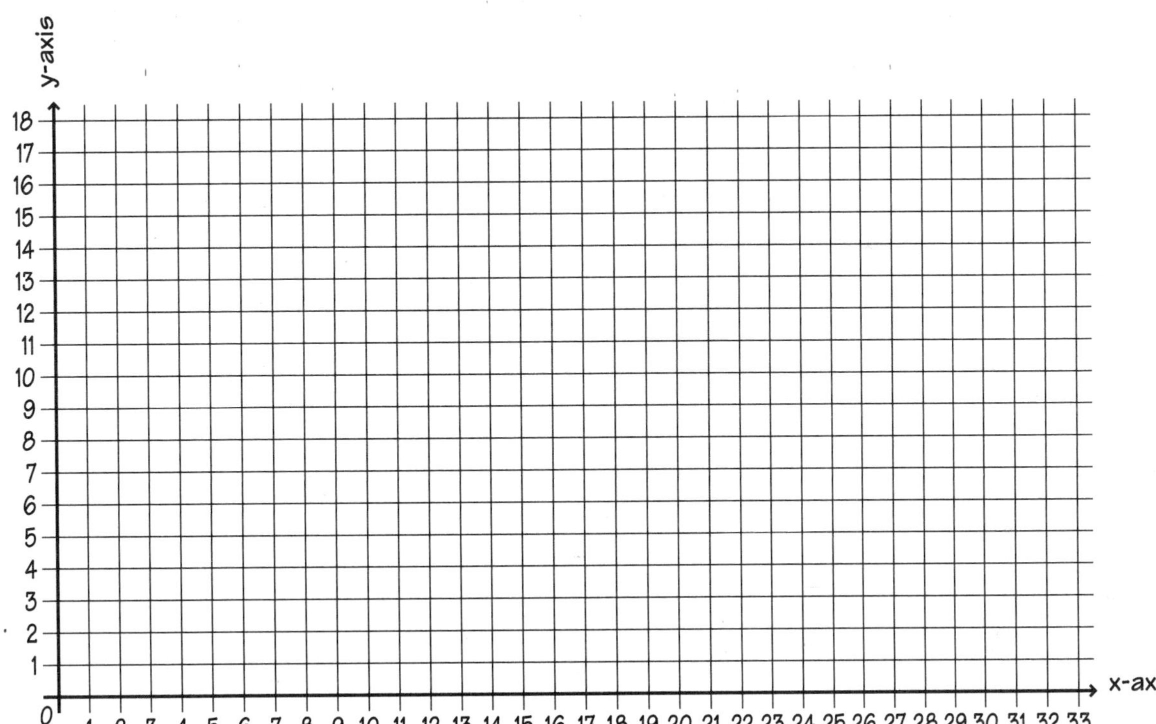

What, No Numbers?

The real-life math problems on these pages require answers, yet they have no numbers!

Directions

1. Present the following problem: *Julio used his savings to buy a bike. The total amount he paid included sales tax. How much of his savings remained after the purchase?*
2. Ask students which operation they would use for each step in the solution and what they would add, subtract, multiply, or divide.
3. Guide students to see that to solve this problem, first they add the amount of the sales tax to the price of the bike, then subtract that sum from the amount of savings. Point out that if the sales tax were given as a percent, they would need to divide to express the percent as a decimal or fraction and then multiply to find that percent of the price of the bike.
4. Suggest to students that to better understand the problem, they can fill in sensible amounts for the unstated numbers. For instance, they might choose $200 for the bike, 5% for the sales tax, and $500 for the amount of savings.
5. Duplicate the reproducible for each individual or pair and distribute. Have students complete the page on their own or with partners. Encourage them to think of a variety of solution plans.

Taking It Further

Ask students to work in pairs. One creates a multi-step problem with no numbers. The other gives the steps in the solution. Or one student provides only numerical data, and the other student writes a sensible problem using that data.

Assessing Skills

- Do students come up with more than one way to solve a problem?
- Can they explain their strategies and answers?

LEARNING OBJECTIVE

Students choose combinations of operations to solve problems for which no numbers are provided.

GROUPING

Individual or pairs

MATERIALS

- *What, No Numbers?* reproducible (p. 289)

Name ______________________ Date ______________

What, No Numbers?

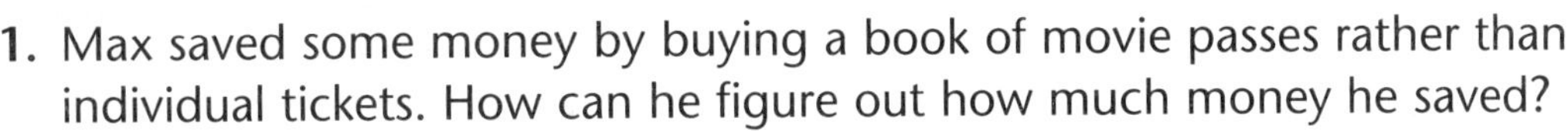

The problems below have no numbers. Decide how you would solve each one. Tell what you would add, subtract, multiply, or divide to find the answer. If it helps you, fill in reasonable numbers.

1. Max saved some money by buying a book of movie passes rather than individual tickets. How can he figure out how much money he saved?

   ____

   ____

2. Inez knows the number of miles she ran last week. She knows how many hours she ran. How can she figure out her rate of speed in miles per hour?

   ____

   ____

3. Ed knows his car's odometer readings (in miles) before and after a trip. He knows the number of gallons of gasoline he used. How can he figure out the number of miles-per-gallon his car got on the trip?

   ____

   ____

4. Pat knows the weight and price of two different-size boxes of dry cat food. How can he figure out which of the two is the better buy?

   ____

   ____

5. Li has a paper route. She delivers a certain number of papers every day. For each paper she delivers, she makes the same amount of money. How can she figure out her hourly wage?

   ____

   ____

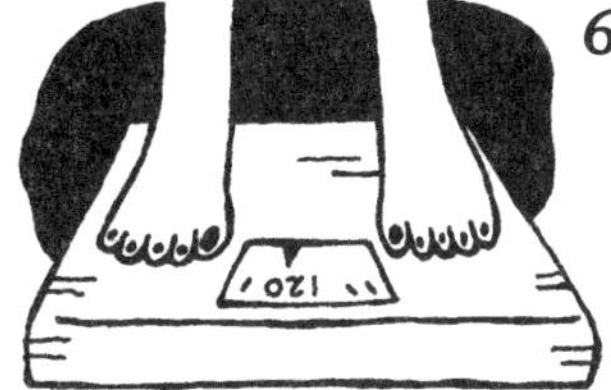

6. Vera weighs more than Eva. You know how much more. You know the mean weight of the two. How can you figure out how much each weighs?

   ____

   ____

Pets Step Up

Correctly interpreting information in store flyers, catalogs, and ads is a real-life skill students need to become smarter shoppers.

Directions

1. Review with students the kinds of information usually provided in ads for consumer products. Discuss the different ways that products are discounted and how that information may be presented.
2. Duplicate the reproducible for each pair and distribute.
3. Instruct partners to answer the questions on the reproducible. Point out that in some cases they'll need to calculate, while in others it may make better sense to use their estimating skills. Encourage students to use the most reasonable calculation method: calculator, paper and pencil, or mental math.
4. Discuss students' answers. If necessary, guide them to explain the strategies they used.

Taking It Further

Invite students to formulate additional questions based on the information in the ad. Or you might have them create their own humorous ads, along with questions, for an interactive bulletin board.

Assessing Skills

* Do students demonstrate an ability to interpret data presented in an ad and show that they can find sale prices given information about discounts?
* Do they choose the most sensible computational method?
* Do students always find exact answers, or do they make estimates when that approach is reasonable and sufficient?

LEARNING OBJECTIVE

Students use information from an advertisement to solve problems involving discounts. They decide whether to find an exact answer or make an estimate.

GROUPING

Pairs

MATERIALS

* *Pets Step Up* reproducible (p. 291)
* calculator (optional)

Name ______________________ Date ______________

Pets Step Up

Educated pets make the best customers. So fur is flying at Claws and Paws Pet Shop because all pet self-help books and DVDs are on sale.

Help your pet use the information from the ad to answer the questions.

BIG BOOK AND DVD SALE!

DVDs	Books
Getting Away With Scratching was \$29.95; now \$5 off	***Life On a Leash: Tips and Strategies*** \$4.50 off original price of \$30
Power Poodles originally \$22; now \$2.50 off	***How to Get More and Better Meals*** was \$14.95; now \$5 off with another purchase
Total Turtle Training $\frac{1}{2}$ off original price of \$15.99	***20 Hours of Sleep—Is That Enough?*** $\frac{1}{4}$ off original price of \$18.88

ALL OUR LOW PRICES INCLUDE SALES TAX!

1. You have a \$50 bill. What is your change if you buy the *Power Poodles* DVD?

____

2. You have \$40. Can you buy *Total Turtle Training* and *Life on a Leash: Tips and Strategies*? If not, how much more money would you need to borrow from your pet?

____

3. Your pet had you spend \$14.16. Which book or DVD did you buy?

____

4. You have \$20 to spend. Order two items that will cost less than that in all.

____

5. You spent just under \$75 on three of the same book or DVD. Which one did you buy?

____

Car for Rent

Rooting through the assortment of rental car options can cause anyone's engine to overheat!

Directions

1. Duplicate the reproducible for each student or pair and distribute.
2. Tell students that they will plan a round-trip using one of several car rental plans. Go over each rental plan with students. To help them understand the plans, you might work through the cost of one or more imaginary trips using each plan. For instance, find and compare costs of a 3-day trip of 1,000 miles, then a 7-day trip of 3,000 miles.
3. Make road atlases available. Have students work in pairs or small groups so that they can help one another read the atlas.
4. Direct students to choose destinations at least several hundred miles from their homes. Discuss all factors that will affect the number of days they'll need the car, such as the distance they're likely to drive in a day and the time they'll spend eating, sleeping, and sightseeing on their trips. As needed, review the distance formula, $d = rt$.
5. Have students complete the page and then share their findings. Ask them how to select the best plan for the different types of trips—a trip that's close to home, a trip of great distance or duration, or one that involves a drop-off at a different location.

LEARNING OBJECTIVE

Students solve a real-life problem by using pricing information, a road atlas, and common sense.

GROUPING

Pairs or small groups

MATERIALS

* *Car for Rent* reproducible (p. 293)
* road atlas for North America (approximately 1 for every 2–3 students)
* calculator (optional)

Taking It Further

Challenge students to research rental plans at actual car agencies. They can find the plan that would work best for their proposed trip.

Assessing Skills

* Have students accurately determined the length of the trip and estimated the time it would take?
* Have they applied each plan correctly to obtain the correct costs?

Name ______________________ Date ______________

Car for Rent

Here's your chance to see the U.S.A.—without leaving your classroom!

The following car rental plans are from Take Off Rent-a-Car.

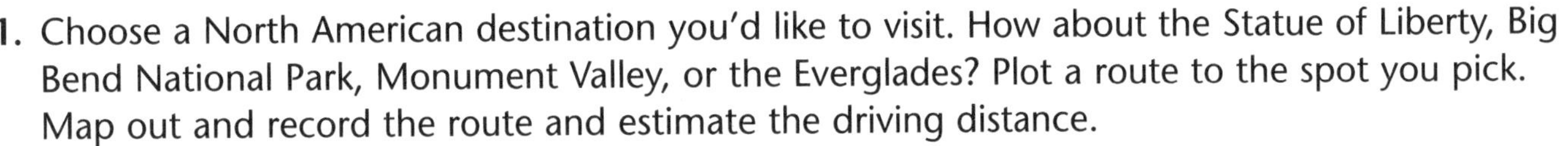

PLAN A	PLAN B	PLAN C
$32.95 per day	$27.95 per day	$45 per day
500 free miles	no free miles	1,500 free miles
then $0.20 a mile	$0.25 a mile	then $0.30 a mile

1. Choose a North American destination you'd like to visit. How about the Statue of Liberty, Big Bend National Park, Monument Valley, or the Everglades? Plot a route to the spot you pick. Map out and record the route and estimate the driving distance.

____

____

____

2. Figure out how long the entire round-trip would take. Remember: You can't drive all day long, and you need to sleep, eat, get gas, and spend some time at the place you're visiting. And don't forget those speed limits!

____

____

____

____

3. Determine the cost of the car rental for your entire round-trip, using each plan. Which plan makes the most sense for you? Why?

____

____

____

____

____

Laces

Some problems or tasks may appear overwhelming at first. But once students break them down into smaller, manageable parts, they can find the answers.

Directions

1. Present the following problem: *About how many feet—the measurement, not the part of the body—of shoelaces are in our school right now?*
2. Invite students to make guesses. Then challenge groups to come up with a series of steps they can use to make a closer approximation of the answer. Groups should record their plans.
3. Emphasize that many approaches are possible and that whatever method groups use, they should be sure that each member participates in a meaningful way.
4. Guide students to record all data as they go.
5. If students are stuck initially, point out that one way to start is to measure the length of a few shoelaces to come up with a typical length to use in the investigation. One approach students can use is to estimate the total shoelace length of their own group or class.
6. Have groups present and discuss their answers and describe their strategies.
7. Compare final estimates with initial guesses.

LEARNING OBJECTIVE

Students do an investigation in which they use small steps to solve a multistep problem.

GROUPING

Cooperative groups

MATERIALS

* ruler or tape measure
* calculator (optional)

Taking It Further

Challenge students to plan a way to estimate the number of pounds of math textbooks in the school, the area of all the windows in the building, the total wattage of all the lights, the number of pieces of pasta the cafeteria uses on macaroni and cheese day, or anything else of interest to them.

Assessing Skills

* Do students have a workable plan for solving the problem?
* Do their estimates make sense?
* Does their presentation fully explain what they did and how they did it?

On the Beaten Path

Sometimes drawing a picture or diagram is the best way to solve a problem. It's certainly a good strategy to use to solve the problem presented below.

Directions

1. Have students record the key data as you read aloud the following problem:

   In MacPherson State Park, a guided nature trail leads from the visitor center to the falls. It's $\frac{1}{3}$ mile from the visitor center to the giant oak and another $\frac{3}{4}$ mile to the abandoned mine. It's half a mile from there to the stream. From the stream it's another $\frac{3}{8}$ mile to the falls. Hikers must stay on the trail at all times. Luke started back from the falls at the same time Lisa started out from the parking lot. Each walked 1 mile and stopped. Who was closer to the mine at that point? Who was closer to the parking lot? [Lisa, by $\frac{1}{24}$ mile; Luke, by $\frac{1}{24}$ mile]
2. Guide students to draw and label a diagram of the trail to solve this problem. As needed, review finding common denominators and renaming fractions. Also reread the problem as necessary.
3. Ask volunteers to share the diagrams they made and then explain how they obtained the answers. Invite students who used other methods to explain their approaches.
4. Make up or invite students to create other problems of this type. You might consider including directionality—3 miles south, then 4.5 miles west, and so on.

Taking It Further

Challenge students to use road atlases to make up problems much like the nature trail problem but that use real information.

Assessing Skills

* Have students accurately recorded the information you presented?
* Do their diagrams show the information correctly?
* Can students explain how they got their answers to the problem?

LEARNING OBJECTIVE

Students use listening skills to record the information in a problem. They draw a diagram to solve the problem.

GROUPING

Individual

MATERIALS

* paper and pencil
* road atlas for North America (optional)

Following Directions

How good are students at following directions, even straightforward ones? Try this activity to find out. The results might surprise you.

Directions

1. Tell students that their challenge in this activity is to follow simple but exact instructions to draw a picture within a frame. Emphasize that the instructions contain specific geometric language and must be followed precisely.
2. Duplicate the two reproducibles and give a set to each student.
3. Alternatively, you may want students to work in pairs; one reads the instructions, the other draws the picture. Or you might choose to read the instructions aloud.
4. Have students post their drawings to compare and discuss them.
5. Invite students to make up their own sets of instructions for classmates to follow to the letter, with the answers drawn on the back. They can post these on the bulletin board. Other students can work on these when time permits.

Taking It Further

Direct students to write out specific sets of instructions for getting from one place (such as school) to another in the neighborhood—but without identifying the destination. Challenge others to follow the directions carefully to identify the destination.

Assessing Skills

- How accurately have students followed the instructions?
- Do students understand where (if anywhere) they fell short and how to fix it?
- Have students who have made up their own sets of directions answered them correctly?

LEARNING OBJECTIVE

Students follow specific instructions to draw a picture.

GROUPING

Individual or pairs

MATERIALS

- *Following Directions* reproducibles (pp. 297–298)
- metric ruler calibrated in millimeters
- pennies
- colored markers or pencils

Name ____________________ Date ____________

Following Directions

Following these directions will definitely make you feel like you've been framed! But you'll have created a work of art you may really want to frame.

Carefully follow these instructions, in order, to draw a picture within the frame. You'll need a metric ruler.

1. From point X, draw a 6-cm line segment toward the center of the frame.
2. Where the segment ends, draw a circle the size of a penny. Make the segment end at the top of this circle.
3. Within the circle, write the customary unit of length you would use to give the distance between two state capitals.
4. From the bottom of the circle, draw a line segment 40 mm long toward the right edge of the frame, parallel to the bottom edge.
5. At the end of this segment, draw a small square. Write your age in months and days to the right of the square.
6. From the upper right corner of the square, draw a line segment to the midpoint shown at the top edge of the frame. Label that point Y.
7. From point Y, draw a line segment that ends about 0.3 dm from the bottom left corner of the frame. Label the end of this segment Z.
8. Using point Z as the upper left corner, draw a rectangle with a base of 75 mm and a height of 15 mm. Print your name inside it.
9. Draw a line segment to connect the bottom of the circle to the top of the rectangle at a point $\frac{2}{3}$ of the way from point Z.
10. Measure the length of this segment to the nearest centimeter. Write the measurement to the right of the segment.

Name ____________________ Date ____________________

Following Directions

Piece of the Pie

If nobody cares about the size of the pieces, it will take fewer cuts than students think to slice a pizza.

Directions

1. Say that a student named Roland claims he can divide a round pizza for 11 friends by making only 4 straight cuts. Ask students to figure out if this can be true. Remind them that the pieces need not be the same size.
2. Point out that although using trial and error, a big circle, and a straightedge is one way of proving Roland right or wrong, another way is to find and extend a pattern. Ask students to make and complete a table showing the greatest number of pieces that can be formed by 0 cuts, 1 cut, 2 cuts, 3 cuts, and so on. Until they recognize the pattern, students can make drawings to help them fill in the table. You might have volunteers create and display drawings for the greatest number of pieces formed by 1, 2, and 3 straight cuts.
3. Have students discuss the pattern that emerges for the greatest number of pieces per number of cuts. [The difference between the greatest number of pieces formed with each successive cut increases by 1: 0 cuts = 1 piece; 1 cut = 2 pieces; 2 cuts = 4 pieces; 3 cuts = 7 pieces; 4 cuts = 11 pieces; 5 cuts = 16 pieces; 6 cuts = 22 pieces; for instance, 2 – 1 = 1, 4 – 2 = 2, 7 – 4 = 3, 11 – 7 = 4, and so on.] See the answer, bottom right.
4. Ask students to draw large circles on sheets of paper and to try to draw all the different ways of making pieces with 4 cuts, 5 cuts, and 6 cuts. But first, guide them to come up with this rule of thumb they can apply when making the cuts: the more intersections there are, the more pieces there will be.

Taking It Further

Ask students to figure out the fewest number of straight cuts needed to divide a pizza for a not-too-hungry class of 27. [7 cuts = 29 pieces]

Assessing Skills

- Do students discover the pattern for the maximum number of pieces formed by straight cuts? Can they apply this understanding to solve problems about a greater numbers of cuts?
- Are students able to draw all different ways to make pieces using 3, 4, 5, and 6 cuts?

LEARNING OBJECTIVE

Students figure out and extend a pattern. They apply their visual reasoning skills to explore the pattern.

GROUPING

Pairs

MATERIALS

- paper and pencils
- straightedge
- compass (optional)

ANSWER

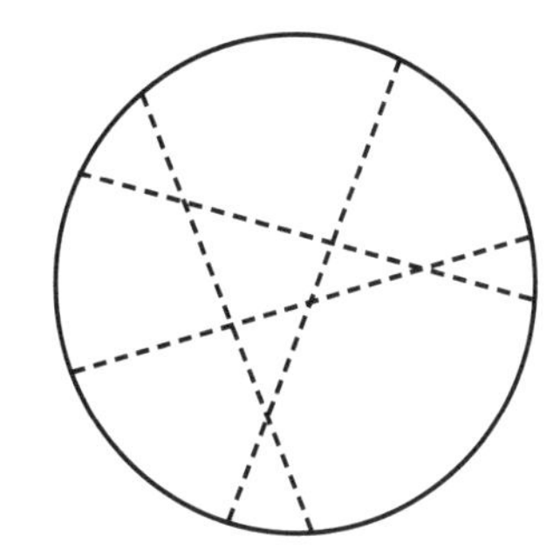

Mapmaker, Mapmaker

On a political map, regions that share borders often have different colors. Mathematicians have proved that no map needs more than four colors.

Directions

1. Draw and display the three "maps" in step 2. Leave out the numbers. Tell students that regions sharing a border must have different colors. As needed, discuss and demonstrate what sharing a border means. Guide students to understand that regions that touch at only one point can have the same color. The Four Corners of the United States where Utah, Arizona, New Mexico, and Colorado join is an example; Utah and New Mexico or Arizona and Colorado could both be the same color. You may wish to have a globe or world atlas available for reference.
2. Then have students copy the maps below. Ask students to figure out the minimum number of colors needed to color each one. Allow time to go over their answers.

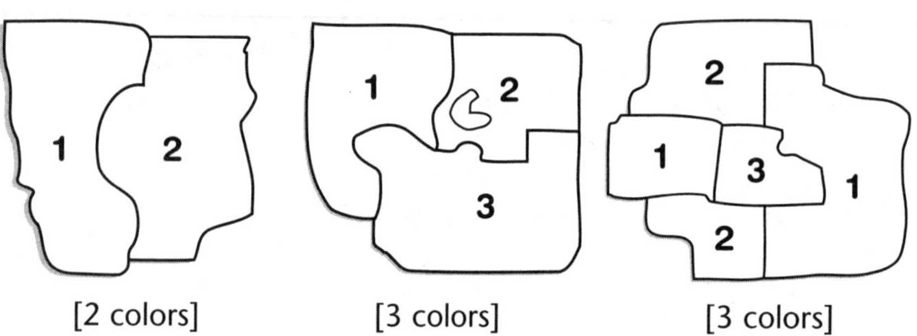

3. Duplicate the reproducible for each student and distribute, along with the colored pencils. Have them complete the page on their own.
4. Invite students to post their completed maps on the bulletin board.

LEARNING OBJECTIVE

Students color maps using only a given number of colors.

GROUPING

Individual

MATERIALS

* colored dry-erase pens, markers, or chalk
* colored pencils
* *Mapmaker, Mapmaker* reproducible (p. 301)
* globe or world atlas (optional)

Taking It Farther

Challenge students to create three of their own maps—one that needs two colors, one that needs three, and one that needs four. Compile the uncolored maps in a folder. Invite students to color the maps as indicated.

Assessing Skills

* Can students color the maps according to the directions?
* What generalizations can they make about the number of different colors a map needs?

Name ______________________ Date ______________

Mapmaker, Mapmaker

Red, yellow, orange, blue, purple—which four colors would you use to color a map of the world?

Color the maps using only the given number of colors.

1. Use 3 colors.

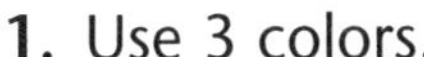

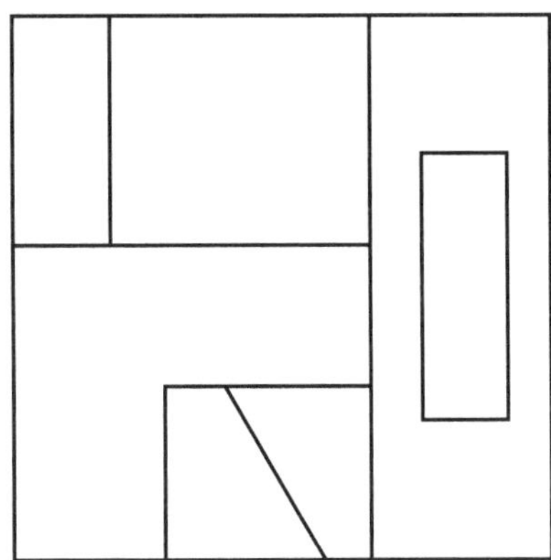

2. Use 4 colors.

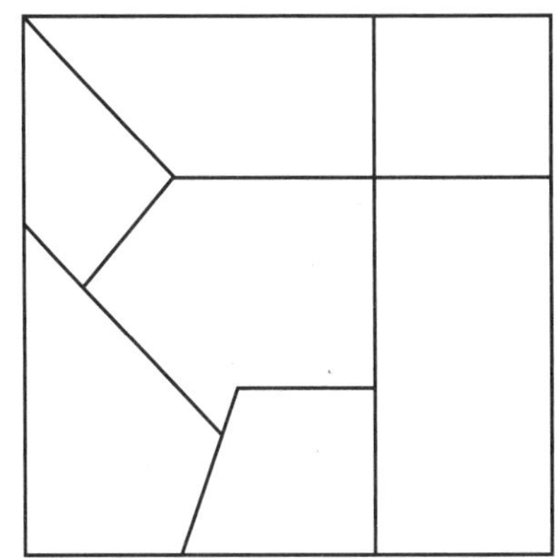

3. Color this map using 4 colors.

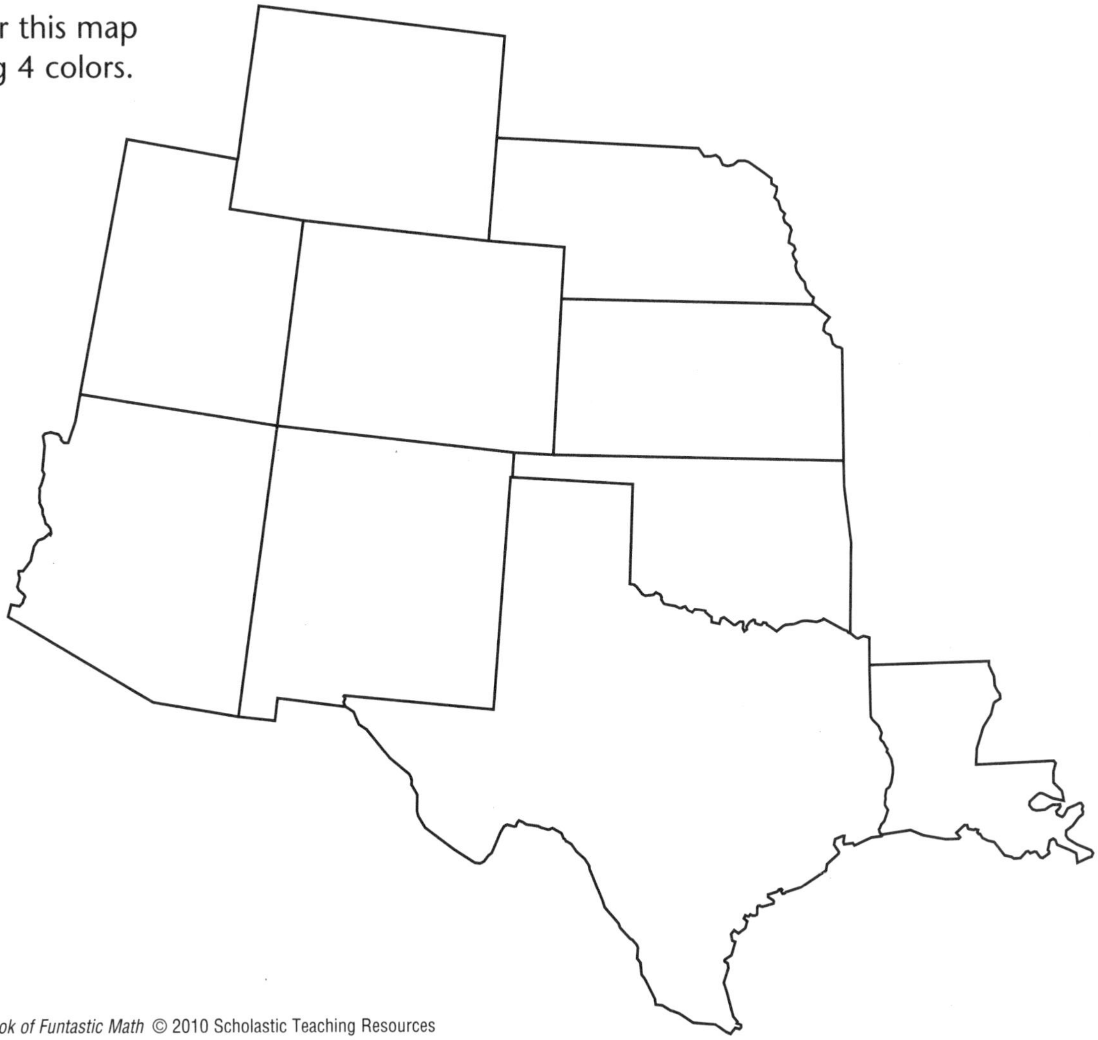

Think Again!

Satchel Paige, the legendary pitcher, said another player was so fast, he could turn out the light by his bedroom door and be in bed before the room was dark!

Directions

1. Share Satchel Paige's claim with students. Challenge them to explain why the story may not be as far-fetched as it seems. If students don't suggest it, point out that the player could have turned out the light during the daytime!
2. Guide students to understand that although some problems are created purposely to mislead, problem solvers can stay ahead of them by trying to avoid mistaken inferences. Present the following problem as an example: *Two coins total 30¢. One is not a nickel. What are the coins?* Guide students to recognize that the solution—a quarter and a nickel (the other coin is the nickel) becomes clear once you change the way you look at it. Suggest that students think to themselves, "What exactly does this problem say? What does it *not* say?"
3. Duplicate the reproducible for each student or pair and distribute.
4. You may want to help students who struggle with the first problem on the reproducible by pointing out that they needn't assume that the lines must stay within the array. For the second and third problems, both classic brain teasers, point out that several answers are possible. Accept any responses students can justify.

LEARNING OBJECTIVE

Students check for hidden assumptions and change their points of view, if necessary, to solve nonroutine problems.

GROUPING

Individuals or pairs

MATERIALS

* *Think Again!* reproducible (p. 303)

Taking It Further

Challenge students to collect and publish a variety of similar math brain teasers for schoolmates and families. They can interview friends or family members, or do research in the library and on the Internet.

Assessing Skills

* Are students able to identify hidden assumptions?
* Do they arrive at reasonable answers to problems 2 and 3?

Date

Think Again!

Solve these puzzlers. If these brain teasers seem unsolvable at first, think again! Good luck!

1. Without lifting your pencil from the paper, draw four line segments to connect the dots in the array.

2. An egg dropped from a height of 15 feet does not break. How is this possible?

3. You see two parallel ski tracks coming down a snowy slope. At one point, the tracks separate to go around a tree: one track goes around to the left and the other track goes around to the right. Then the tracks come together again and continue on, side by side, down the slope. What might have caused this peculiar sight?

Logically Speaking

Some events may or may not happen. See if students can describe the chances that an event will occur.

Directions

1. Present the following statement to students: *The sun will set tomorrow.* Ask if this event is "certain," "likely," "unlikely," or "impossible." Have students defend their responses. Then repeat the process for this statement: *You will listen to the radio this week.*
2. Tell students that they're going to read several statements. Then they will evaluate each one to determine the likelihood that it will occur.
3. Duplicate the reproducible for each student and distribute. Depending on the ability level of your class, you might want to add "very likely" and "somewhat likely" to the list of possible answers.
4. Discuss students' answers. Encourage them to justify their responses, particularly when these differ from the answers most classmates give.
5. Then invite students to write and share statements they've formulated. Have others respond to them before asking for the answer the writer had in mind.

Taking It Further

Create an interactive bulletin board based on this activity. Divide the space into six regions: *certain, very likely, likely, somewhat likely, unlikely, impossible.* Ask students to write statements on index cards and post them in the appropriate regions. Encourage them to read each other's statements and rearrange any they believe are misplaced.

Assessing Skills

* Do students understand the distinctions among the different descriptions?
* Are they able to make reasonable assessments of the likelihood of the events?

LEARNING OBJECTIVE

Students apply logical thinking, common sense, and an intuitive understanding of probability to describe the chances that an event will happen.

GROUPING

Individual

MATERIALS

* *Logically Speaking* reproducible (p. 305)
* index cards

Name ______________________ Date ______________

Logically Speaking

What are the chances that you'll fly to Mars in your lifetime? No way, you say? But are you sure?

Describe the chances of each of the following events happening by choosing the best description from these choices: ***certain, likely, unlikely, impossible.***

1. There will be oxygen in the air tomorrow. ______________
2. It will snow sometime next week. ______________
3. Someone in your class will be a senator one day. ______________
4. Someone in your class will live in another country one day. ______________
5. A giraffe will walk down your block this year. ______________
6. You'll have homework this week. ______________
7. There is life elsewhere in the universe. ______________
8. Your favorite performer will appear in your area. ______________
9. You'll get three heads if you flip a coin three times. ______________
10. You'll see an eclipse this month. ______________
11. You will eat a strange food this week. ______________
12. Scientists will discover something this year that will change your life. ______________
13. The school cafeteria will serve lobster for lunch. ______________
14. Dolphins will someday be able to speak Chinese. ______________
15. In your lifetime, you will work with a robot. ______________

Let's Be Reasonable

How well do students know American geography? Well, do they know where the "middle of nowhere" is?

Directions

1. Tell students that although they may think they've been to the middle of nowhere, or even live there themselves, the people in one small American town know better—they *do* live there. Inform your young skeptics that every year, on the last weekend in June, the people of that town proudly hold a Middle of Nowhere Celebration.
2. Duplicate the reproducible for each student and distribute. Explain that their task is to think logically in order to make sensible guesses to complete statements about American geography. Good guesses will lead them to the middle of nowhere!
3. When students finish, you may want to have them discuss why some choices make sense and others do not. Refer them to an up-to-date almanac or other source to settle any geographical disagreements.

Taking It Farther

Invite students to create their own "crack-the-code" activities that require applying critical thinking and common sense to geography or other social studies concepts.

Assessing Skills

- Do students make reasonable guesses?
- Are they able to explain the logic they used to make their choices?

LEARNING OBJECTIVE

Students make reasonable guesses about geographic information.

GROUPING

Individual

MATERIALS

- *Let's Be Reasonable* reproducible (p. 307)
- United States almanac (optional)
- calculator (optional)

Name ______________________ Date ______________

Let's Be Reasonable

Just exactly where is the middle of nowhere?

To find out, first circle the best answer for each statement. Then write the letter above the number in the code at the bottom.

1. California is the state with the largest population, about ______.
   V. 3,200 **W.** 32 million **X.** 320 million

2. On the other hand, Wyoming has a population of about ______.
   T. 480,000 **U.** 48,000 **V.** 4,800

3. Alaska has the most coastline, about ______ mi.
   L. 558,000 **M.** 55,800 **N.** 5,580

4. The lowest point in the nation, Death Valley, is ______ ft below sea level.
   N. 0.282 **O.** 282 **P.** 2,820

5. The height of Mt. McKinley, the highest in the country, is ______ ft.
   D. 2,320 **E.** 20,320 **F.** 200,320

6. Yellowstone, the first national park, was founded in ______.
   A. 1872 **B.** 1802 **C.** 1772

7. The smallest state, Rhode Island, has an area of ______ sq mi.
   S. 1,545 **T.** 41,545 **U.** 241,545

8. Texas, the second largest, has an area of ______ sq mi.
   G. 86,861 **H.** 268,601 **I.** 6,168,601

9. Crater Lake, the deepest in the nation, is ______ ft deep.
   L. 32 **M.** 932 **N.** 1,932

10. Oklahoma has the largest Native American population, about ______.
    Q. 2,500 **R.** 250,000 **S.** 25 million

11. The number of Americans under age 18 is about ______.
    H. 1 million **I.** 65 million **J.** 200 million

___	___	___	___	___	___	___	___	___	___	___
6	11	3	7	1	4	10	2	8	9	5

Chili Challenge

What's Mexican food without the chilies?

Directions

1. Talk with students about the zesty flavors chilies add to dishes. Point out that there are many kinds of chilies, from the mild poblano to the hyper-hot habañero.
2. Then present the following problem for students to work on independently: *Imagine that 4 people line up for a chili taste test. In turn, one person after the next, they taste each of 5 different kinds of chilies: ancho, poblano, serrano, chipotle, and jalapeño. Each person takes 2 minutes at each tasting station—the chilies are hot, and tasters need time to hose down their taste buds! How long does it take all 4 people to pass through the line and complete the taste test?* [16 minutes]
3. Discuss students' strategies and solutions. Note that some will use logical reasoning. They can figure out that each of the 4 chili tasters needs 10 minutes to do the test—5 varieties of chilies for 2 minutes each. The last person in line has to wait for three people to finish tasting the first kind of chili—that's another 6 minutes, so the taste test takes 16 minutes.
4. Other students might make a table, such as the one started below, to solve the problem. Each number represents one of the 4 people.

	Ancho	Poblano	Serrano	Chipotle	Jalapeño
2 min	1				
4 min	2	1			
6 min	3	2	1		
8 min	4	3	2	1	
10 min		4	3	2	1

Taking It Farther

Invite students to formulate problems—to solve by using logical reasoning, by making a table, or by another method—about people doing a series of tasks or waiting in lines.

Assessing Skills

* Do students use an organized, logical approach to solve the problem?
* Do they use a combination of strategies?

LEARNING OBJECTIVE

Students use logical reasoning or other strategies to solve a problem.

GROUPING

Individual or pairs

MATERIALS

None

Toast French

Anyone can whip up some French toast—provided he or she knows the directions. Can students make French toast from a scrambled set of directions?

Directions

1. Tell students that it can be easy to prepare a meal when the steps are clearly written and listed in the right order. Then present the following steps for making French toast, pointing out that the steps are out of order. You might write the steps on the board and read them aloud for students to record or make a list and distribute copies of it.
2. Allow time for students to examine the list. Ask them to suggest steps left off the list such as shopping for bread or other ingredients, cleaning up, and so on. Then have them rearrange the steps into a sensible order. Explain to students that more than one order is possible. [Sample order: d, i, c, j, k, h, a, e, b, g, f]

The Steps

a. Melt butter in the frying pan.
b. Place the bread in the frying pan.
c. Crack the eggs into a bowl.
d. Collect the utensils you'll need: bowl, frying pan, fork, spatula.
e. Dip a piece of bread into the egg mixture.
f. Pour syrup over French toast.
g. Turn over bread when one side is browned.
h. Heat the frying pan.
i. Get the eggs from the refrigerator.
j. Beat the eggs.
k. Add sugar and cinnamon to eggs.

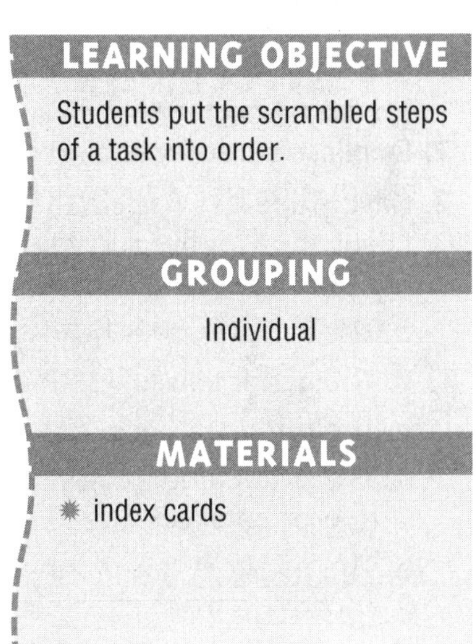

LEARNING OBJECTIVE

Students put the scrambled steps of a task into order.

GROUPING

Individual

MATERIALS

* index cards

Taking It Further

Let students use index cards to create their own set of scrambled directions for doing something. Classmates can unscramble them.

Assessing Skills

* Are students able to place the steps in a sensible order?
* Are they able to explain the choices they made?

Talent Show

Anyone in show business will tell you that performers can be picky. If entertainers don't get their way, the show's director may need to duck!

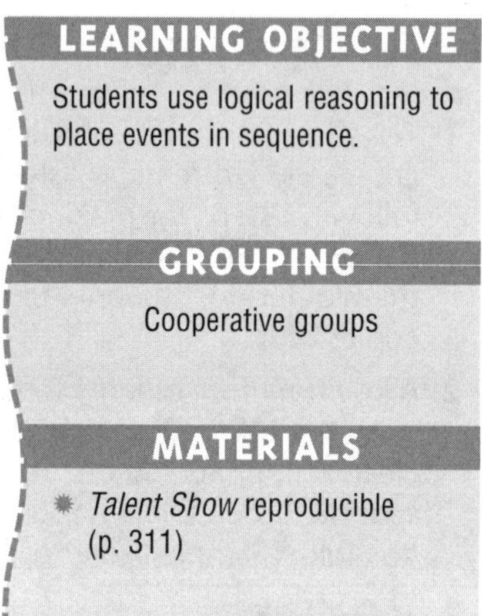

Directions

1. Duplicate, distribute, and discuss the reproducible.
2. Have students imagine that they're in charge of putting together a talent show of five fussy performing pets. Then present this list of all the pets' peeves:
   a. The hamster does headstands. He's a ham and wants to go last.
   b. The gerbil tells jokes. She's jumpy and won't go first.
   c. The puppy fetches. That's boring. Get this act over with early on.
   d. The kitten juggles yarn. She won't perform just before or after the dog or parakeet.
   e. The parakeet does funny impersonations. She won't follow a comic.
3. Instruct students to complete the program for the pet talent show.
4. Have students compare their programs and discuss how they figured out a sequence of acts that meets all the performers' demands.

Taking It Further

Challenge students to formulate a sequencing puzzle of their own. You might brainstorm a list of topics and discuss suggestions for coming up with parameters.

Assessing Skills

Do students' programs account for all the performers' demands and the time requirements?

Name ____________________ Date ____________

Talent Show

Plan a schedule for a pet talent show by filling in the program below. Use the information given about your performers and this key requirement—all acts last about 15 minutes, no longer. (After all, how long would you want to listen to a gerbil's jokes?)

Pet Talent Show

Act	Time
Intermission for Pet Exercise and Water Break (20 minutes)	12 noon

Problem Solving & Logic Problem Bank

Use the quick skill-builders as self-starters, homework, or just for a fun break from the textbook!

1. MAGIC MARBLES

You have 50 red marbles, 50 white marbles, and 50 blue marbles. You have four identical jars. How would you distribute all the marbles into the jars so that, if you were blindfolded and the jars were rearranged, you'd have the best chance of reaching into one jar and choosing a red marble?

2. AN AGE-OLD QUESTION

The sum of the ages of the three Perez sisters is 50. Rosa is the youngest, Elena is the middle sister, and Felicia is the oldest—10 years older than Rosa. Five years ago, their ages were prime numbers. How old was each then?

3. PENNIES FOR A PENCIL?

A pen and a pencil together cost $5.10. The pen costs $5 more than the pencil. How much does each cost?

4. BE REASONABLE

Use the numbers 45, 4, and 184 to fill in the blanks in a way that is reasonable. Then answer the question.

All ________ students in the grade are going by bus to the play. Will _______ buses be enough if each can hold _______ students?

5. WHO'S YOUNGER?

Anna is younger than Billy, and older and shorter than Carl. Billy is younger and taller than Diane. Diane is taller than Carl. Of the four, who is the oldest, the youngest, the tallest, and the shortest?

6. WHAT'S THE POINT?

In the basketball league Ivy belongs to, 2 points are awarded for every shot made and 3 points are deducted for every shot missed. In one game, Ivy took 40 shots but scored 0 points. How many shots did she make? How many did she miss?

7. TIME TO PRACTICE

Five musicians from TOAN-DEF met to rehearse. They arrived at 10-minute intervals. None came at the same time. Andre was the last to arrive, at 10:00. Kent wasn't the first to get there. Reba arrived between the times that Kent and Karl did. Suki arrived 30 minutes before Karl. What time did each musician arrive at the rehearsal?

8. TIME FLIES

Luisa noticed that in 7 years she'll be half her mother's age. If, 3 years ago, Luisa was $\frac{1}{3}$ her mother's age, how old is her mother now?

9. WORKING TOGETHER

Kevin can do a job in 4 hours. It takes Kendra 2 hours to do the same job. If they do the job together, how long will it take them?

10. TIME TO LAUGH

At a convention of comics, there were jokesters (J), pranksters (P), and cut-ups (C). Seventy jokesters were in attendance, and there were:

20 who were both C and J but not P.

20 who were C but neither J nor P.

15 who were both C and P but not J.

35 who were P but neither C nor J.

20 who were J and P but not C.

30 who were J but neither P nor C.

How many comics made the audience laugh for more than 15 seconds?

Answer Key

Page 21:

10 triangles

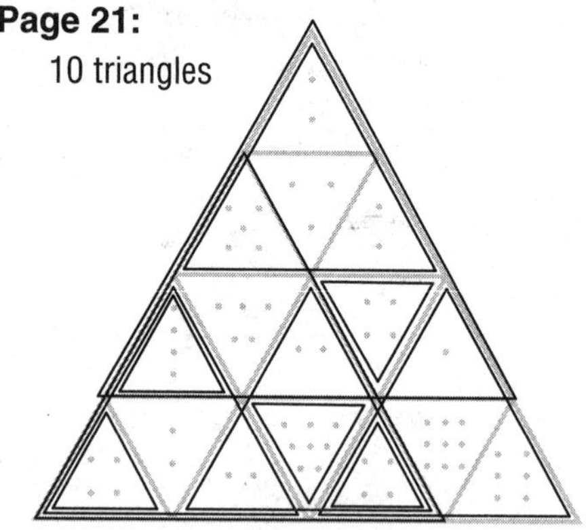

Page 29:

$8\overline{)3,719} \rightarrow 8\overline{)4,000} = 500$

$57 \div 3 \rightarrow 60 \div 3 = 20$

$711 \div 9 \rightarrow 720 \div 9 = 80$

$7\overline{)462} \rightarrow 7\overline{)490} = 70$

$5,680 \div 6 \rightarrow 5,400 \div 6 = 900$

$5\overline{)16,102} \rightarrow 5\overline{)15,000} = 3,000$

$4\overline{)2,620} \rightarrow 4\overline{)2,400} = 600$

$42,888 \div 9 \rightarrow 45,000 \div 9 = 5,000$

$8\overline{)741} \rightarrow 8\overline{)720} = 90$

$3,707 \div 9 \rightarrow 3,600 \div 9 = 400$

Page 33:

1. 10 days
2. 100 miles per hour
3. 70 miles an hour
4. 38 pounds
5. 68 miles per hour
6. 360 calories
7. 150 feet
8. 639 muscles; 40 percent

Page 37:

3; 60; 13; 12; 3; 101; 12; 7; 24; 2; 12; 20,000; 4; 8

Page 40:

1. 12 R3, Soldier
2. 48 R1, Teacher
3. 66, Actor
4. 93 R4, Newspaperman
5. 54, Tailor
6. 93 R6, Teacher
7. 36, Peanut farmer
8. 151, Writer

Page 42:

12,696 ÷ 3 = 4,232 (Nellie Bly)

2,130 ÷ 2 = 1,065 (Sarah Edmonds)

14,790 ÷ 5 = 2,958 (Elizabeth Blackwell)

18,921 ÷ 3 = 6,307 (Ida B. Wells)

25,914 ÷ 6 = 4,319 (Lydia Pinkham)

Page 46:

7 x 3 = 21
21 x 4 = 84
84 x 1 = 84
84 x 3 = 252
252 x 3 = 756
756 x 2 = 1,512
1,512 x 3 = 4,536
4,536 x 1 = 4,536
4,536 x 12 = 54,432

Page 52:

1. 883, True **2.** 482, False
3. 323, True **4.** 895, True
5. 118, False **6.** 623, True
7. 607, True

Pages 63–67:

1. Across	Down
a. 24	**a.** 22
c. 65	**b.** 48
e. 288	**d.** 57
g. 72	**f.** 82
i. 24	**h.** 208
k. 35	**j.** 42
m. 248	**l.** 54
o. 45	**n.** 440
q. 100	**p.** 51

2. Skull = 29; Spine = 26; Chest = 25; Hands = 54; Arms = 10; Legs and Feet = 62; Total = 206

3. 23 2-pound bags and 16 5-pound bags

4. Row 1—3; Row 2—28, 12, 20, 32; Row 3—2, 7, 5, 8; Row 4—0, 0, 0, 0, 0; Row 5—10, 35, 15, 40; Row 6—12, 42, 18, 30, 48

5. 18 × 35; 15 × 83; 51 × 38; 35 × 81

6. triangle = 3, square = 8, hexagon = 16, circle = 4

7. 5,952 — 5,808
6,048 — 5,952
5,808 — 6,048

8. 99 × 999 = 98,901; 5

9. 14 × 86 = 1,204; 38 × 17 = 646; 78 × 124 = 9,672

10.

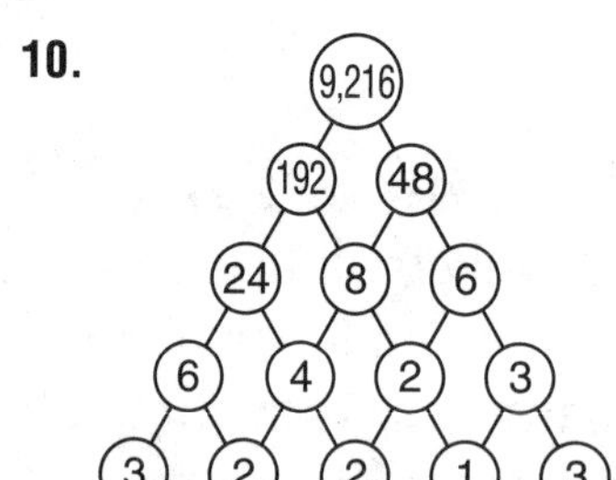

11. a. $95.25; **b.** 32 tuna, 41 turkey, and 20 egg

12. The following rooms should be shaded—576 × 1; 36 × 16; 24 × 24; 52 × 36; 105 × 10; 144 × 13; 36 × 16; 48 × 12; 25 × 42; 18 × 32; 78 × 24.

13. 3 × 3 = 9; 6 × 9 = 54

14. Target 1: 12 × 66 = 792; Target 2: 29 × 41 = 1,189; Target 3: 38 × 125 = 4,750

15. A—5 × 6 = 30; B—5 × 2 = 10; C—3 × 6 = 18; D—3 × 2 = 6; total number = 64 squares; 8 × 8 = 64

16. 11 × 10 = 110; 11 × 11 = 121; 11 × 12 = 132; 11 × 13 = 143; 11 × 14 = 154; 11 × 15 = 165; 11 × 16 = 176; 11 × 17 = 187; 11 × 18 = 198; 11 × 19 = 209

Page 69:

Mary Celeste $\frac{1}{3}$ ($\frac{10}{30}$, $\frac{3}{9}$)

Avengers $\frac{4}{5}$ ($\frac{8}{10}$, $\frac{40}{50}$)

Atlantis $\frac{1}{2}$ ($\frac{50}{100}$, $\frac{6}{12}$)

USS *Cyclops* $\frac{2}{7}$ ($\frac{6}{21}$, $\frac{4}{14}$)

Page 74:

Dark blue:

$\frac{19}{38}$, $\frac{6}{12}$, $\frac{7}{14}$, $\frac{25}{50}$, $\frac{11}{22}$, $\frac{50}{100}$, $\frac{17}{34}$, $\frac{4}{8}$

Red:

$\frac{7}{21}$, $\frac{10}{30}$, $\frac{3}{9}$, $\frac{4}{12}$

Light blue:

$\frac{2}{8}$, $\frac{25}{100}$, $\frac{10}{40}$, $\frac{13}{52}$, $\frac{3}{12}$, $\frac{4}{16}$, $\frac{8}{32}$, $\frac{7}{28}$

Page 81:

Possible Answers:

First row, from left:

$\frac{4}{4} - \frac{1}{4} = \frac{3}{4}$; $\frac{4}{6} - \frac{3}{6} = \frac{1}{6}$;

$\frac{7}{9} - \frac{2}{9} = \frac{5}{9}$; $\frac{9}{10} - \frac{2}{10} = \frac{7}{10}$

Second row, from left:

$\frac{1}{3} + \frac{1}{3} = \frac{2}{3}$; $\frac{3}{13} + \frac{4}{13} = \frac{7}{13}$;

$\frac{3}{12} + \frac{4}{12} = \frac{7}{12}$; $\frac{5}{18} - \frac{4}{18} = \frac{1}{18}$

Third row, from left:
$\frac{3}{7} + \frac{1}{7} = \frac{4}{7}$; $\frac{2}{5} - \frac{1}{5} = \frac{1}{5}$;
$\frac{7}{50} + \frac{12}{50} = \frac{19}{50}$; $\frac{5}{8} - \frac{1}{8} = \frac{4}{8} = \frac{1}{2}$

Fourth row, from left:
$\frac{11}{12} - \frac{1}{12} = \frac{10}{12} = \frac{5}{6}$;
$\frac{1}{30} + \frac{7}{30} = \frac{8}{30} = \frac{4}{15}$;
$\frac{3}{15} + \frac{2}{15} = \frac{5}{15} = \frac{1}{3}$;
$\frac{3}{8} - \frac{1}{8} = \frac{2}{8} = \frac{1}{4}$

Page 85:

$\frac{5}{21}$ (L), $\frac{5}{12}$ (I), $\frac{23}{30}$ (O), $\frac{17}{24}$ (N), $\frac{7}{8}$ (S), $\frac{17}{18}$ (A), $\frac{17}{24}$ (N), $\frac{1}{30}$ (D), $\frac{2}{3}$ (C), $\frac{11}{15}$ (H), $\frac{11}{12}$ (E), $\frac{11}{12}$ (E), $\frac{1}{2}$ (T), $\frac{17}{18}$ (A), $\frac{11}{15}$ (H), $\frac{7}{8}$ (S), $\frac{5}{8}$ (!)—LIONS AND CHEETAHS!

Page 93:

The shapes with the following decimals should be shaded:
0.3, 0.25, 16.5, 1.2, 0.14, 4.49, 0.7, 0.07, 15.8, 3.3, 0.71, 33.9.

Page 96:

1. 37.51 **2.** 55.93 **3.** 26.84
4. 42.24 **5.** 8.24 **6.** 11.37

Page 100:

1. 3.44
2. 4.6
3. 41.7
4. 4016.32
5. 947.36
6. 6.5
7. 56.4
8. 1.35
9. 1.006
10. 45.63
11. 15.3
12. 317.9
13. 3007.55
14. 6.19
15. 6.99

				4					
		4	0	1	6	.	3	2	
6	.	5		.			0		
		.		7			0		
		6			3	1	7	.	9
1	.	3	5				.		4
5			6				5		7
.			.		6		5		.
3	.	4	4		.				3
		.			1	.	0	0	6
		6	.	9	9				

Page 102:

1. **a.** 0.38 (Mercury)
b. 0.38 (Mars)
c. 0.91 (Venus)
d. 0.93 (Saturn)
e. 0.93 (Uranus)
f. 1.00 (Earth)
g. 1.14 (Neptune)
h. 2.34 (Jupiter)
2. Jupiter
3. Mercury and Mars
4. Saturn and Uranus; Mercury and Mars
5. 280,000 pounds

Page 104:

1. 129.00 (Calvin Coolidge)
2. 42.05 (James Garfield)
3. 1.7 (Ulysses S. Grant)
4. 144.00 (Zachary Taylor)
5. 2.80 (Zachary Taylor)
6. 3.00 (Martin Van Buren)

Page 107:

1. 6.1947
2. 679.14
3. 97.416
4. 6.9174
5. 9.6147
6. 9.7246
7. 67.914 or 67.941

Page 114:

4 items for $6.00
Majestic Doll $2.95
Toy Sewing Machine . . $2.25
China Tea Set. $0.75
Dominoes. $0.05

6 items for $5.00
Majestic Doll $2.95
Mechanical Warship. . . $0.43
Laughing Camera. $0.32
China Tea Set. $0.75
Dominoes. $0.05
Chess Game. $0.50

Page 118:

Across	Down
3. 12.54	**1.** 34.17
4. 4.7	**2.** 8.8
5. 9.8	**3.** 17.82
6. 27.1	**4.** 4.28
7. 8.2	**5.** 9.12
8. 29.01	**9.** 9.1
11. 13.6	**10.** 1.68
	12. 3.7

Pages 120–123:

1. 93.93
2. 120 books
3. Four darts landed on $\frac{3}{4}$ and one dart landed on $\frac{1}{7}$.
4. 3, $3\frac{1}{2}$, 4, $4\frac{1}{2}$;
$3\frac{1}{4}$, $3\frac{3}{4}$, $4\frac{1}{4}$, $4\frac{3}{4}$;
$8\frac{1}{4}$, $7\frac{1}{2}$, $6\frac{3}{4}$, 6;
$6\frac{3}{4}$, 8, $9\frac{1}{4}$, $10\frac{1}{2}$
5. $\frac{1}{6} + \frac{1}{6} + \frac{2}{3}$; $\frac{7}{10} + \frac{1}{10} + \frac{1}{5}$;
$\frac{1}{7} + \frac{3}{7} + \frac{3}{7}$
6. 1 dime, 2 nickels, 5 pennies
7. Cecil paid exactly one-third. Amos paid less by $2.00. Patrick paid more by $2.00.
8. 9; 15; 21; 8; 16; 30; 100
9. P = 9, T = 3, M = 1, X = 2, K = 0, O = 8, L = 5, Z = 6, R = 7, V = 4;
93.120 + 85.326 = 178.446
10. A = $\frac{1}{2}$, B = $\frac{1}{4}$, C = $\frac{5}{4}$, D = $\frac{1}{8}$, E = $\frac{1}{16}$, F = $\frac{3}{4}$
11. 44.66

Page 125:

A. inside **B.** outside
C. outside **D.** inside

Page 127:

TIGHTROPE

Page 136:

1. **2.**

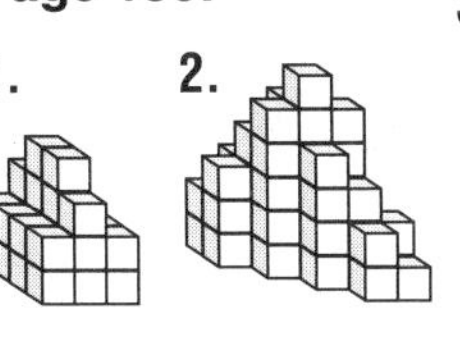

3.

4.

4	4	4
3	4	4
1	2	3

5.

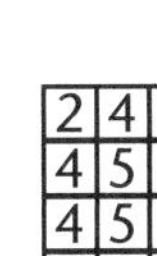

2	4	2
4	5	4
4	5	4
2	4	2

Page 141:

1. segment
2. cone
3. volume
4. perpendicular
5. ray
6. angle
7. pyramid
8. sphere
9. prism
10. vertex
11. point
Gomdan, Yemen

Page 146:

1. about 32 square units
2. The shape is elongated; it's twice as long and the same height as the original.
3. about 64 square units, twice that of the original
4. The shark is squashed; it's twice as high but the same length as the original; area is about 64 square units, twice that of the original.
5. The figure has the same shape as the original.
6. about 128 square units, four times its original size

Page 156:

Across	**Down**
3. months	**1.** carat
6. gallons	**2.** hour
9. millennium	**4.** oz
11. pints	**5.** half gallon
15. decades	**7.** inch
16. minute	**8.** cup
18. acres	**9.** miles
20. cup	**10.** midnight
21. year	**12.** ten
22. ft	**13.** quart
23. ton	**14.** half
24. seconds	**15.** degrees
27. century	**17.** pounds
29. days	**19.** ounce
30. bushel	**21.** yards
31. weeks	**25.** one
	26. six
	28. lb

Page 158:

90 mm	11 cm	0.8 m	500 mm	40 cm	25 cm	0.5 m	0.25 m
200 mm	50 dm	60 cm	1 dm	30 cm	9 mm	1 cm	0.8 m
40 cm	1 cm	700 mm	8 cm	5 cm	4 dm	550 mm	50 cm
400 mm	0.3 m	300 mm	3 dm	40 cm	0.3 m	0.4 cm	300 cm
2 dm	3 dm	40 mm	15 mm	1.1 m	300 mm	9 m	0.5 m
0.3 cm	1 m	30 cm	600 mm	1 dm	8 dm	20 cm	350 mm
50 cm	0.45 m	1 dm	45 cm	2.5 cm	0.1 m	9 dm	15 cm
200 mm	3 dm	50 cm	0.95 m	4 cm	3 cm	0.80 m	40 dm
10 mm	250 mm	600 dm	4.5 dm	0.07 m	600 mm	70 cm	300 mm

Page 160:

Segments measure in cm.

1. 2.0, 2.5, 7.0, 10.0 (DENT/TEND)
2. 2.5, 1.5, 4.0, 7.5 (ECHO)
3. 3.0, 6.0, 0.5, 7.5 (FOAL/LOAF)
4. 10.0, 4.5, 6.5, 2.5, 9.0 (TIMER/REMIT/MITER)
5. 1, 10.5, 3.5, 3.5, 12.5 (BUGGY)
6. 1.5, 0.5, 5.5, 2.5 (CAKE)
7. 5.0, 0.5, 11.5 (JAW)

Page 163:

Answers may vary slightly.

Possible answers:

1. 86 square units
2. 53.5 square units
3. 54 square units
4. 58.5 square units

Page 166:

1. large can costing \$2.10
2. small can costing \$3.70
3. large can costing 75¢
4. small can costing 60¢

Page 172:

1. 9:35 **2.** 8:10 **3.** 1:50 **4.** 3:40
5. 6:55 **6.** 4:20 **7.** 8:01 or 9:01
8. 11:22, 11:23, 11:32, or 11:33
9. 2:45, 2:46, 3:45, or 3:46
10. 3:00 or 9:00

Pages 174–177:

1. Saturday, October 5
2. There is no top or bottom; the twist makes it a one-sided strip!
3. 1,205.76 inches, or about 100.48 feet
4. January 12, 13 hours 46 minutes and 40 seconds into the day or a little bit after 1:46 P.M.
5. 1:50 A.M. Tuesday
6. 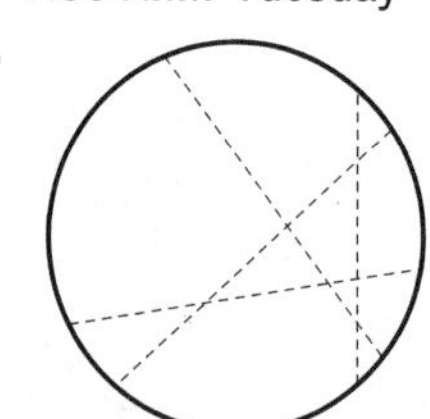
7. 5.71 m; 1,489.37 cm; 65.00 cm; 98.75 m
8. 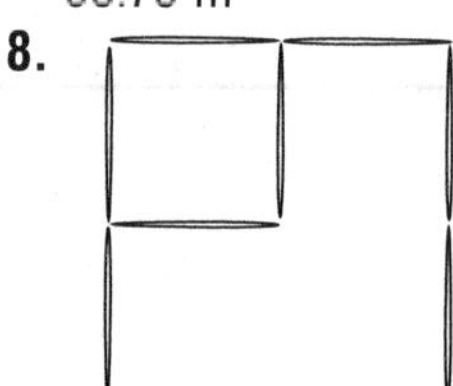
9. 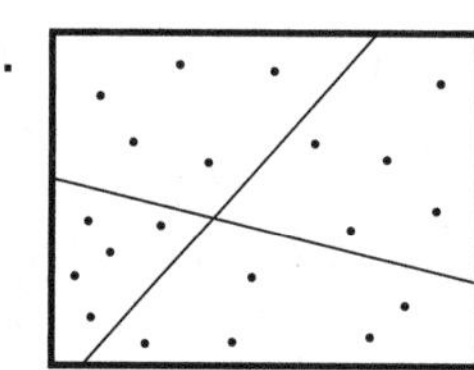
10. 210 blocks
11. 11 hours 59 minutes, from 10:00 to 9:59
12. 204
13. a. b. c. d. e. f. g.

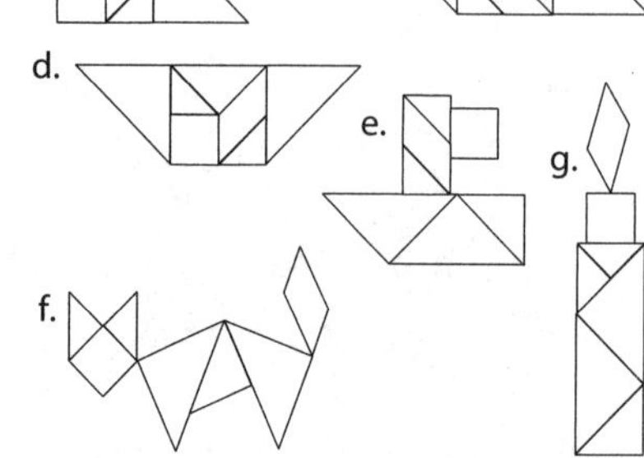

14. rectangular pie costing \$6
15. Answers will vary.
16. Check students' cube structures.
17.

a.

1	3
2	4
2	3
1	2

b.

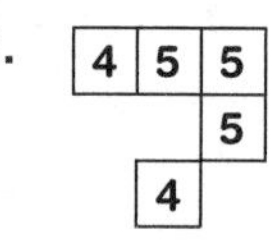

Page 179:

The spinner with the most likely chance would have three sections for the favorite toy and one section for another toy.

Page 184:

1. Row 1—3,1; 6,1; Row 2—3,2; 5,2; Row 3—2,3; 4,3; 6,3; Row 4—3,4; 4,4; 6,4; Row 5—2,5; 4,5; 5,5; 6,5; Row 6—3,6; 5,6
2a. 18 **b.** $\frac{18}{36}$, or $\frac{1}{2}$, or 50%
3a. 18 **b.** $\frac{18}{36}$, or $\frac{1}{2}$, or 50%
4–6. Answers will vary. The game is fair because there is an equal number of ways to get an even or odd number.

Page 186:

START → $\frac{3}{4}$ → 75% → 0.4 → $\frac{2}{5}$ → 83% → 0.83 → 25% → $\frac{1}{4}$ → $\frac{41}{100}$ → 41% → $\frac{3}{8}$ → 0.375 → $\frac{14}{15}$ → 93% → 60% → $\frac{18}{30}$ → 0.26 → 26% → FINISH

Page 192:

1a. 2:00 A.M.
1b. 1:00, 2:00, 3:00, 4:00, 5:00, 6:00, 7:00, 8:00, 9:00, 10:00, 11:00, or 12:00 A.M.; 1:00, 2:00, 3:00, 4:00, 5:00, 6:00, 7:00, 8:00, 9:00, 10:00, 11:00, or 12:00 P.M.
2a. pork chops
2b. macaroni and cheese, pork chops, cotton candy
3a. The spaceship lands.
3b. Mars
4a. The robot brings back rocks from Mars.
4b. 5, 10, 15, 20, 25, 30, 35, 40, 45, 50, 55, 60, 65, 70, 75, 80, 85, 90, 95, 100

Page 194:

1. 6 **2.** 2 **3.** 3

Check students' completed tree diagrams. Outcomes: PLSN, PLSa PShSn, PShSa, StLSn, StLSa, StShSn, StShSa

4. 4 **5.** 4 **6.** 4

Page 200:

1a. 9 ways

1b. Answers may vary.

1c. Sample answer:

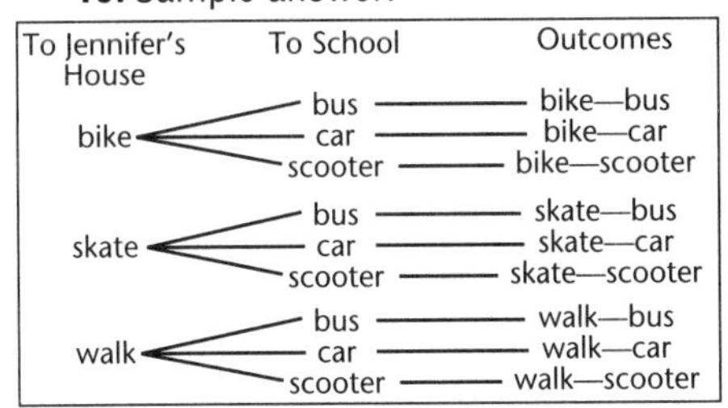

2a. 343 combinations

2b. Answers may vary.

2c. Sample answer: 7 x 7 x 7 = 343 combinations

Page 203:

1a. $P(5, 4)$

1b. 5 x 4 x 3 x 2 = 120 ways

2a. $P(10, 2)$

2b. 10 x 9 = 90 ways

3a. 4 x 3 x 2 x 1 = 24 ways

3b. 4 x 3 x 2 = 24 ways

4a. Answers may vary.

4b. Answers may vary depending on number of presentations chosen, but permutation problem should be set up as: $P(n, 4)$, where n = number of presentations.

4c. Answers may vary, but permutation problem should be set up as: $P(n, 2)$.

Page 205:

1. $\frac{1}{6} + \frac{1}{6} = \frac{2}{6}$, or $\frac{1}{3}$

2. $\frac{1}{6} + \frac{1}{6} + \frac{1}{3} = \frac{4}{6}$, or $\frac{2}{3}$

3. $\frac{1}{6} + \frac{1}{4} = \frac{5}{12}$

4. $\frac{1}{6} + \frac{1}{6} + \frac{1}{4} = \frac{7}{12}$; area model for Maze 2: $\frac{1}{6} + \frac{1}{4} = \frac{5}{12}$.

Upper Path	Wild Woods	$\frac{1}{6}$
	Wild Woods	$\frac{1}{6}$
	Ricardo's Cabin	$\frac{1}{6}$
Lower Path	Ricardo's Cabin	$\frac{1}{4}$
	Wild Woods	$\frac{1}{4}$

Page 207:

1a. 35

1b. 20

1c. 35

1d. $\frac{50}{100}$, or $\frac{1}{2}$

1e. $\frac{20}{100}$, or $\frac{1}{5}$

1f. $\frac{35}{100}$, or $\frac{7}{20}$

2a. 75

2b. $\frac{60}{100}$, or $\frac{3}{5}$

2c. $\frac{25}{100}$, or $\frac{1}{4}$

2d. $\frac{65}{100}$, or $\frac{13}{20}$

2e. $\frac{0}{100}$, or 0

Page 226:

1a. 1

1b. 16

1c. 24

2a. $\frac{1}{47}$

2b. $\frac{16}{32}$, or $\frac{1}{2}$

2c. $\frac{24}{24}$, or $\frac{1}{1}$, or the odds are even.

3a–5b. Answers will vary. Check students' results.

Pages 231–233:

1. $\frac{24}{365}$, 0.066, or 6.6%

2. $6 \times 6 \times 6$, or 216 combinations are possible.

3. Each time a number is rolled, it represents one chocolate chip going to a cookie. For example, rolling a 2 means that cookie number 2 gets one chip.

4. $4 \times 3 \times 2 \times 1 = 24$; 12

5. $\frac{5}{10}$, or $\frac{1}{2}$; $\frac{4}{10}$, or $\frac{2}{5}$; $\frac{4}{6}$, or $\frac{2}{3}$

6a. 1,920 combinations

6b. Answers may vary.

6c. Sample answer: 12 x 4 x 8 x 5 = 1,920 combinations

7a. $\frac{25}{50}$, or $\frac{1}{2}$

7b. $\frac{10}{50}$, or $\frac{1}{5}$

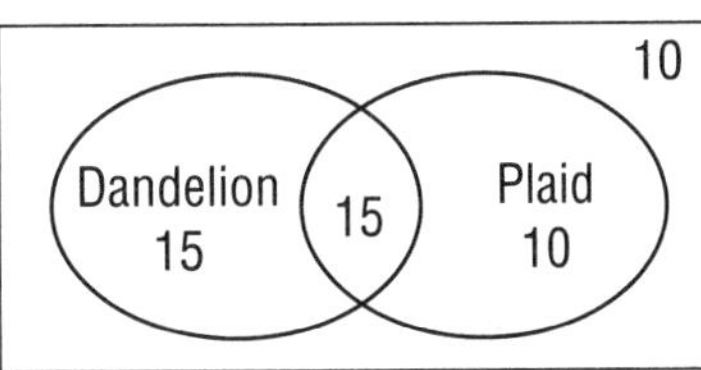

8. Answers will vary.

Page 235:

2. 5 Vermont, Identity property of addition

3. 15×4 Montana, Commutative property of multiplication

4. 8 + (3 + 7) Florida, Associative property of addition

5. $(x + 4)$ Iowa, Identity property of multiplication

6. $y12x$ California, Commutative property of multiplication

7. $5 + v$, Pennsylvania, Commutative property of addition

8. cd Mississippi, Identity property of addition

9. $j + 11$ Illinois, Associative property of addition

Page 238:

$\frac{14}{9}$ $\frac{9}{14}$, $\frac{2}{3}$ $1\frac{1}{2}$, $\frac{1}{6}$ 6, $-\frac{4}{5}$ $-\frac{5}{4}$, $2\frac{1}{8}$

$\frac{8}{17}$, $\frac{32}{2}$ $\frac{1}{16}$, $\frac{2}{20}$ 10

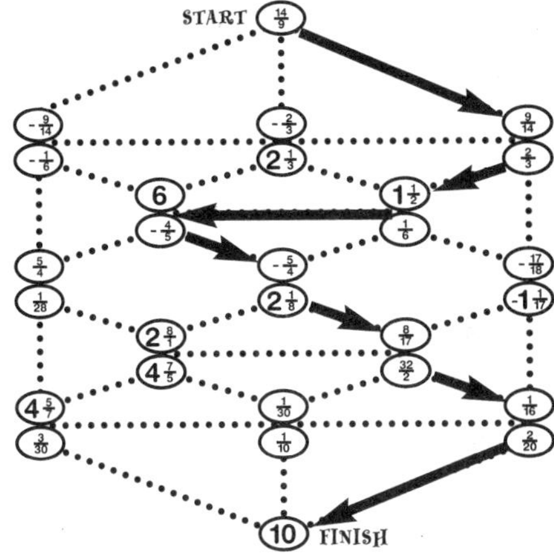

Page 240:

2. $4x$, Fear of Darkness

3. $8p + 8$, Fear of Lightning

4. $6n + 3$, Fear of Snakes

5. $4x + 12$, Fear of Fire

6. $4p + 9$, Fear of Heights

7. $6n + 36$, Fear of Water

8. $8x + 28$, Fear of Light

9. $12p + 30$, Fear of Infinity

10. $9n + 12$, Fear of Dirt

Page 242:

1. 208, Chili

2. 79, Corned beef hash

3. 38, Water

4. 52, Poached eggs on an English muffin

5. 4, Crackers

6. 61, Orange juice

Page 244:

Calculator, 1833; Telephone, 1876; Car, 1889; Toaster, 1918; Frozen Food, 1924; Television, 1927; Computer, 1944; Tupperware, 1945; Velcro, 1948; Audiocassette, 1963; Video Game, 1972

Page 247:

1. True **2.** True **3.** False **4.** True
5. True **6.** True **7.** True **8.** False
9. True **10.** False

Page 251:

1. 72.6 + 2.5t = height **2.** 165.1 cm
3. 192.1 cm **4.** 151.8 cm
5. 195.1 cm

Page 259:

2. 20, "I feel a little ridiculous."
3. 10.68, "I always liked math."
4. 37.8, "I have a nervous stomach."
5. 20.55, "I used to eat mayonnaise sandwiches."
6. 54, "I'm not a couch potato."
7. 30, "I think it's OK to be a movie star."
8. 24.18, "I'm such a mall rat."

Page 265:

A. $x = 10$, $y = 7$
B. $x = 5$, $y = 11$
C. $x = 22$, $y = 36$
Al Steelz is the thief.

Page 267:

75 (via 5) 531 (via 9) 345 (via 23) 432 (via 12) 810 (via 135) 986 (via 29) 1,482 (via 57) 2,108 (via 62) Finish

Page 272:

BECAUSE HE HAD ORDERED PAIRS! (PEARS)

Page 278:

Across	Down
B. 9	**A.** 10
C. 81	**B.** 900
F. 400	**D.** 1,024
H. 289	**G.** 18
I. 324	**H.** 2,601
L. 144	**J.** 22
N. 14	**K.** 441
O. 15	**M.** 25

Page 280:

Page 285:

A. 14 **B.** 63 **C.** 129 **D.** 20 **E.** 27
F. 34 (Fibonacci sequence)
G. 12 **H.** 19 (prime numbers)

Pages 286–287:

1. 1 hour
2. **a.** 8 **b.** 40,000,000 **c.** 100 **d.** 8
3. Jamal is 12. His mother is 36.
4. 23 ostriches, 12 llamas
5. 61 gumdrops
6.

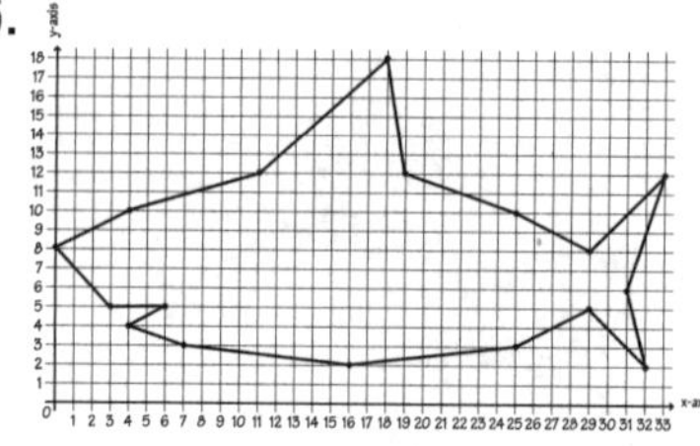

Page 289:

1. Multiply the cost of an individual ticket by the number of tickets in the booklet; subtract what Max paid from that product.
2. Divide the miles Inez ran by the number of hours she ran.
3. Subtract the "before" odometer reading from the "after" reading; divide that result by the number of gallons used.
4. Possible answer: divide the price of each box by its weight—the smaller quotient indicates the better buy.
5. Multiply the profit per paper by the number of papers Li delivers (in a day or week); divide by the number of hours she works (in a day or week).
6. Possible answer: Double the mean weight; subtract the difference in their weights from that sum; divide by 2 to find Eva's weight; add the difference to find Vera's weight.

Page 291:

1. \$30.50
2. yes
3. *20 Hours of Sleep—Is That Enough?*
4. *How to Get More and Better Meals, Total Turtle Training*
5. *Getting Away with Scratching*

Page 298:

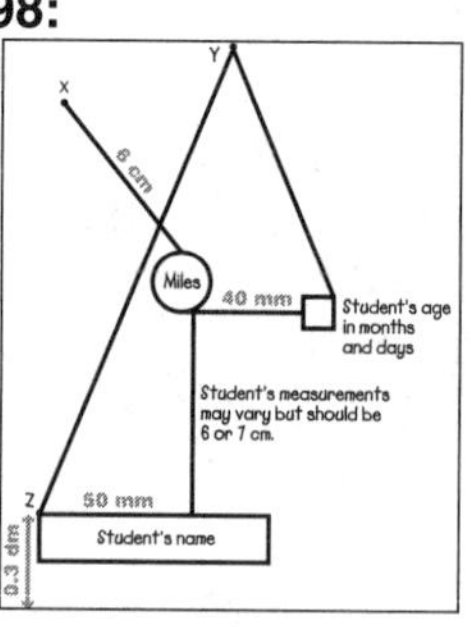

Page 301:

Answers will vary.

Page 303:

1.

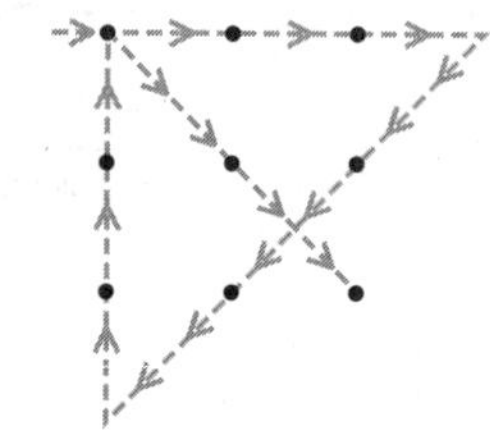

2. Sample answers: The egg is caught after it falls 15 feet, but before it hits the ground; it lands in water; it's hard boiled; it lands in something very soft, like cotton or sand.
3. Answers will vary.

Page 307:

1. W. 32 million **2.** T. 480,000
3. N. 5,580 **4.** O. 282
5. E. 20,320 **6.** A. 1872
7. S. 1,545 **8.** H. 268,601
9. N. 1,932 **10.** R. 250,000
11. I. 65 million Ainsworth, NE

Page 311:

Possible order—puppy, parakeet, gerbil, kitten, hamster; times will vary.

Pages 312–313:

1. Sample answer: Put 1 red marble in each of three jars; put all remaining 147 marbles in the fourth jar.
2. 7, 11, and 17
3. pen, \$5.05; pencil \$0.05
4. 184, 4, 45; no
5. oldest: Diane; youngest: Carl; tallest: Billy; shortest: Anna
6. 24 shots made, 16 shots missed
7. Suki, 9:20; Kent, 9:30; Reba, 9:40; Karl, 9:50; Andre, 10:00
8. 33
9. $1\frac{1}{3}$ hours
10. Who knows?!

 Name ______________________ Date ____________

STUDENT SELF-EVALUATION

In My Opinion

The activity ______________________________ was:
(name of activity)

Easy Hard

because:

My work on this activity was:

poor fair good excellent

because:

I used the following math strategy or strategies:

I would share this tip with someone who is about to do this activity:

Activity ____________________ Date ____________

ASSESSMENT FORM

Student						
UNDERSTANDING						
Identifies the problem or task.						
Understands the math concept.						
SOLVING						
Develops and carries out a plan.						
Uses strategies, models, and tools effectively.						
DECIDING						
Is able to convey reasoning behind decision making.						
Understands why approach did or didn't work.						
LEARNING						
Comments on solution.						
Connects solution to other math or real-world applications.						
Makes general rule about solution or extends it to a more complicated problem.						
COMMUNICATING						
Understands and uses mathematical language effectively.						
COLLABORATING						
Participates by sharing ideas with partner or group members.						
Listens to partner or other group members.						
ACCOMPLISHING						
Shows progress in problem solving.						
Undertakes difficult tasks and perseveres in solving them.						
Is confident of mathematical abilities.						

SCORING RUBRIC

3	2	1
Fully accomplishes the task. Shows full understanding of key mathematical idea(s). Communicates thinking clearly using oral explanation or written, symbolic, or visual means.	Partially accomplishes the task. Shows partial understanding of key mathematical idea(s). Oral or written explanation partially communicates thinking but may be incomplete, misdirected, or not clearly presented.	Does not accomplish the task. Shows little or no grasp of key mathematical idea(s). Recorded work or oral explanation is fragmented and not understandable.